CLYMER®

YAMAHA

YX600 RADIAN & FZ600 • 1986-1990

The world's finest publisher of mechanical how-to manuals

PRIMEDIA
Business Directories & Books

P.O. Box 12901, Overland Park, Kansas 66282-2901

Copyright ©1992 PRIMEDIA Business Magazines & Media Inc.

FIRST EDITION
First Printing November, 1992
Second Printing November, 1995
Third Printing August, 1998
Fourth Printing October, 2002

Printed in U.S.A.

CLYMER and colophon are registered trademarks of PRIMEDIA Business Magazines & Media Inc.

ISBN: 0-89287-577-1

Library of Congress: 92-71764

TECHNICAL PHOTOGRAPHY: Ed Scott and Randy Stephens.

TECHNICAL ILLUSTRATIONS: Mitzi McCarthy.

TOOLS AND EQUIPMENT: K & L Supply Co. at www.klsupply.com.

COVER: Photographed by Mark Clifford, Mark Clifford Photography, Los Angeles, California.

PRODUCTION: Shirley Renicker.

CLYMER PUBLICATIONS
PRIMEDIA Business Magazines & Media
Chief Executive Officer Timothy M. Andrews
President Ron Wall

EDITORIAL

Editor
James Grooms

Technical Writers
Ron Wright
Ed Scott
George Parise
Mark Rolling
Michael Morlan
Jay Bogart

Production Supervisor
Dylan Goodwin

Lead Editorial Production Coordinator
Shirley Renicker

Editorial Production Coordinators
Greg Araujo
Shara Pierceall

Editorial Production Assistants
Susan Hartington
Holly Messinger
Darin Watson

Technical Illustrators
Steve Amos
Robert Caldwell
Mitzi McCarthy
Bob Meyer
Mike Rose

MARKETING/SALES AND ADMINISTRATION

Vice President,
PRIMEDIA Business Directories & Books
Rich Hathaway

Marketing Manager
Elda Starke

Advertising & Promotions Coordinator
Melissa Abbott

Associate Art Directors
Chris Paxton
Tony Barmann

Sales Manager/Marine
Dutch Sadler

Sales Manager/Motorcycles
Matt Tusken

Operations Manager
Patricia Kowalczewski

Sales Manager/Manuals
Ted Metzger

Customer Service Manager
Terri Cannon

Customer Service Supervisor
Ed McCarty

Customer Service Representatives
Susan Kohlmeyer
April LeBlond
Courtney Hollars
Jennifer Lassiter
Ernesto Suarez

Warehouse & Inventory Manager
Leah Hicks

The following books and guides are published by PRIMEDIA Business Directories & Books.

More information available at *primediabooks.com*

CONTENTS

QUICK REFERENCE DATA

TIRE INFLATION PRESSURE (COLD)*

Load	Radian models	Air Pressure FZ600 models
Up to 198 lb. (90 kg)		
Front	26 psi (177 kPa)	26 psi (177 kPa)
Rear	28 psi (196 kPa)	28 psi (196 kPa)
Maximum load limit**		
Front	28 psi (196 kPa)	28 psi (196 kPa)
Rear	32 psi (226 kPa)	36 psi (245 kPa)

*Recommended air pressure for factory equipped tires. Aftermarket tires may require different air pressure.
**Maximum load limit includes total weight of motorcycle with accessories, rider(s) and luggage.

MAINTENANCE AND TUNE-UP TIGHTENING TORQUES

Item	N•m	ft.-lb.
Oil drain plug	43	31
Oil filter union bolt	15	11
Oil gallery check bolt	7	5
Fork top cap bolt	23	17
Handlebar		
Holder bolt (Radian)	20	14
Pinch bolt (FZ600)	20	14
Upper fork bridge bolt		
Radian	23	17
FZ600	20	14
Lower fork bridge bolt	23	17
Rear axle nut	105	75
Camshaft chain tensioner		
Stopper bolt	9	6.5
Locknut	6	4.3
Ignition cover screws	10	7.2
Cylinder head nuts		
Upper	22	16
Lower	10	7.2
Cylinder head cover bolts	10	7.2

FRONT FORK AIR PRESSURE (FZ600 MODELS)

	kPa	psi
Standard air pressure	39	5.7
Minimum air pressure	0	0
Maximum air pressure	98	14

Differential between fork legs 9.8 kPa (1.4 psi) or less

TUNE-UP SUMMARY

Item	Specification
Air filter element	Dry element type
Firing order	1-2-4-3
Ignition timing	Fixed, non-adjustable
Timing mark	"T" mark at idle speed
Valve clearance (cold below 35° C/95° F)	
Intake	0.11-0.15 mm (0.004-0.0059 in.)
Exhaust	0.16-0.20 mm (0.0063-0.008 in.)
Compression pressure (at sea level)	
Standard pressure	1,079 kPa (156 psi)
Minimum pressure	980 kPa (142 psi)
Maximum pressure	1,128 kPa (164 psi)
Maximum difference between cylinders	98 kPa (14 psi)
Spark plug (U.S.)	
Type	ND X24ES-U or NGK D8EA
Gap	0.6-0.7 mm (0.024-0.028 in.)
Tightening torque	17.5 N•m (13 ft-lb.)
Spark plug (UK)	
Type	ND X24ESR-U or NGK D8ES-L
Gap	0.6-0.7 mm (0.024-0.028 in.)
Tightening torque	17.5 N•m (13 ft-lb.)
Idle speed	
Radian models	1,250-1,350 rpm
FZ600 models	1,150-1,250 rpm

REPLACEMENT BULBS

Item	Wattage
U.S. Models	
Headlight	Quartz Halogen
Radian	12V 60/55W (single)
FZ600	12V 35/35W (dual)
Tail/brakelight	12V 8/27W
Turn signals	12V 27W
License plate	12V 3.8 W
Instruments lights	12V 3.4W
Indicator lights	12V 3W
UK FZ600 Models	
Headlight	Quartz Halogen
High beam	12V 60W
Low beam	12V 50W
Tail/brakelight	12V 5/21W
Turn signals	12V 21W
License plate	12V 5W
Instruments lights	12V 3.4W
Indicator lights	12V 3W

INTRODUCTION

This detailed, comprehensive manual covers the Yamaha Radian and FZ600 600 cc inline fours from 1986-1990.

The expert text gives complete information on maintenance, tune-up, repair and overhaul. Hundreds of photos and drawings guide you through every step. The book includes all you will need to know to keep your Yamaha running right. Throughout this book where differences occur among the models, they are clearly identified.

A shop manual is a reference. You want to be able to find information fast. As in all Clymer books, this one is designed with you in mind. All chapters are thumb tabbed. Important items are extensively indexed at the rear of the book. All procedures, tables, photos, etc., in this manual are for the reader who may be working on the bike for the first time or using this manual for the first time. All the most frequently used specifications and capacities are summarized in the *Quick Reference Data* pages at the front of the book.

Keep the book handy in your tool box. It will help you better understand how your bike runs, lower repair costs and generally improve your satisfaction with the bike.

CHAPTER ONE

GENERAL INFORMATION

MANUAL ORGANIZATION

All dimensions and capacities are expressed in English units familiar to U.S. mechanics as well as in metric units. Refer to **Table 1** for Decimal and Metric equivalents.

This chapter provides general information and discusses equipment and tools useful both for preventive maintenance and troubleshooting.

Chapter Two provides methods and suggestions for quick and accurate diagnosis and repair of problems. Troubleshooting procedures discuss typical symptoms and logical methods to pinpoint the trouble.

Chapter Three explains all periodic lubrication and routine maintenance necessary to keep the Yamaha running well. Chapter Three also includes recommended tune-up procedures, eliminating the need to consult chapters constantly on the various assemblies.

Subsequent chapters describe specific systems such as the engine, clutch, transmission, fuel, exhaust, suspension and brakes. Each chapter provides disassembly, repair and assembly procedures in simple step-by-step form.

If a repair is impractical for a home mechanic, it is so indicated. It is usually faster and less expensive to take such repairs to a dealer or competent repair shop. Specifications concerning a particular system are included at the end of the appropriate chapter.

Some of the procedures in this manual specify special tools. In most cases, the tool is illustrated either in actual use or alone. Well equipped mechanics may find they can substitute similar tools already on hand or can fabricate their own.

Tables 1-4 are at the end of this chapter.

NOTES, CAUTIONS AND WARNINGS

The terms NOTE, CAUTION and WARNING have specific meanings in this manual. A NOTE provides additional information to make a step or procedure easier or clearer. Disregarding a NOTE could cause inconvenience, but would not cause equipment damage or personal injury.

A CAUTION emphasizes areas where equipment damage could result. Disregarding a CAUTION could cause permanent mechanical damage; however, personal injury is unlikely.

A WARNING emphasizes areas where personal injury or even death could result from negligence. Mechanical damage may also occur. WARNINGS *are to be taken seriously*. In some cases, serious injury or death has resulted from disregarding similar warnings.

Throughout this manual, keep in mind 2 conventions. "Front" refers to the front of the bike. The front of any component, such as the engine, is the end which faces toward the front of the bike. The "left-" and "right-hand" sides refer to the position of the parts as viewed by a rider sitting on the seat facing forward. For example, the throttle control is on the right-hand side and the clutch lever is on the left-hand side. These rules are simple, but even experienced mechanics occasionally become disoriented.

SAFETY FIRST

Professional mechanics can work for years and never sustain a serious injury. If you observe a few rules of common sense and safety, you can enjoy many hours servicing your own machine. If you ignore these rules, you can hurt yourself or damage the bike.

1. *Never* use gasoline as a cleaning solvent.

2. Never smoke or use a torch in the vicinity of flammable liquids such as cleaning solvent in open containers.

3. If welding or brazing is required on the machine, remove the fuel tank to a safe distance, at least 50 feet away.

4. Use the proper sized wrenches to avoid damage to nuts and injury to yourself.

5. When loosening a tight or stuck nut, think about what would happen if the wrench should slip. Be careful, protect yourself accordingly.

6. Keep your work area clean and uncluttered.

7. Wear safety goggles during all operations involving drilling, grinding or the use of a cold chisel.

8. Never use worn tools.

9. Keep a fire extinguisher handy and be sure it is rated for gasoline and electrical fires.

SERVICE HINTS

Most of the service procedures covered are straightforward and can be performed by anyone reasonably handy with tools. It is suggested, however, that you consider your own capabilities carefully before attempting any operation involving major disassembly of the engine.

Take your time and do the job right. Do not forget that a newly rebuilt engine must be broken in the same as a new one. Keep the rpm within the limits given in your owner's manual when you get back on the road.

1. There are many items available that can be used on your hands before and after working on your bike.

A little preparation prior to getting "all greased up" will help when cleaning up later. Before starting, work Vaseline, soap or a product such as Invisible Glove (**Figure 1**) onto your forearms, into your hands and under your fingernails and cuticles. This will make cleanup a lot easier. For cleanup, use a waterless hand soap such as Sta-Lube and then finish with powdered Boraxo and a fingernail brush (**Figure 2**).

2. Repairs go much faster and easier if the bike is clean before you begin work. There are special cleaners, such as Gunk or Bel-Ray Degreaser (**Figure 3**) for washing the engine and related parts. Just spray or brush on the cleaning solution, let it stand, then rinse it away with a garden hose. Clean all oily or greasy parts with cleaning solvent as you remove them.

> *WARNING*
> *Never use gasoline as a cleaning agent. It presents an extreme fire hazard. Be sure to work in a well-ventilated area when using cleaning solvent. Keep a fire extinguisher, rated for gasoline fires, handy in any case.*

3. Special tools are required for some repair procedures. These may be purchased from a Yamaha dealer or motorcycle shop, rented from a tool rental dealer or fabricated by a mechanic or machinist (often at a considerable savings).

4. Much of the labor charged by mechanics is to remove and disassemble other parts to reach the defective unit. It is usually possible to perform the preliminary operations yourself and then take the defective unit in to the dealer for repair.

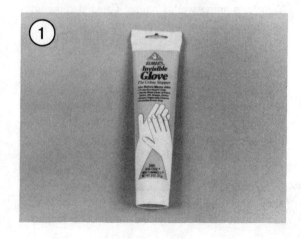

5. Once you have decided to tackle the job yourself, read the entire section *completely* while looking at the actual parts before starting the job, making sure you have identified the proper one. Study the illustrations and text until you have a good idea of what is involved in completing the job satisfactorily. If special tools or replacement parts are required, make arrangements to get them before you start. It is frustrating and time-consuming to get partly into a job and then be unable to complete it.

6. Simple wiring checks can be easily made at home, but knowledge of electronics is almost a necessity for performing tests with complicated electronic testing gear.

7. Whenever servicing the engine or transmission, or when removing a suspension component, the bike should be secured in a safe manner. If the bike is to be parked on the side stand or centerstand, check the stand to make sure it is secure and not damaged. Block the front and rear wheels if they remain on the ground. A small hydraulic jack and a block of wood can be used to raise the chassis. If the transmission is not going to be worked on and the drive chain is

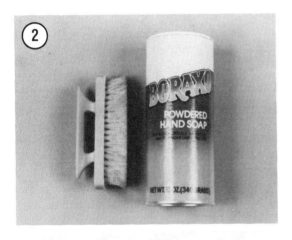

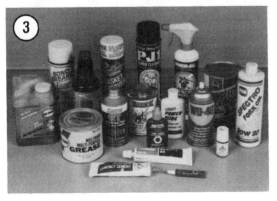

connected to the rear wheel, shift the transmission into first gear.

8. Disconnect the negative battery cable when working on or near the electrical, clutch, or starter systems and before disconnecting any electrical wires. On most batteries, the negative terminal will be marked with a minus (–) sign and the positive terminal with a plus (+) sign.

9. During disassembly of parts, keep a few general cautions in mind. Force is rarely needed to get things apart. If parts are a tight fit, such as a bearing in a case, there is usually a tool designed to separate them. Never use a screwdriver to pry parts with machined surfaces such as crankcase halves. You will mar the surfaces and end up with leaks.

10. Make diagrams (or take a Polaroid picture) wherever similar-appearing parts are found. For instance, crankcase bolts are often not the same length. You may think you can remember where everything came from, but mistakes are costly. There is also the possibility you may be sidetracked and not return to work for days or even weeks, in which interval carefully laid out parts may have become disturbed.

11. Tag all similar internal parts for location and mark all mating parts for position. Record number and thickness of any shims as they are removed. Small parts such as bolts can be identified by placing them in plastic sandwich bags. Seal and label them with masking tape.

12. Wiring should be tagged with masking tape and marked as each wire is removed. Again, do not rely on memory alone.

13. Protect finished surfaces from physical damage or corrosion. Keep gasoline and hydraulic brake fluid off plastic parts and painted and plated surfaces.

14. Frozen or very tight bolts and screws can often be loosened by soaking with penetrating oil, such as WD-40 or Liquid Wrench, then sharply striking the bolt head a few times with a hammer and punch (or screwdriver for screws). Avoid heat unless absolutely necessary, since it may melt, warp or remove the temper from many parts.

15. No parts, except those assembled with a press fit, require unusual force during assembly. If a part is hard to remove or install, find out why before proceeding.

16. Cover all openings after removing parts to keep dirt, small tools, etc., from falling in.

17. Wiring connections and brake components should be kept clean and free of grease and oil.

18. When assembling 2 parts, start all fasteners, then tighten evenly.

19. When assembling parts, be sure all shims and washers are installed exactly as they came out.

20. Whenever a rotating part butts against a stationary part, look for a shim or washer.

21. Use new gaskets if there is any doubt about the condition of the old ones. A thin coat of oil on gaskets may help them seal effectively.

22. Heavy grease can be used to hold small parts in place if they tend to fall out during assembly. However, keep grease and oil away from electrical and brake components.

23. High spots may be sanded off a piston with sandpaper, but fine emery cloth and oil will do a much more professional job.

24. Carbon can be removed from the head, the piston crown and the exhaust port with a dull screwdriver. Do *not* scratch machined surfaces. Wipe off the surface with a clean cloth when finished.

25. The carburetors are best cleaned by disassembling them and soaking the parts in a commercial carburetor cleaner. Never soak gaskets and rubber parts in these cleaners. Never use wire to clean out jets and air passages; they are easily damaged. Use compressed air to blow out the carburetor *after* the float has been removed.

26. A baby bottle makes a good measuring device for adding oil to the front forks. Get one that is graduated in fluid ounces and cubic centimeters. After it has been used for this purpose, do *not* let a small child drink out of it as there will always be an oil residue in it.

27. Some operations require the use of a press. It would be wiser to have these performed by a shop equipped for such work, rather than trying to do the job yourself with makeshift equipment. Other procedures require precise measurements. Unless you have the skills and equipment required, it would be better to have a qualified repair shop make the measurements for you.

SPECIAL TIPS

Because of the extreme demands placed on a bike, several points should be kept in mind when performing service and repair. The following items are general suggestions that may improve the overall life of the machine and help avoid costly failures.

1. Use a locking compound such as Loctite Threadlocker No. 242 (blue) on all bolts and nuts, even if they are secured with lockwashers. This type of Loctite does not harden completely and allows easy removal of the bolt or nut. A screw or bolt lost from an engine cover or bearing retainer could easily cause serious and expensive damage before its loss is noticed. Make sure the threads are clean and free of grease and oil. Clean with contact cleaner before applying the Loctite. When applying Loctite, use a small amount. If too much is used, it can work its way down the threads and stick parts together not meant to be stuck. Keep a tube of Loctite in your tool box. When used properly it is cheap insurance.

2. Use a hammer-driven impact tool to remove and install all bolts, particularly engine cover screws. These tools help prevent the rounding off of bolt heads and ensure a tight installation.

3. When replacing missing or broken fasteners (bolts, nuts and screws), especially on the engine or

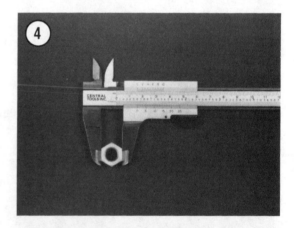

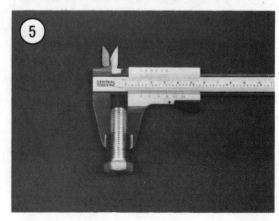

frame components, always use Yamaha replacement parts. They are specially hardened for each application. The wrong 50-cent bolt could easily cause serious and expensive damage, not to mention rider injury.

4. When installing gaskets in the engine, always use Yamaha replacement gaskets *without* sealer, unless designated. These gaskets are designed to swell when they come in contact with oil. Gasket sealer will prevent the gaskets from swelling as intended, which can result in oil leaks. These Yamaha gaskets are cut from material of the precise thickness needed. Installation of a too thick or too thin gasket in a critical area could cause engine damage.

TORQUE SPECIFICATIONS

Torque specifications throughout this manual are given in Newton meters (N•m) and foot-pounds (ft.-lb.). Newton meters have been adopted in place of meter kilograms (mkg) in accordance with the International Modernized Metric System. Tool manufacturers offer torque wrenches calibrated in both Newton meters and foot-pounds.

Existing torque wrenches calibrated in meter kilograms can be used by performing a simple conversion. All you have to do is move the decimal point one place to the right; for example, 4.7 mkg = 47 N•m. This conversion is accurate enough for mechanical work even though the exact mathematical conversion is 3.5 mkg = 34.3 N•m.

Refer to **Table 2** for standard torque specifications for various size screws, bolts and nuts that may not

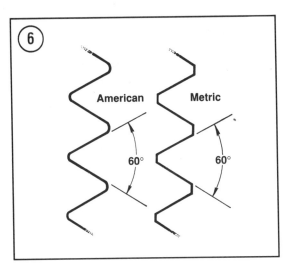

be listed in the respective chapters. To use the table, first determine the size of the bolt or nut. Use a vernier caliper and measure across the flats of the nut (**Figure 4**) and across the threads for a bolt (**Figure 5**).

FASTENERS

The materials and designs of the various fasteners used on your Yamaha are not arrived at by chance or accident. Fastener design determines the type of tool required to work the fastener. Fastener material is carefully selected to decrease the possibility of physical failure.

Threads

Nuts, bolts and screws are manufactured in a wide range of thread patterns. To join a nut and bolt, the diameter of the bolt and the diameter of the hole in the nuts must be the same. It is just as important that the threads on both be properly matched.

The best way to tell if the threads on 2 fasteners are matched is to turn the nut on the bolt (or the bolt into the threaded hole in the piece of equipment), with your fingers only. Be sure both pieces are clean. If much force is required, check the thread condition on each fastener. If the thread condition is good but the fastener jams, the threads are not compatible. A thread pitch gauge can also be used to determine pitch. Yamaha motorcycles are manufactured with metric standard fasteners. The threads are cut differently from those of American fasteners (**Figure 6**).

Most threads are cut so that the fastener must be turned *clockwise* to tighten it. These are called right-hand threads. Some fasteners have left-hand threads; they must be turned *counterclockwise* to be tightened. Left-hand threads are used in locations where normal rotation of the equipment would tend to loosen a right-hand threaded fastener. When left-hand threads are used in this manual they are identified in the text.

Machine Screws

There are many different types of machine screws. **Figure 7** shows a number of screw heads requiring different types of turning tools. Heads are also designed to protrude above the metal (round or hex) or to be slightly recessed in the metal (flat). See **Figure 8**.

Bolts

Commonly called bolts, the technical name for these fasteners is cap screws. Metric bolts are described by the diameter and pitch (or the distance between each thread). For example a M8 × 1.25 bolt is one that has a diameter of 8 millimeters and a distance of 1.25 millimeters between each thread. The measurement across 2 flats on the head of the bolt indicates the proper wrench size to be used. Use a vernier caliper and measure across the threads (**Figure 5**) to determine the bolt diameter.

Nuts

Nuts are manufactured in a variety of type and sizes. Most are hexagonal (6-sided) and fit on bolts, screws and studs with the same diameter and pitch.

Figure 9 shows several types of nuts. The common nut is generally used with a lockwasher. Self-locking nuts have a nylon insert which prevents the nut from loosening; no lockwasher is required. Wing nuts are designed for fast removal by hand. Wing nuts are used for convenience in non-critical locations.

To indicate the size of a nut, manufacturers specify the diameter of the opening and the threads per inch. This is similar to bolt specifications, but without the length dimension. The measurement across 2 flats on the nut indicates the proper wrench size to be used. **Figure 4** shows how to determine bolt diameter.

Prevailing Torque Fasteners

Several types of bolts, screws and nuts incorporate a system that develops an interference between the bolt, screw, nut or tapped hole threads. Interference is achieved in various ways: by distorting threads, coating threads with dry adhesive or nylon, distorting the top of an all-metal nut, using a nylon insert in the center or at the top of a nut, etc.

Prevailing torque fasteners offer greater holding strength and better vibration resistance. Some prevailing torque fasteners can be reused if in good condition. Others, like the nylon insert nut, form an initial locking condition when the nut is first installed; the nylon forms closely to the bolt thread pattern, thus reducing any tendency for the nut to loosen. When the nut is removed, its locking efficiency is greatly reduced. For greatest safety it is recommended that you install new prevailing torque fasteners whenever they are removed.

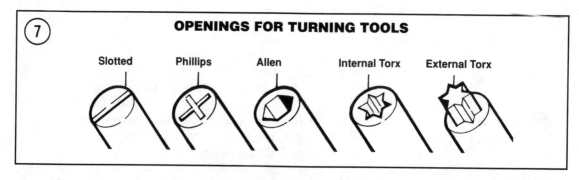

(7) OPENINGS FOR TURNING TOOLS

Slotted   Phillips   Allen   Internal Torx   External Torx

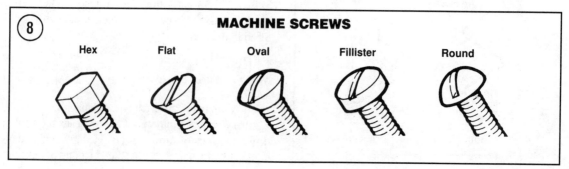

(8) MACHINE SCREWS

Hex   Flat   Oval   Fillister   Round

Washers

There are 2 basic types of washers: flat washers and lockwashers. Flat washers are simple discs with a hole to fit a screw or bolt. Lockwashers are designed to prevent a fastener from working loose due to vibration, expansion and contraction. **Figure 10** shows several types of washers. Washers are also used in the following functions:

a. As spacers.

b. To prevent galling or damage of the equipment by the fastener.

c. To help distribute fastener load during torquing.

d. As fluid seals (copper or laminated washers).

Note that flat washers are often used with a fastener to provide a smooth bearing surface. This allows the fastener to be turned easily with a tool.

Cotter Pins

Cotter pins (**Figure 11**) are used to secure special kinds of fasteners. The threaded stud must have a hole in it; the nut or nut lock piece has castellations around which the cotter pin ends wrap. Cotter pins should not be reused after removal as the ends may break and the cotter pin could then fall out.

Circlips

Circlips (or snap rings) can be of internal or external design. They are used to retain items on shafts (external type) or within tubes (internal type). In some applications, circlips of varying thickness are used to control the end play of parts assemblies. These are often called selective circlips. Circlips should be replaced during installation, as removal weakens and deforms them.

Two basic types of circlips are available: machined and stamped circlips. Machined circlips can be installed in either direction (shaft or housing) because both faces are machined, thus creating two sharp edges. Stamped circlips (**Figure 12**) are manufactured with one sharp edge and one rounded edge. When installing stamped circlips in a thrust situation

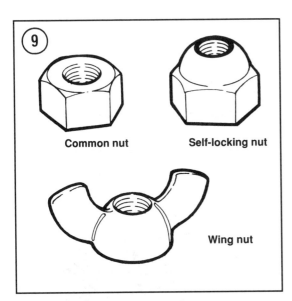

Common nut   Self-locking nut

Wing nut

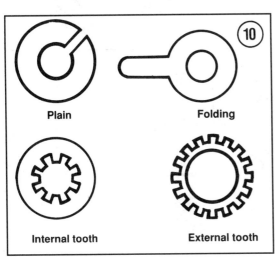

Plain   Folding

Internal tooth   External tooth

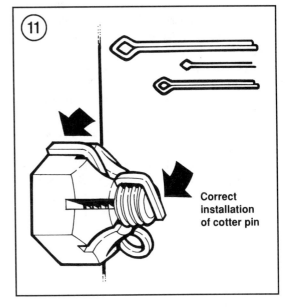

Correct installation of cotter pin

(transmission shafts, fork tubes, etc.), the sharp edge must face away from the part producing the thrust (**Figure 13**). When installing circlips, observe the following:

  a. Compress or expand the circlip only enough to install or remove it.
  b. After the circlip is installed, make sure it is completely seated in its groove.

LUBRICANTS

Periodic lubrication assures long life for any type of equipment. The *type* of lubricant used is just as important as the lubrication service itself, although in an emergency the wrong type of lubricant is better than none at all. The following paragraphs describe the types of lubricants most often used on motorcycle equipment. Be sure to follow the motorcycle's manufacturer's recommendations for lubricant types.

Generally, all liquid lubricants are called "oil." They may be mineral-based (including petroleum bases), natural based (vegetable and animal bases), synthetic-based or emulsions (mixtures). "Grease" is an oil to which a thickening base has been added so that the end product is semi-solid. Grease is often classified by the type of thickener added; lithium soap is commonly used.

Engine Oil

Oil for motorcycle and automotive engines is graded by the American Petroleum Institute (API) and the Society of Automotive Engineers (SAE) in several categories. Oil containers display these ratings on the top of the can or on the bottle label (**Figure 14**).

API oil grade is indicated by letters; oils for gasoline engines are identified by an "S." The engines covered in this manual require a minimum of SE or SF graded oil.

Viscosity is an indication of the oil's thickness. The SAE uses numbers to indicate viscosity; thin oils have low numbers while thick oils have high numbers. A "W" after the number indicates that the viscosity testing was done at a low temperature to simulate cold-weather operation. Engine oils fall into the 5W-30 and 20W-50 range.

Multi-grade oils (for example 10W-40) maintain the same viscosity at low temperatures and at high

temperatures. This allows the oil to perform efficiently across a wide range of engine operating conditions. The lower the number, the better the engine will start in cold climates. Higher numbers are usually recommended for engines running in hot weather conditions.

Grease

Greases are graded by the National Lubricating Grease Institute (NLGI). Greases are graded by number according to the consistency of the grease; these range from No. 000 to No. 6, with No. 6 being

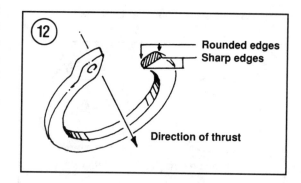

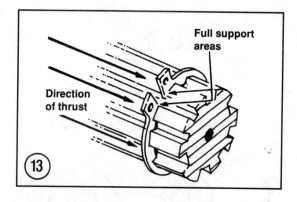

the most solid. A typical multipurpose grease is NLGI No. 2. For specific applications, equipment manufacturers may require grease with an additive such as molybdenum disulfide (MOS2).

EXPENDABLE SUPPLIES

Certain expendable supplies are required during maintenance and repair work. These include grease, oil, gasket cement, wiping rags and cleaning solvent. Ask your dealer for the special locking compounds, silicone lubricants and other products (**Figure 3**) which make vehicle maintenance simpler and easier. Cleaning solvent or kerosene is available at some service stations or hardware stores.

PARTS REPLACEMENT

Yamaha makes frequent changes during a model year—some minor, some relatively major. When you order parts from the dealer or other parts distributor, always order by engine and frame number. Write the numbers down and carry them with you. Compare new parts to old before purchasing them.

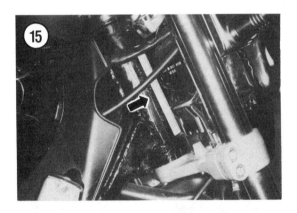

If they are not alike, have the parts manager explain the difference to you.

SERIAL NUMBERS

You must know the model serial number and VIN number for registration purposes and when ordering replacement parts.

The frame serial number and vehicle identification number (VIN) is stamped on the right-hand side of the steering head (**Figure 15**). The engine serial number is located on the top right-hand surface of the crankcase (**Figure 16**).

BASIC HAND TOOLS

Many tools are required to maintain a bike in top riding condition. You may already have some of these tools for home or car repairs. There are also tools made especially for bike repairs; these you will have to purchase. In any case, a wide variety of quality tools will make bike repairs easier and more effective.

Top-quality tools are essential; they are also more economical in the long run. If you are now starting to build your tool collection, stay away from the "advertised specials" featured at some parts houses, discount stores and chain drug stores. These are usually a poor grade tool that can be sold cheaply and that is exactly what they are—*cheap*. They are usually made of inferior material and are thick, heavy and clumsy. Their rough finish makes them difficult to clean and they usually don't last very long. The Stanley line, available from most hardware stores is a good all-around line of tools and will last you a lifetime if you take care of them. Also be careful when lending tools to "friends"—make sure they return them promptly; if not, your collection will soon disappear.

Quality tools are made of alloy steel and are heat treated for greater strength. They are lighter and better balanced than cheap ones. Their surface is smooth, making them a pleasure to work with and easy to clean. The initial cost of good quality tools may be more but it is cheaper in the long run. Don't try to buy everything in all sizes in the beginning; do it a little at a time until you have the necessary tools.

Keep your tools clean and in a tool box. Keep them organized with the sockets and related drives together and the open-end and box-end wrenches together, etc. After using a tool, wipe off dirt and grease with a clean cloth and place the tool in its correct place. Doing this will save a lot of time you would have spent trying to find a socket buried in a bunch of clutch parts.

The following tools are required to perform virtually any repair job on a bike. Each tool is described and the recommended size given for starting a tool collection. **Table 3** includes the tools that should be on hand for simple home repairs and/or major overhaul as shown in **Figure 17**. Additional tools and some duplicates may be added as you become more familiar with the bike. Almost all motorcycles and bikes (with the exception of the U.S. built Harley and some English bikes) use metric size bolts and nuts. If you are starting your collection now, buy metric sizes.

Screwdrivers

The screwdriver is a very basic tool, but if used improperly it will do more damage than good. The slot on a screw has a definite dimension and shape. A screwdriver must be selected to conform with that shape. Use a small screwdriver for small screws and a large one for large screws or the screw head will be damaged.

Two basic types of screwdrivers are required to repair the bike—a common (flat blade) screwdriver (**Figure 18**) and the Phillips screwdriver (**Figure 19**).

Screwdrivers are available in sets which often include an assortment of common and Phillips blades. If you buy them individually, buy at least the following:

    a. Common screwdriver—5/16 × 6 in. blade.

    b. Common screwdriver—3/8 × 12 in. blade.

    c. Phillips screwdriver—size 2 tip, 6 in. blade.

Use screwdrivers only for driving screws. Never use a screwdriver for prying or chiseling. Do not try to remove a Phillips or Allen head screw with a common screwdriver; you can damage the head so that the proper tool will be unable to remove it.

Keep screwdrivers in the proper condition and they will last longer and perform better. Always keep the tip of a common screwdriver in good condition. **Figure 20** shows how to grind the tip to the proper shape if it becomes damaged. Note the parallel sides of the tip.

Pliers

Pliers come in a wide range of types and sizes. Pliers are useful for cutting, bending and crimping. They should never be used to cut hardened objects or to turn bolts or nuts. **Figure 21** shows several pliers useful in bike repairs.

Each type of pliers has a specialized function. Gas pliers are general purpose pliers and are used mainly for holding things and for bending. Vise-grips are used as pliers or to hold objects very tight like a vise.

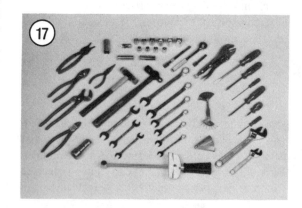

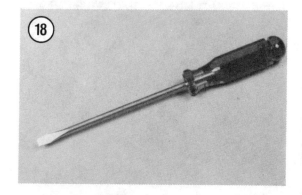

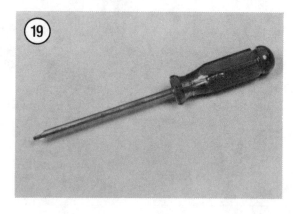

Needlenose pliers are used to hold or bend small objects. Channel lock pliers can be adjusted to hold various sizes of objects; the jaws remain parallel to grip around objects such as pipe or tubing. There are many more types of pliers. The ones described here are most suitable for bike repairs.

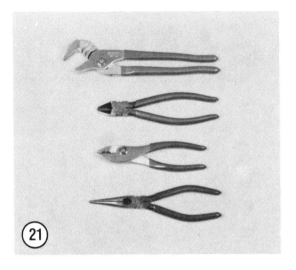

Box-end and Open-end Wrenches

Box-end and open-end wrenches are available in sets or separately in a variety of sizes. The size number stamped near the end refers to the distance between 2 parallel flats on the hex head bolt or nut.

Box-end wrenches are usually superior to open-end wrenches. Open-end wrenches grip the nut on only 2 flats. Unless they fit well, they may slip and round off the points on the nut. The box-end wrench grips all 6 flats. Both 6-point and 12-point openings on box-end wrenches are available. The 6-point gives superior holding power; the 12-point allows a shorter swing.

Combination wrenches (**Figure 22**) which are open on one side and boxed on the other are also available. Both ends are the same size.

Adjustable (Crescent) Wrenches

An adjustable wrench (also called crescent wrench) can be adjusted to fit nearly any nut or bolt

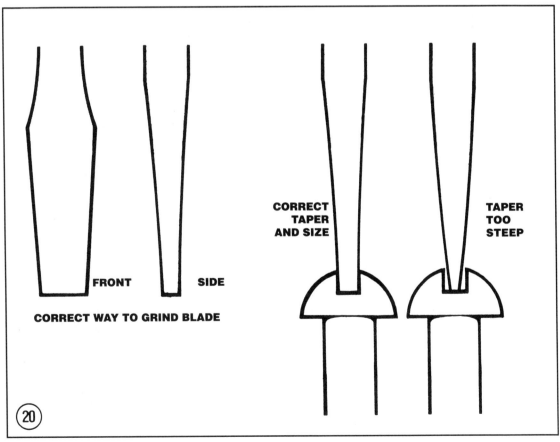

head. See **Figure 23**. However, it can loosen and slip, causing damage to the nut and injury to your knuckles. Use an adjustable wrench only when other wrenches are not available.

Adjustable wrenches come in sizes ranging from 4-18 in. overall. A 6 or 8 in. wrench is recommended as an all-purpose wrench.

Socket Wrenches

This type is undoubtedly the fastest, safest and most convenient to use. See **Figure 24**. Sockets which attach to a ratchet handle are available with 6-point or 12-point openings and 1/4, 3/8, 1/2 and 3/4 inch drives. The drive size indicates the size of the square hole which mates with the ratchet handle.

Allen Wrenches

Allen wrenches (**Figure 25**) are available in sets or separately in a variety of sizes. These sets come in SAE and metric size, so be sure to buy a metric set.

Torque Wrench

A torque wrench is used with a socket to measure how tightly a nut or bolt is installed. They come in a wide price range and with either 3/8 or 1/2 in. square drive (**Figure 26**). The drive size indicates the size of the square drive which mates with the socket. Purchase one that measures 0-280 N•m (0-200 ft.-lb.)

Impact Driver

This tool might have been designed with the bike in mind. See **Figure 27**. It makes removal of engine and clutch parts easy and eliminates damage to bolts and screw slots. Impact drivers are available at most large hardware, motorcycle or auto parts stores.

Circlip Pliers

Circlip pliers (sometimes referred to as snap-ring pliers) are necessary to remove the circlips used on the transmission shaft assemblies and the transmission assemblies. See **Figure 28**.

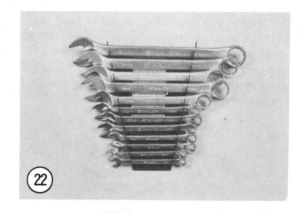

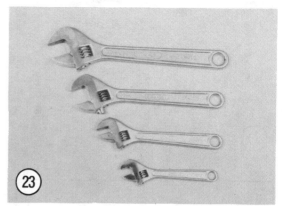

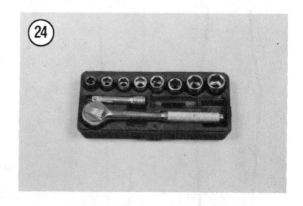

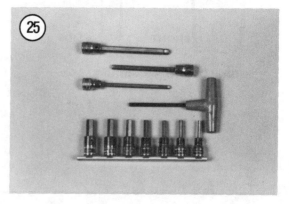

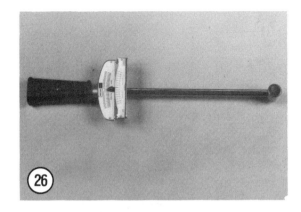

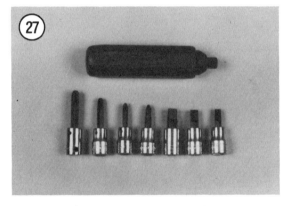

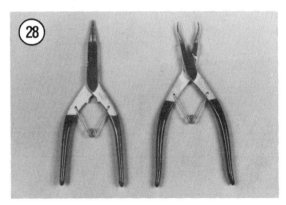

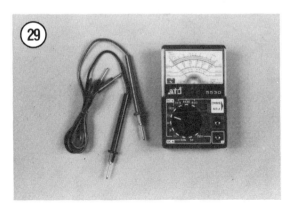

Hammers

The correct hammer is necessary for bike repairs. Use only a hammer with a face (or head) of rubber or plastic or the soft-faced type that is filled with buck shot. These are sometimes necessary in engine tear-downs. *Never* use a metal-faced hammer on the bike as severe damage will result in most cases. You can always produce the same amount of force with a soft-faced hammer.

Ignition Gauge

This tool has both flat and wire measuring gauges and is used to measure spark plug gap. This device is available at most auto or motorcycle supply stores.

Other Special Tools

A few other special tools may be required for major service. These are described in the appropriate chapters and are available either from a Yamaha dealer or other manufacturers as indicated.

TUNE-UP AND TROUBLESHOOTING TOOLS

Multimeter or Volt-ohm Meter

This instrument (**Figure 29**) is invaluable for electrical system troubleshooting and service. A few of its functions may be duplicated by homemade test equipment, but for the serious mechanic it is a must. Its uses are described in the applicable sections of the book.

Strobe Timing Light

This instrument is necessary for tuning. By flashing a light at the precise instant the spark plug fires, the position of the timing mark can be seen. Marks on the alternator flywheel line up with the stationary mark on the crankcase while the engine is running.

Suitable lights range from inexpensive neon bulb types to powerful xenon strobe lights (**Figure 30**). Neon timing lights are difficult to see and must be used in dimly lit areas. Xenon strobe timing lights can be used outside in bright sunlight. Both types work on the bike; use according to the manufacturer's instructions.

Portable Tachometer

A portable tachometer is necessary for tuning. Ignition timing and carburetor adjustments must be performed at the specified engine speed. The best instrument for this purpose is one with a low range of 0-1,000 or 0-2,000 rpm and a high range of 0-4,000 rpm. Extended range (0-6,000 or 0-8,000 rpm) instruments lack accuracy at lower speeds. The instrument should be capable of detecting changes of 25 rpm on the low range.

Compression Gauge

A compression gauge (**Figure 31**) measures the engine compression. The results, when properly interpreted, can indicate general ring and valve condition. They are available from motorcycle or auto supply stores and mail order outlets.

MECHANIC'S TIPS

Removing Frozen Nuts and Screws

When a fastener rusts and cannot be removed, several methods may be used to loosen it. First, apply penetrating oil such as Liquid Wrench or WD-40 (available at any hardware or auto supply store). Apply it liberally and let it penetrate for 10-15 minutes. Rap the fastener several times with a small hammer; do not hit it hard enough to cause damage. Reapply the penetrating oil if necessary.

For frozen screws, apply penetrating oil as described, then insert a screwdriver in the slot and rap the top of the screwdriver with a hammer. This loosens the rust so the screw can be removed in the

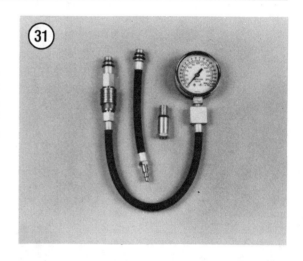

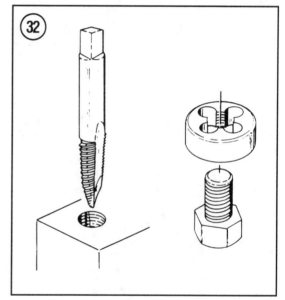

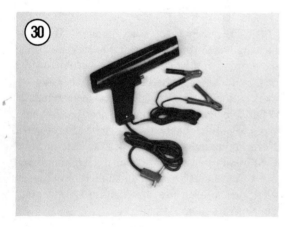

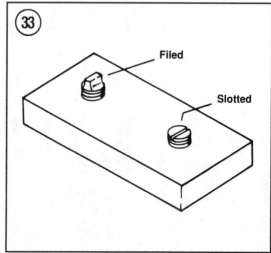

Filed

Slotted

normal way. If the screw head is too chewed up to use a screwdriver, grip the head with Vise-grip pliers and twist the screw out.

Remedying Stripped Threads

Occasionally, threads are stripped though carelessness or impact damage. Often the threads can be cleaned up by running a tap (for internal threads on nuts) or die (for external threads on bolts) through or over the threads. See **Figure 32**.

Removing Broken Screws or Bolts

When the head breaks off a screw or bolt, several methods are available for removing the remaining portion.

If a large portion of the remainder projects out, try gripping it with Vise-grip pliers. If the projecting portion is too small, file it to fit a wrench or cut a slot in it to fit a screwdriver. See **Figure 33**.

If the head breaks off flush, use a screw extractor. To do this, centerpunch the remaining portion of the

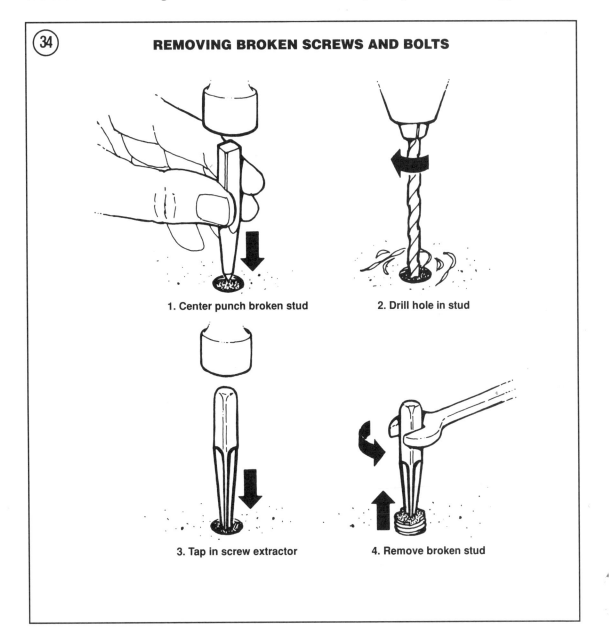

REMOVING BROKEN SCREWS AND BOLTS

1. Center punch broken stud

2. Drill hole in stud

3. Tap in screw extractor

4. Remove broken stud

screw or bolt. Drill a small hole in the screw and tap the extractor into the hole. Back the screw out with a wrench on the extractor. See **Figure 34**.

RIDING SAFETY

General Tips

1. Read your owner's manual and know your machine.
2. Check the throttle and brake controls before starting the engine.
3. Know how to make an emergency stop.
4. Never add fuel while anyone is smoking in the area or when the engine is running.
5. Never wear loose scarves, belts or boot laces that could catch on moving parts.
6. Always wear eye and head protection and protective clothing to protect your *entire* body. Today's riding apparel is very stylish and you will be ready for action as well as being well protected.
7. Riding in the winter months requires a good set of clothes to keep your body dry and warm, otherwise your entire trip may be miserable. If you dress properly, moisture will evaporate from your body. If you become too hot and if your clothes trap the moisture, you will become cold. Even mild temperatures can be very uncomfortable and dangerous when combined with a strong wind or traveling at high speed. See **Table 4** for wind chill factors. Always dress according to what the wind chill factor is, not the ambient temperature.
8. Never allow anyone to operate the bike without proper instruction. This is for their bodily protection and to keep your machine from damage or destruction.

9. Use the "buddy system" for long trips, just in case you have a problem or run out of gas.
10. Never attempt to repair your machine with the engine running except when necessary for certain tune-up procedures.
11. Check all of the machine components and hardware frequently, especially the wheels and the steering.

Operating Tips

1. Never operate the bike in crowed areas or steer toward people.
2. Avoid dangerous terrain.
3. Cross highways (where permitted) at a 90° angle after looking in both directions. Post traffic guards if crossing in groups.
4. Do not ride the bike on or near railroad tracks. The bike engine and exhaust noise can drown out the sound of an approaching train.
5. Keep the headlight, turn signal lights and taillight free of dirt.
6. Always steer with both hands.
7. Be aware of the terrain and avoid operating the bike at excessive speed.
8. Do not panic if the throttle sticks. Turn the engine stop switch to the OFF position.
9. Do not tailgate. Rear end collisions can cause injury and machine damage.
10. Do not mix alcoholic beverages or drugs with riding—*ride straight*.
11. Check your fuel supply regularly. Do not travel farther than your fuel supply will permit you to arrive at the next fuel stop.

Table 1 DECIMAL AND METRIC EQUIVALENTS

Fractions	Decimal in.	Metric mm	Fractions	Decimal in.	Metric mm
1/64	0.015625	0.39688	33/64	0.515625	13.09687
1/32	0.03125	0.79375	17/32	0.53125	13.49375
3/64	0.046875	1.19062	35/64	0.546875	13.89062
1/16	0.0625	1.58750	9/16	0.5625	14.28750
5/64	0.078125	1.98437	37/64	0.578125	14.68437
3/32	0.09375	2.38125	19/32	0.59375	15.08125
7/64	0.109375	2.77812	39/64	0.609375	15.47812
1/8	0.125	3.1750	5/8	0.625	15.87500
9/64	0.140625	3.57187	41/64	0.640625	16.27187
5/32	0.15625	3.96875	21/32	0.65625	16.66875
11/64	0.171875	4.36562	43/64	0.671875	17.06562
3/16	0.1875	4.76250	11/16	0.6875	17.46250
13/64	0.203125	5.15937	45/64	0.703125	17.85937
7/32	0.21875	5.55625	23/32	0.71875	18.25625
15/64	0.234375	5.95312	47/64	0.734375	18.65312
1/4	0.250	6.35000	3/4	0.750	19.05000
17/64	0.265625	6.74687	49/64	0.765625	19.44687
9/32	0.28125	7.14375	25/32	0.78125	19.84375
19/64	0.296875	7.54062	51/64	0.796875	20.24062
5/16	0.3125	7.93750	13/16	0.8125	20.63750
21/64	0.328125	8.33437	53/64	0.828125	21.03437
11/32	0.34375	8.73125	27/32	0.84375	21.43125
23/64	0.359375	9.12812	55/64	0.859375	22.82812
3/8	0.375	9.52500	7/8	0.875	22.22500
25/64	0.390625	9.92187	57/64	0.890625	22.62187
13/32	0.40625	10.31875	29/32	0.90625	23.01875
27/64	0.421875	10.71562	59/64	0.921875	23.41562
7/16	0.4375	11.11250	15/16	0.9375	23.81250
29/64	0.453125	11.50937	61/64	0.953125	24.20937
15/32	0.46875	11.90625	31/32	0.96875	24.60625
31/64	0.484375	12.30312	63/64	0.984375	25.00312
1/2	0.500	12.70000	1	1.00	25.40000

Table 2 TIGHTENING TORQUES*

Nut	Bolt	ft.-lb.	N·m
10 mm	6 mm	4.5	6
12 mm	8 mm	11	15
14 mm	10 mm	22	30
17 mm	12 mm	40	55
19 mm	14 mm	51	85
22 mm	16 mm	94	130

* This table lists general torque for standard fasteners with standard ISO pitch threads.

Table 3 HOME WORKSHOP TOOLS

Tool	Size or Specifications
Screwdriver	
Common	5/16 × 8 in. blade
Common	3/8 × 12 in. blade
Phillips	Size 2 tip, 6 in. overall

(continued)

Table 3 HOME WORKSHOP TOOLS (continued)

Tool	Size or Specifications
Pliers	
Slip-joint	6 in. overall
Vise-grip	10 in. overall
Needlenose	6 in. overall
Channel lock	12 in. overall
Snap ring	–
Wrenches	
Box-end set	5-17 mm, plus 24/28 mm
Open-end set	5-17 mm, plus 24/28 mm
Crescent	6 in. and 12 in. overall
Socket set	1/2 in. drive ratchet with 5-17 mm sockets
Other special tools	
Strap wrench	–
Impact wrench	1/2 in. drive with assorted bits
Torque wrench	1/2 in. drive 0-50 ft.-lb.
Ignition gauge	–

Table 4 WIND CHILL FACTORS

Estimated Wind Speed in MPH	Actual Thermometer Reading (°F)*											
	50	40	30	20	10	0	-10	-20	-30	-40	-50	-60
	Equivalent Temperature (°F)*											
Calm	50	40	30	20	10	0	–10	–20	–30	–40	–50	–60
5	48	37	27	16	6	–5	–15	–26	–36	–47	–57	–68
10	40	28	16	4	–9	–21	–33	–46	–58	–70	–83	–95
15	36	22	9	–5	–18	–36	–45	–58	–72	–85	–99	–112
20	32	18	4	–10	–25	–39	–53	–67	–82	–96	–110	–124
25	30	16	0	–15	–29	–44	–59	–74	–88	–104	–118	–133
30	28	13	–2	–18	–33	–48	–63	–79	–94	–109	–125	–140
35	27	11	–4	–20	–35	–49	–67	–82	–98	–113	–129	–145
40	26	10	–6	–21	–37	–53	–69	–85	–100	–116	–132	–148
**	Little Danger (for properly clothed person)			Increasing Danger			Great Danger • Danger from freezing of exposed flesh •					

* To convert Fahrenheit (°F) to Celsius (°C), use the following formula: °C = 5/9 × (°F - 32).
**Wind speeds greater than 40 mph have little additional effect.

TROUBLESHOOTING

Diagnosing mechanical problems is relatively simple if you use orderly procedures and keep a few basic principles in mind.

The troubleshooting procedures in this chapter analyze typical symptoms and show logical methods of isolating causes. These are not the only methods. There may be several ways to solve a problem, but only a systematic, methodical approach can guarantee success.

Never assume anything. Do not overlook the obvious. If you are riding along and the engine suddenly quits, check the easiest, most accessible problems first. Is there gasoline in the tank? Is the fuel shutoff valve in the ON position? Has a spark plug wire cap(s) become loose? Check the ignition switch and key. Sometimes the weight of the key ring may turn the ignition off suddenly.

If nothing obvious turns up in a quick check, look a little further. Learning to recognize and describe symptoms will make repairs easier for you or a mechanic at the shop. Describe problems accurately and fully. Saying that "it won't run" isn't the same as saying "it quit at high speed and won't start" or that "it sat in my garage for 3 months and then wouldn't start."

Gather as many symptoms together as possible to aid in diagnosis. Note whether the engine lost power gradually or all at once. Remember that the more complicated a machine is, the easier it is to troubleshoot because symptoms point to specific problems.

After the symptoms are defined, areas which could cause the problems are tested and analyzed. Guessing at the cause of a problem may provide the solution, but it can easily lead to frustration, wasted time and a series of expensive, unnecessary parts replacements.

You do not need fancy equipment or complicated test gear to determine whether repairs can be attempted at home. A few simple checks could save a large repair bill and time lost while the bike sits in a dealer's service department. On the other hand, be realistic and don't attempt repairs beyond your abilities. Service departments tend to charge a lot for putting together a disassembled engine that may have been abused. Some dealers won't even take on such a job—so use common sense and don't get in over your head.

OPERATING REQUIREMENTS

An engine needs 3 basics to run properly: correct fuel-air mixture, compression and a spark at the correct time. If one or more are missing, the engine just won't run. The electrical system is the weakest link of the 3 basics. More problems result from electrical breakdowns than from any other source.

Keep that in mind before you begin tampering with carburetor adjustments and the like.

If the bike has been sitting for any length of time and refuses to start, check and clean the spark plugs and then look to the gasoline delivery system. This includes the fuel tank, fuel shutoff valve and the fuel line to the carburetors and the vacuum line to the fuel shutoff valve. Gasoline deposits may have formed and gummed up the carburetor's jets and air passages. Gasoline tends to lose its potency after standing for long periods. Condensation may contaminate the fuel with water. Drain the old fuel and try starting with fresh.

EMERGENCY TROUBLESHOOTING

When the bike is difficult to start or won't start at all, it does not help to wear down the battery with the starter. Check for obvious problems even before getting out your tools. Go down the following list step by step. Do each one; you may be embarrassed to find your engine stop switch is stuck in the OFF position, but that is better than wearing down the battery. If it still will not start, refer to the appropriate troubleshooting procedure which follows in this chapter.

> *WARNING*
> *Do not use an open flame to check in the tank. A serious explosion is certain to result.*

1. Is there fuel in the tank? Open the filler cap (**Figure 1**) and rock the bike. Listen for fuel sloshing around.

2. Is the fuel shutoff valve (**Figure 2**) in the ON position and is the vacuum line to the valve from the engine still connected?

3. Make sure the engine stop switch (**Figure 3**) is not in the OFF position.

4. Are the spark plug wire caps (**Figure 4**) on tight? Push all four of them on and slightly rotate them to clean the electrical connection between the plug and the connector.

5A. On Radian models, is the choke in the correct position? The lever should be moved toward the *left* (**Figure 5**) or toward the hand grip for a cold engine and moved in toward the *right* (**Figure 6**) for a warm engine.

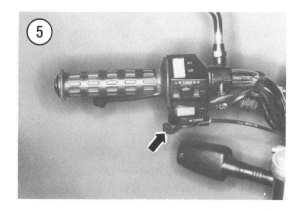

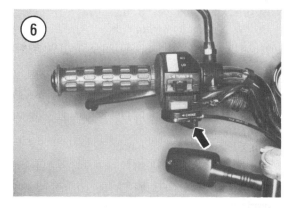

5B. On FZ600 models, the lever on the carburetor assembly should be moved *forward* (**Figure 7**) for a cold engine and moved *back* (**Figure 8**) for a warm engine.

ENGINE STARTING

An engine that refuses to start or is difficult to start is very frustrating. More often than not, the problem is very minor and can be found with a simple and logical troubleshooting approach.

The following items show a beginning point from which to isolate engine starting problems.

Engine Fails to Start

Perform the following spark test to determine if the ignition system is operating properly.

1. Remove one of the spark plugs from the cylinder head.

2. Connect the spark plug wire and connector to the spark plug and touch the spark plug's base to a good ground such as the engine cylinder head (**Figure 9**). Make sure the spark plug is against some bare metal, not a painted surface. Position the spark plug so you can see the electrodes.

3. Crank the engine over with the starter. A fat blue spark should be evident across the plug's electrodes.

> *WARNING*
> *If it is necessary to hold the high voltage lead, do so with an insulated pair of pliers. The high voltage generated by the ignition pulse generator and ignitor unit could produce serious or fatal shocks.*

4. If the spark is good, check for one or more of the following possible malfunctions:

    a. Obstructed fuel line.

    b. Low compression.

    c. Leaking head gasket.

    d. Choke not operating properly.

    e. Throttle not operating properly.

5. If spark is not good, check for one or more of the following:

    a. Weak ignition coil.

    b. Weak or faulty ignitor unit.

    c. Broken or shorted high tension lead to the spark plug(s).

    d. Loose electrical connections.

    e. Loose or broken ignition coil ground wire.

Engine Is Difficult to Start

Check for one or more of the following possible malfunctions:

    a. Fouled spark plug.

    b. Improperly adjusted choke.

    c. Contaminated fuel system.

    d. Improperly adjusted carburetor.

    e. Weak ignition coil.

    f. Weak or faulty ignitor unit.

    g. Incorrect type ignition coil.

    h. Poor compression.

    i. Moisture in the ignitor unit electrical connector(s).

Engine Will Not Crank

Check for one or more of the following possible malfunctions:

    a. Discharged battery.

    b. Broken starter gears.

    c. Seized piston(s).

    d. Seized crankshaft bearings.

    e. Broken connecting rod(s).

    f. Locked-up transmission or clutch assembly.

ENGINE PERFORMANCE

In the following check list, it is assumed that the engine runs, but is not operating at peak performance. This will serve as a starting point from which to isolate a performance malfunction.

The possible causes for each malfunction are listed in a logical sequence and in order of probability.

Engine Will Not Start or Is Hard To Start

    a. Fuel tank empty.

    b. Obstructed fuel line or fuel shutoff valve.

    c. Sticking float valve in carburetor(s).

    d. Carburetors incorrectly adjusted.

    e. Improper choke operation.

    f. Fouled or improperly gapped spark plugs.

    g. Weak ignition pickup coil.

    h. Weak or faulty ignitor unit.

    i. Ignition timing incorrect (faulty component in system).

    j. Broken or shorted ignition coil.

    k. Improper valve timing.

    l. Moisture in the ignitor unit electrical connector(s).

    m. Clogged air filter element.

    n. Contaminated fuel.

Engine Will Not Idle or Idles Erratically

    a. Carburetor(s) incorrectly adjusted.

    b. Fouled or improperly gapped spark plugs.

    c. Leaking head gasket or vacuum leak.

    d. Weak ignition pickup coil.

    e. Weak or faulty ignitor unit.

    f. Ignition timing incorrect (faulty component in system).

    g. Moisture in the ignitor unit electrical connector(s).

    h. Improper valve timing.

    i. Obstructed fuel line or fuel shutoff valve.

Engine Misses at High Speed

    a. Fouled or improperly gapped spark plugs.

    b. Improper ignition timing (faulty component in system).

    c. Improper carburetor main jet selection.

    d. Clogged jets in the carburetor(s).

    e. Weak ignition coil.

    f. Weak ignition pickup coil.

    g. Weak or faulty ignitor unit.

h. Moisture in the ignitor unit electrical connector(s).

i. Improper valve timing.

j. Obstructed fuel line or fuel shutoff valve.

Engine Continues to Run with Ignition Off

a. Excessive carbon build-up in engine.

b. Vacuum leak in intake system.

c. Contaminated or incorrect fuel octane rating.

Engine Overheating

a. Obstructed cooling fins on the cylinder block and/or cylinder head.

b. Improper ignition timing (faulty component in system).

c. Improper spark plug heat range.

d. Engine oil level low.

Engine Misses at Idle

a. Fouled or improperly gapped spark plugs.

b. Spark plug caps faulty.

c. Ignition cable insulation deteriorated (shorting out).

d. Moisture in the ignitor unit electrical connector(s).

e. Dirty or clogged air filter element.

f. Carburetor(s) incorrectly adjusted (too lean or too rich).

g. Choke valves stuck.

h. Clogged jet(s) in the carburetor.

i. Carburetor float height incorrect.

Engine Backfires— Explosions in Mufflers

a. Fouled or improperly gapped spark plugs.

b. Spark plug caps faulty.

c. Ignition cable insulation deteriorated (shorting out).

d. Ignition timing incorrect.

e. Moisture in the ignitor unit electrical connector(s).

f. Improper valve timing.

g. Contaminated fuel.

h. Burned or damaged intake and/or exhaust valves.

i. Weak or broken intake and/or exhaust valve springs.

Pre-ignition (Fuel Mixture Ignites Before Spark Plug Fires)

a. Hot spot in combustion chamber (piece of carbon).

b. Valve(s) stuck in guide.

c. Overheating engine.

Smoky Exhaust and Engine Runs Roughly

a. Carburetor mixture too rich.

b. Choke not operating correctly.

c. Water or other contaminants in fuel.

d. Clogged fuel line.

e. Clogged air filter element.

Engine Loses Power at Normal Riding Speed

a. Carburetors incorrectly adjusted.

b. Engine overheating.

c. Improper ignition timing (faulty component in system).

d. Weak ignition pickup unit.

e. Weak or faulty ignitor unit.

f. Incorrectly gapped spark plugs.

g. Weak ignition coil.

h. Obstructed mufflers.

i. Dragging brake(s).

Engine Lacks Acceleration

a. Carburetor mixture too lean.

b. Clogged fuel line.

c. Improper ignition timing (faulty component in system).

d. Improper valve clearance.

e. Dragging brake(s).

ENGINE NOISES

1. *Knocking or pinging during acceleration—* Caused by using a lower octane fuel than recommended. May also be caused by poor fuel. Pinging

can also be caused by spark plugs of the wrong heat range. Refer to *Spark Plug Selection* in Chapter Three.

2. *Slapping or rattling noises at low speed or during acceleration*—May be caused by piston slap (excessive piston to cylinder wall clearance).

3. *Knocking or rapping while decelerating*—Usually caused by excessive rod bearing clearance.

4. *Persistent knocking and vibration*—Usually caused by excessive main bearing clearance.

5. *Rapid on-off squeal*—Compression leak around cylinder head gasket or spark plugs.

EXCESSIVE VIBRATION

This can be difficult to find without disassembling the engine. Usually this is caused by loose engine mounting hardware.

FRONT SUSPENSION AND STEERING

Poor handling may be caused by improper tire pressure, a damaged or bent frame or front steering components, a worn front fork assembly, worn wheel bearings or dragging brakes.

BRAKE PROBLEMS

Sticking disc brakes may be caused by a stuck piston(s) in a caliper assembly(ies) or warped pad shim or disc(s).

A sticking drum brake may be caused by worn or weak return springs, dry pivot and cam bushings or improper adjustment. Grabbing brakes may be caused by greasy linings which must be replaced. Brake grab may also be caused by an out-of-round drum. Glazed linings will cause loss of stopping power.

CHAPTER THREE

LUBRICATION, MAINTENANCE AND TUNE-UP

A motorcycle, even in normal use, is subjected to tremendous heat, stress and vibration. When neglected, any bike becomes unreliable and actually dangerous to ride.

To gain the utmost in safety, performance and useful life from the Yamaha Radian and FZ600, it is necessary to make periodic inspections and adjustments. Frequently, minor problems are found during these inspections that are simple and inexpensive to correct at the time. If they are not found and corrected at this time they could lead to major and more expensive problems later on.

Start by doing simple tune-up, lubrication and maintenance. Tackle more involved jobs as you become more acquainted with the bike.

Tables 1-6 are located at the end of this chapter.

NOTE
Where differences occur relating to the United Kingdom (UK) models, they are identified. If there is no (UK) designation relating to a procedure, photo or illustration, it is identical to the United States (U.S.) models.

ROUTINE CHECKS

The following simple checks should be performed at each stop at a service station for gas.

Engine Oil Level

Refer to *Engine Oil Level Check* under *Periodic Lubrication* in this chapter.

General Inspection

1. Quickly inspect the engine for signs of oil or fuel leakage.
2. Check the tires for embedded stones. Pry them out with a suitable tool.
3. Make sure all lights work.

NOTE
At least check the brake light. It can burn out at any time. Motorists cannot stop as quickly as you and need all the warning you can give.

Tire Pressure

Tire pressure must be checked with the tires cold. Correct tire pressure varies with the load you are carrying or if you have a passenger. See **Table 1**.

Battery

The electrolyte level must be between the upper and lower level marks on the case (**Figure 1**). For complete details see *Battery Removal, Installation and Electrolyte Level Check* in this chapter.

Check the level more frequently in hot weather; electrolyte will evaporate rapidly as heat increases.

Crankcase Breather Hose

Inspect the hose for cracks and deterioration and make sure that the hose clamps are tight (**Figure 2**).

Evaporative Emission
Control System
(California Models)

Inspect the hoses to make sure they are not kinked or bent and that they are securely connected to their respective parts.

Lights and Horn

With the engine running, check the following.
1. Pull the front brake lever on and check that the brake light comes on.
2. Push the rear brake pedal down and check that the brake light comes on soon after you have begun depressing the pedal.
3. Turn the ignition switch ON. Press the headlight dimmer switch to both the HI and LO positions and check to see that both headlight elements are working.
4. Turn the turn signal switch to the left and right positions and check that all 4 turn signals are working.
5. Push the horn button and make sure that the horn blows loudly.
6. If, during the test, the rear brake pedal traveled too far before the brakelight came on, adjust the rear brakelight switch as described in Chapter Eight.
7. If the horn or any of the lights failed to operate properly, refer to Chapter Eight.

PRE-CHECKS

The following checks should be performed prior to the first ride of the day.
1. Inspect all fuel lines and fittings for wetness.
2. Make sure the fuel tank is full of fresh gasoline.
3. Make sure the engine oil level is correct.

4. Check the operation of the front and rear brakes. Add hydraulic fluid to the front or rear (FZ600 models) brake master cylinder if necessary.
5. Check the operation of the clutch. If necessary, adjust the clutch free-play as described in this chapter.
6. Check the throttle and the rear brake pedal. Make sure they operate properly with no binding.
7. Inspect the front and rear suspension; make sure they have a good solid feel with no looseness.
8. Check tire pressure. Refer to **Table 1**.
9. Check the exhaust system for damage or leaks.
10. Check the tightness of all fasteners, especially engine mounting hardware.

SERVICE INTERVALS

The services and intervals shown in **Table 2** are recommended by the factory. Strict adherence to these recommendations will ensure long service from the Yamaha. If the bike is run in an area of high

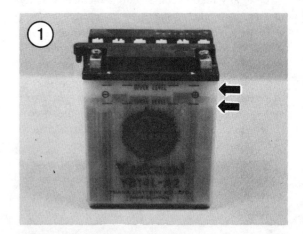

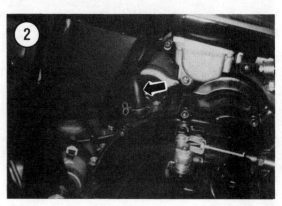

humidity, the lubrication services must be done more frequently to prevent possible rust damage.

For convenience when maintaining your motorcycle, most of the services shown in these tables are described in this chapter. However, some procedures which require more than minor disassembly or adjustment are covered elsewhere in the appropriate chapter.

TIRES AND WHEELS

Tire Pressure

Tire pressure should be checked and adjusted to maintain the smoothness of the tire, good traction and handling and to get the maximum life out of the tire. A simple, accurate gauge (**Figure 3**) can be purchased for a few dollars and should be carried in your motorcycle tool kit. The appropriate tire pressures are shown in **Table 1**.

> *NOTE*
> *After checking and adjusting the air pressure, make sure to install the air valve cap. The cap prevents small peb-*

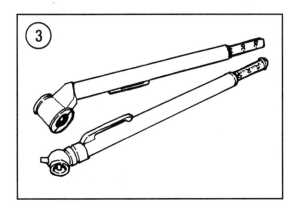

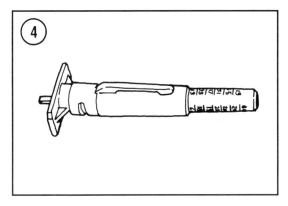

bles and dirt from collecting in the valve stem; this could allow air leakage or result in incorrect tire pressure readings.

Tire Inspection

The tires take a lot of punishment so inspect them periodically for excessive wear, cuts, abrasions, etc. If you find a nail or other object in the tire, mark its location with a light crayon prior to removing it. This will help locate the hole for repair. Refer to Chapter Nine for tire changing and repair information.

Check local traffic regulations concerning minimum tread depth. Measure the tread depth at the center of the tire tread using a tread depth gauge (**Figure 4**) or small ruler. Yamaha recommends that original equipment tires be replaced when the tread depth has worn to 1.0 mm (0.04 in.) or less.

Rim Inspection

Frequently inspect the wheel rims. If a rim has been damaged, it might have been enough to knock it out of alignment. Improper wheel alignment can cause severe vibration and result in an unsafe riding condition.

BATTERY

The battery is an important component in your Yamaha's electrical system. It is also the one most frequently neglected. In addition to checking and correcting the battery electrolyte level on a weekly basis, the battery should be cleaned and inspected at periodic intervals.

The battery used on your Yamaha should be checked periodically for electrolyte level, state of charge and corrosion. During hot weather periods, frequent checks are recommended. If the electrolyte level is below the fill line, add distilled water as required. To assure proper mixing of the water and acid, operate the engine immediately after adding water. *Never* add battery acid instead of water; this will shorten the battery's life.

> *CAUTION*
> *If it becomes necessary to remove the battery vent tube when performing any of the following procedures, make sure*

to route the tube correctly during installation to prevent acid from spilling onto
surrounding parts.

NOTE
Recycle your old battery. *When you replace the old battery, be sure to turn in
the old battery at that time. The lead
plates and the plastic case can be recycled. Most motorcycle dealers will accept your old battery in trade when you
purchase a new one, but if they will not,
many automotive supply stores cer-
tainly will. **Never** place an old battery
in your household trash since it is ille-
gal, in most states, to place any acid or
lead (heavy metal) contents in landfills.
There is also the danger of the battery
being crushed in the trash truck and
spraying acid on the truck operator.*

**Removal, Installation and
Electrolyte Level Check
(Radian Models)**

The battery is the heart of the electrical system.
Check and service the battery at the interval indicated in **Table 2**. The majority of electrical system
troubles can be attributed to neglect of this vital
component.

1. Remove the right-hand side cover (A, **Figure 5**).

NOTE
*It is not necessary to remove nor discon-
nect the voltage regulator from the
mounting cover. On later models, the
voltage regulator is not located here, it
is mounted on the front fork down tubes.*

2. Remove the screws securing the battery
cover/voltage regulator mounting cover (B, **Figure
5**). Move the cover out of the way.
3. First disconnect the battery negative (–) lead and
then the positive (+) lead from the battery terminals
(A, **Figure 6**).
4. Turn the battery to gain access to the breather tube,
then disconnect the breather tube from the battery
(B, **Figure 6**). Leave the breather tube routed
through the frame.

CAUTION
*Be careful not to spill battery electrolyte
on plastic, painted or plated surfaces.*

*The liquid is highly corrosive and will
damage the finish. If it is spilled, wash
it off immediately with soapy water and
thoroughly rinse with clean water.*

5. Carefully slide the battery up slightly and out of
the battery box.
6. The electrolyte level should be maintained between the 2 marks on the battery case (**Figure 1**).

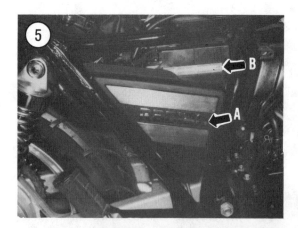

WARNING
Protect your eyes, skin and clothing. If electrolyte gets into your eyes, flush your eyes thoroughly with clean water and get prompt medical attention.

7. Remove the caps (**Figure 7**) from the battery cells and add distilled water to correct the level. Never add electrolyte (acid) to correct the level.

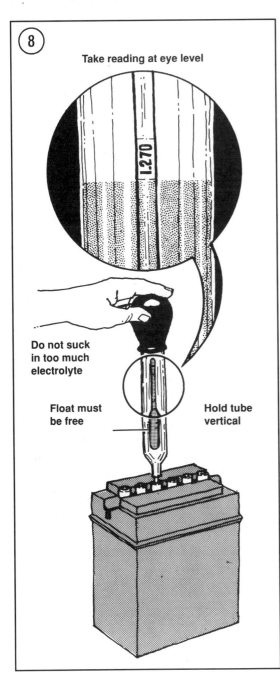

Take reading at eye level

1.270

Do not suck in too much electrolyte

Float must be free

Hold tube vertical

NOTE
If distilled water has been added, reinstall the battery caps and gently shake the battery for several minutes to mix the existing electrolyte with the new water.

8. After the fluid level has been corrected and the battery allowed to stand for a few minutes, remove the battery caps and check the specific gravity of the electrolyte with a hydrometer (**Figure 8**). See *Battery Testing* in this chapter.

9. After the battery has been refilled, recharged or replaced, install it by reversing these removal steps.

CAUTION
If you removed the breather tube from the frame, be sure to route the open end so that residue will not drain onto any part of the bike's frame. The breather tube must be free of bends or twists as any restrictions may pressurize the battery and damage it.

Removal, Installation and Electrolyte Level Check (FZ600 Models)

The battery is the heart of the electrical system. Check and service the battery at the interval indicated in **Table 2**. The majority of electrical system troubles can be attributed to neglect of this vital component.

1. Remove the rider and passenger seats as described under *Seat Removal/Installation* in Chapter Twelve.

2. First disconnect the battery negative (–) lead and then the positive (+) lead from the battery terminals (A, **Figure 9**).

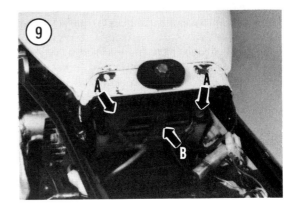

3. Unhook the rubber retaining strap (B, **Figure 9**) from the top of the battery.

4. Disconnect the breather tube from the battery. Leave the breather tube routed through the frame.

CAUTION
Be careful not to spill battery electrolyte on plastic, painted or plated surfaces. The liquid is highly corrosive and will damage the finish. If it is spilled, wash it off immediately with soapy water and thoroughly rinse with clean water.

5. Carefully slide the battery toward the back and out of the battery box.

6. The electrolyte level should be maintained between the 2 marks on the battery case (**Figure 1**).

WARNING
Protect your eyes, skin and clothing. If electrolyte gets into your eyes, flush your eyes thoroughly with clean water and get prompt medical attention.

7. Remove the cap from the battery cells and add distilled water to correct the level. Never add electrolyte (acid) to correct the level.

NOTE
If distilled water has been added, re-install the battery caps and gently shake the battery for several minutes to mix the existing electrolyte with the new water.

CAUTION
If distilled water has been added to a battery in freezing or near freezing weather, add it to the battery, dress warmly and then ride the bike for a minimum of 30 minutes. This will help mix the water thoroughly into the electrolyte in the battery. Distilled water is lighter than electrolyte and will float on top of the electrolyte if it is not mixed in properly. If the water stays on the top, it may freeze and fracture the battery case, ruining the battery.

8. After the fluid level has been corrected and the battery allowed to stand for a few minutes, remove the battery caps and check the specific gravity of the electrolyte with a hydrometer (**Figure 8**). See *Battery Testing* in this chapter.

9. After the battery has been refilled, recharged or replaced, install it by reversing these removal steps.

CAUTION
If you removed the breather tube from the frame, be sure to route the open end so that residue will not drain onto any part of the bike's frame. The breather tube must be free of bends or twists as any restrictions may pressurize the battery and damage it.

Testing

Hydrometer testing is the best way to check battery condition. Use a hydrometer with numbered graduations from 1.100 to 1.300 rather than one with color-coded bands. To use the hydrometer, squeeze the rubber ball, insert the tip into the cell and release the pressure on the ball. Draw enough electrolyte to float the weighted float inside the hydrometer. Note the number in line with the surface of the electrolyte; this is the specific gravity for this cell. Squeeze the rubber ball again and return the electrolyte to the cell from which it came.

The specific gravity of the electrolyte in each battery cell is an excellent indication of that cell's condition. A fully charged cell will read from 1.260-1.280, while a cell in good condition reads from 1.230-1.250 and anything below 1.140 is discharged.

Specific gravity varies with temperature. For each 10° the electrolyte temperature exceeds 27° C (80° F), add 0.004 to readings indicated on the hydrometer. Subtract 0.004 for each 10° below 27° C (80° F).

If the cells test in the poor range, the battery requires recharging. The hydrometer is useful for checking the progress of the charging operation. **Table 3** shows approximate state of charge.

Charging

WARNING
During the charging process, highly explosive hydrogen gas is released from the battery. The battery should be charged only in a well-ventilated area away from any open flames (including pilot lights on home gas appliances). Do not allow any smoking in the area. Never check the charge by arcing (con-

necting pliers or other metal objects) across the terminals; the resulting spark can ignite the hydrogen gas.

CAUTION
Always remove the battery from the bike's frame before connecting the battery charger. Never recharge a battery in the bike's frame; the corrosive mist that is emitted during the charging process will corrode all surrounding surfaces.

1. Connect the positive (+) charger lead to the positive (+) battery terminal and the negative (–) charger lead to the negative (–) battery terminal.
2. Remove all vent caps from the battery, set the charger to 12 volts and switch the charge ON. If the output of the charger is variable, it is best to select a low setting—1 1/2 to 2 amps.

CAUTION
The electrolyte level must be maintained at the upper level during the charging cycle; check and refill as necessary.

3. After the battery has been charged for about 8 hours, turn the charger OFF, disconnect the leads and check the specific gravity of each cell. It should be within the limits specified in **Table 3**. If it is, and remains stable for 1 hour, the battery is considered charged.
4. Clean the battery terminals, electrical cable connectors and surrounding case and reinstall the battery in the frame, reversing the removal steps. Coat the battery terminals with Vaseline or silicone spray to retard corrosion and decomposition of the terminals.

CAUTION
Route the breather tube so that it does not drain onto any part of the frame. The breather tube must be free of bends or twists as any restriction may pressurize the battery and damage it.

New Battery Installation

When replacing the old battery with a new one, be sure to charge it completely (specific gravity 1.260-1.280) before installing it in the bike. Failure to do

so or using the battery with a low electrolyte level will permanently damage the new battery.

PERIODIC LUBRICATION

Oil

Oil is graded according to its viscosity, which is an indication of how thick it is. The Society of Automotive Engineers (SAE) system distinguishes oil viscosity by numbers. Thick oils have higher viscosity numbers than thin oils. For example, an SAE 5 oil is a thin oil while an SAE 90 oil is relatively thick.

Grease

A good-quality grease (preferably waterproof) should be used. Water does not wash grease off parts as easily as it washes oil off. In addition, grease maintains its lubricating qualities better than oil on long and strenuous rides. In a pinch, though, the wrong lubricant is better than none at all. Correct the situation as soon as possible.

Engine Oil Level Check

Engine oil level is checked with the oil level inspection window, located at the engine right-hand crankcase cover.
1. Place the bike on level ground.
2. Start the engine and let it reach operating temperature; 15-20 minutes of stop-and-go riding is usually sufficient.
3. Shut off the engine and let the oil settle for 1-2 minutes.
4. Have an assistant hold the bike in the true vertical position. A false reading will be given if the bike is tipped either to the right or left.
5. Look at the oil level inspection window on the right-hand side of the engine. The oil level should be between the 2 lines (**Figure 10**).
6A. On Radian models, if the level is below the lower line, remove the oil fill cap (**Figure 11**) and add the recommended weight engine oil (**Figure 12**) to correct the level. Reinstall the fill cap and tighten securely.
6B. On FZ600 models, if the level is below the lower line, perform the following:

a. Remove the right-hand lower fairing as described under *Lower Fairing Removal/Installation (FZ600 Models)* in Chapter Twelve.

b. Remove the oil fill cap (**Figure 11**) and add the recommended weight engine oil (**Figure 12**) to correct the level.

c. Reinstall the fill cap and tighten securely.

Engine Oil and Oil Filter Change

Change the engine oil and the oil filter at the same time at the factory-recommended oil change interval indicated in **Table 2**. This assumes that the motorcycle is operated in moderate climates. In extreme climates, oil should be changed every 30 days. The time interval is more important than the mileage interval because acids formed by combustion blowby will contaminate the oil even if the motorcycle is not run for several months. If the motorcycle is operated under dusty conditions, the oil will get dirty more quickly and should be changed more frequently than recommended.

Use only a high-quality detergent motor oil with a minimum API classification of SE or SF. The classification is stamped on top of the can or printed on the label on the plastic bottle (**Figure 13**). Try to use the same brand of oil at each change. Use of oil additives is not recommended as it may cause clutch slippage. Refer to **Figure 12** for correct oil viscosity to use under anticipated ambient temperatures (not engine oil temperature).

To change the engine oil and filter you will need the following:

a. Drain pan.

b. Funnel.

c. Can opener or pour spout (oil cans only).

d. 19 mm wrench (drain plug).

e. 12 mm oil filter bolt.

f. 3 U.S. quarts of oil.

g. Oil filter element.

> *NOTE*
> *Never dispose of motor oil in the trash, on the ground, or down a storm drain. Many service stations accept used motor oil and waste haulers provide curbside used motor oil collection. Do not combine other fluids with motor oil to be recycled. To locate a recycler, con-*

tact the American Petroleum Institute (API) at ***www.recycleoil.org***.

Radian models

Refer to **Figure 14** for this procedure.

1. Start the engine and let it reach operating temperature; 15-20 minutes of stop-and-go riding is usually sufficient.

2. Turn the engine off and place the bike on level ground on the centerstand.

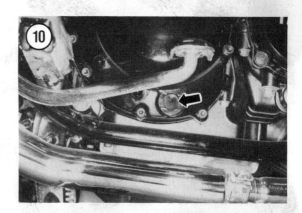

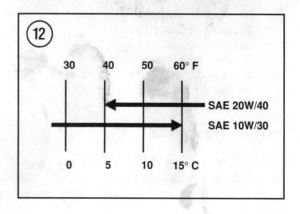

3. Place a drain pan under the front portion of the crankcase and remove the drain plug (A, **Figure 15**). Remove the oil filler cap (**Figure 11**); this will speed up the flow of oil.

4. Let the oil drain for at least 15-20 minutes.

5. Inspect the sealing washer on the crankcase drain plug. Replace if its condition is in doubt.

6. Install the drain plug and washer and tighten to the torque specification listed in **Table 4**.

7. To remove the oil filter, perform the following:

> *WARNING*
> *Protect your hands since the exhaust system is very close to the oil filter.*

> *NOTE*
> *Before removing the oil filter cover, thoroughly clean off all dirt and oil residue around it.*

a. To remove the oil filter, unscrew the union bolt (B, **Figure 15**) securing the oil filter cover to the engine.

b. Remove the cover, the filter and spring. Place the old filter in a plastic bag and close it to prevent residual oil from draining out. Don't lose the spring in the end of the filter.

c. Clean the filter cover and union bolt in solvent and thoroughly dry.

d. Inspect the O-ring seal in the end of the cover (**Figure 16**). Replace if necessary.

e. Clean off the oil filter mating surface on the crankcase with a shop rag and cleaning solvent (**Figure 17**). Remove any sludge or road dirt. Wipe it dry with a clean, lint-free cloth.

f. Inspect the O-ring seal in the end of the cover bolt (**Figure 18**). Replace if necessary.

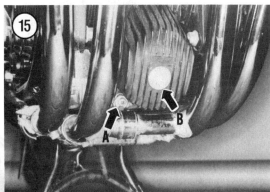

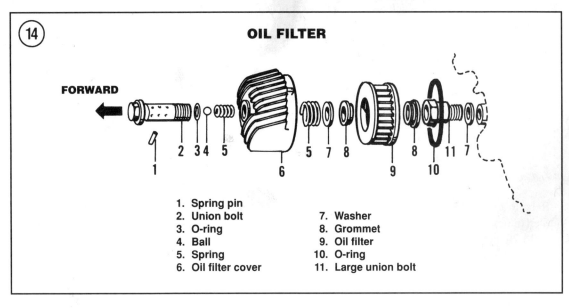

OIL FILTER

FORWARD

1. Spring pin
2. Union bolt
3. O-ring
4. Ball
5. Spring
6. Oil filter cover
7. Washer
8. Grommet
9. Oil filter
10. O-ring
11. Large union bolt

g. Apply a light coat of clean engine oil to the O-ring seal on the filter cover (**Figure 16**).

> *NOTE*
> *Make sure the rubber grommets (**Figure 19**) in each side of the filter do not dislodge or tear during installation.*

h. Install the union bolt into the cover then install the spring (**Figure 20**), washer (**Figure 21**) and oil filter (**Figure 22**) onto the union bolt.

i. Correctly position the cover and filter onto the crankcase. Align the tab on the cover with the notch in the crankcase and install the cover assembly onto the crankcase. Tighten the union bolt to the torque specification listed in **Table 4**.

8. During oil filter removal, some oil may drip onto the exhaust pipes. Prior to starting the engine, wipe off any spilled oil with a shop cloth. If necessary, spray some aerosol electrical contact cleaner on the pipes to remove the oil residue. If the oil is not cleaned off, it will smoke once the exhaust pipes get hot.

9. Insert a funnel into the oil fill hole and fill the engine with 2.6 U.S. quarts (2.46 liters, 2.16 Imp. qt.) of the correct viscosity oil (**Figure 12**).

10. Install the oil fill cap.

11. Start the engine, let it run at idle speed and check for leaks.

12. Turn the engine off and check for correct oil level; adjust as necessary.

13. On models so equipped, to make sure the oil is flowing correctly, perform the following:

a. Loosen the oil gallery check bolt (**Figure 23**) on the right-hand end of the cylinder head.

b. Start the engine and let it idle until oil starts to seep out of the bolt threads. If no oil comes out within 1 minute, shut off the engine and correct the problem.

c. Shut the engine off and tighten the bolt to the torque specification in **Table 4**.

FZ600 models

Refer to **Figure 14** for this procedure.

1. Start the engine and let it reach operating temperature; 15-20 minutes of stop-and-go riding is usually sufficient.

2. Turn the engine off and place the bike on level ground.

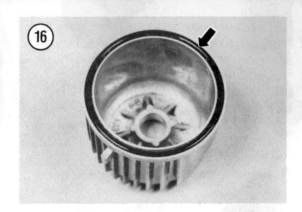

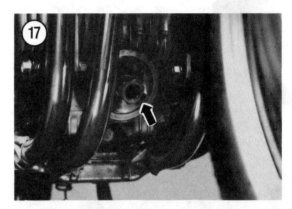

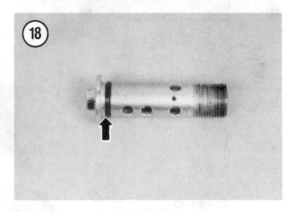

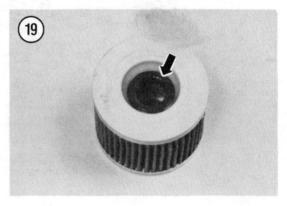

3. Remove both lower fairings as described under *Lower Fairing Removal/Installation* in Chapter Twelve. Remove the lower fairing mounting brackets.

4. Remove the exhaust system (A, **Figure 24**) as described under *Exhaust System (FZ600 Models)* in Chapter Seven.

5. Place wood block(s) under the engine to support the bike securely.

6. Place a drain pan under the left-hand rear corner of the engine and remove the drain plug. Remove the oil filler cap (**Figure 11**); this will speed up the flow of oil.

7. Let the oil drain for at least 15-20 minutes.

8. Inspect the sealing washer on the crankcase drain plug. Replace if its condition is in doubt.

9. Install the drain plug and washer and tighten to the torque specification listed in **Table 4**.

10. If the oil filter is going to be replaced, perform the following:

NOTE
Before removing the oil filter cover, thoroughly clean off all dirt and oil residue around it.

a. To remove the oil filter, unscrew the union bolt securing the oil filter cover (B, **Figure 24**) to the engine.

b. Remove the cover, the filter and spring. Place the old filter in a plastic bag and close it to prevent residual oil from draining out. Don't lose the spring in the end of the filter.

c. Clean the filter cover and union bolt in solvent and thoroughly dry.

d. Inspect the O-ring seal in the end of the cover (**Figure 16**). Replace if necessary.

e. Clean off the oil filter mating surface on the oil cooler adaptor with a shop rag and cleaning solvent. Remove any sludge or road dirt. Wipe it dry with a clean, lint-free cloth.

f. Inspect the O-ring seal in the end of the cover union bolt (**Figure 18**). Replace if necessary.

g. Apply a light coat of clean engine oil to the O-ring seal on the filter cover (**Figure 16**).

NOTE
*Make sure the rubber grommets (**Figure 19**) in each side of the filter do not dislodge or tear during installation.*

h. Install the union bolt into the cover then install the spring (**Figure 20**), washer (**Figure 21**) and oil filter (**Figure 22**) onto the union bolt.

i. Correctly position the cover and filter onto the crankcase. Align the tab on the cover with the notch in the crankcase and install the cover assembly onto the crankcase. Tighten the union bolt to the torque specification listed in **Table 4**.

11. Insert a funnel into the oil fill hole and fill the engine with 2.75 U.S. quarts (2.6 liters, 2.29 Imp. qt.) of the correct viscosity oil (**Figure 12**).

12. Install the oil fill cap.

13. Install the exhaust system.

14. Start the engine, let it run at idle speed and check for leaks.

15. Turn the engine off and check for correct oil level; adjust as necessary.

16. Install the lower fairings as described in Chapter Twelve.

Front Fork Oil Change
(Radian Models)

It is a good practice to change the fork oil at the interval listed in **Table 2** or once a year. If it becomes contaminated with dirt or water, change it immediately.

To gain access to the fork caps, it is necessary to remove the handlebar assembly from the upper fork bridge.

1. Place the bike on the centerstand.

2. Disconnect the battery negative lead as described in this chapter.

CAUTION
Cover the fuel tank with shop cloths or plastic to protect it from accidental spillage of brake fluid. Wash any brake fluid from painted or plated surfaces immediately as it will destroy the finish. Use soapy water and rinse thoroughly.

3. Remove the Allen bolts securing the handlebar holders (A, **Figure 25**). Remove both holders.

4. Carefully pull the handlebar assembly (B, **Figure 25**) up and slightly toward the rear. Do not pull too hard as the electrical cables may be damaged. Place it on the fuel tank.

5. Loosen the upper fork bridge bolt (C, **Figure 25**).

6. Remove the upper fork cap bolt (D, **Figure 25**) and spring seat.

7. Place a drip pan under the fork.

CAUTION
Cover the brake discs with shop cloths or plastic. Do not allow the fork oil to contact the discs. If any oil comes in contact with them, clean off with lacquer thinner or electrical contact

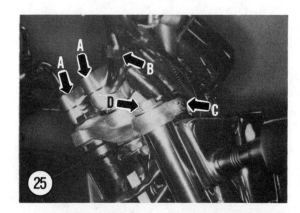

cleaner. Remove all oil residue from the
discs or the brake will be useless.

8. Remove the drain screw (**Figure 26**) and allow the fork oil to drain for at least 5 minutes. Never reuse fork oil, discard it but do *not* mix in with any engine oil that is going to be recycled.

9. Place a shop cloth around the top of the fork tube and the upper fork bridge to catch remaining fork oil while the fork spring is removed. Withdraw the fork spring from the fork tube.

CAUTION
When repeating Step 6 for the other fork leg, the front suspension will collapse when the fork cap bolt is removed, pushing the fork spring out of the top of the fork tube. Protect yourself accordingly.

10. Repeat Steps 5-9 for the other fork tube.

11. With both the bike's wheels on the ground, have an assistant steady the bike. Move the front end up and down several times to expel all remaining oil from the fork tubes.

12. Place wood block(s) under the frame to support the bike securely with the front wheel off the ground.

13. Install both drain screws and tighten securely.

14. Fill the fork tube with 320 cc (10.8 U.S. oz.) of SAE 10 fork oil.

15. Install the fork springs into the fork tubes with the closer wound coils toward the top.

16. Inspect the O-ring seal on the fork cap bolt; replace if necessary.

17. Install the spring seat and the fork cap bolt while pushing down on the spring. Start the bolt slowly, don't cross-thread it. Tighten to the torque specification listed in **Table 4**.

18. Tighten the upper fork bridge bolt to the torque specification listed in **Table 4**.

19. Repeat Steps 14-18 for the other fork assembly.

20. Install the handlebar into position and install the handlebar holders with the punch mark facing forward (**Figure 27**), then install the bolts.

21. Correctly position the handlebar assembly and tighten the upper holder bolts to the torque specification listed in **Table 4**. Tighten the front bolts first then the rear.

22. Connect the battery negative lead.

23. Road test the bike and check for leaks.

Front Fork Oil Change
(FZ600 Models)

It is a good practice to change the fork oil at the interval listed in **Table 2** or once a year. If it becomes contaminated with dirt or water, change it immediately.

1. Remove the lower fairing on each side as described under *Lower Fairing Removal/Installation* in Chapter Twelve. Remove the lower fairing mounting brackets.

2. Remove the exhaust system as described under *Exhaust System Removal/Installation (FZ600 Models)* in Chapter Seven.

3. Place wood block(s) under the crankcase to support the bike securely with the front wheel off the ground.

4. Remove the air valve dust cap (**Figure 28**) from the fork top cap bolt.

WARNING
Release the air pressure gradually. If it is released too fast, fork oil will spurt out with the air. Protect your eyes and clothing accordingly.

5. Depress the valve stem (**Figure 29**) with a small screwdriver and *bleed off all air pressure* within the fork tube. Remove the valve stem from the valve.

6. Loosen the handlebar pinch bolt (A, **Figure 30**) then the fork cap bolt (B, **Figure 30**).

7. Place a drip pan under the fork.

CAUTION
Cover the brake discs with shop cloths or plastic. Do not allow the fork oil to contact the discs. If any oil comes in contact with them, clean off with lacquer thinner or electrical contact cleaner. Remove all oil residue from the discs or the brake will be useless.

8. Remove the drain screw (**Figure 31**) and allow the fork oil to drain for at least 5 minutes. Never reuse fork oil, discard it but do not mix in with any engine oil that is going to be recycled.

9. Place a shop cloth around the top of the fork tube, the handlebar and the upper fork bridge to catch remaining fork oil while the fork spring is removed. Withdraw the fork spring from the fork tube.

10. Repeat Steps 4-9 for the other fork tube.

11. Remove the wood block(s) from under the engine.

12. With both the bike's wheels on the ground, have an assistant steady the bike. Move the front end up and down several times to expel all remaining oil from the fork tubes.

13. Reinstall the wood block(s) under the engine to support the bike securely with the front wheel off the ground.

14. Install both drain screws and tighten securely.

15. Fill the fork tube with 315 cc (11.1 U.S. ounces) of SAE 10 fork oil.

16. Install the fork springs into the fork tubes with the closer wound coils toward the top.

17. Inspect the O-ring seal on the fork cap bolt; replace if necessary.

18. Install the spring seat and the fork cap bolt while pushing down on the spring. Start the bolt slowly, don't cross-thread it. Tighten to the torque specification listed in **Table 4**.

19. After the fork cap bolt is tightened to the specific torque the valve must face inboard at a 45° angle (**Figure 32**). If the air valve position is incorrect, perform the following:

   a. Loosen the upper and lower fork bridge bolts.

   b. Rotate the upper fork tube until air valve location is correct.

   c. Align the top surface of the fork tube with the top surface of the upper fork bridge (**Figure 33**) and tighten the fork bridge bolts to the torque specification listed in **Table 4**.

d. Tighten the handlebar pinch bolt (A, **Figure 30**) to the torque specification listed in **Table 4**.

20. Install the valve stem into the air valve.

21. Repeat Steps 15-20 for the other fork assembly.

22. Install the exhaust system as described in Chapter Seven.

NOTE
When checking or pressurizing the front forks, the front wheel must be off the ground.

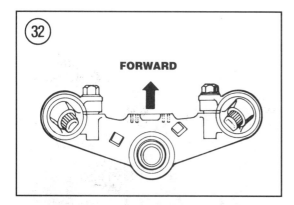

FORWARD

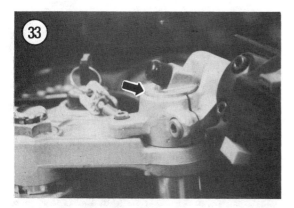

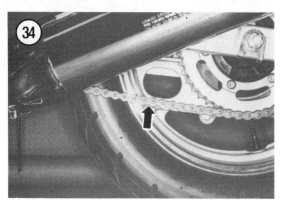

WARNING
*Never use any type of compressed gas as an explosion may be lethal. Never heat the front fork assembly with a torch or place it near an open flame or extreme heat as this will also result in an explosion. **Never** exceed the maximum air pressure listed in **Table 5**.*

23. Inflate the front forks to the recommended air pressure listed in **Table 5**. Do not use compressed air; only use a hand-operated air pump. For optimum handling the air pressure in both forks should be the same. The difference in air pressure between the 2 forks should be 9.8 kPa (1.4 psi) or less.

24. Install the lower fairing stays and the lower fairings on each side as described in Chapter Twelve.

25. Road test the bike and check for leaks.

Drive Chain Lubrication

Oil the drive chain at the interval indicated in **Table 2** or sooner if it becomes dry.

1A. On FZ600 models, perform the following:

NOTE
Place a suitable size aftermarket swing arm stand under the rear swing arm and support the bike with the rear wheel off the ground. If a swing arm stand is unavailable, perform the following.

a. Remove both lower fairings as described under *Lower Fairing Removal/Installation (FZ600 Models)* in Chapter Twelve.

b. Remove the exhaust system as described under *Exhaust System Removal/Installation (FZ600 Models)* in Chapter Seven.

c. Place wood block(s) under the engine to support the bike securely with the rear wheel off the ground.

1B. On Radian models, place wood block(s) under the engine or frame to support the bike securely with the rear wheel off the ground.

2A. On Radian models, lubricate the bottom run (**Figure 34**) of the drive chain with a good grade of chain lubricant carefully following the manufacturer's instructions. Concentrate on getting the oil down between the side plates of the chain links, into the pins, bushings and rollers.

2B. On FZ600 models, oil the bottom run (**Figure 34**) with a good grade of commercial chain lubricant formulated for O-ring chains (or SAE 10W/30 engine oil). Concentrate on getting the oil down between the side plates of the chain links.

3. Rotate the rear wheel to bring the unoiled portion of the chain within reach. Continue until all the chain is lubricated.

4. On FZ600 models, if removed, perform the following:

   a. Install the exhaust system as described in Chapter Seven.

   b. Install the lower fairing on each side, both side covers and the rider and passenger seats as described in Chapter Twelve.

Control Cables

The control cables should be lubricated at the interval listed in **Table 2**. They should also be inspected at this time for fraying and the cable sheath checked for chafing. The cables are relatively inexpensive and should be replaced when found to be faulty.

The control cables can be lubricated either with oil or any popular cable lubricants and a cable lubricator. The first method requires more time and the complete lubrication of the entire cable is less certain.

On the throttle cable it is necessary to remove the screws securing the right-hand switch assembly together to gain access to the throttle cable end.

Oil method

1. Disconnect the cable from the clutch (**Figure 35**) and the throttle grip assembly (**Figure 36**).

2. Make a cone of stiff paper and tape it to the end of the cable sheath (**Figure 37**).

3. Hold the cable upright and pour a small amount of thin oil (SAE 10W-30) into the cone. Work the cable in and out of the sheath for several minutes to help the oil work its way down to the end of the cable.

> *NOTE*
> *To avoid a mess, place a shop cloth at the end of the cable to catch the oil as it runs out.*

4. Remove the cone, reconnect the cable and adjust the cable(s) as described in this chapter.

> *NOTE*
> *While the throttle cable is removed and the switch assembly disassembled, apply a light coat of grease to the metal surfaces of the throttle grip assembly.*

Lubricator method

1. Disconnect the cable from the clutch (**Figure 35**) and the throttle grip assembly (**Figure 36**).

2. Attach a lubricator following the manufacturer's instructions (**Figure 38**).

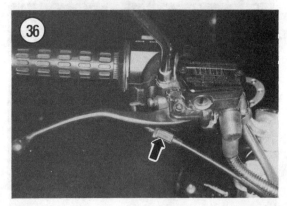

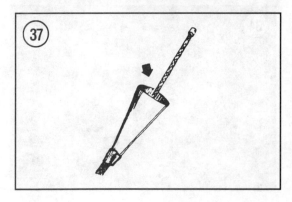

3. Insert the nozzle of the lubricant can in the lubricator, press the button on the can and hold down until the lubricant begins to flow out of the other end of the cable.

4. Remove the lubricator, reconnect the cable(s) and adjust the cable as described in this chapter.

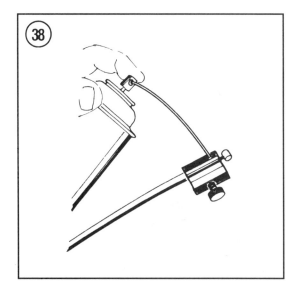

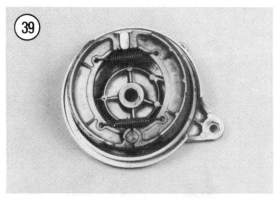

Rear Brake Cam Lubrication (Radian Models)

Lubricate the brake cam whenever the rear wheel is removed.

1. Remove the rear wheel as described in Chapter Ten.

2. Remove the brake backing plate assembly from the rear wheel hub.

3. Wipe away the old grease, being careful not to get any on the brake shoes.

> *CAUTION*
> *Use only a high-temperature grease. Other types, when heated from braking, run onto the brake shoe linings, causing loss of rear braking.*

4. Sparingly apply high-temperature grease to the camming surfaces of the camshaft, the camshaft groove, the brake shoe pivots and the end of the springs (**Figure 39**).

5. Install the brake backing plate assembly into the rear wheel hub.

6. Install the rear wheel as described in Chapter Ten.

7. Adjust the rear brake free-play as described in this chapter.

Speedometer Cable Lubrication

Lubricate the speedometer cable every year or whenever needle operation is erratic.

1. Disconnect the cable from the backside of the speedometer (**Figure 40**).

2. Pull the cable from the sheath.

3. If the existing grease is contaminated, thoroughly clean off all old grease.

4. Thoroughly coat the cable with a good grade of multi-purpose grease and reinstall it into the cable sheath.

> *NOTE*
> *If the cable does not seat into the drive unit, it is necessary to disconnect the cable from the speedometer drive housing (**Figure 41**).*

5. Make sure the cable is correctly seated into the drive unit on the front wheel hub.

Miscellaneous Lubrication Points

Lubricate the clutch lever, front brake lever, side stand pivot point and the footpeg pivot points. Use SAE 10W-40 engine oil.

PERIODIC MAINTENANCE

Preliminary Drive Chain Inspection

Before adjusting the drive chain, it should be inspected for wear. This procedure describes how to check a drive chain for excessive stretch while it is installed on the bike.

1. Place the bike on the centerstand or sidestand.

2. Pull the drive chain rearward at the point midway down the rear sprocket (**Figure 42**). If more than one-half of each tooth on the sprocket is uncovered, the drive chain should be removed and further inspected as described in this section.

> *CAUTION*
> *Drive chain stretch is caused by a loss of metal from the drive chain's bushings and pins. This can result in chain breakage which could cause a serious accident while riding the bike.*

Drive Chain Adjustment

The drive chain should be checked and adjusted at the interval listed in **Table 2** or more often if ridden in wet or dusty conditions. The correct amount of chain free play, when pushed up midway between the sprockets on the lower chain run, is 20-30

mm (0.8-1.2 in.). See **Figure 43**. If the adjustment is necessary, perform the following.

1. Place the bike on the centerstand or sidestand.

2. Place the transmission in NEUTRAL.

3A. On Radian models, perform the following:

    a. Remove the cotter pin and loosen the axle nut (**Figure 44**).

    b. Loosen the locknut and turn the adjuster nuts (**Figure 45**) in either direction, in equal

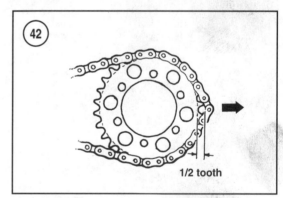

1/2 tooth

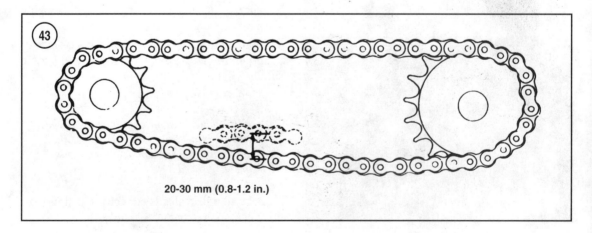

20-30 mm (0.8-1.2 in.)

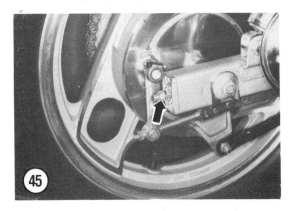

amounts, to either increase or decrease drive chain tension. After adjustment is complete, make sure the notch on the rear axle special washers are on the same scale mark (**Figure 46**) on the swing arm on both sides.

3B. On FZ600 models, perform the following:

    a. Remove the cotter pin and loosen the axle nut (A, **Figure 47**).

    b. Loosen the locknut and turn the adjuster nut (B, **Figure 47**) in either direction, in equal amounts, to either increase or decrease drive chain tension. After adjustment is complete, make sure the notch on the rear axle special washers are on the same scale mark (**Figure 48**) on the swing arm on both sides.

4. Roll the bike forward to rotate the rear wheel to move the chain to another position and recheck the free play; chains rarely wear or stretch evenly and, as a result, the free play will not remain constant over the entire length.

WARNING
Excessive free play can result in chain breakage which could cause a serious accident.

5. If the chain cannot be adjusted within the specified limits, it is excessively worn and stretched and should be replaced. Always replace both sprockets when replacing the drive chain; never install a new chain over worn sprockets.

6. When the adjustment is correct, sight along the chain from the rear sprocket to see that it is correctly aligned. It should leave the top of the rear sprocket in a straight line (A, **Figure 49**). If it is cocked to one side or the other (B or C, **Figure 49**), the rear wheel is incorrectly aligned and must be corrected by turn-

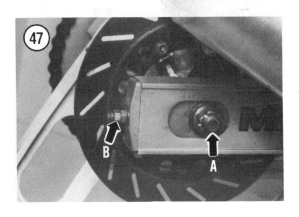

ing the adjusters counter to one another until the chain and sprocket are correctly aligned.

7. Tighten the rear axle nut to the torque specification listed in **Table 4**.

8. Install a new cotter pin and bend both ends over completely. Always install a new cotter pin—never reuse a cotter pin.

Drive Chain Cleaning, Inspection and Lubrication

Clean and lubricate the drive chain at the interval indicated in **Table 2**, or more frequently if ridden in dusty or muddy terrain.

1. Remove the drive chain as described under *Drive Chain Removal/Installation* in Chapter Ten.

> *CAUTION*
> *The factory drive chain is equipped with O-rings between the side plates (**Figure 50**) that seal lubricant between the pins and bushings. To prevent damaging these O-rings, use only kerosene for cleaning. Do not use gasoline or other solvents that will cause the O-ring to swell or deteriorate.*

2. Immerse the drive chain in a pan of kerosene or non-flammable solvent.

3. Allow it to soak for about half an hour. Move it around and flex it during this period so that the dirt between the links, pins and plates may work its way out.

4. On Radian model drive chains, scrub the rollers and side plates with a soft brush and rinse away

loosened grit. Rinse it a couple of times to make sure all dirt is washed out. Wipe the drive chain dry with a shop cloth.

5. Hang the drive chain from a piece of wire and allow it to air-dry.

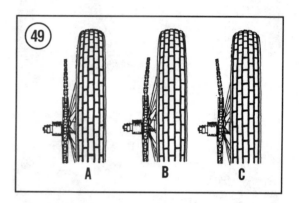

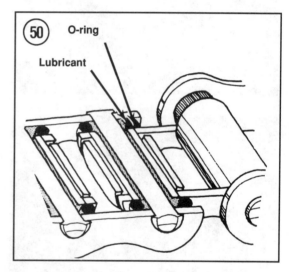

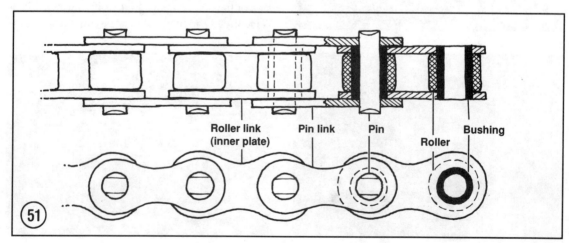

6. After cleaning the chain, examine it carefully for wear or damage. If any signs are visible, replace the chain.

7. Check the inner faces of the inner plates (**Figure 51**). They should be lightly polished on both sides. If they show considerable wear on both sides, the sprockets are not aligned. Adjust alignment as described in this chapter.

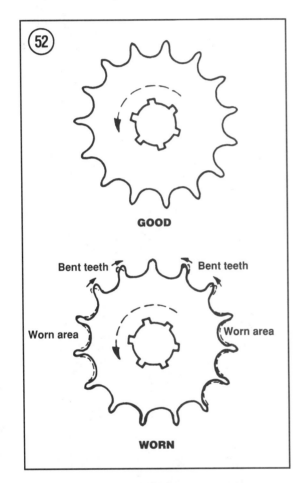

GOOD

Bent teeth   Bent teeth

Worn area   Worn area

WORN

8. While the drive chain is removed, check both the drive and the driven sprockets (**Figure 52**). If any wear is visible on the teeth, replace the sprocket(s). Never install a new chain over worn sprockets or a worn chain over new sprockets.

9A. On Radian models, lubricate the drive chain with a good grade of chain lubricant carefully following the manufacturer's instructions. Concentrate on getting the oil down between the side plates of the chain links, into the pins, bushings and rollers.

9B. On FZ600 models, oil the bottom run with a good grade of commercial chain lubricant formulated for O-ring chains (or SAE 10W/30 engine oil). Concentrate on getting the oil down between the side plates of the chain links.

10. Reinstall the drive chain as described under *Drive Chain Removal/Installation* in Chapter Ten.

11. Adjust the drive chain tension and check alignment as described in this chapter.

Drive Chain Slider
Inspection/Replacement

A drive chain slider (**Figure 53**) is attached to the left-hand side of the swing arm near the pivot point. There are no factory-specified wear limit dimensions for the slider. If the slider is worn unevenly or if the wear groove is worn more than halfway through the material, replace the slider.

1. Remove the swing arm as described under *Swing Arm Removal/Installation* in Chapter Ten.

2. Remove the screw, washer and collar securing the slider to the swing arm.

3. Remove the slider and install a new slider.

4. Tighten the screws securely.

5. Install the swing arm as described under *Swing Arm Removal/Installation* in Chapter Ten.

Disc Brake Fluid Level

The fluid level should be up between the upper and lower mark within the reservoir. If the brake fluid level reaches the lower level mark, visible through the viewing port (**Figure 54**) on the front master cylinder and the transparent reservoir (**Figure 55**) on the rear master cylinder (FZ600 models), the fluid level must be corrected by adding fresh brake fluid.

1. Place the bike on level ground and position the handlebars so the front master cylinder reservoir is level.

2. On FZ600 models, remove the right-hand side cover in order to check the rear master cylinder.

3. Clean any dirt from the area around the top cover prior to removing the cover.

4. Remove the screws securing the front top cover or unscrew the rear cap. Remove the top cover and the diaphragm. Refer to **Figure 56** for the front master cylinder or **Figure 57** for the rear master cylinder.

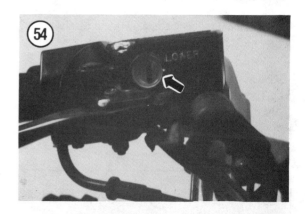

WARNING
Use brake fluid from a sealed container and clearly marked DOT 3 or DOT 4 only (specified for disc brakes). Others may vaporize and cause brake failure. Do not intermix different brands or types of brake fluid as they may not be compatible. Do not intermix a silicone based (DOT 5) brake fluid as it can cause brake component damage leading to brake system failure.

CAUTION
Be careful when handling brake fluid. Do not spill it on painted or plated surfaces or plastic parts as it will destroy the surface. Wash the area immediately with soapy water and thoroughly rinse it off.

5. Add brake fluid until the level is to the upper level line within the master cylinder reservoir. Refer to **Figure 56** for the front master cylinder or **Figure 57** for the rear master cylinder. Use fresh brake fluid from a sealed brake fluid container.

6. Reinstall the diaphragm and the top cover. Tighten the screws securely on the front master cylinder. On rear disc brakes, tighten the cap securely.

Disc Brake Lines

Check brake lines between the master cylinder and the brake calipers. If there is any leakage, tighten the connections and bleed the brakes as described under *Bleeding the System* in Chapter Eleven. If this does not stop the leak or if a brake line is obviously damaged, cracked or chafed, replace the brake line(s) and bleed the system.

3

Disc Brake Pad Wear

Inspect the brake pads for excessive or uneven wear, scoring and oil or grease on the friction surface. Look into the caliper assembly (**Figure 58**) and check the location of the wear indicator in relation to the disc (**Figure 59**). Replace both pads if the wear

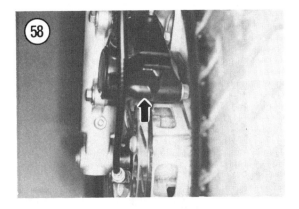

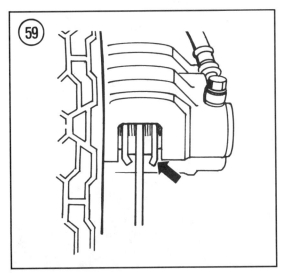

line on the pads reaches the brake disc. On the front brake, replace both pads in both calipers at the same time.

If any of these conditions exist, replace the pads as described in Chapter Eleven.

Disc Brake Fluid Change

Every time the reservoir cap is removed, a small amount of dirt and moisture enters the brake fluid. The same thing happens if a leak occurs or any part of the hydraulic system is loosened or disconnected. Dirt can clog the system and cause unnecessary wear. Water in the brake fluid vaporizes at high temperature, impairing the hydraulic action and reducing the brake's stopping ability.

To maintain peak performance, change the brake fluid as indicated in **Table 2**. To change brake fluid, follow the *Bleeding the System* procedure in Chapter Eleven. Continue adding new fluid to the master cylinder and bleeding out at the calipers until the fluid leaving each caliper is clean and free of contaminants.

> *WARNING*
> *Use brake fluid from a sealed container and clearly marked DOT 3 or DOT 4 only (specified for disc brakes). Others may vaporize and cause brake failure. Do not intermix different brands or types of brake fluid as they may not be compatible. Do not intermix a silicone based (DOT 5) brake fluid as it can cause brake component damage leading to brake system failure.*

Front Brake Lever Adjustment

Free play is the distance the lever travels from the at-rest position to the point at which the master cylinder is depressed by the lever adjuster. An adjuster is provided to maintain the front brake lever free play.

1. Loosen the adjuster locknut. Turn the adjuster (**Figure 60**) to obtain the specified free play of the following:

    a. Radian models: 2-5 mm (0.08-0.20 in).

    b. FZ600 models: 0-1 mm (0.00-0.04 in).

2. Tighten the locknut.

3. Rotate the front wheel and check for brake drag. Also operate the brake lever several times to make

sure it returns to the at-rest position immediately after release.

4. Slide the rubber boot back into position.

Rear Drum Brake Shoe Wear

Inspect the rear brake shoe for wear by depressing the rear brake pedal and check the wear indicator on the brake hub (**Figure 61**). If the indicator reaches to the wear limit, replace the brake shoes as described in Chapter Ten.

Rear Brake Pedal Height Adjustment

The rear brake pedal height should be adjusted at the interval listed in **Table 2** or anytime the brake shoes or pads are replaced. The top of the brake pedal should be positioned below the top surface of the footpeg the following amount:

a. Radian models: 15 mm (0.59 in.).
b. FZ600 models: 40 mm (1.57 in.).

1. Place the bike on the centerstand or sidestand.
2. Make sure the brake pedal is in the at-rest position.
3A. On Radian models, to change height position, loosen the locknut (A, **Figure 62**) and turn the adjuster in or out (B, **Figure 62**) until the correct height is achieved. Tighten the locknut (A) securely.
3B. On FZ600 models, to change height position, loosen the locknut (A, **Figure 63**) and turn the master cylinder pushrod (B, **Figure 63**) in either direction until the correct height is achieved. Tighten the locknut (A) securely.
4. Check and adjust the rear brake pedal free play (Radian models) as described in this chapter.

Rear Brake Pedal Free Play Adjustment (Radian Models)

The rear drum brake pedal free play should be adjusted after the rear brake pedal height has been adjusted. Free play is the distance the rear brake pedal travels from the at-rest position to the applied position when the pedal is depressed lightly by hand. The brake pedal should be adjusted so the pedal has 20-30 mm (0.8-1.18 in.) of free play.

NOTE
This type of adjustment is not necessary on rear disc brake models.

1. Adjust the rear brake pedal height as described in this chapter.
2. Make sure the brake pedal is in the at-rest position.
3. Turn the adjust nut (**Figure 64**) on the end of the brake rod until the correct amount of free play is achieved.
4. Rotate the rear wheel and check for brake drag.
5. Operate the brake pedal several times to make sure the brake pedal returns to the at-rest position immediately after release.

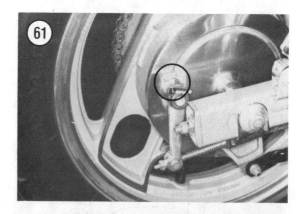

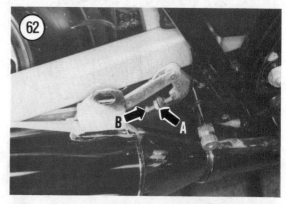

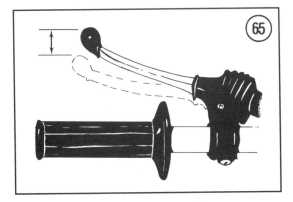

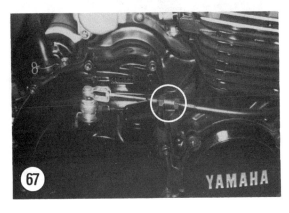

6. Adjust the rear brake light switch as described in Chapter Eight.

Clutch Adjustment

Adjust the clutch at the interval indicated in **Table 2**. For the clutch to engage and disengage fully, there must be the following amount of free play between the tip of the lever (**Figure 65**):

    a. Radian models: 10-15 mm (0.4-0.6 in.).

    b. FZ600 models: 8-12 mm (0.3-0.5 in.).

1. Minor adjustments can be made at the upper adjuster at the hand lever. Loosen the locknut (A, **Figure 66**) and turn the adjuster (B, **Figure 66**) in or out to obtain the correct amount of free play.

> *NOTE*
> *If the proper amount of free play cannot be achieved at the hand lever, additional adjustment can be made at the clutch actuating lever on the right-hand crankcase cover.*

2. On FZ600 models, remove the right-hand lower fairing as described under *Lower Fairing Removal/Installation* in Chapter Twelve.

3. Major adjustment is made at the clutch actuating lever as follows:

    a. At the clutch lever turn the adjuster (B, **Figure 66**) in all the way toward the hand grip.

    b. At the right-hand crankcase cover, loosen the locknut and turn the adjuster (**Figure 67**) until the correct amount of free play can be achieved.

    c. Tighten the locknut (A, **Figure 66**).

4. If necessary, do some final adjusting at the clutch lever as described in Step 1.

5. After adjustment is complete, check that the locknut is tight at the clutch actuating lever on the crankcase cover.

6. On FZ600 models, install the right-hand lower fairing.

7. Road test the bike to make sure the clutch fully disengages when the lever is pulled in; if it does not, the bike will creep in gear when stopped. Also make sure the clutch fully engages; if it does not, the clutch will slip, particularly when accelerating in high gear.

8. If the proper amount of adjustment cannot be achieved using this procedure, the cable has stretched to the point where it needs replacing. Refer to Chapter Five for complete procedure.

Throttle Operation/Adjustment

The throttle cable should have 2-5 mm (0.08-0.20 in.) of free play. If adjustment is necessary, perform the following:

1. At the throttle grip, loosen the cable locknut (A, **Figure 68**) and turn the adjuster (B, **Figure 68**) in either direction until the correct amount of free play is achieved.

2. If the proper amount of adjustment cannot be achieved using this procedure, the cable has stretched to the point where it needs replacing. Refer to *Throttle Cable Replacement* in Chapter Seven.

3. Check the throttle cable from the throttle grip to the carburetor. Make sure it is not kinked or chafed. Replace as necessary.

4. Make sure the throttle grip rotates freely from a fully closed to a fully open position. Check with the handlebar at center, at full right and at full left. If necessary, remove the throttle grip and apply a lithium base grease to the rotating surfaces.

WARNING
*With the engine idling, move the handlebar from side to side. If idle speed increases during this movement, the throttle cable may need adjusting or may be incorrectly routed through the frame. Correct this problem immediately. Do **not** ride the bike in this unsafe condition.*

Fuel and Vacuum Line Inspection

On FZ600 models, remove the right-hand side cover as described under *Side Cover Removal/Installation* in Chapter Twelve.

Inspect the fuel line (A, **Figure 69**) and vacuum line (B, **Figure 69**) for cracks or deterioration; replace if necessary. Make sure the hose clamps are in place and holding securely.

WARNING
A damaged or deteriorated fuel line presents a very dangerous fire hazard to both the rider and the vehicle if fuel should spill onto a hot engine or exhaust pipe.

Crankcase Breather System

Inspect the breather hose (**Figure 70**) from the top of the crankcase to the air filter air case. If it is cracked or starting to deteriorate, it must be replaced. Make sure the hose clamps are in place and holding securely.

Evaporative Emission Control System (California Models Only)

Fuel vapor from the fuel tank is routed into a charcoal canister when the engine is stopped. When the engine is started these vapors are drawn, through the vacuum controlled valves, into the carburetors and into the engine to be burned. Make sure all vacuum hoses are correctly routed and attached. Inspect the hoses and replace any if necessary.

Refer to Chapter Seven for detailed information on the evaporative emission control system and for vacuum hose routing.

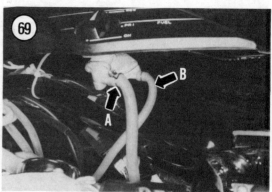

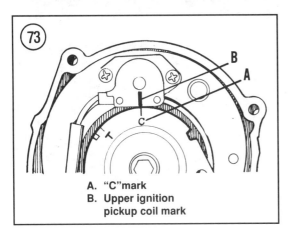

A. "C"mark
B. Upper ignition
   pickup coil mark

Exhaust System

Check for leakage at all fittings. Tighten all bolts and nuts. Replace any gaskets if necessary. Refer to *Exhaust System* in Chapter Seven.

Camshaft Chain Tensioner Adjustment

3

The camshaft chain tensioner should be adjusted at the interval listed in **Table 2** or whenever it becomes noisy.

1. On FZ600 models, remove the lower fairing on each side as described under *Lower Fairing Removal/Installation* in Chapter Twelve.

2. Remove the spark plugs as this will make it easier to turn the engine over by hand.

3A. On 1986-1988 models, perform the following:

   a. Remove the screws securing the ignition cover and remove the cover (**Figure 71**).

   b. Slowly rotate the crankshaft *counterclockwise* using a wrench on the nut on the left-hand end of the crankshaft (**Figure 72**). Stop turning when the "C" mark aligns with the upper ignition pickup coil mark (**Figure 73**).

3B. On 1989 and 1990 models, perform the following:

   a. Remove the screws securing the ignition cover and remove the cover (**Figure 71**).

   b. Slowly rotate the crankshaft *counterclockwise* using a wrench on the bolt securing the alternator rotor. Stop turning when the "C" mark on the rotor aligns with the upper fixed pointer on the crankcase (**Figure 74**).

4. Loosen the tensioner locknut and loosen the stopper bolt (**Figure 75**). The tensioner will automatically move to adjust the camshaft chain tension.

5. Tighten the stopper bolt, then the locknut to the torque specifications listed in **Table 4**.

6. Install the ignition cover and screws. Tighten the screws to the torque specifications listed in **Table 4**.

7. On FZ600 models, install the lower fairing on each side.

Air Filter Element

The air filter element should be removed and cleaned at the interval listed in **Table 2**. The air filter element should be replaced at the interval listed in **Table 2** or sooner if soiled, severely clogged or broken in any area.

The air filter removes dust and abrasive particles from the air before the air enters the carburetors and the engine. Without the air filter, very fine particles could enter into the engine and cause rapid wear of the piston rings, cylinders and bearings and might clog small passages in the carburetors. Never run the bike without the air filter element installed.

Proper air filter servicing can do more to ensure long service from your engine than almost any other single item.

Aftermarket Air Filters

If you modify the intake system and install individual aftermarket air filters, there will be a void left where the stock air filter air case was located. The stock air filter air case is the holding fixture for the ignition system's ignitor unit which is a very expensive part. The air case not only holds the ignitor unit in place but it also positions it between the top of the air case and the bottom of the seat in a location which helps keep it dry.

If you have performed this intake system modification, secure the ignitor unit so it will not bounce around within this void and also waterproof the

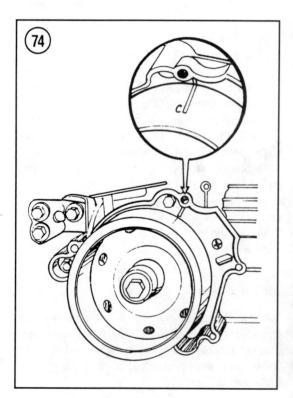

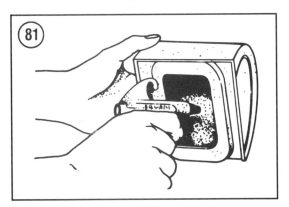

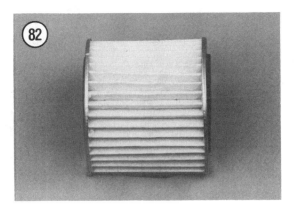

electrical connectors by packing them with a dielectric compound or place the unit within a waterproof envelope to keep out rain or moisture.

If the electrical connectors become wet, it will make the bike either impossible to start, difficult to start or will cause the ignition system to cut out at any rpm while the engine is running.

Air Filter Element Removal/Cleaning/Installation (Radian Models)

1. Place the bike on the centerstand.

2. Remove the carburetor cover (**Figure 76**) and the left-hand side cover (**Figure 77**).

3. Remove the screws securing the air filter cover and remove the cover (**Figure 78**).

4. Withdraw the element assembly from the air box (**Figure 79**).

5. Wipe out the interior of the air box (**Figure 80**) with a shop rag dampened with cleaning solvent. Remove any foreign matter that may have passed through a broken element.

6. Gently tap the air filter element to loosen the dust.

> *CAUTION*
> *In the next step, do not direct compressed air toward the outside surface of the element. If air pressure is directed to the outside surface it will force the dirt and dust into the pores of the element thus restricting air flow.*

7. Apply compressed air toward the *inside surface* of the element to remove all loosened dirt and dust from the element (**Figure 81**).

8. Inspect the element (**Figure 82**); if it is torn or damaged in any area it must be replaced. Do *not* run the bike with a damaged element as it may allow dirt to enter the engine.

9. Install the new air filter element and make sure the element is correctly seated into the air box so there is no air leak. The gasket surface (**Figure 83**) must fit directly on to the air box surface.

10. Install the cover and screws and tighten securely.

11. Install the left-hand side cover and the carburetor cover.

Air Filter Element
Removal/Cleaning/Installation
(FZ600 Models)

1. Remove the rider and passenger seats as described under *Seat Removal/Installation (FZ600 Models)* in Chapter Twelve.

2. Remove the side cover on each side as described under *Side Cover Removal/Installation* in Chapter Twelve.

3. Remove the fuel tank as described under *Fuel Tank Removal/Installation (FZ600 Models)* in Chapter Seven.

4. Remove the screws securing the air filter cover (**Figure 84**) and move the cover out of the way.

5. Withdraw the element assembly from the air box (**Figure 85**).

6. Wipe out the interior of the air box with a shop rag dampened with cleaning solvent. Remove any foreign matter that may have passed through a broken element.

7. Gently tap the air filter element to loosen the dust.

> *CAUTION*
> *In the next step, do not direct compressed air toward the outside surface of the element. If air pressure is directed to the outside surface it will force the dirt and dust into the pores of the element thus restricting air flow.*

8. Apply compressed air toward the *inside surface* of the element to remove all loosened dirt and dust from the element.

9. Inspect the element; if it is torn or damaged in any area it must be replaced. Do *not* run the bike with a damaged element as it may allow dirt to enter the engine.

10. Install the new air filter element and make sure the element is correctly seated into the air box so there is no air leak.

11. Install the fuel tank as described in Chapter Seven.

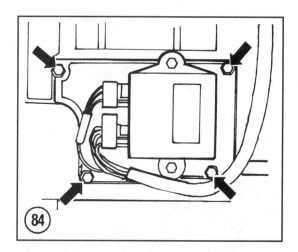

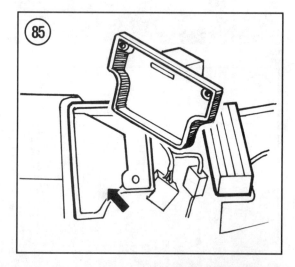

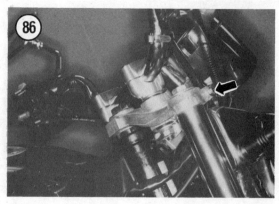

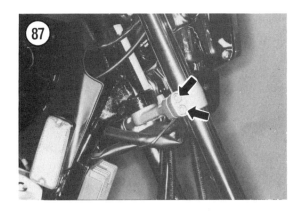

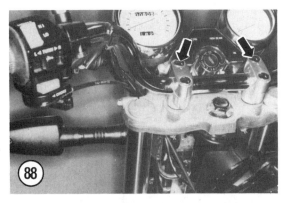

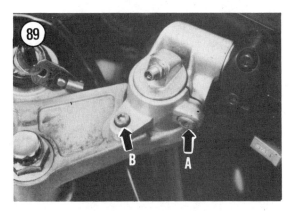

12. Install the rider and passenger seats as described in Chapter Twelve.

Wheel Bearings

There is no factory-recommended mileage interval for cleaning and repacking the wheel bearings. They should be inspected and serviced, if necessary, every time the wheel is removed or whenever there is a likelihood of water contamination. The correct service procedures are covered in Chapter Nine and Chapter Ten.

Front Suspension Check

1. Apply the front brake and pump the forks up and down as vigorously as possible. Check for smooth operation and check for any oil leaks.

2. Make sure the upper (**Figure 86**) and lower (**Figure 87**) fork bridge bolts are tight.

3A. On Radian models, make sure the bolts (**Figure 88**) securing the handlebar assembly is tight and that the handlebar is secure.

3B. On FZ600 models, make sure the pinch bolts (A, **Figure 89**) and holder bolts (B, **Figure 89**) securing the handlebars are tight and that each handlebar is secure.

4. Make sure the front axle pinch bolt nut (A, **Figure 90**) and axle (B, **Figure 90**) are tight.

> *CAUTION*
> *If any of the previously mentioned bolts and nuts are loose, refer to Chapter Nine for correct procedures and torque specifications.*

Rear Suspension Check

1A. On FZ600 models, perform the following:

   a. Remove the lower fairing on each side as described under *Lower Fairing Removal/Installation* in Chapter Twelve. Remove the lower fairing mounting brackets.

   b. Remove the exhaust system as described under *Exhaust System Removal/Installation (FZ600 Models)* in Chapter Seven.

   c. Place wood block(s) under the crankcase to support the bike securely with the front wheel off the ground.

1B. On Radian models, place a wood block(s) under each side of the frame to support it securely with the rear wheel off the ground.

2. Push hard on the rear wheel (sideways) to check for side play in the rear swing arm bearings. Remove the wood block(s).

3. Make sure the swing arm pivot bolt nut (**Figure 91**) is tight.

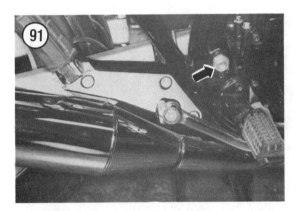

4A. On Radian models, check the tightness of the upper (**Figure 92**) and lower (**Figure 93**) mounting bolts and nuts on the shock absorber.

4B. On FZ600 models, perform the following:

    a. Check the tightness of the upper (**Figure 94**) and lower (**Figure 95**) mounting bolts and nuts on the shock absorber.

    b. Check the tightness of the rear shock linkage.

5. Make sure the rear axle nut is tight and that the cotter pin is in place (**Figure 96**).

6A. On Radian models, check the tightness of the rear drum brake torque arm bolts and nuts (**Figure 97**). Make sure the cotter pins are in place.

6B. On FZ600 models, check the tightness of the rear caliper torque arm bolt (**Figure 98**).

> *CAUTION*
> *If any of the previously mentioned bolts and nuts are loose, refer to Chapter Ten for correct procedures and torque specifications.*

7. On FZ600 models, perform the following:

    a. Install the exhaust system as described in Chapter Seven.

    b. Install the lower fairing mounting brackets and the upper and lower fairing on each side as described in Chapter Twelve.

Nuts, Bolts and Other Fasteners

Constant vibration can loosen many of the fasteners on the motorcycle. Check the tightness of all fasteners, especially those on:

    a. Engine mounting hardware.

    b. Engine crankcase covers.

    c. Handlebar and front forks.

    d. Gearshift lever.

    e. Brake pedal and lever.

    f. Sprocket bolts and nuts.

    g. Exhaust system.

    h. Body panels (FZ600 models).

    i. Lighting equipment.

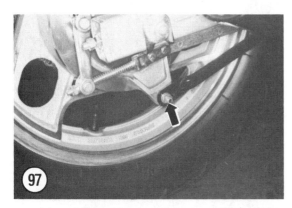

Steering Head Adjustment Check

Check the steering head bearings for looseness at the interval listed in **Table 2**.

Place a wood block(s) under each side of the frame to support it securely with the front wheel off the ground.

Hold on to the front fork tube and gently rock the fork assembly back and forth. If you feel looseness, refer to Chapter Nine.

TUNE-UP

Perform a complete tune-up at the interval listed in **Table 2** for normal riding. More frequent tune-ups may be required if the bike is ridden in stop-and-go traffic. The purpose of the tune-up is to restore the performance lost due to normal wear and deterioration of parts.

The spark plugs should be routinely replaced at every other tune-up or if the electrodes show signs of erosion. In addition, this is a good time to clean the air filter element. Have the new parts on hand before you begin.

Because the different systems in an engine interact, the procedures should be done in the following order:

    a. Tighten the cylinder head nuts.

    b. Adjust valve clearances.

    c. Run a compression test.

    d. Check the ignition timing.

    e. Synchronizing carburetors and set the idle speed.

Table 5 summarizes tune-up specifications.

To perform a tune-up on your Yamaha, you will need the following tools and equipment:

    a. Spark plug wrench.

    b. Socket wrench and assorted sockets.

    c. Flat feeler gauge.

    d. Special tool for changing valve lifter shims (Yamaha U.S. part No. YM-01245, UK part No. 90890-01245).

    e. Compression gauge.

    f. Spark plug wire feeler gauge and gapper tool.

    g. Ignition timing light.

    h. Carburetor synchronizing tool—to measure manifold vacuum.

Cylinder Head Nut Tightening

The cylinder head nuts should be tightened after the first 600 miles (1,000 km) of the purchase of a new bike, after the cylinder head has been removed for service and at every tune-up. The engine must be at room temperature for this procedure (95° F/35° C or cooler).

1A. On FZ600 models, perform the following:

    a. Remove the lower fairing on each side as described under *Lower Fairing Removal/Installation* in Chapter Twelve. Remove the lower fairing mounting brackets.

    b. Remove the exhaust system as described under *Exhaust System Removal/Installation (FZ600 Models)* in Chapter Seven.

    c. Place wood block(s) under the crankcase to support the bike securely.

1B. On Radian models, place a wood block(s) under each side of the frame to support it securely.

2. Remove the seat as described under *Seat Removal/Installation* in Chapter Twelve.

3. Remove the fuel tank as described under *Fuel Tank Removal/Installation* in Chapter Seven.

4. Remove the bolt securing the horn and remove the horn.

5. Disconnect all spark plug caps and wires (A, **Figure 99**).

6. Using a crisscross pattern, loosen then remove the Allen bolts securing the cylinder head cover (B, **Figure 99**). **Figure 100** shows the different length Allen bolts, grommets and washers used.

7. Remove the cylinder head cover and gaskets.

8. First, using a crisscross pattern, loosen all cylinder head upper and lower nuts.

9. Tighten all cylinder head upper nuts in the torque pattern shown in **Figure 101**. Tighten to the torque specification listed in **Table 4**.

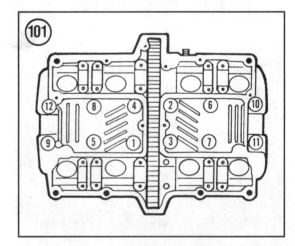

10. Tighten the lower cylinder head front nuts (**Figure 102**) and rear nuts (**Figure 103**) to the torque specifications listed in **Table 4**.

11. Leave off all parts that have been removed and adjust the valves as described in this chapter

Valve Clearance Measurement

Valve clearance measurement and adjustment must be performed with the engine cool, at room temperature (below 95° F/35° C). The correct valve clearance is as follows:

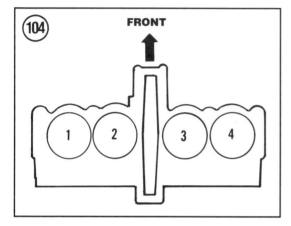

FRONT

YAMAHA

a. Exhaust valves: 0.16-0.20 mm (0.0063-0.008 in.).

b. Intake valves: 0.11-0.15 mm (0.004-0.0059 in.).

The exhaust valves are located at the front of the engine and the intake valves are located at the rear of the engine.

1. Perform Steps 1-10 of *Cylinder Head Nut Tightening* in this chapter.

2. Remove all spark plugs. This will make it easier to rotate the engine.

NOTE
*The cylinders are numbered 1, 2, 3 and 4 from the left-to-right as shown in **Figure 104**. The left-hand side refers to a rider sitting on the seat looking forward.*

NOTE
Measure the valve clearance in this sequence; cylinder No. 1, No. 2, No. 4 and then No. 3.

3A. On 1986-1988 models, perform the following:

a. Remove the screws securing the ignition cover (**Figure 105**) and remove the cover and gasket.

b. Rotate the crankshaft *counterclockwise* with a wrench on the nut on the left-hand end of the crankshaft (**Figure 106**).

c. Rotate the engine until the "T" mark (C, **Figure 107**) on the timing plate aligns with the *top* pickup coil (A, **Figure 107**) with the No. 1 piston at top dead center on the compression

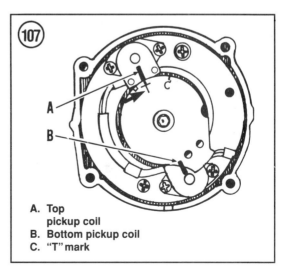

A. Top pickup coil
B. Bottom pickup coil
C. "T" mark

stroke. The piston is at TDC when the camshaft lobes face away from each other as shown in **Figure 108**.

3B. On 1989-1990 models, perform the following:

a. Remove the bolts securing the alternator cover/coil assembly.

b. Rotate the crankshaft *counterclockwise* with a wrench on the alternator rotor bolt on the left-hand end of the crankshaft (**Figure 109**).

c. Rotate the engine until the "T" mark on the rotor aligns with the fixed pointer on the crankcase (**Figure 110**) with the No. 1 piston at top dead center on the compression stroke. The piston is at TDC when the camshaft lobes face away from each other as shown in **Figure 108**.

4. With the engine in this position, check the clearance of the intake and exhaust valves of the No. 1 cylinder. Insert a flat feeler gauge between the camshaft lobe and the lifter surface (**Figure 111**). Measure the clearance with a metric feeler gauge as it will be easier to calculate pad replacement. When the clearance is correct, there will be a slight drag on the feeler gauge when it is inserted and withdrawn. The correct valve clearance is as follows:

a. Exhaust valves: 0.16-0.20 mm (0.0063-0.008 in.).

b. Intake valves: 0.11-0.15 mm (0.004-0.0059 in.).

Note the clearance as it will be used in the next procedure.

5A. On 1986-1988 models, rotate the crankshaft *counterclockwise* using a wrench on the nut located on the left side of the crankshaft (**Figure 106**). Rotate the engine until the "T" mark on the timing plate is aligned with the center of the *bottom* pickup coil (B, **Figure 107**), and the No. 2 piston is at top dead center on its compression stroke. The piston is at top dead center on its compression stroke when the camshaft lobes for the No. 2 cylinder are facing away from each other as shown in **Figure 108**.

5B. On 1989-1990 models, turn the crankshaft *counterclockwise* exactly 180° using a wrench on the alternator rotor bolt (**Figure 109**). The "T" mark on the alternator rotor (**Figure 110**) should be 180° from the mark on the crankcase and the No. 2 piston should be at top dead center on its compression stroke. The piston is at top dead center on its compression stroke when the camshaft lobes for the No.

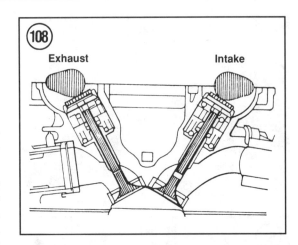

(108) Exhaust　　　　　　　　　　Intake

(109)

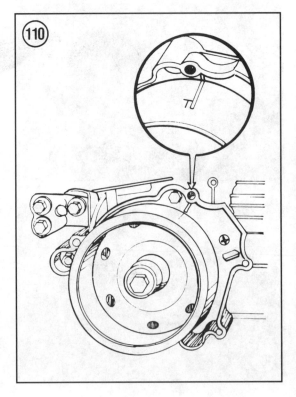

(110)

2 cylinder are facing away from each other as shown in **Figure 108**.

6. With the engine in this position, check the clearance of the intake and exhaust valves of the No. 2 cylinder. Insert a flat feeler gauge between the camshaft lobe and the lifter surface (**Figure 111**). Measure the clearance with a metric feeler gauge as it will be easier to calculate pad replacement. When the clearance is correct, there will be a slight drag on the feeler gauge when it is inserted and withdrawn. The correct valve clearance is as follows:

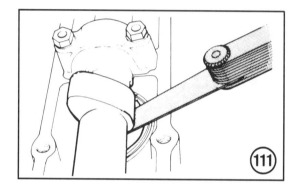

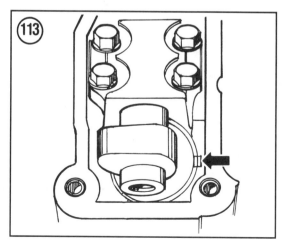

a. Exhaust valves: 0.16-0.20 mm (0.0063-0.008 in.).

b. Intake valves: 0.11-0.15 mm (0.004-0.0059 in.).

Note the clearance as it will be used in the next procedure.

7. Repeat Step 3 and Step 4 for the No. 4 cylinder.

8. Repeat Step 5 and Step 6 for the No. 3 cylinder.

Valve Clearance Adjustment

To correct the valve clearance, the shim on top of the valve lifter must be replaced with one of the correct thickness. These shims are available in 25 different thicknesses from No. 200 (2.00 mm) to No. 320 (3.20 mm) in increments of 0.05 mm. They are available from Yamaha dealers. The thickness is marked on the face that contacts the lifter body.

A special tool, the Yamaha Tappet Adjusting tool (**Figure 112**), (U.S. part No. YM-01245, UK part No. 90890-01245) is necessary for this procedure. It is attached to the cylinder head, next to the valve being adjusted, with one of the Allen bolts used to secure the cylinder head cover. This tool holds the valve lifter down so the adjusting shim can be removed and replaced.

There is no set order to follow in adjusting the valves since the number of valves requiring adjustment varies.

1. The top of the valve lifter has a slot (**Figure 113**) and this slot must be positioned away from the outer edge of the cylinder head where the special tool is to be installed.

2. Rotate the crankshaft *counterclockwise* with a wrench on the nut on the left-hand end of the crankshaft (**Figure 106**) until the camshaft lobe fully depresses the valve lifter (valve is completely open).

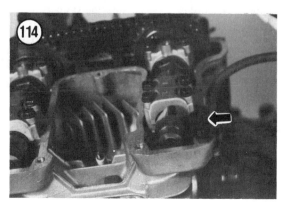

3. Install the special Yamaha tool, using one of the cylinder head cover Allen bolts, as shown in **Figure 114**. Make sure the tool blade touches only the lifter body (**Figure 115**), not the shim.

> *CAUTION*
> *Do not allow the camshaft lobe to come in contact with the valve adjusting tool as it may fracture the cylinder head. To avoid camshaft contact with the tool, rotate the intake camshaft **clockwise** and the exhaust camshaft **counterclockwise**, as viewed from the left-hand side looking directly at the No. 1 cylinder (Figure 116).*

4. Carefully rotate the camshaft lobe off of the shim so the shim can be removed. Remove the shim from the valve lifter with a small screwdriver or needlenose pliers (**Figure 117**).

5. Turn the shim over and note the number. Confirm the thickness with a micrometer measurement.

6. For correct shim thickness selection proceed as follows:

> *NOTE*
> *The following numbers are examples only. Use the actual clearance measurement as noted in the previous procedure, correct clearance specification and existing shim number from your engine.*

Actual measured clearance	0.50 mm
Minimum specified clearance	−0.19
Equals excess clearance	0.31
Existing shim number	220
Plus excess clearance	+31
Equals new shim number	251
Round off to nearest pad number	250

7. Install the new shim into the valve lifter with the number facing down. Make sure the shim is positioned correctly within the recess in the valve lifter.

8. Carefully rotate the engine until the camshaft lobe comes in contact with the new shim and lifter (see CAUTION following Step 3). Remove the Yamaha adjusting tool.

9. Rotate the engine several times to make sure the shim has properly seated into the valve lifter.

10. Recheck the clearance of this valve as described under *Valve Clearance Measurement* in this chapter. If clearance is incorrect, repeat these steps until proper clearance is achieved.

11. Repeat this procedure for all valves requiring adjustment.

12. Discard the old shims. They have become worn and their numbers are no longer accurate.

13. Install the cylinder head cover and gasket.

14. Install the Allen bolts, washers and grommets. Tighten the Allen bolts and hex bolts in a crisscross pattern to the torque specification listed in **Table 4**.

15. Install all spark plugs and connect all spark plug caps and wires.

16. Install the bolt securing the horn and tighten securely.

17A. On 1986-1988 models, install the ignition cover and gasket. Install and tighten the screws securely.

17B. On 1989-1990 models, install the alternator cover/coil assembly and tighten the bolts securely.

18. Install the fuel tank as described in Chapter Seven.

19. Install the seat as described in Chapter Twelve.

20. On FZ600 models, perform the following:

    a. Install the exhaust system as described in Chapter Seven.

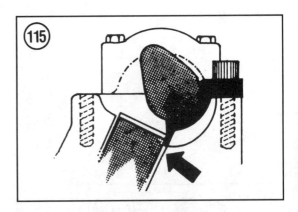

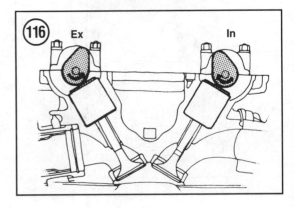

b. Install the lower fairing mounting brackets and the lower fairing on each side as described in Chapter Twelve.

Compression Test

Check the cylinder compression at the interval indicated in **Table 2**. Record the results and compare them to the results at the next interval. A running record will show trends in deterioration so that corrective action can be taken before complete failure.

The results, when properly interpreted, can indicate general cylinder, piston ring and valve condition.

1. Warm the engine to normal operating temperature, then shut it off. Make sure the choke valve and throttle valve are completely open.

2. On FZ600 models, remove the lower fairing on each side as described under *Lower Fairing Removal/Installation* in Chapter Twelve.

3. Remove all spark plugs.

4. Connect the compression tester to one cylinder following the manufacturer's instructions (**Figure 118**).

5. Have an assistant crank the engine over until there is no further rise in pressure.

6. Remove the tester and record the reading.

7. Repeat for all four cylinders.

8. Install the spark plugs.

9. On FZ600 models, install the lower fairing on each side as described in Chapter Twelve.

When interpreting the results, actual readings are not as important as the difference between the readings. The recommended cylinder compression pressure and the maximum allowable difference between cylinders are listed in **Table 6**. Greater differences than those listed in **Table 6** indicate broken rings, leaky or sticking valves, a blown head gasket or a combination of all. If the compression readings do not differ between the cylinders by more than 10 psi, the rings and valves are in good condition.

If a low reading (10% or more) is obtained, it indicates valve or ring trouble. To determine which, pour about a teaspoon of engine oil through the spark plug hole onto the top of the piston. Turn the engine over once to clear the oil, then take another compression test and record the reading. If the compression returns to normal, the valves are good but the rings are defective. If the compression does not increase, the valves require servicing. A valve(s) could be hanging open but not burned or a piece of carbon could be on a valve seat.

Spark Plug Selection

Spark plugs are available in various heat ranges, hotter or colder than plugs originally installed at the factory.

Select plugs of a heat range designed for the loads and temperature conditions under which the bike will be run. The use of incorrect heat ranges can cause seized pistons, scored cylinder walls or damaged piston crowns.

In general, use a hot plug for low speeds, low engine loads and low temperatures. Use a cold plug for high speeds, high engine loads and high temperatures. The plug should operate hot enough to burn off unwanted deposits, but not so hot that it is damaged or causes preignition. A spark plug of the correct heat range will show a light tan color on the portion of the insulator within the cylinder after the plug has been in service.

The reach (length) of a plug is also important (**Figure 119**). A longer than normal plug could interfere with the valves and pistons, causing permanent and severe damage. The recommended spark plugs are listed in **Table 6**.

Spark Plug Removal/Cleaning

1. On FZ600 models, remove the lower fairing on each side as described under *Lower Fairing Removal/Installation* in Chapter Twelve.

2. Grasp each spark plug lead (**Figure 120**) as near the plug as possible and carefully pull it off the plug. If the boot is stuck to the plug, twist it slightly to break it loose.

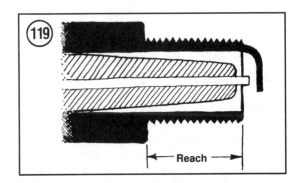

> *CAUTION*
> *If any dirt falls into the cylinder when the plugs are removed, it could cause serious engine damage.*

3. Use compressed air and blow away any dirt that may have passed by the rubber boot on the spark plug lead and accumulated in the spark plug well.

4. Remove spark plugs with a spark plug wrench. Keep the spark plugs in the order that they were removed. If anything turns up during the inspection step, you will then know which cylinder it came from.

> *NOTE*
> *If plugs are difficult to remove, apply penetrating oil such as WD-40 or Liquid Wrench around base of plugs and let it soak in about 10-20 minutes.*

5. Inspect the spark plug carefully. Look for a plug with broken center porcelain, excessively eroded electrodes and excessive carbon or oil fouling. Replace such a plug. If deposits are light, the plug may be cleaned in solvent with a wire brush or in a special spark plug sandblast cleaner. Regap the plug as explained in this chapter.

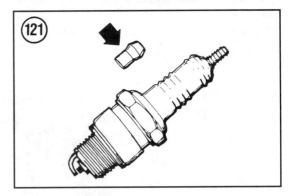

Spark Plug Gapping and Installation

A new plug should be carefully gapped to ensure a reliable, consistent spark. You must use a special spark plug gapping tool with a wire feeler gauge.

1. Remove the new plug from the box. Do *not* screw on the small piece (**Figure 121**) that is sometimes loose in the box, it is not to be used.

2. Insert a wire feeler gauge between the center and the side electrode of each plug (**Figure 122**). The correct gap is 0.6-0.7 mm (0.024-0.028 in.). If the gap is correct, you will feel a slight drag as you pull the wire through. If there is no drag or the gauge

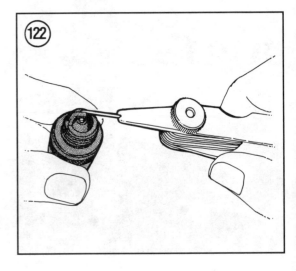

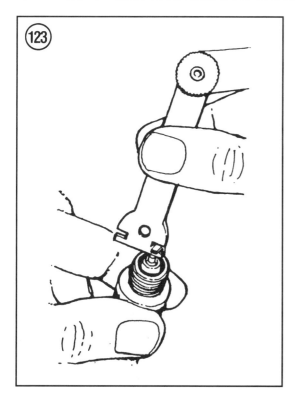

won't pass through, bend the side electrode *with the gapping tool* (**Figure 123**) to set the proper gap.

3. Put a *small* drop of oil or aluminum anti-seize compound on the threads of the spark plug (**Figure 124**).

4. Screw each spark plug in by hand until it seats. Very little effort is required. If force is necessary, you have the plug cross-threaded; unscrew it and try again.

5. Tighten the spark plugs an additional 1/2 turn after the gasket has made contact with the head. If you are reinstalling old, regapped plugs and are reusing the old gasket, only tighten an additional 1/4 turn.

NOTE
Do not overtighten. This will only squash the gasket and destroy its sealing ability.

6. Install the spark plug leads; make sure the leads are on tight.

7. On FZ600 models, install the lower fairing on each side as described in Chapter Twelve.

Reading Spark Plugs

Much information about engine and spark plug performance can be determined by careful examination of the spark plugs. This information is only valid after performing the following steps.

1. Ride the bike a short distance at full throttle in any gear.

2. Turn the engine stop switch (**Figure 125**) to the OFF position before closing the throttle and simultaneously pull in the clutch or shift to NEUTRAL; coast and brake to a stop.

3. Remove one spark plug at a time and examine it. Compare it to **Figure 126**. If the insulator is white or burned, the plug is too hot and should be replaced with a colder one. A too-cold plug will have sooty or oily deposits ranging in color from dark brown to black. Replace with a hotter plug and check for too-rich carburetion or evidence of oil blowby at the piston rings. If the plug has a light tan or gray colored deposit and no abnormal gap wear or electrode erosion is evident, the plug and the engine are running properly. If the plug exhibits a black insulator tip, a damp and oily film over the firing end and a carbon layer over the entire nose, it is oil fouled. An oil fouled plug can be cleaned, but it is better to replace it.

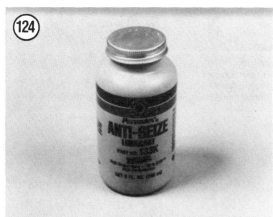

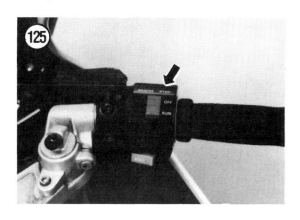

SPARK PLUG CONDITION

NORMAL

- Identified by light tan or gray deposits on the firing tip.
- Can be cleaned.

GAP BRIDGED

- Identified by deposit buildup closing gap between electrodes.
- Caused by oil or carbon fouling. If deposits are not excessive, the plug can be cleaned.

OIL FOULED

- Identified by wet black deposits on the insulator shell bore and electrodes.
- Caused by excessive oil entering combustion chamber through worn rings and pistons, excessive clearance between valve guides and stems, or worn or loose bearings. Can be cleaned. If engine is not repaired, use a hotter plug.

CARBON FOULED

- Identified by black, dry fluffy carbon deposits on insulator tips, exposed shell surfaces and electrodes.
- Caused by too cold a plug, weak ignition, dirty air cleaner, too rich a fuel mixture, or excessive idling. Can be cleaned.

LEAD FOULED

- Identified by dark gray, black, yellow, or tan deposits or a fused glazed coating on the insulator tip.
- Caused by highly leaded gasoline. Can be cleaned.

WORN

- Identified by severely eroded or worn electrodes.
- Caused by normal wear. Should be replaced.

FUSED SPOT DEPOSIT

- Identified by melted or spotty deposits resembling bubbles or blisters.
- Caused by sudden acceleration. Can be cleaned.

OVERHEATING

- Identified by a white or light gray insulator with small black or gray brown spots and with bluish-burnt appearance of electrodes.
- Caused by engine overheating, wrong type of fuel, loose spark plugs, too hot a plug, or incorrect ignition timing. Replace the plug.

PREIGNITION

- Identified by melted electrodes and possibly blistered insulator. Metallic deposits on insulator indicate engine damage.
- Caused by wrong type of fuel, incorrect ignition timing or advance, too hot a plug, burned valves, or engine overheating. Replace the plug.

4. Repeat for all 4 spark plugs. Replace as a set if any are bad.

Ignition Timing
(1986-1988 Models)

NOTE
Yamaha does not provide any information relating to the 1989-1990 models for this procedure.

Ignition timing is factory set and is not adjustable (the base plate screw holes are not slotted). The following procedure is to be used to check that all components within the ignition system are operating correctly.

It is only necessary to check the timing on the No. 1 cylinder. If this cylinder is correct, the other three cylinders will automatically be correct.

NOTE
Prior to running this procedure, check all electrical connections within the ignition system. Make sure all connections are free of corrosion and are tight and that all ground connections are tight.

1. Place the bike on the centerstand or sidestand.
2. Remove the screws securing the ignition cover on the left-hand end of the crankshaft and remove the cover and gasket.
3. Connect a portable tachometer following the manufacturer's instructions. The bike's tachometer is not accurate enough in the low rpm range for this procedure.

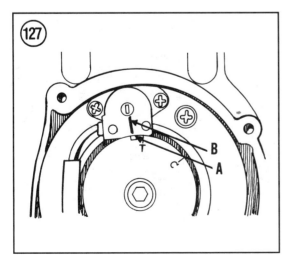

4. Connect the timing light to the left-hand No. 1 cylinder following the manufacturer's instructions.
5. Check and tighten if necessary, the timing plate mounting screws.
6. Start the engine and let it reach normal operating temperature. Bring the engine to idle speed (**Table 6**) and aim the timing light at the timing marks on the timing plate.
7. The firing range mark (A, **Figure 127**) on the timing plate should align with the upper ignition pickup coil mark (B, **Figure 127**). If the timing mark is incorrect and the mounting screws are tight, refer to the ignition system section in Chapter Eight for probable causes. The ignition timing cannot be adjusted.

Carburetor Idle Mixture

The idle mixture (pilot screw) is preset at the factory and *is not to be reset*. Do not adjust the pilot screw unless the carburetors have been overhauled. If so, refer to Chapter Seven for service procedures.

Carburetor Synchronization

NOTE
Prior to synchronizing the carburetors, the ignition timing must be checked and be correct and the valve clearance properly adjusted.

1. On FZ600 models, remove the lower fairing on each side as described under *Lower Fairing Removal/Installation* in Chapter Twelve.
2. Place the bike on the centerstand or side stand.
3. Start the engine and let it reach normal operating temperature. Shut the engine off.
4. Remove the seat(s) as described under *Seat Removal/Installation* in Chapter Twelve.
5. Remove both side covers.
6. Remove the bolt securing the fuel tank at the rear. Prop up the rear of the tank.
7. Remove the plug (**Figure 128**) from each cylinder head vacuum port adjacent to the carburetor intake tubes.
8. Connect the vacuum tubes from the synchronizing tool to the vacuum ports following the manufacturer's instructions.
9. Restart the engine and let it idle at the idle speed listed in **Table 6**. Adjust the idle speed if necessary as described in this chapter.

NOTE
The carburetors are numbered the same as the cylinders are with the No. 1, 2, 3 and 4 from the left-to-right as shown in **Figure 129**. *The left-hand side refers to a rider sitting on the seat looking forward.*

10. The carburetors are synchronized if all have the same gauge readings. If not, proceed as follows.

11. Synchronize the No. 1 carburetor to the No. 2 carburetor by turning screw "A" in **Figure 129** until both gauges read the same.

12. Rev the engine several times for a fraction of a second and check the synchronization again. Readjust if necessary.

13. Synchronize the No. 4 carburetor to the No. 3 carburetor by turning screw "C" in **Figure 129** until both gauges read the same.

14. Rev the engine several times for a fraction of a second and check the synchronization again. Readjust if necessary.

15. Synchronize the No. 2 carburetor to the No. 3 carburetor by turning screw "B" in **Figure 129** until both gauges read the same.

16. Rev the engine several times for a fraction of a second and check the synchronization again. Readjust if necessary.

17. Adjust the idle speed as described in this chapter.

18. Shut the engine off.

19. Remove the vacuum gauge tubes and install the plugs into the cylinder head ports.

20. Lower the fuel tank, install the rear bolt and tighten securely.

21. On FZ600 models, install the lower fairing on each side as described in Chapter Twelve.

22. Install both side covers.

23. Install the seat as described in Chapter Twelve.

Carburetor Idle Speed Adjustment

Before making this adjustment, the air filter element must be clean and the engine must have adequate compression. See *Compression Test* in this chapter. Otherwise this procedure cannot be done properly.

1. Start the engine and let it reach normal operating temperature. Make sure the choke knob is in the open position.

2. On FZ600 models, remove the lower fairing on each side as described under *Lower Fairing Re-*

moval/Installation in Chapter Twelve. Remove the lower fairing mounting brackets.

3. Place the bike on the centerstand or side stand.

4. Connect a portable tachometer following the manufacturer's instructions.

5. Turn the idle adjust knob (**Figure 130**) in or out to adjust idle speed.

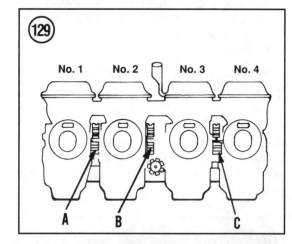

No. 1   No. 2   No. 3   No. 4

A   B   C

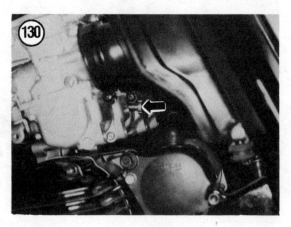

6. The correct idle speed is listed in **Table 6**.

7. Open and close the throttle a couple of times; check for variations in idle speed. Readjust if necessary.

WARNING
With the engine running at idle speed, move the handlebar from side to side.

If the idle speed increases during this movement, the throttle cable may need adjusting or it may be incorrectly routed through the frame. Correct this problem immediately. Do not ride the bike in this unsafe condition.

8. On FZ600 models, install the lower fairing on each side as described in Chapter Twelve.

3

Table 1 TIRE INFLATION PRESSURE (COLD)*

Radian models	Load FZ600 models	Air Pressure
Up to 198 lb. (90 kg)		
Front	26 psi (179 kPa)	26 psi (179 kPa)
Rear	28 psi (193 kPa)	28 psi (193 kPa)
Maximum load limit**		
Front	28 psi (193 kPa)	28 psi (193 kPa)
Rear	32 psi (220 kPa)	36 psi (248 kPa)

*Recommended air pressure for factory equipped tires. Aftermarket tires may require different air pressure.
**Maximum load limit includes total weight of motorcycle with accessories, rider(s) and luggage.

Table 2 SERVICE INTERVALS

U.S. MODELS*	
Every 300 miles (300 km)	Check and adjust (if necessary) drive chain slack Lubricate drive chain

**Initial 600 miles (1,000 km)
    or 1 month**
	Adjust camshaft chain tension
	Change engine oil and filter
	Check carburetor synchronization;
	  adjust if necessary
	Check the brake lever and pedal free play;
	  adjust if necessary
	Check clutch able free play; adjust if necessary
	Check brake pad and lining thickness
	Check hydraulic fluid level in brake
	  master cylinder(s)
	Lubricate all control cables
	Check operation of side stand switch;
	  lubricate if necessary

**Initial 4,400 miles (7,000 km); there-
    after every 3,800 miles (6,000 km)**
	Adjust camshaft chain tension
	Inspect crankcase breather hose for cracks or
	  loose hose clamps; drain out all residue
	Inspect fuel line for chafed, cracked or swollen ends
	Inspect all vacuum lines for chafed or cracked ends
	Check exhaust system for leakage

(continued)	

Table 2 SERVICE INTERVALS (continued)

U.S. MODELS* (continued)	
Initial 4,400 miles (7,000 km); thereafter every 3,800 miles (6,000 km) (continued)	Check carburetor synchronization; adjust if necessary
	Check engine idle speed; adjust if necessary
	Change engine oil and filter
	Clean air filter element; replace if damaged
	Check the brake lever and pedal free play; adjust if necessary
	Check brake pad and lining thickness
	Lubricate all control cables
	Lubricate brake and clutch lever pivot points
	Lubricate brake pedal and shift pedal pivot shafts
	Lubricate side stand and centerstand (Radian) pivot points
	Check front fork operation and check for oil seal leakage
	Check steering play; adjust if necessary
	Check wheel bearing operation
	Check battery specific gravity and electrolyte level
	Check operation of side stand switch; lubricate if necessary
Initial 4,400 miles (7,000 km) or 7 months; then every 7,600 miles (12,000 km) or 13 months	Check spark plugs; adjust gap and clean
Initial 8,200 miles (13,000 km) or 13 months; then every 7,600 miles (12,000 km) or 12 months	Replace spark plugs
	Replace alternator brushes (1986-1988)
Every 15,200 miles (24,000 km)	Repack the steering head bearings
Every 15,800 miles (25,000 km) or 25 months	Check valve clearance; adjust if necessary
	Lubricate swing arm pivot shaft
	Lubricate rear suspension linkage (FZ600 models)
UK MODELS*	
Every 300 miles (300 km)	Check and adjust (if necessary) drive chain slack
	Lubricate drive chain
Initial 600 miles (1,000 km) or 1 month	Adjust camshaft chain tension
	Change engine oil and filter
	Check carburetor synchronization; adjust if necessary
	Check the brake lever and pedal free play; adjust if necessary
	Check clutch cable free play; adjust if necessary
	Check brake pad and lining thickness
	Check hydraulic fluid level in brake master cylinder(s)
	Lubricate all control cables
	Check operation of side stand switch (1987); lubricate if necessary
Every 4,000 miles (6,000 km) or 6 months	Adjust camshaft chain tension

(continued)

Table 2 SERVICE INTERVALS (continued)

	UK MODELS* (continued)
Every 4,000 miles (6,000 km) or 6 months (continued)	Inspect crankcase breather hose for cracks or loose hose clamps; drain out all residue Inspect fuel line for chafed, cracked or swollen ends Inspect all vacuum lines for chafed or cracked ends Check exhaust system for leakage Check spark plugs; adjust gap and clean; replace if necessary Check carburetor synchronization; adjust if necessary Check engine idle speed; adjust if necessary Change engine oil Clean air filter element; replace if damaged Check the brake lever and pedal free play; adjust if necessary Check brake pad and lining thickness Lubricate all control cables Lubricate brake and clutch lever pivot points Lubricate brake pedal and shift pedal pivot shafts Lubricate side stand and centerstand (Radian) pivot points Check front fork operation and check for oil seal leakage Check steering play; adjust if necessary Check wheel bearing operation Check battery specific gravity and electrolyte level Check operation of side stand switch (1986); lubricate if necessary
Every 8,000 miles (12,000 km) or 12 months	Check valve clearance; adjust if necessary Change engine oil and filter Lubricate swing arm pivot shaft Lubricate rear suspension linkage Replace alternator brushes
Every 16,000 miles (24,000 km) or 24 months	Repack the steering head bearings

* This Yamaha factory maintenance schedule should be considered as a guide to general maintenance and lubrication intervals. Harder than normal use and exposure to mud, water, sand, high humidity, etc. will naturally dictate more frequent attention to most maintenance items.

Table 3 STATE OF CHARGE

Specific Gravity	State of Charge
1.110-1.130	Discharged
1.140-1.160	Almost discharged
1.170-1.190	One-quarter charged
1.200-1.220	One-half charged
1.230-1.250	Three-quarters charged
1.260-1.280	Fully charged

Table 4 MAINTENANCE AND TUNE-UP TIGHTENING TORQUES

Item	N·m	ft.-lb.
Oil drain plug	43	31
Oil filter union bolt	15	11
Oil gallery check bolt	7	5
Fork top cap bolt	23	17
Handlebar		
Holder bolt (Radian)	20	14
Pinch bolt (FZ600)	20	14
Upper fork bridge bolt		
Radian	23	17
FZ600	20	14
Lower fork bridge bolt	23	17
Rear axle nut	105	75
Camshaft chain tensioner		
Stopper bolt	9	6.5
Locknut	6	4.3
Ignition cover screws	10	7.2
Cylinder head nuts		
Upper	22	16
Lower	10	7.2
Cylinder head cover bolts	10	7.2

Table 5 FRONT FORK AIR PRESSURE (FZ600 MODELS)

	kPa	psi
Standard air pressure	39	5.7
Minimum air pressure	0	0
Maximum air pressure	98	14
Differential between fork legs 9.8 kPa (1.4 psi) or less		

Table 6 TUNE-UP SUMMARY

Item	Specification
Air filter element	Dry element type
Firing order	1-2-4-3
Ignition timing	Fixed, non-adjustable
Timing mark	Firing range mark at idle speed
Valve clearance (cold below 35° C/95° F)	
Intake	0.11-0.15 mm (0.004-0.0059 in.)
Exhaust	0.16-0.20 mm (0.0063-0.008 in.)
Compression pressure (at sea level)	
Standard pressure	1,079 kPa (156 psi)
Minimum pressure	980 kPa (142 psi)
Maximum pressure	1,128 kPa (164 psi)
Maximum difference between cylinders	98 kPa (14 psi)
Spark plug (U.S.)	
Type	ND X24ES-U or NGK D8EA
Gap	0.6-0.7 mm (0.024-0.028 in.)
Tightening torque	17.5 N·m (13 ft-lb.)
Spark plug (UK)	
Type	ND X24ESR-U or NGK D8ES-L
Gap	0.6-0.7 mm (0.024-0.028 in.)
Tightening torque	17.5 N·m (13 ft-lb.)
Idle speed	
Radian models	1,250-1,350 rpm
FZ600 models	1,150-1,250 rpm

CHAPTER FOUR

ENGINES

The Yamaha Radian and FZ600 bikes are equipped with an air cooled, 4-stroke, 4 cylinder engine with double overhead camshafts. The camshafts are chain-driven from the sprocket on the center of the crankshaft.

This chapter provides complete service and overhaul procedures including information for removal, disassembly, inspection, service and reassembly of the engine. Although the clutch and transmission are located within the engine, the clutch is covered in Chapter Five and the transmission is covered in Chapter Six to simplify this material.

Refer to **Table 1** for complete engine specifications and **Table 2** for torque specifications. **Tables 1-3** are located at the end of this chapter.

Before starting any work, re-read Chapter One of this book. You will do a better job with this information fresh in your mind.

Throughout the text there is frequent mention of the right-hand and left-hand side of the engine. This refers to the engine as it sits in the bike's frame, *not* as it sits on your workbench. The right- and left-hand refers to a rider sitting on the seat facing forward.

> *NOTE*
> *Where differences occur relating to the United Kingdom (UK) models they are identified. If there is no (UK) designation relating to a procedure, photo or illustration, it is identical to the United States (U.S.) models.*

ENGINE PRINCIPLES

Figure 1 explains how the engine works. This will be helpful when troubleshooting or repairing the engine.

SERVICING ENGINE IN FRAME

The following components can be serviced while the engine is mounted in the frame (the bike's frame is a great holding fixture for breaking loose stubborn bolts and nuts):

    a. Carburetor assembly.
    b. Exhaust system.
    c. Alternator and starter.
    d. Camshafts and cylinder head.
    e. Cylinder block.
    f. Pistons.
    g. Clutch assembly.
    h. External shift mechanism.

ENGINE REMOVAL/INSTALLATION

1. Remove the seat(s) as described under *Seat Removal/Installation* in Chapter Twelve.

2. On FZ600 models, remove the lower fairing as described under *Lower Fairing Removal/Installation* in Chapter Twelve. Remove the lower fairing mounting brackets.

4-STROKE PRINCIPLES

(1)

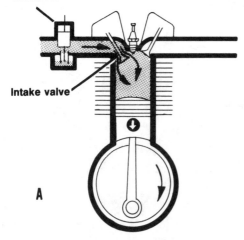

A

As the piston travels downward, the exhaust valve is closed and the intake valve opens, allowing the new air-fuel mixture from the carburetor to be drawn into the cylinder. When the piston reaches the bottom of its travel (BDC), the intake valve closes and remains closed for the next 1 1/2 revolutions of the crankshaft.

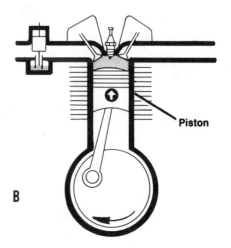

B

While the crankshaft continues to rotate, the piston moves upward, compressing the air-fuel mixture.

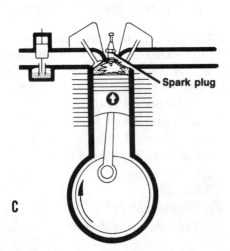

C

As the piston almost reaches the top of its travel, the spark plug fires, igniting the compressed air-fuel mixture. The piston continues to top dead center (TDC) and is pushed downward by the expanding gases.

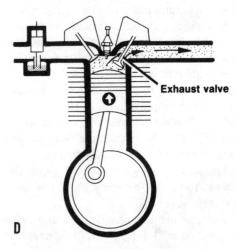

D

When the piston almost reaches BDC, the exhaust valve opens and remains open until the piston is near TDC. The upward travel of the piston forces the exhaust gases out of the cylinder. After the piston has reached TDC, the exhaust valve closes and the cycle starts all over again.

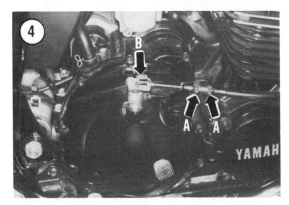

3. Remove the fuel tank as described under *Fuel Tank Removal/Installation* in Chapter Seven.

4. Remove the battery as described under *Battery Removal/Installation* in Chapter Three.

5. Remove the exhaust system as described under *Exhaust System Removal/Installation* in Chapter Seven.

6. Disconnect the breather hose (**Figure 2**) from the crankcase.

7. Disconnect the spark plug leads (**Figure 3**) and tie them up out of the way.

8. Remove the carburetor assembly as described under *Carburetor Removal/Installation* in Chapter Seven.

9. Drain the engine oil and remove the oil filter as described under *Engine Oil and Filter Change* in Chapter Three. The oil filter must be removed in order for the engine to clear the frame later on in this procedure.

10. Loosen the locknuts (A, **Figure 4**) on the clutch cable and disconnect the cable from the lever (B, **Figure 4**) on the clutch cover.

11. Remove the gearshift lever (A, **Figure 5**).

12. Remove the bolts securing the drive sprocket cover (B, **Figure 5**) and remove the cover.

13. Have an assistant apply the rear brake. Remove the bolts (**Figure 6**) securing the drive sprocket. Rotate the sprocket holding plate so the tabs clear the shaft splines and remove the holding plate.

14. To provide slack in the drive chain, perform the following:

    a. Remove the cotter pin and loosen the rear axle nut (A, **Figure 7**).

    b. Loosen the drive chain adjuster locknut and nut (B, **Figure 7**) on each side of the swing arm.

4

c. Push the rear wheel forward to achieve slack in the drive chain.

15. Remove the drive chain and drive sprocket from the transmission shaft.

16. Refer to Chapter Eight and disconnect the following electrical connectors:

    a. Alternator.

    b. Neutral indicator.

    c. Oil level indicator switch.

    d. Side stand indicator.

    e. Starter motor.

    f. Pickup coil leads (1986-1988 models).

17. On FZ600 models, remove the oil cooler and mounting brackets from the frame as described in this chapter.

18. On California models, disconnect the hoses (A, **Figure 8**) and remove the evaporation canister (B, **Figure 8**) from the frame.

NOTE
If you are just removing the engine and are not planning to disassemble it, do not perform Step 19.

19. If the engine is going to be disassembled, remove the following parts while the engine is still in the frame. Remove the following as described in this chapter unless otherwise noted:

    a. Alternator and starter (Chapter Eight).

    b. Camshafts and cylinder head.

    c. Cylinder block.

    d. Pistons.

    e. Pick-up coil assembly (1986-1988 models).

    f. Clutch assembly (Chapter Five).

    g. External shift mechanism (Chapter Six).

20. Take a final look all over the engine to make sure everything has been disconnected.

21. Place a suitable size jack, with a piece of wood to protect the crankcase, under the engine. Apply a small amount of jack pressure up on the engine.

NOTE
*There are many different bolt sizes and lengths, different combinations of washers, conical washers, lockwashers and different spacer lengths. It is suggested that when **each set** of bolts, nuts, washers, spacers and holding plates is removed that you place them in a separate plastic bag or box to keep them separated. This will save a lot of time when installing the engine.*

CAUTION
Continually adjust jack pressure during engine removal and installation to prevent damage to the mounting bolt threads and hardware.

22A. On Radian models, remove the following:

    a. Front upper holding plate-to-engine bolt (A, **Figure 9**).

    b. Front upper holding plate-to-frame bolts (B, **Figure 9**).

    c. Front lower bolts and lockwashers (C, **Figure 9**).

    d. Rear lower through bolt, nut and spacers (D, **Figure 9**).

22B. On FZ600 models, remove the following:

    a. Front middle through bolt and nut (A, **Figure 10**).

    b. Front lower bolts, washers, nuts (B, **Figure 10**).

    c. Allen bolts (C, **Figure 10**) securing the subframe to the frame and remove the sub frame (D, **Figure 10**).

    d. Rear lower through bolt (E, **Figure 10**), nut and spacer.

4

NOTE
Don't lose the spacers between the frame and the engine. Be sure to reinstall them.

CAUTION
The following steps require the aid of a helper to remove the engine assembly from the frame safely. Due to the weight of the engine, it is suggested that at least one helper, preferably 2 assist you in the removal of the engine.

23A. On Radian models, gradually raise the engine assembly to clear the frame and pull the engine out through the right-hand side of the frame. Take the engine to a workbench for further disassembly.

23B. On FZ600 models, gradually lower the engine assembly to clear the remaining portions of the frame and pull the engine out through the right-hand side of the frame. Take the engine to a workbench for further disassembly.

24. Install by reversing these removal steps while noting the following.

25. Tighten the mounting bolts to the torque specifications in **Table 2**.

26. Replace the oil filter then fill the engine with the recommended type and quantity of oil; refer to Chapter Three.

27. Adjust the clutch as described under *Clutch Adjustment* in Chapter Three.

28. Adjust the drive chain as described under *Drive Chain Adjustment* in Chapter Three.

29. Start the engine and check for leaks.

CYLINDER HEAD AND CAMSHAFTS

This section describes the removal, inspection and installation of the cylinder head and camshaft components. The valves and valve components are covered in a separate section.

Removal

Refer to **Figure 11** and **Figure 12** for this procedure. The cylinder head and camshafts can be removed with the engine in the frame.

1. Place the bike on the side stand.

2. Remove the seat(s) as described under *Seat Removal/Installation* in Chapter Twelve.

3. On FZ600 models, remove the side covers and lower fairings as described under *Lower Fairing Removal/Installation (FZ600 Models)* in Chapter Twelve.

4. Disconnect the battery negative lead. Refer to Chapter Three.

5. Remove the fuel tank as described under *Fuel Tank Removal/Installation* in Chapter Seven.

6. Remove the carburetor assembly as described under *Carburetor Removal/Installation* in Chapter Seven.

7. Disconnect all spark plug caps and wires (**Figure 13**) and tie them up out of the way.

8. Remove all spark plugs. This will make it easier to rotate the engine.

9. Using a crisscross pattern, loosen then remove the Allen bolts or hex-head bolts (**Figure 14**) securing the cylinder head cover. **Figure 15** shows the different length bolts, grommets and washers used. Don't lose the washers and rubber washers under the bolts.

10. Remove the cylinder head cover and gasket.

11. Remove the nut and bolt securing the camshaft drive chain tensioner (**Figure 16**). Remove the tensioner assembly and gasket.

⑪ **CYLINDER HEAD**

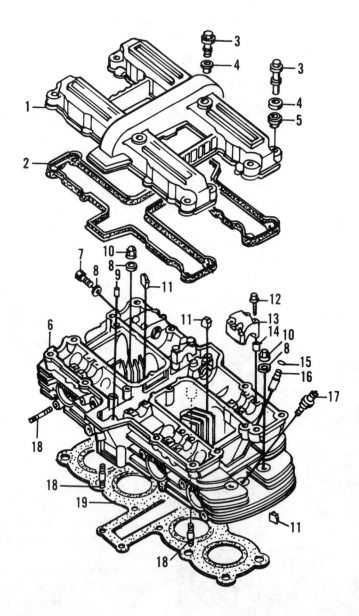

1. Cylinder head cover
2. Gasket
3. Bolt
4. Washer
5. Rubber isolator
6. Cylinder head
7. Bolt
8. Gasket
9. Dowel pin
10. Cap nut

11. Rubber silencer
12. Bolt
13. Bearing cap
14. Locating dowel
15. Valve guide ring
16. Valve guide
17. Spark plug
18. Threaded stud
19. Cylinder head gasket

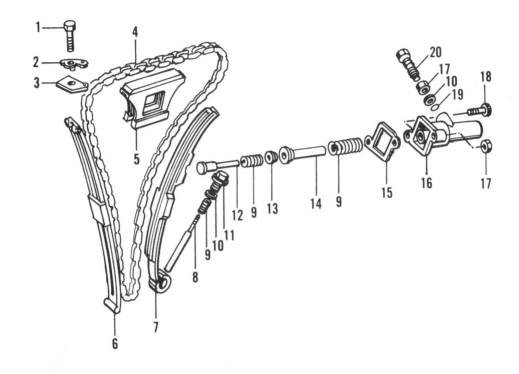

CAMSHAFT CHAIN TENSIONER

1. Bolt
2. Lockwasher
3. Plate
4. Drive chain
5. Center guide
6. Front chain guide
7. Rear chain guide
8. Stopper
9. Spring
10. Washer
11. Bolt
12. Tensioner rod (small)
13. Damper
14. Tensioner rod (large)
15. Gasket
16. Tensioner body
17. Nut
18. Bolt
19. O-ring
20. Bolt

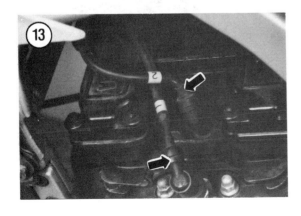

12A. On 1986-1988 models, perform the following:

   a. Remove the screws securing the ignition cover on the left-hand end of the crankshaft and remove the cover and gasket.

   b. Rotate the crankshaft *counterclockwise* with a wrench on the nut on the left-hand end of the crankshaft (**Figure 17**).

   c. Rotate the engine until the "T" mark on the timing plate aligns with the *top* pickup coil (**Figure 18**) with the engine at top dead center on the compression stroke. The cylinder is at TDC when the camshaft lobes face away from each other as shown in **Figure 19**.

12B. On 1989-1990 models, perform the following:

   a. Remove the bolts securing the alternator cover/coil assembly (**Figure 20**).

   b. Rotate the crankshaft *counterclockwise* with a wrench on the alternator rotor bolt on the left-hand end of the crankshaft (**Figure 21**).

   c. Rotate the engine until the "T" mark on the rotor aligns with the fixed pointer on the crankcase (**Figure 22**) with the engine at top dead center on the compression stroke. The cylinder is at TDC when the camshaft lobes face away from each other as shown in **Figure 19**.

13. Remove the camshaft drive chain center guide (**Figure 23**).

> *NOTE*
> *Each camshaft bearing cap has its own unique mark and must be reinstalled in the same location.*

14. Using a crisscross pattern, loosen then remove the bolts securing the 2 center camshaft bearing caps on both the intake and exhaust camshafts (**Figure 24**). Remove both bearing caps. These inner cam-

shaft bearing caps are marked with an "I" (intake) or "E" (exhaust) and with an arrow pointing toward the right-hand or clutch side of the engine as shown in **Figure 25**. Don't lose the locating dowels in each cap.

15. Remove the exposed camshaft sprocket bolt on each camshaft.

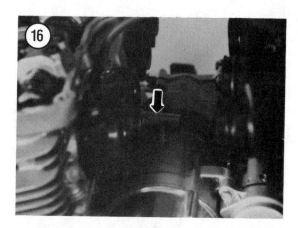

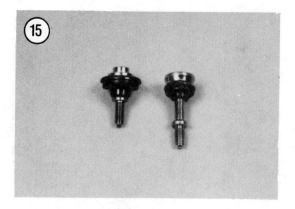

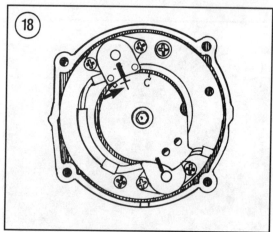

CAUTION
If the crankshaft must be rotated after the camshaft sprockets are removed, pull up on the camshaft chain and keep it taut while rotating the crankshaft. Make certain that the drive chain is positioned correctly on the crankshaft timing sprocket. If this is not done, the drive chain may become kinked and may damage both the chain and the timing sprocket on the crankshaft.

16. Rotate the crankshaft *counterclockwise* until the other camshaft sprocket bolts are exposed. Remove the remaining 2 sprocket bolts.

17. Slide the sprockets to the right-hand side and off of the camshaft shoulders.

NOTE
Each camshaft bearing cap has its own unique mark and must be reinstalled in the same location.

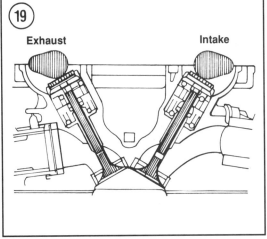

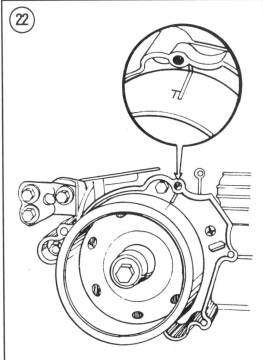

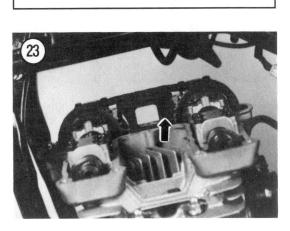

18. Remove the remaining camshaft bearing caps. The outer camshaft bearing caps are marked with a No. 1 (left-hand side) or No. 4 (right-hand side) and with an "I" (intake) or "E" (exhaust) as shown in **Figure 26**. Don't lose the locating dowels in each cap.

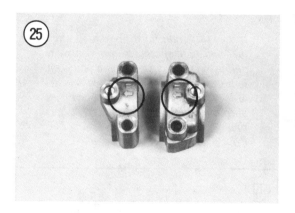

19. Disengage the camshaft drive chain from one camshaft sprocket and remove that camshaft from the cylinder head.

20. Tie a piece of wire to the camshaft drive chain (**Figure 27**) and to the frame. This will prevent the chain from falling down into the crankcase after the other camshaft is removed.

> *CAUTION*
> *If the crankshaft must be rotated when the camshafts are removed, pull up on the camshaft chain and keep it taut while rotating the crankshaft. Make certain that the drive chain is positioned correctly on the crankshaft timing sprocket. If this is not done, the drive chain may become kinked and may damage both the chain and the timing sprocket on the crankshaft.*

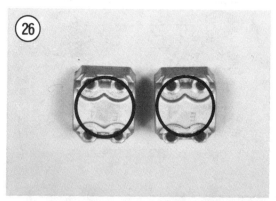

21. Disengage the camshaft drive chain from the other camshaft sprocket and remove the camshaft from the cylinder head.

> *CAUTION*
> *Never use a magnetic tool to lift out the valve lifters or adjustment shims. They are hardened steel and are easily magnetized. A magnetized part will attract and hold metal particles which will cause excessive wear.*

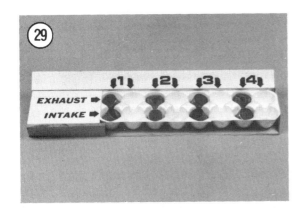

CAUTION
The valve lifters and adjustment shims must be installed into their original locations upon reassembly.

22. Remove the valve lifters and adjustment shims at this time to prevent the accidental mixup if they should come out while removing the cylinder head as follows:

    a. Remove them one at a time with a suction cup tool (**Figure 28**) and place them in a container such as an egg container (**Figure 29**).

    b. Mark the container with the specific cylinder number (No. 1-4) and intake and exhaust.

    c. The No.1 cylinder is on the left-hand side; the exhaust valves are at the front of the cylinder head and the intake are at the rear.

23. Bend down the raised tab on the lockwasher. Remove the bolt, lockwasher and plate (**Figure 30**) securing the camshaft drive chain front guide to the cylinder head.

24. Pull the drive chain front guide straight up and out of the cylinder head and cylinder block (**Figure 31**).

25. Loosen all cylinder head nuts 1/2 turn at a time as follows:

    a. First loosen the lower front (**Figure 32**) and rear (**Figure 33**) nuts.

    b. Then loosen the upper nuts in the sequence shown in **Figure 34**.

    c. After all nuts have been loosened, remove the nuts and washers.

26. Loosen the cylinder head by tapping around the perimeter with a rubber or soft-faced mallet. If necessary, *gently* pry the head loose with a broad-tipped screwdriver.

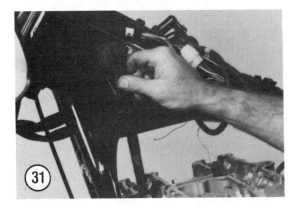

CAUTION
Remember the cooling fins are fragile
and may be damaged if tapped or pried
on too hard. Never use a metal hammer.

27. Lift the cylinder head straight up and off the cylinder block and crankcase studs. Guide the camshaft chain through the opening in the cylinder head and retie the wire to the exterior of the engine (A, **Figure 35**). This will prevent the drive chain from falling down into the crankcase.

28. Remove the cylinder head gasket and discard it. Don't lose the locating dowels.

29. Place a clean shop cloth into the camshaft chain opening (B, **Figure 35**) in the cylinder block to prevent the entry of foreign matter.

Cylinder Head Inspection

1. Remove all traces of gasket material from the cylinder head mating surfaces (A, **Figure 36**).

2. *Without removing the valves,* remove all carbon deposits from the combustion chambers (B, **Figure 36**) and valve ports with a wire brush. A blunt screwdriver or chisel may be used if care is taken not to damage the head, valves and spark plug threads.

3. Examine the spark plug threads in the cylinder head for damage. If damage is minor or if the threads are dirty or clogged with carbon, use a spark plug thread tap (**Figure 37**) and clean the threads following the manufacturer's instructions. If thread damage is severe, refer further service work to a Yamaha dealer or competent machine shop.

4. After the carbon is removed from the combustion chambers and the valve intake and exhaust ports,

clean the entire head in cleaning solvent. Blow dry with compressed air.

5. Clean away all carbon from the piston crowns. Do not remove the carbon ridge at the top of the cylinder bore.

6. Check for cracks in the combustion chamber and exhaust ports. A cracked cylinder head must be replaced.

7. After the cylinder head has been thoroughly cleaned, place a straightedge across the cylinder head/cylinder gasket surface at several points. Measure the warp by inserting a flat feeler gauge between the straightedge and the cylinder head at

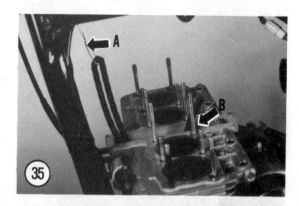

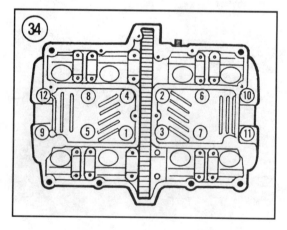

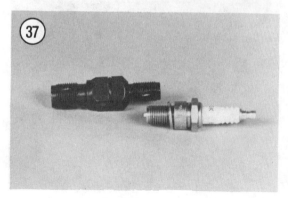

each location. There should be no warpage; if a small amount is present, it can be resurfaced by a dealer or qualified machine shop. Replace the cylinder head and cylinder head cover as a set if the gasket surface is warped to or beyond the limit listed in **Table 1**.

8. Check the cylinder head cover mating surface (**Figure 38**) using the procedure in Step 7. There should be no warpage.

9. Check the valves and valve guides as described in this chapter.

10. Inspect the camshaft end seals (**Figure 39**). Make sure they fit tightly; if not replace them.

NOTE
Each intake pipe is unique and must be reinstalled at the correct location on the cylinder head. Mark each pipe prior to removal to ensure proper installation.

11. If necessary, remove the screws securing the intake pipes onto the cylinder head. Install the intake pipes and tighten the screws securely.

Camshaft Inspection

1. Check the camshaft bearing journals for wear or scoring (**Figure 40**).

2. Check the camshaft lobes (**Figure 41**) for wear. The lobes should show no signs of scoring and the edges should be square. Slight damage may be removed with a silicone carbide oilstone. Use No. 100-120 grit stone initially, then polish with a No. 280-320 grit stone.

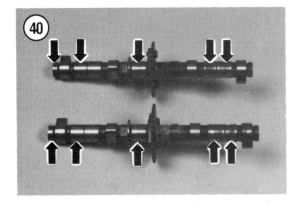

3. Even though the camshaft lobe surface appears to be satisfactory, with no visible signs of wear, the camshaft lobes must be measured as follows:

 a. Use a micrometer and measure the camshaft lobe long length (**Figure 42**). Compare to the dimensions given in **Table 3** and if worn to the service limit or less the camshaft(s) must be replaced.

 b. Use a micrometer and measure the camshaft lobe short length (**Figure 43**). Compare to the dimensions given in **Table 3** and if worn to the service limit or less the camshaft(s) must be replaced.

4. If the camshaft is within specifications in Steps 1-3, place the camshaft on a set of V-blocks and check its runout with a dial indicator (**Figure 44**). Compare to the dimension given in **Table 1**. If the runout is to the service limit or more, the camshaft(s) must be replaced.

5. Inspect the camshaft bearing surfaces in the cylinder head (**Figure 45**) and camshaft bearing caps. They should not be scored or excessively worn. Replace the cylinder head and camshaft bearing caps if the bearing surfaces are worn or scored.

6. Inspect the camshaft sprocket teeth for wear; replace if necessary.

7. Inspect the center guide as described in this chapter.

Camshaft Bearing
Clearance Measurement

This procedure requires the use of a Plastigage set. The camshafts must be installed into the cylinder head. Before installing the camshafts, wipe all oil residue from each camshaft bearing journal and bearing surface in the cylinder head and camshaft bearing caps.

1. Install the camshafts into the cylinder head. Do not engage the drive chain onto the sprockets.

2. Install all locating dowels into the camshaft bearing caps.

3. Place a strip of Plastigage material on top of each camshaft bearing journal (**Figure 46**), parallel to the camshaft.

> *NOTE*
> *Each camshaft bearing cap has its own unique mark as noted in Step 14 and Step 18 of **Removal**. Each bearing cap must be reinstalled in its original location.*

4. Place the bearing caps into their correct positions and install the bolts. Tighten the bolts finger-tight at first, then tighten in 2-3 stages in a crisscross pattern to the final torque specification listed in **Table 2**.

> *CAUTION*
> *Do not rotate the camshafts with the Plastigage material in place.*

5. Loosen the bearing cap bolts in 2-3 stages in a crisscross pattern. Carefully remove all bearing caps.

6. Measure the width of the flattened Plastigage material (**Figure 47**) at the widest point, according to the manufacturer's instructions.

> *CAUTION*
> *Be sure to remove all traces of Plastigage material from the groove in each bearing cap. If any material is left in the engine it can plug up an oil control orifice and cause severe engine damage.*

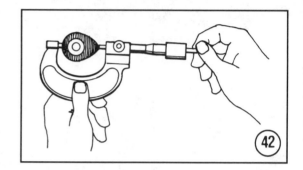

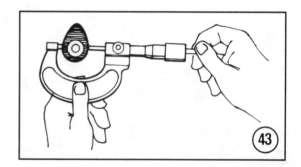

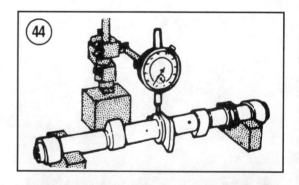

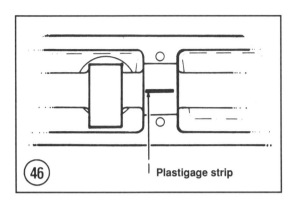

Plastigage strip

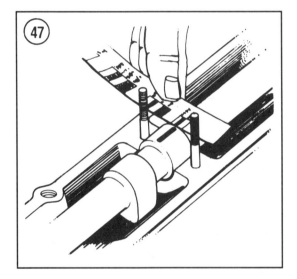

7. Remove *all* Plastigage material from the camshafts and the bearing caps.

8. If the oil clearance is greater than specified in **Table 1**, measure the bearing journals and compare to the dimension listed in **Table 1**. If the journal is less than the dimension specified, replace the camshaft(s). If the camshaft(s) is within specifications, the cylinder head and bearing caps must be replaced as a set.

Camshaft Drive Chain Guide Inspection

1. Inspect the center guide (**Figure 48**) for wear or deterioration. If it is worn or starting to deteriorate, it must be replaced. If the center guide is worn or damaged in any way, this may indicate improper drive chain adjustment.

2. If the chain guide is worn, check the condition of the two vertical camshaft drive chain tensioner guides. Shine a flashlight down into the drive chain cavity in the cylinder head and block. If necessary, replace them.

3. To remove the front guide, remove the cylinder head as described in this chapter (**Figure 49**).

4. To remove the rear guide, remove the cylinder block as described in this chapter. Loosen the holding bolt (A, **Figure 50**) and remove the rear guide (B, **Figure 50**).

5. Inspect both drive chain guides (**Figure 51**) and replace if necessary.

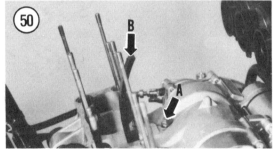

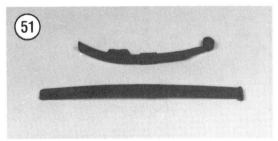

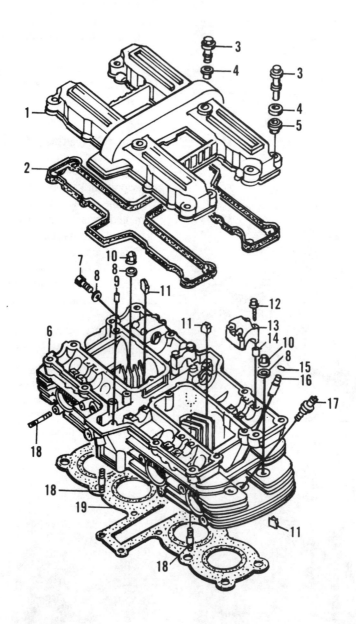

52

CYLINDER HEAD

1. Cylinder head cover
2. Gasket
3. Bolt
4. Washer
5. Rubber isolator
6. Cylinder head
7. Bolt
8. Gasket
9. Dowel pin
10. Cap nut
11. Rubber silencer
12. Bolt
13. Bearing cap
14. Locating dowel
15. Valve guide ring
16. Valve guide
17. Spark plug
18. Threaded stud
19. Cylinder head gasket

Cylinder Head Installation

Refer to **Figure 52** and **Figure 53** for this procedure.

1. Remove the shop rag from the camshaft chain opening in the cylinder block.

2. Install a new cylinder head gasket.

3. If removed, install the locating dowels in the locations shown in **Figure 54**.

4. Install a new O-ring (A, **Figure 54**) onto the locating dowels on the 2 right-hand crankcase studs.

5. Untie the wire securing the drive chain to the frame.

CAUTION
In Step 6A and Step 6B, pull up on the camshaft chain and keep it taut while rotating the crankshaft. Make certain that the drive chain is positioned correctly on the crankshaft timing sprocket. If this is not done, the drive chain may become kinked and may damage both the chain and the timing sprocket on the crankshaft.

6A. On 1986-1988 models, perform the following:

    a. Hold up on the drive chain and rotate the crankshaft *counterclockwise* with a wrench on

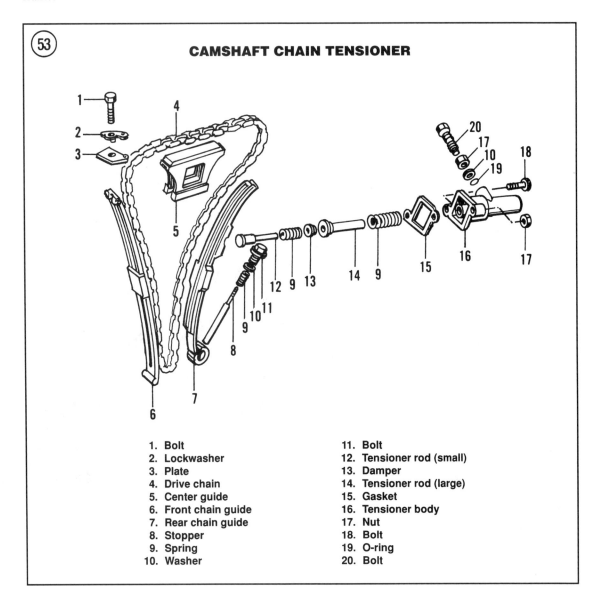

CAMSHAFT CHAIN TENSIONER

1. Bolt	11. Bolt
2. Lockwasher	12. Tensioner rod (small)
3. Plate	13. Damper
4. Drive chain	14. Tensioner rod (large)
5. Center guide	15. Gasket
6. Front chain guide	16. Tensioner body
7. Rear chain guide	17. Nut
8. Stopper	18. Bolt
9. Spring	19. O-ring
10. Washer	20. Bolt

the nut on the left-hand end of the crankshaft (**Figure 55**).

b. Rotate the engine until the No. 1 piston (left-hand cylinder) is at top dead center (TDC) (**Figure 56**). The cylinder is at TDC when the "T" mark on the timing plate aligns with the *top* pickup coil (**Figure 57**) and the piston is at its uppermost point in its travel.

6B. On 1989-1990 models, perform the following:

a. Hold up on the drive chain and rotate the crankshaft *counterclockwise* with a wrench on the alternator rotor bolt on the left-hand end of the crankshaft (**Figure 58**).

b. Rotate the engine until the No. 1 piston (left-hand cylinder) is at top dead center (TDC) (**Figure 56**). The cylinder is at TDC when the "T" mark on the rotor aligns with the fixed pointer on the crankcase (**Figure 59**) and the piston is at its uppermost point in its travel.

7. Carefully slide the cylinder head onto the cylinder block. Feed the camshaft drive chain through the chain cavity in the cylinder head and secure the other end of the wire again.

8. Apply oil to the threads of the crankcase threaded studs.

NOTE
If the washers are difficult to install on the center studs, use a screwdriver as

56

54

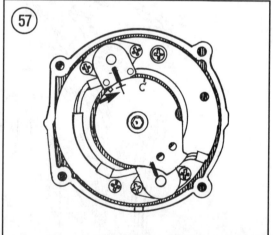

57

55

58

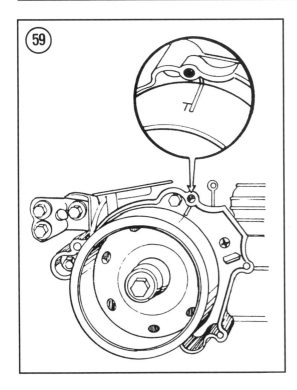

shown in **Figure 60** to help guide the washer down onto the stud.

9. Install the cylinder head's upper 12 washers and nuts. Install the 2 copper washers on the right-hand outside studs (**Figure 61**). Install steel washers on the remaining studs. Tighten the nuts finger-tight at this time.

10. Tighten the 12 upper nuts in the torque pattern shown in **Figure 62** to the torque specification listed in **Table 2**.

11. Install the lower 4 nuts and washers on the front (**Figure 63**) and rear (**Figure 64**) of the cylinder head.

12. Tighten the nuts to the torque specification listed in **Table 2**.

13. Install the camshaft drive chain front chain guide (**Figure 65**). Then twist the guide and insert it down into the front of the cylinder block and into its holder.

NOTE
Once the front chain guide has been installed, check with a flashlight and

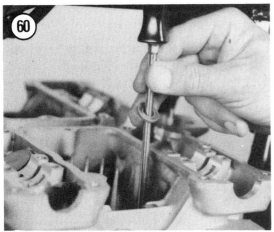

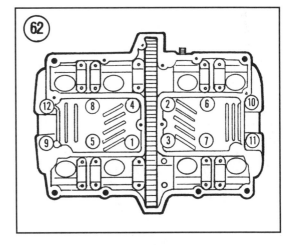

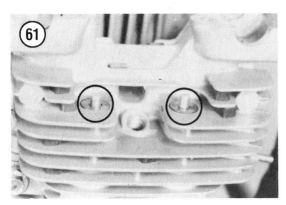

*mirror (**Figure 66**) to make sure the end
of the guide seats correctly in its holder.*

14. Install camshaft chain guide lockwasher and
bolt, then tighten securely. Bend up the lockwasher
tab against the bolt head.

15. Install the valve lifters and adjustment shims into
their *original positions* as noted during disassembly.

16. Lubricate all bearing surfaces in the cylinder
head (**Figure 67**) and bearing caps with assembly
oil.

17. Make sure the No. 1 piston is still at TDC (**Figure
56**).

18. Slide a sprocket onto each camshaft and install
the two assemblies through the camshaft chain. Refer to identification marks cast into the camshafts:
"I" for intake and "E" for exhaust. The exhaust
camshaft is installed at the front of the engine. Install
with the sprocket flange toward the left-hand side
and the sprocket on the right-hand side (A, **Figure
68**).

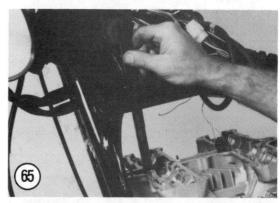

19. Temporarily position each camshaft in the cylinder head so the dot (B, **Figure 68**) next to the center
bearing cap is almost straight up.

20. Align the bolt holes in both sprockets with the
holes in the sprocket flange on both camshafts. Do
not place the sprockets onto the shoulder of the
camshaft at this time, rest them next to the shoulder.
Engage the drive chain onto both sprockets.

21. Make sure the locating dowels are in place in the
camshaft bearing caps.

> *CAUTION*
> *The bearing caps must be installed in
> their **original** positions because they
> were machined (line bored) along with
> the cylinder head during manufactur-
> ing.*

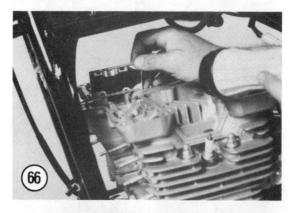

> *NOTE*
> *Do not install the No. 3 bearing caps at
> this time as they would cover up cam-
> shaft sprocket bolt holes. The No. 3
> bearing caps will be installed later in
> this procedure.*

22. Install the exhaust and intake No. 1, No. 2 and
No. 4 bearing caps, washers and bolts in their *original positions* as noted during disassembly and as
follows:

   a. The outside bearing caps are numbered 1-4
      and marked with an "E" (exhaust) or "I" (in-
      take) (**Figure 69**).

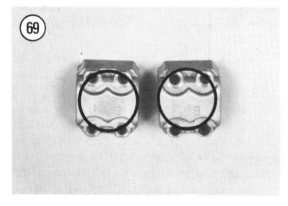

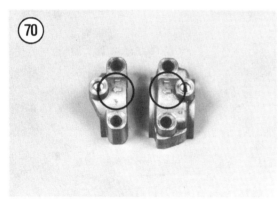

b. The inside bearing caps are marked with an "E" (exhaust) or "I" (intake) with arrows pointing toward the right-hand (clutch) side of the engine (**Figure 70**).

23. Tighten the bearing cap bolts gradually in 2 stages working from the center out in a crisscross pattern to the final torque listed in **Table 2**.

CAUTION
*Be extremely careful when rotating the camshaft using the hex shoulder (**Figure 71**). Make sure the open-end wrench does not come in contact with the cylinder head as it may fracture it. Do not rotate either camshaft more than 1/8 turn or the valves and pistons will contact each other and may be damaged.*

24. Use an open-end wrench on the camshaft hex shoulder, carefully rotate each camshaft slightly until the dot aligns with the center of the bearing cap (**Figure 72**).

25. Correctly position the camshaft drive chain onto the *exhaust* camshaft as follows:
    a. Lift the camshaft drive chain off the exhaust camshaft sprocket.
    b. Pull the drive chain upward and make sure it engages the crankshaft sprocket.
    c. Pull up on the front of the drive chain tightly, make sure the sprocket bolts align, then place the drive chain back onto the exhaust camshaft sprocket.
    d. Rest the sprocket on the camshaft, do not place it on the shoulder at this time.

26. Correctly position the camshaft drive chain onto the *intake* camshaft as follows:
    a. Lift the camshaft drive chain off the intake camshaft sprocket.

b. Pull the drive chain upward and make sure it engages the crankshaft sprocket.

c. Pull the drive chain toward the rear to remove the slack, make sure the sprocket bolts align, then place the drive chain back onto the intake camshaft sprocket.

d. Rest the sprocket onto the camshaft, do not place it onto the shoulder at this time.

NOTE
In the next step make sure the camshaft drive chain is properly centered within the chain guide and tensioner guide.

27. Hold onto each camshaft sprocket and drive chain and place both sprockets onto the shoulder of each camshaft. Maintain the tension between the crankshaft timing sprocket and the exhaust sprocket and between the exhaust sprocket and intake sprocket.

28. Align the bolt holes in the sprockets and the sprocket flange on the camshafts.

CAUTION
The sprocket bolts are hardened shoulder bolts. Substitution of lesser quality bolts may cause severe engine damage if they should break or work loose.

29. Install one bolt into each sprocket and tighten finger-tight.

CAUTION
Very expensive damage could result from improper camshaft drive chain to camshafts alignment. Recheck your work several times to be sure alignment is correct.

30. At this point recheck that each camshaft dot timing mark on the camshaft aligns with the center bearing cap timing mark arrow. Readjust the drive chain on the sprockets if necessary until alignment is correct and with the proper tension applied to the camshaft drive chain as indicated in Step 26.

31. Lift up on the center of the drive chain and install the center guide (**Figure 73**).

32A. On 1986-1988 models, perform the following:

a. Rotate the crankshaft *counterclockwise* with a wrench on the nut on the left-hand end of the crankshaft (**Figure 74**).

b. Rotate the engine until the "T" mark on the timing plate aligns with the *top* pickup coil (**Figure 57**).

32B. On 1989-1990 models, perform the following:

a. Rotate the crankshaft *counterclockwise* with a wrench on the alternator rotor bolt on the left-hand end of the crankshaft (**Figure 58**).

b. Rotate the engine until the "T" mark on the rotor aligns with the fixed pointer on the crankcase (**Figure 59**).

33. Loosen the camshaft drive chain tensioner holding bolt, compress the tensioner and spring and tighten the bolt to hold the tensioner in the retracted position.

34. Install the tensioner assembly and a new gasket. Tighten the mounting bolt and nut and tighten to the torque specification listed in **Table 2**.

35. Loosen the tensioner holding bolt. There should be an audible click as the tensioner is released and comes in contact with the drive chain. Make sure it does move into the drive chain; if not, remove it and correct any binding. Tighten the holding bolt to the torque specification listed in **Table 2**. Tighten the

holding bolt locknut to the torque specification listed in **Table 2**.

> *CAUTION*
> *If there is any binding while rotating the crankshaft, **stop**. Determine the cause before proceeding.*

36. After installation is complete, rotate the crankshaft *counterclockwise* until the remaining sprocket bolt holes are exposed. Install the 2 remaining bolts and tighten to the torque specification listed in **Table 2**.

37. Again rotate the crankshaft *counterclockwise* until the sprocket bolt installed in Step 28 is exposed. Tighten these 2 bolts to the torque specification listed in **Table 2**.

38A. On 1986-1988 models, perform the following:

    a. Rotate the crankshaft *counterclockwise* with a wrench on the nut on the left-hand end of the crankshaft (**Figure 74**).

    b. Rotate the engine until the No. 1 piston (left-hand cylinder) is at top dead center (TDC) (**Figure 56**). The cylinder is at TDC when the "T" mark on the timing plate aligns with the *top* pickup coil (**Figure 57**) and the piston is at its uppermost point in its travel.

38B. On 1989-1990 models, perform the following:

    a. Rotate the crankshaft *counterclockwise* with a wrench on the alternator rotor bolt on the left-hand end of the crankshaft (**Figure 58**).

    b. Rotate the engine until the No. 1 piston (left-hand cylinder) is at top dead center (TDC) (**Figure 56**). The cylinder is at TDC when the "T" mark on the rotor aligns with the fixed pointer on the crankcase (**Figure 59**) and the piston is at its uppermost point in its travel.

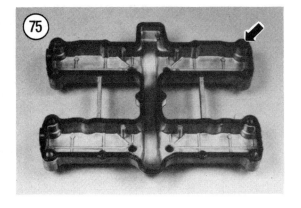

> *CAUTION*
> *Very expensive damage could result from improper camshaft drive chain to camshafts alignment. Recheck your work several times to be sure alignment is correct.*

39. With the engine in this position, recheck that each camshaft dot timing mark on the camshaft aligns with the center bearing cap timing mark arrow. Readjust the drive chain on the camshaft sprockets if necessary until alignment is correct.

40. Fill the oil pockets in the cylinder head with new engine oil so the cam lobes are submerged in the oil.

41. Make sure the locating dowels are in place in the No. 3 camshaft bearing caps.

42. Install the exhaust and intake No. 3 bearing caps, washers and bolts. Tighten the bolts to the torque specification listed in **Table 2**.

43. Check the valve clearance as described under *Valve Clearance* in Chapter Three.

44. Inspect the rubber gasket (**Figure 75**) around the perimeter of the cylinder head cover. If it is starting to deteriorate or harden it should be replaced.

45. Install the cylinder head cover. Make sure the gasket is correctly seated onto the cylinder head.

46. Install the Allen bolts, grommets and washers. Be sure to install the bolts in the correct locations as their length varies. Tighten finger-tight at this time.

47. Tighten the Allen bolts in a crisscross pattern to the torque specification listed in **Table 2**.

48. Install all spark plugs and connect all spark plug caps and wires. See Chapter Three.

49. Install the carburetor assembly as described in Chapter Seven.

50. Install the fuel tank as described in Chapter Seven.

51. Connect the battery negative lead. Refer to Chapter Three.

52. On FZ600 models, install the side covers and lower fairings as described in Chapter Twelve.

53. Install the seat(s) as described in Chapter Twelve.

VALVES AND VALVE COMPONENTS

General practice among those who do their own service is to remove the cylinder head and take it to a machine shop or dealer for inspection and service. Since the cost is relative to the required effort and equipment, this is the best approach even for the experienced mechanics.

This procedure is included for those who chose to do their own valve service.

Refer to **Figure 76** for this procedure.

Valve Removal

1. Remove the cylinder head as described in this chapter.

2. If not already removed, remove the valve lifters and adjustment shims as follows:

    a. Remove them one at a time with a suction cup tool (**Figure 28**) and place them in a container such as an egg container (**Figure 29**).

    b. Mark the container with the specific cylinder number (No. 1-4) and intake and exhaust.

    c. The No.1 cylinder is on the left-hand side; the exhaust valves are at the front of the cylinder head and the intake are at the rear.

3. Compress the valve springs with a valve compressor tool placed directly over the valve retainer (**Figure 77**).

> *CAUTION*
> *To avoid loss of spring tension, do not compress the springs any more than necessary to remove the keepers.*

4. Tighten the compressor tool until the valve keepers separate. Lift out the valve keepers with needlenose pliers.

5. Gradually release the compressor tool. Remove the valve compressor tool.

6. Remove the valve spring retainer and valve springs.

7. Prior to removing the valve, remove any burrs from the valve stem (**Figure 78**). Otherwise the valve guide will be damaged.

8. Remove the valve.

9. Remove the valve spring seat.

10. Repeat for all intake and exhaust valves.

11. Mark all parts (**Figure 79**) as they are disassembled so that they will be installed in their original locations.

12. If necessary, remove the oil seal from each valve guide.

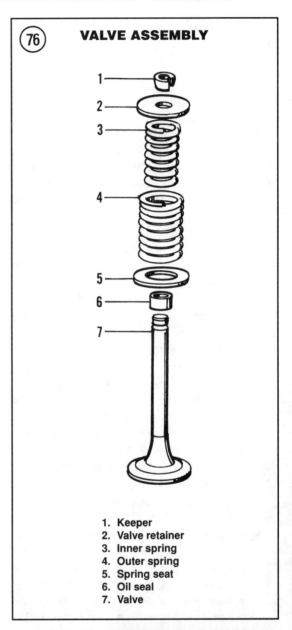

VALVE ASSEMBLY

1. Keeper
2. Valve retainer
3. Inner spring
4. Outer spring
5. Spring seat
6. Oil seal
7. Valve

Valve Inspection

1. Clean the valves with a wire brush and solvent.

2. Inspect the contact surface of each valve for burning or pitting (**Figure 80**). Unevenness of the contact surface is an indication that the valve is not serviceable. The valve contact surface *cannot* be ground and must be replaced if defective.

3. Inspect each valve stem for wear and roughness and measure the vertical runout of the valve stem as shown in **Figure 81**. The runout should not exceed the service limit listed in **Table 1**.

4. Measure each valve stem for wear (**Figure 82**). If worn to the wear limit listed in **Table 1** or less, the valve must be replaced.

5. Measure the thickness of the valve face (A, **Figure 83**) with a vernier caliper. If worn to the wear limit listed in **Table 1** or less, the valve must be replaced.

6. Measure the bevel on the end of the valve stem (B, **Figure 83**) with a vernier caliper. If worn to the wear limit listed in **Table 1** or less, the valve must be replaced.

7. Inspect the valve stem end for mushrooming. Measure the valve stem length (C, **Figure 83**) with a vernier caliper. If worn to the wear limit listed in **Table 1** or less, the valve must be replaced.

8. Remove all carbon and varnish from each valve guide with a stiff spiral wire brush.

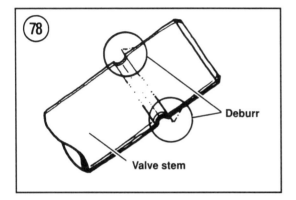

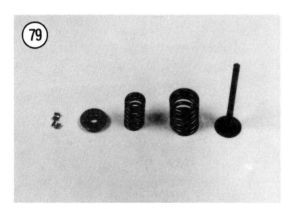

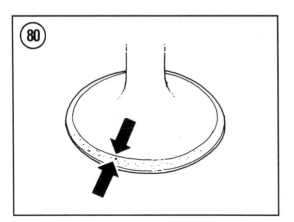

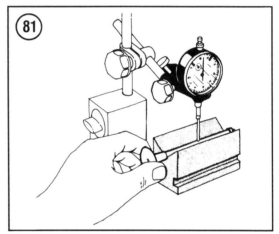

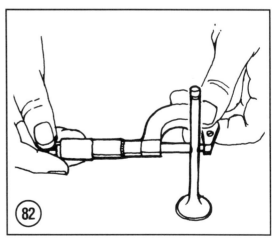

4

9. Measure each valve guide at the top, middle and bottom with a small hole gauge (**Figure 84**). If worn to the wear limit listed in **Table 1** or less, the valve guide must be replaced.

10. Subtract the valve stem measurement made in Step 4 from the valve guide dimensions made in Step 9. The difference is the valve guide-to-valve stem clearance. See **Table 1** for correct clearance. Replace any valve or guide that is not within specifications.

> *NOTE*
> *If you do not have the special measuring equipment for Step 9, perform Step 11. Step 11 assumes that all valve stems have been measured and are within specifications. Replace any valves with worn valve stems prior to performing Step 11.*

11. Insert each valve in its guide. Hold the valve with the head just slightly off the valve seat and rock it sideways in 2 directions, "X" and "Y," perpendicular to each other as shown in **Figure 85**. If the valve rocks more than slightly, the valve guide is probably worn. If the valve stem is worn, replace the valve. If the valve stem is within tolerances, replace the valve guide.

12. Measure each valve spring free length with a vernier caliper (**Figure 86**). All should be within the length specified in **Table 1** with no signs of bends or distortion. Replace defective springs in pairs (inner and outer).

13. Measure the tilt of all valve springs as shown in **Figure 87**. If distorted to the wear limit listed in **Table 1** or less, the valve spring must be replaced.

14. Check the valve spring retainer and valve keepers. If they are in good condition they may be reused; replace as necessary.

15. Inspect the valve seats. If worn or burned, they must be reconditioned as described in this chapter.

Valve Installation

1. If removed, install a new seal on each valve guide.

2. Install the valve seat.

3. Coat the valve stems with molybdenum disulfide grease. To avoid damage to the valve stem seal, install and turn the valve slowly while inserting the valve into the cylinder head.

4. Install the valve springs with their closer wound coils facing the cylinder head and install the valve spring retainer.

5. Install the valve spring retainer on top of the valve springs.

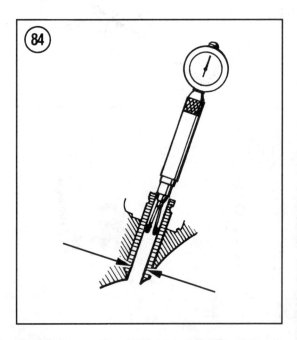

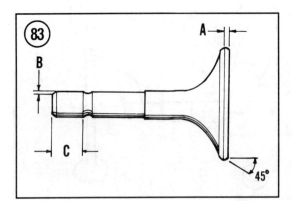

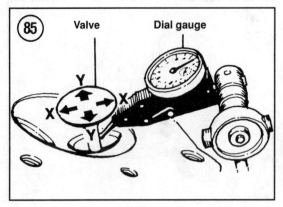

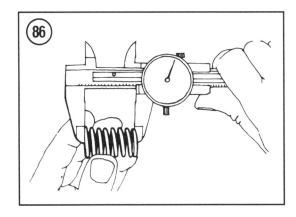

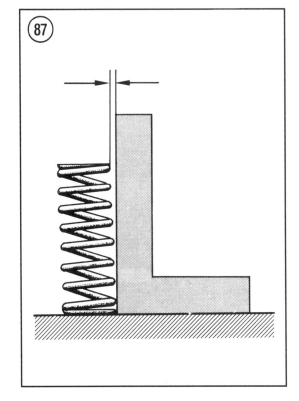

CAUTION
To avoid loss of spring tension, do not compress the springs any more than necessary to install the keepers.

6. Compress the valve springs with a compressor tool (**Figure 88**) and install the valve keepers. Make sure the keepers fit snugly into the rounded groove in the valve stem.

7. Remove the compression tool.

8. After all springs have been installed, gently tap the end of the valve stem (**Figure 89**) with a soft aluminum or brass drift and hammer. This will ensure that the keepers are properly seated.

9. Repeat for all valve assemblies.

10. Install the cylinder head as described in this chapter.

Valve Guide Replacement

When valve guides are worn so that there is excessive valve stem-to-guide clearance or valve tipping, the guides must be replaced. This job should only be done by a dealer as special tools are required as well as considerable expertise. If the valve guide is replaced; also replace the respective valve.

The following procedure is provided if you choose to perform this task yourself.

CAUTION
*There **may** be a residual oil or solvent odor left in the oven after heating the cylinder head. If you use a household oven; first check with the person who uses the oven for food preparation to avoid getting into trouble.*

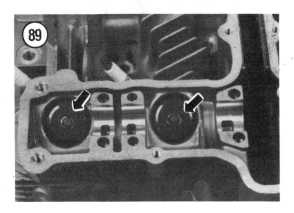

NOTE
Mark each intake pipe relating to cylinder number prior to removal to ensure proper installation. If installing new intake pipes, refer to marks made on the old intake pipes to ensure proper installation location. There are 2 different bolt pattern configurations and the pipes must be installed on the correct side of the cylinder head.

1. Remove the screws securing the intake pipes onto the cylinder head. Remove all intake pipes prior to placing the cylinder head in the oven.

2. While heating the cylinder head, place the new valve guides in a freezer (or refrigerator) if possible. Chilling them will slightly reduce their overall diameter while the hot cylinder head is slightly larger due to heat expansion. This will make valve guide installation much easier.

CAUTION
Do not heat the cylinder head with a torch (propane or acetylene); never bring a flame into contact with the cylinder head or valve guide. The direct heat will destroy the case hardening of the valve guide and will likely cause warpage of the cylinder head.

3. The valve guides are installed with a slight interference fit. Place the cylinder head in a heated oven (or on a hot plate). Heat the cylinder head to a temperature of 100° C (212° F). An easy way to check the proper temperature is to drop tiny drops of water on the cylinder head; if they sizzle and evaporate immediately, the temperature is correct.

4. Remove the cylinder head from the oven and hold onto it with kitchen pot holders, heavy gloves or heavy shop cloths—*it is very hot.*

5. Turn the cylinder head upside down on wood blocks. Make sure the cylinder is properly supported on the wood blocks.

6. From the combustion chamber side of the cylinder head, drive out the old valve guide (**Figure 90**) with a hammer and valve guide remover. Use Yamaha special tool, Valve Guide Remover, (U.S. part No. YM-04064, UK part No. 90890-04064). Remove the valve guide and the special tool.

7. Remove and discard the valve guide and the ring. *Never* reinstall a valve guide or ring that has been removed as it is no longer true nor within tolerances.

8. Install a new ring onto the valve guide.

CAUTION
Failure to apply fresh engine oil to both the valve guide and the valve guide hole in the cylinder head will result in damage to the cylinder head and/or the new valve guide.

9. Apply fresh engine oil to the new valve guide and the valve guide hole in the cylinder head.

10. From the top side (camshaft side) of the cylinder head, drive in the new valve guide (**Figure 91**) with a hammer, valve guide installer (Yamaha special tool, Valve Guide Installer, U.S. part No. YM-04065, UK part No. 90890-04065) and remover (Yamaha special tool, Valve Guide Remover, U.S. part No. YM-04064, UK part No. 90890-04064).

11. Drive the valve guide in until it completely seats in the cylinder head. Remove the special tools.

12. After installation, ream the new valve guide as follows:

    a. Use Yamaha special tools, 6 mm (0.24 in.) Valve Guide Reamer, (U.S. part No. YM-

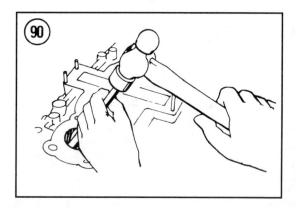

04066, UK part No. 90890-04066) and appropriate handle (**Figure 92**).

b. Apply cutting oil to both the new valve guide and the valve guide reamer during the reaming operation.

CAUTION
Always *rotate the valve guide reamer* ***clockwise****. If the reamer is rotated counterclockwise, a good valve guide will be damaged.*

c. Rotate the reamer *clockwise*. Continue to rotate the reamer and work it down through the entire length of the new valve guide. Continue to apply additional cutting oil during this procedure.

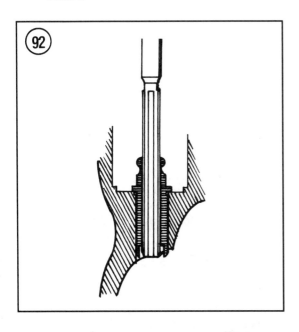

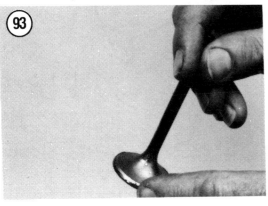

d. Rotate the reamer *clockwise* until the reamer has traveled all the way through the new valve guide.

e. Rotate the reamer *clockwise* and withdraw the reamer from the valve guide. Remove the reamer.

13. If necessary, repeat Steps 1-12 for any other valve guides.

14. Thoroughly clean the cylinder head and valve guides with solvent to wash out all metal particles. Dry with compressed air.

15. Reface the valve seats as described in this chapter.

16. Install the intake pipes and tighten the bolts securely.

Valve Seat Inspection

1. Remove the valves as described in this chapter.

2. The most accurate method for checking the valve seal is to use Prussian Blue or machinist dye, available from auto parts stores or machine shops. To check the valve seal with Prussian Blue or machinist dye, perform the following:

a. Thoroughly clean off all carbon deposits from the valve face with solvent or detergent, then thoroughly dry.

b. Spread a thin layer of Prussian Blue or machinist dye evenly on the valve face (**Figure 93**).

c. Moisten the end of a suction cup valve tool (**Figure 94**) and attach it to the valve. Insert the valve into the guide.

d. Using the suction cup tool, tap the valve up and down in the cylinder head. Do *not* rotate the valve or a false indication will result.

e. Remove the valve and examine the impression left by the Prussian Blue or machinist dye. If

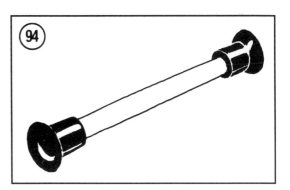

the impression left in the dye (on the valve or in the cylinder head) is not even and continuous and the valve seat width (**Figure 95**) is not within specified tolerance listed in **Table 1**, the cylinder head valve seat must be reconditioned.

3. Closely examine the valve seat in the cylinder head (**Figure 96**). It should be smooth and even with a polished seating surface.

4. Measure the valve seat width (**Figure 97**). Compare to the wear limit listed in **Table 1**.

5. If the valve seat is okay, install the valves as described in this chapter.

6. If the valve seat is not correct, recondition the valve seat in the cylinder head as described in this chapter.

Valve Seat Reconditioning

Special valve cutter tools and considerable expertise are required to recondition the valve seats in the cylinder head properly. You can save considerable money by removing the cylinder head and taking just the cylinder head to a dealer or machine shop and having the valve seats ground.

The following procedure is provided if you choose to perform this task yourself.

The Yamaha valve seat cutters and handle set (U.S. part No. YM-91043, UK part No. 90890-91043) is available from a Yamaha dealer or from machine shop supply outlets. Follow the manufacturer's instruction in regard to operating the cutter. You will need valve seat cutters of the following angles; 0°, 45° and a 60° and an appropriate handle.

The valve seats for both the intake valves and exhaust valves are machined to the same angles. The valve contact surface is cut to a 45° angle and the area above the contact surface (closest to the combustion chamber) is cut to a 60° angle (**Figure 98**).

1. Use the 45° angle side of the cutter, install the cutter and the T-handle.

2. Using the 45° cutter, descale and clean the valve seat with one or two turns (**Figure 99**).

> *CAUTION*
> *Measure the valve seat contact area in the cylinder head after each cut to make sure the contact area is correct and to prevent removing too much material. If*

too much material is removed, the cylinder head must be replaced.

3. If the seat is still pitted or burned, turn the 45° cutter additional turns until the surface is clean.

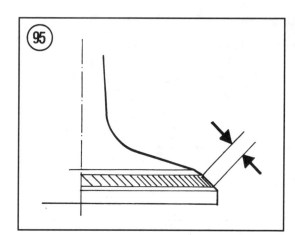

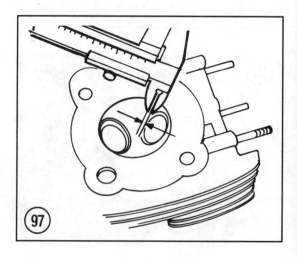

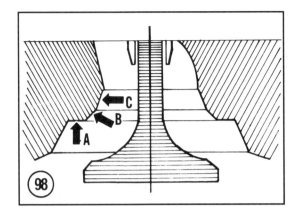

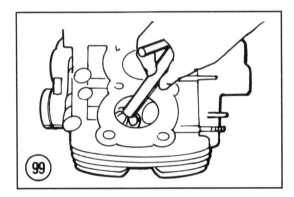

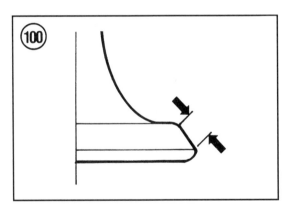

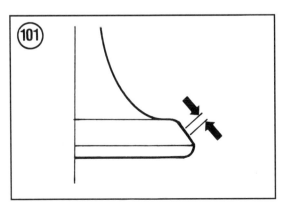

Refer to the previous CAUTION to avoid removing too much material from the cylinder head.

4. Remove the valve cutter and T-handle from the cylinder head.

5. Inspect the valve seat-to-valve face impression as follows:

    a. Spread a thin layer of Prussian Blue or machinist dye evenly on the valve face.

    b. Moisten the end of a suction cup valve tool and attach it to the valve. Insert the valve into the guide.

    c. Using the suction cup tool, tap the valve up and down in the cylinder head. Do *not* rotate the valve or a false indication will result.

    d. Remove the valve and examine the impression left by the Prussian Blue or machinist dye.

    e. Measure the valve seat width as shown in **Figure 97**. Refer to **Table 1** for the seat width specifications.

6. If the contact area is centered on the valve but is too wide (**Figure 100**), use either the 60° or the 0° cutter and remove a portion of the valve seat material to narrow the contact area.

7. If the contact area is centered on the valve but is too narrow (**Figure 101**), use the 45° cutter and remove a portion of the valve seat material to increase the contact area.

8. If the contact area is too narrow and up close to the valve head (**Figure 102**), first use the 0° cutter and then use the 45° cutter to center the contact area.

9. If the contact area is too narrow and down away from the valve head (**Figure 103**), first use the 60° cutter and then use the 45° cutter to center the contact area.

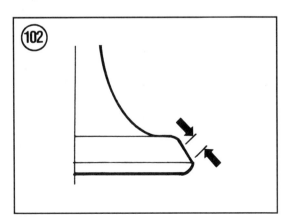

10. After the desired valve seat position and width are obtained, use the 45° side of the cutter and T-handle and *very lightly* clean off any burrs that may have been caused by the previous cuts—remove only enough material as necessary.

11. Check that the finish has a smooth and velvety surface (**Figure 96**), it should *not* be shiny or highly polished. The final seating will take place when the engine is first run.

12. Repeat Steps 1-11 for all remaining valve seats.

13. After the valve seat has been reconditioned, lap the seat and valve as described in this chapter.

Valve Seat Lapping

Valve lapping is a simple operation which can restore the valve seal without machining if the amount of wear or distortion is not too great. Lapping is also recommended after the valve seat has been serviced.

1. Smear a light coating of fine grade valve lapping compound such as Carborundum or Clover Brand on the seating surface of the valve (**Figure 93**).

2. Insert the valve into the cylinder head.

3. Wet the suction cup of the lapping stick (**Figure 104**) and stick it onto the valve head.

4. Lap the valve to the valve seat as follows:

   a. Lap the valve by rotating the laping stick between your hands (**Figure 105**) in both directions.

   b. Every 5 to 10 seconds, *stop* and rotate the valve 180° in the valve seat.

   c. Continue lapping until the contact surfaces of the valve (**Figure 106**) and valve seat (**Figure 96**) are a uniform grey. Stop as soon as they turn this color to avoid removing too much material.

5. Thoroughly clean the cylinder head and all valve components in solvent, then detergent and hot water.

6. After the lapping has been completed and the valve assemblies have been reinstalled into the cylinder head, the valve seal should be tested. Check the seal of each valve by pouring solvent into each of the intake and exhaust ports. The solvent should not flow past the valve head and the valve seat. Perform on all sets of valves. If the fluid leaks past any of the seats, disassemble that valve assembly and repeat the lapping procedure until there is no leakage.

7. After the cylinder head and valve components are cleaned in detergent and hot water, apply a light coat of engine oil to all bare metal surfaces to prevent any rust formations.

Valve Lifters and Shims

> *CAUTION*
> *Do not intermix the valve lifters and shims during inspection. They must be reinstalled into their original positions in the cylinder head upon reassembly.*

1. Inspect the sides of the valve lifter body for scratches and scoring. If it is damaged in any way, replace it.

2. Inspect the valve lifter cavity in the cylinder head in which it travels. If the damage is severe, the cylinder head may have to be replaced.

3. Check the valve lifter's top ridge that retains the adjustment shim. Make sure the shim seats correctly into the recess but not too loose. Replace any parts as necessary.

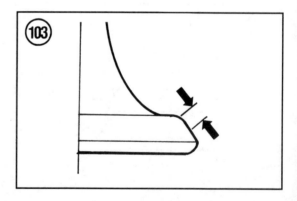

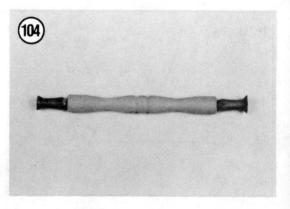

CYLINDER BLOCK

Removal

Refer to **Figure 107** for this procedure.

1. Remove the cylinder head as described in this chapter.

2. If not already removed, remove the cylinder head gasket and the locating dowels.

3. Loosen the nut and washer (**Figure 108**) securing the front portion of the cylinder block to the crankcase. You cannot remove the nut at this time due to interference with the engine front mount spacer.

> *CAUTION*
> *Remember the cooling fins are fragile and may be damaged if tapped or pried on too hard. Never use a metal hammer.*

4. Loosen the cylinder block by tapping around the perimeter with a rubber or plastic mallet. If necessary, *gently* pry the cylinder loose with a broad-tipped screwdriver.

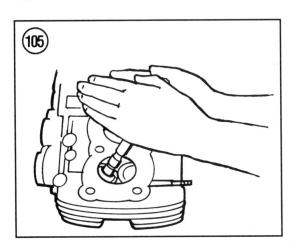

5. Slightly raise the cylinder block, then remove the nut and washer (**Figure 108**) loosened in Step 3.

6. Pull the cylinder block straight up and off of the pistons and crankcase studs. Work the camshaft chain wire through the opening in the cylinder block. Reattach the wire to the exterior of the crankcase (A, **Figure 109**).

7. Remove the cylinder base gasket and O-rings, discard them.

8. Remove the locating dowels and O-rings from the 2 right-hand crankcase studs.

> *NOTE*
> *Piston holding fixtures may be purchased or homemade of wood to the dimensions in **Figure 110**.*

9. Place a piston holding fixture under the 2 pistons (B, **Figure 109**) protruding out of the crankcase opening.

10. Stuff clean shop cloths into the crankcase openings and under the pistons to prevent the entry of foreign matter and small objects.

Inspection

The following procedure requires the use of highly specialized and expensive measuring instruments. If such equipment is not readily available, have the measurements performed by a dealer or qualified machine shop.

1. Apply a gasket remover or use solvent and soak the old cylinder head gasket material stuck to the cylinder block. If necessary use a broad-tipped *dull* chisel and gently scrape off all gasket residue. Do not gouge the sealing surface as oil leaks will result.

2. Measure the cylinder bore with a cylinder gauge (**Figure 111**) or inside micrometer at the points shown in **Figure 112**. Measure in 2 axes—in line with the piston-pin and at 90° to the pin. If the taper or out-of-round is 0.05 mm (0.002 in.) or greater in one cylinder, the cylinder block must be rebored to the next oversize and new pistons and piston rings installed. Rebore all 4 cylinders even though only one may be worn.

> *NOTE*
> *The new pistons should be obtained before the cylinders are rebored so that the pistons can be measured; slight manufacturing tolerances must be taken into*

account to determine the actual size and working clearance.

3. Check the cylinder walls for scratches; if evident, the cylinders should be rebored.

NOTE
*The maximum wear limit on the cylinders is listed in **Table 1**. If any cylinder is worn to this limit, the cylinder block*

must be replaced. Never rebore a cylinder(s) if the finished rebore diameter will be this dimension or greater.

NOTE
After having the cylinder block rebored, wash it thoroughly in hot soapy water. This is the best way to clean the cylinders of all fine grit material left from the bore job. After washing the cylinder

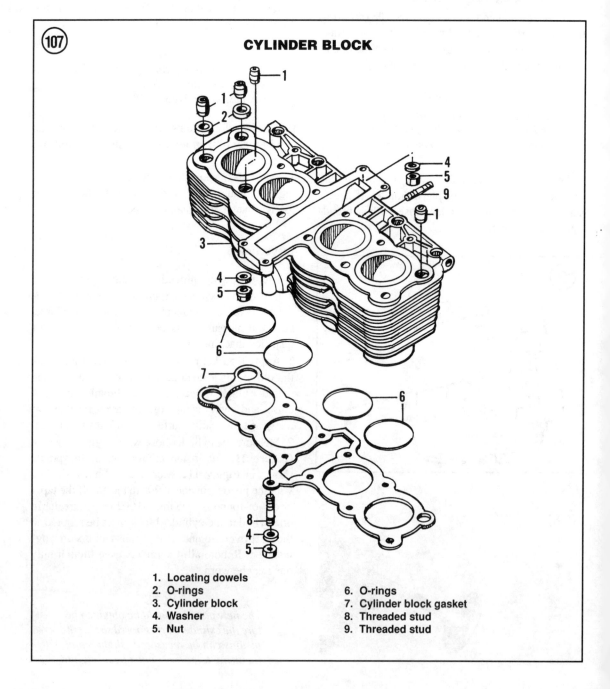

CYLINDER BLOCK

1. Locating dowels
2. O-rings
3. Cylinder block
4. Washer
5. Nut
6. O-rings
7. Cylinder block gasket
8. Threaded stud
9. Threaded stud

block, run a clean white cloth through each cylinder, the cloth should show no traces of dirt or other debris. If the rag is dirty, the cylinder(s) is not clean enough and must be re-washed. After

the cylinder block is thoroughly cleaned, dry and lubricate each cylinder wall with clean engine oil to prevent the cylinder liners from rusting.

Installation

1. Check that the top surface of the crankcase and the bottom surface of the cylinder block are clean prior to installing a new base gasket.
2. Install a new cylinder base gasket.
3. Install the locating dowels and new O-rings onto the right-hand end crankcase studs (**Figure 113**).

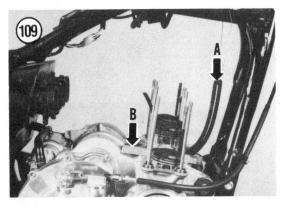

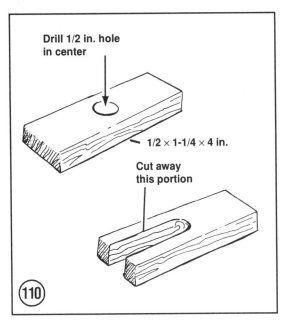

Drill 1/2 in. hole in center

1/2 × 1-1/4 × 4 in.

Cut away this portion

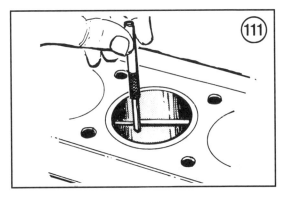

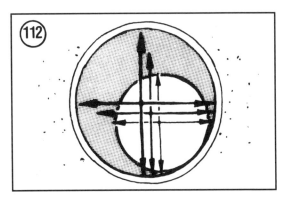

4. Install a piston holding fixture under the 2 center pistons.

5. Make sure the end gaps of the piston rings are *not* lined up with each other—they must be staggered. Lightly oil the piston rings and the inside of the cylinder block bores with assembly oil.

6. Carefully feed the camshaft chain and wire up through the opening in the cylinder block and tie it to the engine.

7. Start the cylinder block down over the center pistons and crankcase studs (**Figure 114**). Compress each piston ring with your fingers as it enters the cylinder block.

8. Slide the cylinder block down until it bottoms on the piston holding fixtures.

9. Remove the piston holding fixtures and slightly slide the cylinder down until you can install the washer and nut at the front of the cylinder block.

10. Push the cylinder the rest of the way down until it bottoms out on the crankcase.

11. Tighten the nut (**Figure 108**) to the torque specification listed in **Table 2**.

12. Install the cylinder head as described in this chapter.

13. Follow the *Break-in Procedure* in this chapter if the cylinder block was rebored or honed or if new pistons or piston rings were installed.

PISTONS, PISTON PINS AND PISTON RINGS

The pistons are made of an aluminum alloy. The piston pins are made of steel and are a precision fit. The piston pin is held in place by a clip at each end.

Piston Removal

1. Remove the cylinder head and cylinder block as described in this chapter.

2. Lightly mark the top of the piston with an identification number (1 through 4), starting with the No. 1 piston on the left-hand side and working across to the right. The left-hand side refers to a rider sitting on the seat facing forward. These marks will make it easier to assure that the pistons will be installed into the correct cylinder bores during installation.

WARNING
The edges of all piston rings are very sharp. Be careful when handling them to avoid cutting fingers.

3. Remove the top ring with a ring expander tool or by spreading the ends with your thumbs just enough to slide the ring up over the piston (**Figure 115**). Repeat for the remaining rings.

4. Before removing the piston, hold the rod tightly and rock the piston (**Figure 116**). Any rocking motion (do not confuse with the normal sliding motion) indicates wear on the piston pin, piston pin bore or connecting rod small-end bore (more likely a combination of these).

NOTE
Wrap a clean shop cloth under the piston so that the piston pin clip will not fall into the crankcase.

5. Remove the clip from each side of the piston pin bore (**Figure 117**) with a small screwdriver or scribe.

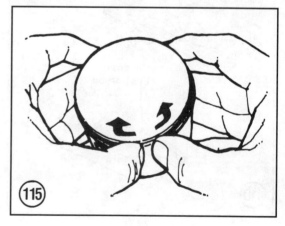

Hold your thumb over one edge of the clip when removing it to prevent the clip from springing out.

6. Use a proper size wooden dowel or socket extension and push out the piston pin. Mark the piston pin

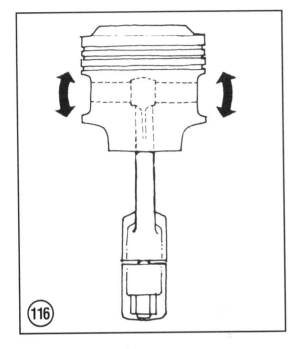

in relation to the piston so that it will be reassembled into the same set.

CAUTION
Be careful when removing the pin to avoid damaging the connecting rod. If it is necessary to tap the pin gently to remove it, be sure that the piston is properly supported so that lateral shock is not transmitted to the lower connecting rod bearing.

7. If the piston pin is difficult to remove, heat the piston and pin with a butane torch. The pin will probably push right out. Heat the piston to only about 140° F (60° C), i.e., until it is too warm to touch, but not excessively hot. If the pin is still difficult to push out, use a homemade tool as shown in **Figure 118**.

8. Lift the piston off the connecting rod.

9. If the piston is going to be left off for some time, place a piece of foam insulation tube over the end of the rod to protect it.

10. Repeat Steps 3-9 for the remaining pistons.

Inspection

1. Carefully clean the carbon from the piston crown with a chemical remover or with a soft scraper (**Figure 119**). Do not remove or damage the carbon ridge around the circumference of the piston above the top ring. If the pistons, rings and cylinders are found to be dimensionally correct and can be reused, removal of the carbon ring from the top of the piston or the carbon ridge from the top of the cylinder block wall will promote excessive oil consumption in this cylinder.

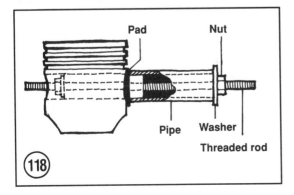

Pad   Nut

Pipe   Washer

Threaded rod

CAUTION
Do not wire brush the piston skirts.

2. Examine each ring groove for burrs, dented edges and wide wear. Pay particular attention to the top compression ring groove as it usually wears more than the other grooves.

3. If damage or wear indicates piston replacement, select a new piston as described under *Piston Clearance* in this chapter.

4. Oil the piston pin and install it in the connecting rod. Slowly rotate the piston pin and check for radial and axial play (**Figure 120**). If any play exists, the piston pin should be replaced, providing the rod bore is in good condition.

5. Oil the piston pin and install it in the piston. Slowly rotate the piston pin and check for radial and axial play (**Figure 121**). If any play exists, the piston pin should be replaced, providing the piston bore is in good condition.

6. Check the piston skirt for galling and abrasion which may have been caused by piston seizure. If a piston(s) shows signs of partial seizure (bits of aluminum build-up on the piston skirt), the pistons should be replaced and the cylinders bored (if necessary) to reduce the possibility of engine noise and further piston seizure.

Piston Clearance

1. Make sure the pistons and cylinder walls are clean and dry.

2. Measure the inside diameter of the cylinder bore at a point 13 mm (1/2 in.) from the upper edge with a bore gauge (**Figure 122**).

3. Measure the outside diameter of each piston across the skirt at right angles to the piston pin. Measure at a distance 7.0 mm (0.276 in.) up from the bottom of the piston skirt (**Figure 123**).

4. Piston clearance is the difference between the maximum piston diameter and the minimum cylinder diameter. Subtract the dimension of the piston from the cylinder dimension and compare to the dimension listed in **Table 1**. If the clearance exceeds that specified, the cylinders should be rebored to the next oversize and new pistons installed.

5. To establish a final overbore dimension with new pistons, add the piston skirt measurement to the specified clearance. This will determine the dimension for the cylinder overbore size. Remember, do not exceed the cylinder maximum service limit inside diameter indicated in **Table 1**.

Piston Installation

1. Apply molybdenum disulfide grease to the inside surface of the connecting rods.

NOTE
New piston pin clips should be installed during assembly. Install the clips with

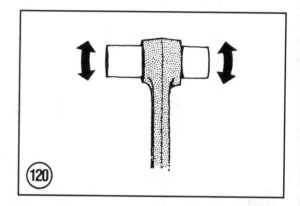

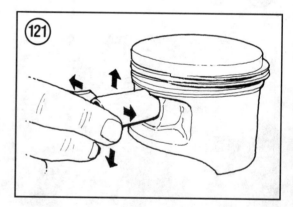

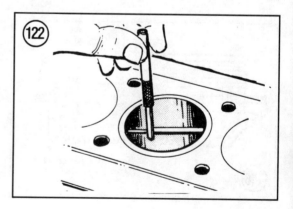

the gap away from the cutout in the piston.

2. Install one piston pin clip in each piston on the side that faces toward the center of the engine. The arrow on top of the piston must point toward the front of the engine.

3. Oil the piston pin with assembly oil or fresh engine oil and install the piston pin in the piston until its end extends slightly beyond the inside of the boss.

4. Place the piston over the connecting rod. If you are reusing the same pistons and connecting rods, match the pistons to the rods from which they came. If the cylinders were bored, install the pistons as marked by the machinist. Remember that the arrow on top of the piston must point toward the front of the engine.

CAUTION
When installing the piston pin in Step 5 do not push the pin in too far, or the piston pin clip installed in Step 2 will be

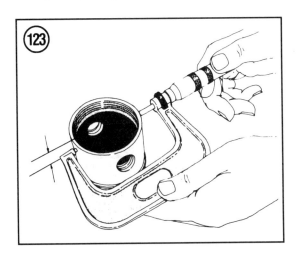

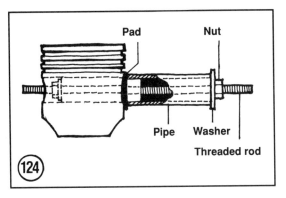

forced into the piston metal, destroying the clip groove and loosening the clip.

5. Line up the piston pin with the hole in the connecting rod. Push the piston pin into the connecting rod. It may be necessary to move the piston around until the piston pin enters the connecting rod. Do not use force during installation or damage may occur. Push the piston pin in until it touches the pin clip on the other side of the piston.

6. If the piston pin does not slide easily, use the homemade tool (**Figure 124**) used during removal but eliminate the piece of pipe. Pull the piston pin in until it stops.

7. After the piston is installed, recheck and make sure that the arrow on top of the piston is pointing toward the front of the engine.

NOTE
In the next step, install the second clip with the gap away from the cutout in the piston.

8. Install the second piston pin clip into the groove in the piston. Make sure both piston pin clips are seated in the grooves in the piston.

9. Check the installation by rocking the piston back and forth around the pin axis and from side to side along the axis. It should rotate freely back and forth but not from side to side.

10. Repeat Steps 3-9 for the remaining pistons.

11. Install the piston rings as described in this chapter.

12. Install the cylinder and cylinder head as described in this chapter.

Piston Ring Replacement

WARNING
The edges of all piston rings are very sharp. Be careful when handling them to avoid cutting fingers.

1. Measure the side clearance of each ring in its groove with a flat feeler gauge (**Figure 125**) and compare to dimensions given in **Table 1**. If the clearance is greater than specified, the rings must be replaced. If the clearance is still excessive with the new rings, the piston(s) must also be replaced.

2. Remove the old top ring by spreading the ends with your thumbs just enough to slide the ring up

over the piston (**Figure 126**). Repeat for the remaining rings.

3. Carefully remove all carbon buildup from the ring grooves with a broken piston ring (**Figure 127**). Inspect the grooves carefully for burrs, nicks or broken and cracked lands. Recondition or replace the piston if necessary.

4. Roll each ring around its piston groove as shown in **Figure 128** to check for binding. Minor binding may be cleaned up with a fine-cut file.

5. Measure the thickness of each ring with a micrometer and compare to dimensions given in **Table 1**. If the thickness is less than specified, the ring(s) must be replaced.

6. Place each ring, one at a time, into the cylinder and push it in about 20 mm (3/4 in.) with the crown of the piston to ensure that the ring is square in the cylinder bore. Measure the gap with a flat feeler gauge (**Figure 129**) and compare to dimensions in **Table 1**. If the gap is greater than specified, the rings should be replaced.

7. When installing new rings, measure their end gap as described in Step 6 and compare to dimensions given in **Table 1**. If the end gap is greater than specified, return the rings for another set(s).

NOTE
*Install the 1st and 2nd rings with their manufacturing marks (e.g "R") mark facing up (**Figure 130**).*

8. Install the oil ring spacer first, then both side rails. If reassembling used parts, install the side rails as they were removed.

9. Install the second compression ring, then the top—by carefully spreading the ends of the ring with your thumbs and slipping the ring over the top of the

piston. Remember that the manufacturing marks on the piston rings are toward the top of the piston.

10. Make sure the rings are seated completely in their grooves all the way around the piston and that the ends are distributed around the piston as shown

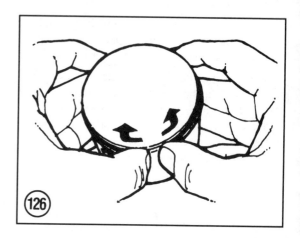

(126)

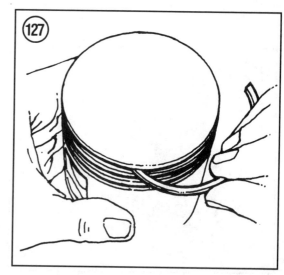

(127)

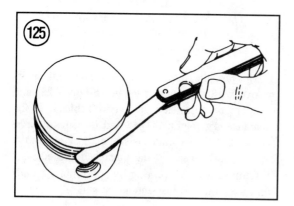

(125)

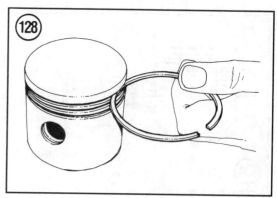

(128)

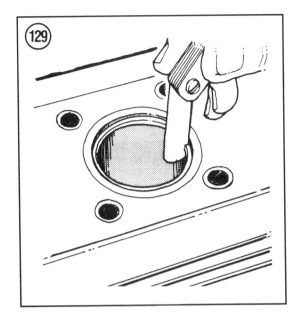

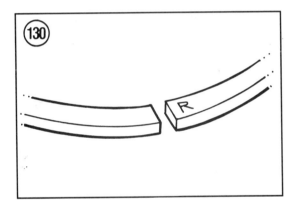

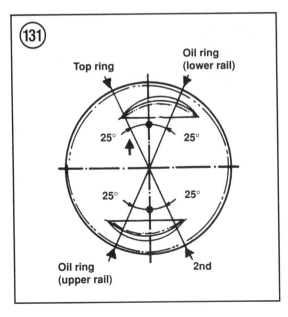

Oil ring (lower rail)

Top ring

25°   25°

25°   25°

Oil ring (upper rail)   2nd

in **Figure 131**. The important thing is that the ring gaps are not aligned with each other when installed to prevent compression pressures from escaping past them during initial start-up.

11. If installing oversized rings, check the top and second ring number and the oil control ring color to make sure the correct rings are being installed. The top and second ring oversize numbers should be the same as the piston oversize numbers as follows:

    a. Piston oversize No. 2: ring No. 2.

    b. Piston oversize No. 4: ring No. 4.

12. If installing oversized oil rings, check the paint color spot to make sure the correct oil rings are being installed. The paint color spots are as follows:

    a. Piston oversize No. 2: blue color.

    b. Piston oversize No. 4: yellow color.

13. If new rings are installed, the cylinders must be deglazed or honed. This will help to seat the new rings. Refer honing service to a Yamaha dealer or competent machine shop. After honing, measure the end clearance of each ring (**Figure 129**) and compare to dimensions in **Table 1**.

> *CAUTION*
> *If the cylinders were deglazed or honed, thoroughly clean each cylinder as described under* **Cylinder Block Inspection** *in this chapter.*

14. Follow the *Break-in Procedure* in this chapter if new pistons or new piston rings have been installed or the cylinders were rebored or honed.

OIL PUMP

Removal/Installation

The oil pump can be removed with the engine in the frame.

1. Remove the clutch assembly as described under *Clutch Assembly Removal/Disassembly* in Chapter Five.

2. Remove the circlip (A, **Figure 132**) securing the oil pump drive sprocket (B, **Figure 132**) to the oil pump.

3. Remove the oil pump drive sprocket from the oil pump.

4. Remove the bolts securing the oil pump assembly (**Figure 133**) to the crankcase and remove the oil pump assembly.

5. Remove the two O-ring seals (**Figure 134**) from the receptacles in the crankcase. Discard the O-ring seals.

6. Inspect the oil pump as described in this chapter.

CAUTION
To prevent loss of oil pressure and to prevent an oil leak, always install new O-ring seals between the crankcase and the oil pump.

7. Install *new* O-ring seals (**Figure 134**).

8. Install the oil pump onto the crankcase.

9. Apply Loctite Threadlocker to the mounting bolts prior to installation. Install the bolts and tighten to the torque specification listed in **Table 2**.

10. Align the flat on the oil pump drive sprocket with the flat on the oil pump drive shaft and install the oil pump drive sprocket onto the oil pump.

11. Install the circlip (A, **Figure 132**) securing the oil pump drive sprocket to the oil pump drive shaft. Make sure the circlip is properly seated in the groove in the drive shaft.

12. Install the clutch assembly as described in Chapter Five.

Disassembly/Inspection/Assembly

Refer to **Figure 135** for this procedure.

NOTE
Replacement parts are not available for all models and years. Check for parts availability from your Yamaha dealer for your specific model.

1. Inspect the oil pump housing and cover for cracks or damage.

2. Remove the screw (**Figure 136**) securing the oil pump cover to the housing and remove the cover (**Figure 137**).

3. Remove the drive shaft (**Figure 138**) and dowel pin.

4. Remove the inner and outer rotor and separate all parts (**Figure 139**).

5. Clean all parts in solvent and thoroughly dry with compressed air.

6. Check the inner and outer rotors for scratches or abrasions. Replace both parts if evidence of this is found.

7. Check the drive shaft and both the cover and rotor housing for internal and external damage. Replace if necessary.

8. Install the outer rotor into the rotor housing and check the clearance between the housing and the rotor (**Figure 140**) with a flat feeler gauge. Compare to the dimensions in **Table 1** and if the clearance is greater than specified, replace the worn part(s).

9. Install the inner rotor and check the clearance between the inner rotor tip and the outer rotor (**Figure 141**) with a flat feeler gauge. Compare to the

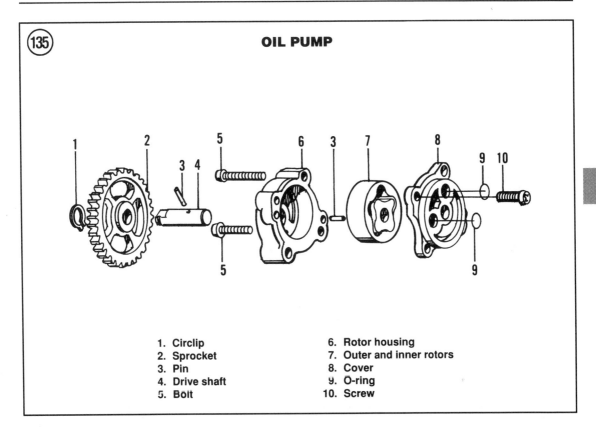

OIL PUMP

1. Circlip
2. Sprocket
3. Pin
4. Drive shaft
5. Bolt
6. Rotor housing
7. Outer and inner rotors
8. Cover
9. O-ring
10. Screw

4

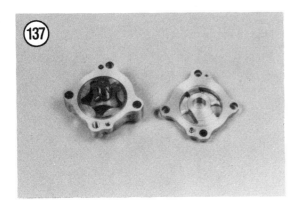

dimensions in **Table 1** and if the clearance is greater than specified, replace the worn part(s).

10. Remove the inner and outer rotors from the housing.

11. Coat all parts with clean engine oil prior to assembly.

12. Install the drive shaft into the housing (**Figure 142**) with the sprocket flat end going in first.

13. Install the inner rotor (**Figure 143**) and align its slots with the pin hole in the drive shaft (**Figure 144**).

14. Insert the pin through the driveshaft (**Figure 145**), then push the shaft down until the pin engages the slot in the inner rotor.

15. Install the outer rotor (**Figure 146**).

16. Make sure the pin (A, **Figure 147**) is in place on the top surface of the rotor housing.

17. Install the cover onto the housing and align the pin with the hole in the housing (B, **Figure 147**).

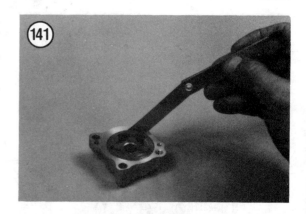

CAUTION
Make sure the cover is completely seated on the rotor housing prior to installing the cover bolt. If not, determine the problem and correct it prior to installing and tightening the bolt. Do not try to pull the cover down onto the housing with the bolt as the oil pump may be locked up. If so, it will be unable to rotate, rendering the oil pump useless.

18. Install the bolt securing the cover and tighten securely.

19. After the bolt is tightened, install the sprocket (**Figure 148**) and rotate the drive shaft and make sure it rotates freely with no binding. If there is any binding problem, correct it at this time—do not install an oil pump that does not rotate freely.

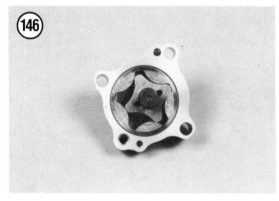

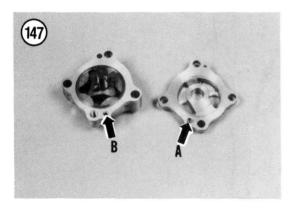

OIL COOLER AND MOUNTING BRACKET (FZ600 MODELS)

Removal/Installation

Refer to **Figure 149** for this procedure.

1. Remove the lower fairings on each side as described under *Lower Fairing Removal/Installation* in Chapter Twelve.

2. Drain the engine oil and remove the oil filter as described under *Engine Oil and Filter Change* in Chapter Three.

3. Remove the exhaust system (A, **Figure 150**) as described under *Exhaust System (FZ600) Removal/Installation* in Chapter Seven.

4. Remove the large union bolt and washer securing the oil filter adaptor to the crankcase. Pull the adaptor away from the crankcase.

5. Remove the Allen bolt (B, **Figure 150**) and clamp securing both oil lines to the center bracket. Don't lose the metal spacer between the clamp and the center bracket.

6. Remove the bolts and washers securing the oil cooler (C, **Figure 150**) to the frame mounting bracket. Don't lose the collar within each rubber grommet on the frame mounting bracket.

7. Carefully lower the oil cooler out of the upper mount and remove the oil cooler and oil line assembly from the frame and engine. Protect your clothing as some residual oil may drain out of the assembly as it's being removed.

8. To remove the mounting bracket, remove the bolts, lockwashers and washers on each side securing the mounting bracket to the frame and remove it. Don't lose the rubber grommets in the mounting holes in the bracket.

9. Install by reversing these removal steps while noting the following:

    a. Clean off all road dirt and oil residue from the oil filter adaptor mating surface on the crankcase.

    b. Install a new O-ring seal onto the backside of the oil filter adaptor.

    c. Tighten the center bracket bolt and oil cooler mounting bolts securely.

    d. Install the large union bolt and tighten to the torque specification listed in **Table 2**.

    e. Refill the engine with the recommended type and quantity oil as described in Chapter Three.

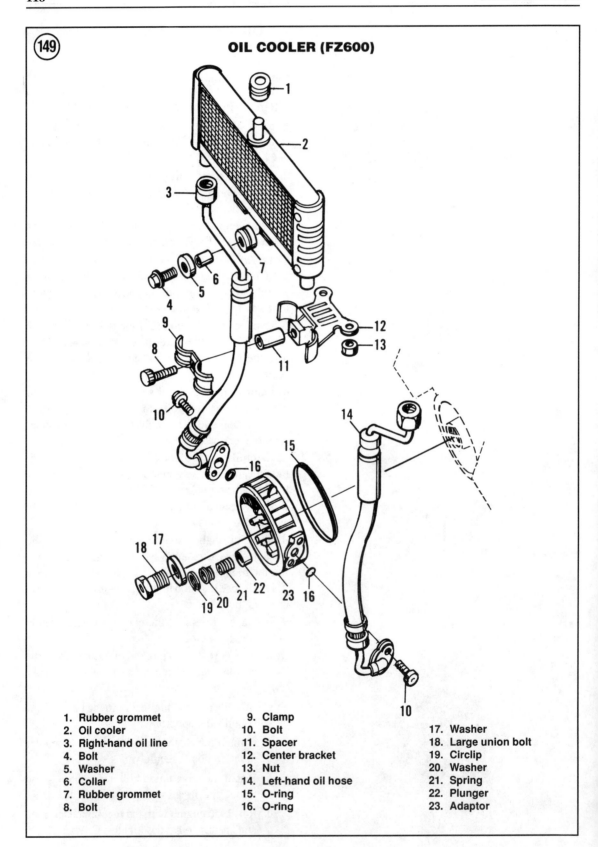

OIL COOLER (FZ600)

1. Rubber grommet
2. Oil cooler
3. Right-hand oil line
4. Bolt
5. Washer
6. Collar
7. Rubber grommet
8. Bolt
9. Clamp
10. Bolt
11. Spacer
12. Center bracket
13. Nut
14. Left-hand oil hose
15. O-ring
16. O-ring
17. Washer
18. Large union bolt
19. Circlip
20. Washer
21. Spring
22. Plunger
23. Adaptor

Disassembly/Cleaning/Assembly

Refer to **Figure 149** for this procedure.

1. Remove the bolts securing the lower portion of the oil line to the oil filter adaptor.

2. Remove the oil line and discard the O-ring seal from the backside of the oil line fitting.

3. Unscrew the large nut securing the upper portion of the oil line to the oil cooler. Remove the oil line from the oil cooler.

4. Repeat Steps 1-3 for the other oil line.

5. Carefully clean off all road dirt and any oil residue from the oil cooler cooling fins.

6. Inspect the oil lines for deterioration, cracks, cuts or damage. Replace if necessary.

7. If the engine oil was contaminated, perform the following:

    a. Flush out the oil lines with solvent and blow out with compressed air.

    b. Flush out the oil cooler with light weight oil. Tip it from side to side to drain as much old and new oil as possible. Repeat if necessary until the oil draining out is free of contamination.

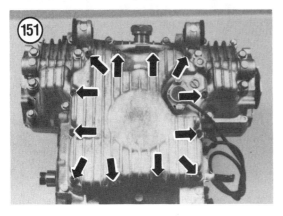

8. Clean the oil filter adaptor with solvent and dry with compressed air.

NOTE
Do not tighten the large nut securing the oil lines to the oil cooler until the oil cooler assembly has been installed on the engine and frame. The oil lines must be in a relaxed position until the assembly is installed on the bike.

9. Connect the upper portion of the oil lines to the oil cooler and tighten the large nuts just enough to hold the lines in place—do not tighten at this time.

10. Install new O-ring seals onto the backside of the fitting on the lower portion of the oil line.

11. Install the lower portion of the oil lines to the oil cooler adaptor and tighten the bolts securely.

12. Lay this assembly on a flat surface and straighten the oil lines so they lay next to each other in their normal installed position. Tighten the large nuts finger-tight at this time. Do not tighten completely until the oil cooler assembly has been installed onto the engine and frame.

13. Install the oil cooler assembly as described in this chapter, then tighten the large nuts securely.

OIL PAN, STRAINER AND RELIEF VALVE

Removal/Inspection/Installation

1. Remove the engine from the frame as described in this chapter.

CAUTION
If the cylinder head and cylinder block have been removed, place the crankcase on wood blocks to protect the crankcase studs.

2. Turn the engine upside down on the workbench.

3. Remove the Allen bolts (**Figure 151**) securing the oil pan to the lower crankcase. Note the location of the electrical wire clips (**Figure 152**) so they can be installed in the same location during installation.

4. Remove the oil pan and gasket. Discard the gasket as a new one must be installed.

CAUTION
Do not damage the strainer screen during removal.

5. Carefully pry up on the oil pickup strainer screen (**Figure 153**) and remove it.

6. Remove the 2 Allen bolts (**Figure 154**) securing the oil pickup strainer housing and remove it and the gasket (**Figure 155**). Discard the gasket as a new one must be installed.

7. Remove the oil relief valve (**Figure 156**) assembly from the lower crankcase.

8. Thoroughly clean the oil pickup strainer and screen in solvent and dry with compressed air.

9. Inspect the screen for damage or holes; replace as necessary.

10. Check the relief valve assembly for wear or damage; replace as necessary. Replace the O-ring if it has lost its resiliency or is starting to deteriorate.

11. Inspect the oil pan for dents, cracks or other damage; repair or replace as required.

12. Remove all traces of old gasket material from the oil pan and the mating surface on the lower crankcase.

13. Install the oil relief valve (**Figure 156**) and O-ring assembly into the lower crankcase.

14. Position the oil pickup strainer housing with the arrow (**Figure 157**) facing toward the front of the engine.

15. Install the oil pickup strainer housing, new gasket and bolts. Tighten the bolts to the torque specification listed in **Table 2**.

16. Position the oil pickup strainer screen with the cutout portion facing toward the rear of the engine (**Figure 153**) and install it. Make sure it is correctly seated in the housing.

17. Install a new pan gasket and the oil pan.

18. Apply Loctite Threadlocker to the oil pan Allen bolt threads prior to installation.

19. Install the oil pan bolts. Be sure to install the electrical wire clips (**Figure 152**) in the correct location as noted during removal. Tighten the bolts to the torque specification listed in **Table 2**.

LOW OIL LEVEL SWITCH

The low oil level switch is located in the bottom of the oil pan. It is not necessary to remove the engine from the frame in order to remove the oil level switch. The engine is shown removed in this procedure for clarity.

Removal/Installation

1. On FZ600 models, perform the following:
   a. Remove the lower fairing from each side as described under *Lower Fairing Removal/Installation* in Chapter Twelve.
   b. Remove the exhaust system as described under *Exhaust System Removal/Installation* in Chapter Seven.

2. Place the bike on the centerstand (Radian models) or side stand (FZ600 models).

3. Drain the engine oil and remove the oil filter as described under *Engine Oil and Filter Change* in Chapter Three.

4. Disconnect the low oil level switch single electrical connector containing one black/red wire.

5. Release the electrical wire from the clip on the oil pan (**Figure 152**).

6. Remove the 2 screws (**Figure 158**) securing the low oil level switch to the oil pan and remove it and the gasket. Discard the gasket as a new one must be installed.

7. Clean off all old gasket residue from the oil pan and the oil level switch body.

8. Install a new oil level switch and gasket.

9. Install the bolts and tighten securely.

10. Secure the electrical wire to the clips on the oil pan and reconnect the electrical connector.

11. Refill the engine with the recommended type and quantity oil as described in Chapter Three.

12. On FZ600 models, install the exhaust system as described in Chapter Seven and the lower fairings as described in Chapter Twelve.

PRIMARY DRIVE GEAR

Removal/Inspection/Installation

1. Perform Steps 1-8 of *Clutch Removal/Disassembly* in Chapter Five.

2. Straighten the tab on the lockwasher behind the nut.

3. Have an assistant apply the rear brake.

4. Loosen the nut (**Figure 159**) securing the primary drive gear.

5. Perform Steps 10-22 of *Clutch Removal/Disassembly* in Chapter Five.

6. Remove the nut and lockwasher (A, **Figure 160**) and the primary drive gear (B, **Figure 160**) and

collar from the starter gear shaft. Discard the lock-washer as a new one must be installed.

7. Inspect the gear for chipped or missing teeth. If the primary gear is damaged, inspect the teeth on the clutch outer housing for wear or damage. Replace the gear if necessary.

8. Install the collar, a *new* lockwasher and the primary drive gear onto the starter gear shaft.

9. Perform Steps 1-18 of *Clutch Assembly/Installation* in Chapter Five.

10. Make sure the transmission is still in gear and have an assistant apply the rear brake.

11. Tighten the nut to the toque specification listed in **Table 2**.

12. Bend down one of the tabs on the lockwasher against the flat on the nut.

13. Perform Steps 19-27 of *Clutch Assembly/Installation* in Chapter Five.

CRANKCASE

Service to the lower end requires that the crankcase assembly be removed from the motorcycle frame.

Disassembly

1. On 1989-1990 models, remove the screws securing the left-hand rear cover. Remove the cover and gasket.

2. While the engine is still in the frame, remove the cylinder head, cylinder block, pistons, electric starter, alternator, signal generator and clutch assembly as described in this and other related chapters.

3. Remove the engine as described in this chapter.

4. Set the engine on the workbench right side up.

NOTE
When removing the crankcase bolts in the following steps, keep the upper crankcase bolts separate from the lower crankcase bolts to prevent mixup during reassembly.

5. Loosen all of the bolts in the upper crankcase 1/2 turn at a time. Refer to **Figure 161** and start with the highest number first. The bolt numbers are marked on the case adjacent to the bolt hole (**Figure 162**). After loosening the bolts, remove all of them.

6. Turn the engine over on the workbench on several wood blocks. This is to protect the protruding connecting rod ends and the crankcase studs.

7. Remove the oil pan, gasket and oil pickup strainer assembly as described in this chapter.

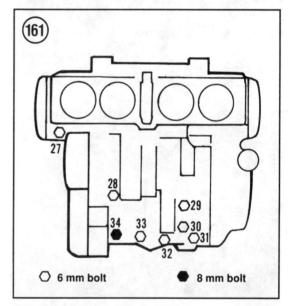

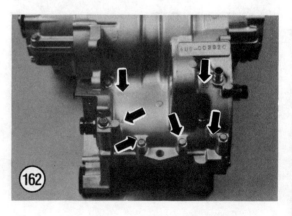

CAUTION
Always remove the 8 mm bolts in the crankshaft area last (bolt Nos. 1-10, Figure 163).

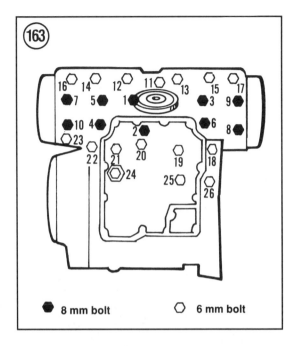

8 mm bolt   ○ **6 mm bolt**

8. Loosen all of the bolts in the lower crankcase 1/2 turn at a time. Refer to **Figure 163** and start with the highest number first. The bolt numbers are marked on the case adjacent to the bolt hole. After loosening the bolts, remove all of them. The 8 mm bolts (crankshaft area) have a washer under each one, don't lose them.

9. Double check that you have removed all of the upper and lower crankcase bolts.

10. Tap the lower crankcase with a plastic mallet and separate the 2 halves.

CAUTION
*If it is necessary to pry the halves apart, do it **very carefully** so that you do not mar the gasket surfaces. If you do, the cases will leak oil and must be replaced.*

11. Lift the lower crankcase off of the upper crankcase. Turn the lower crankcase over immediately and be careful that the crankshaft main bearing inserts do not fall out. If any do, reinstall them immediately and into their original positions if possible.

12. Remove the locating dowel and O-ring (**Figure 164**) from the upper crankcase half.

13. Remove both transmission assemblies from the upper crankcase half. Remove the transmission locating C-rings (**Figure 165**).

14. Remove the starter clutch assembly as described in this chapter.

15. Lift the crankshaft/connecting rod assembly out of the upper crankcase.

16. Remove the internal shift mechanism as described under *Internal Gearshift Mechanism Removal/Installation* in Chapter Six.

NOTE
Start with the No. 1 cylinder on the left-hand side. The left-hand side refers to the engine as it sits in the bike's frame, not as it sits on your workbench.

17. Remove the crankshaft main bearing inserts (**Figure 166**) from the upper and lower crankcase halves. Mark the backside of the inserts with a number (No. 1, 2, 3, 4 and 5) and with a "U" (upper) or "L" (lower) crankcase half so they can be reinstalled in their original positions.

18. Remove the bolts securing the upper (**Figure 167**) and lower (**Figure 168**) Hy-Vo chain guides and remove both of them.

19. Remove the bolts securing the Hy-Vo chain tensioner (**Figure 169**) to the lower crankcase half and remove the assembly.

Inspection

1. Thoroughly clean the inside and outside of both crankcase halves with cleaning solvent. Dry with compressed air. Make sure there is no solvent residue left in the cases as it will contaminate the new engine oil.

2. Remove all old gasket sealing material from both case half mating surfaces.

3. Carefully inspect the cases for cracks and fractures. Also check the areas around the stiffening ribs, around bearing bosses and threaded holes. If damage is found, have it repaired by a shop specializing in the repair of precision aluminum castings or replace the crankcase halves as a set.

4. Make sure the crankcase studs are tight. Yamaha does not provide a torque specification for the studs.

Assembly

1. Install the upper (**Figure 167**) and lower (**Figure 168**) Hy-Vo chain guides and install the bolts and tighten securely.

2. Install the Hy-Vo chain tensioner (**Figure 169**) to the lower crankcase half. Apply Loctite Threadlocker to the bolt threads prior to installation, then install and tighten to the torque specification listed in Table 2.

> *NOTE*
> *If reusing the old bearing inserts, make sure that they are installed in the same location as noted during* **Removal**.

3. Install the crankshaft main bearing inserts into the crankcase halves in the same location. Make sure each insert tab is notched correctly (**Figure 170**) in the crankcase halves.

4. Install the starter clutch assembly as described in this chapter.

5. Install the internal shift mechanism as described under *Internal Gearshift Mechanism Removal/Installation* in Chapter Six.

6. Install the crankshaft/connecting rod and chain assembly into the upper crankcase as described in this chapter.

7. Install the C-rings (**Figure 165**) into the upper crankcase.

8. Install both transmission assemblies into the upper crankcase half.

9. Install the locating dowel and O-ring (**Figure 164**) into the upper crankcase half.

10. Make sure the crankshaft main bearing inserts are in place in the lower crankcase half.

11. Shift the transmission into NEUTRAL.

12. Make sure case half sealing surfaces are perfectly clean and dry. Clean off with an aerosol elec-

trical contact cleaner and wipe off with a lint-free cloth.

NOTE
On U.S. models, use a gasket sealer similar to Three Bond, Yamabond No. 4, Quick Gasket (part No. ACC-11001-05-01), Gasgacinch Gasket Sealer, or equivalent. When selecting an equivalent, avoid thick and hard setting materials. On UK models, use Yamabond No. 1215 (part No. 90890-85505) or equivalent.

CAUTION
Failure to apply sealant to the following areas in Step 13 may result in reduced oil pressure and crankshaft bearing damage.

13. Apply a light coat of gasket sealer, or equivalent, to the following surfaces:

  a. Sealing surfaces of the lower crankcase half. Cover only flat surfaces, *not curved bearing surfaces*.

  b. To each sealing surface next to the main bearing inserts (**Figure 171**). Apply sealant to within 2.5 mm (0.10 in.) of the insert.

  c. Adjacent to the oil gallery O-ring (**Figure 164**). Apply sealant to within 2.5 mm (0.10 in.) of the O-ring.

Make the coating as thin as possible, but still completely covered, or the case can shift and hammer out bearings.

14. Make sure the Hy-Vo chain tensioner (**Figure 169**) plunger is seated correctly in its guide.

15. Hold the Hy-Vo chain tensioner plunger in place and turn the lower crankcase over.

CAUTION
If the Hy-Vo chain tensioner plunger is dislodged when the lower crankcase half is turned over and during installation, the engine will be damaged.

16. Position the lower crankcase onto the upper crankcase. Set the front portion down first and lower the area while making sure the No. 2 shift fork engages properly in the correct slot in the transmission gear. Join both halves and tap them together lightly with a plastic mallet—do not use a metal hammer as it will damage the case.

CAUTION
Crankcase halves should fit together without force. If the crankcase halves do not fit together completely, do not attempt to pull them together with the crankcase bolts. Separate the crankcase halves and investigate the cause of the interference. If the transmission shafts were disassembled, recheck to make sure that a gear is not installed backwards. Do not risk damage by trying to force the cases together.

17. Before installing the bolts, slowly spin the transmission shafts and shift the transmission through all gears using the shift drum. Make sure the shift forks are operating properly and that you can shift through all gears. This is the time to find that something may be installed incorrectly—not after the crankcase is completely assembled.

18. Apply a light coat of oil to all crankcase bolts prior to installation.

NOTE
A number is cast into the lower crankcase next to each crankcase bolt hole (Figure 162).

19. Install the main bearing 8 mm bolts and washers (Nos. 1-10, **Figure 163**).

NOTE
If you don't remember the correct location of the bolts, place all of the bolts in the bolt holes. All bolt heads should stick up out of the crankcase the same distance. If necessary, interchange the bolts until they all protrude the same distance. When this is achieved, the bolts are installed in the correct holes.

20. Install the remaining 6 mm bolts (Nos. 11-26, **Figure 163**). Be sure to place the electrical wire clamp under the No. 26 bolt.

21. Tighten the main bearing bolt in the ascending order of the numbers cast into the lower crankcase (**Figure 163**). Tighten in 2-3 stages until you reach the final torque specification listed in **Table 2**.

22. Install the oil pickup strainer assembly and the oil pan as described in this chapter.

23. Turn the engine over on the workbench.

24. Apply a light coat of oil to all crankcase bolts prior to installation.

NOTE
A number is cast into the lower crankcase next to each crankcase bolt hole (Figure 162).

NOTE
If you don't remember the correct location of the bolts, place all of the bolts in the bolt holes. All bolt heads should stick up out of the crankcase the same distance. If necessary, interchange the bolts until they all protrude the same

distance. When this is achieved, the bolts are installed in the correct holes.

25. Install the upper crankcase 6 mm bolts (Nos. 27-33, **Figure 161**) and 8 mm bolt (No. 34, **Figure 161**). Be sure to place the electrical ground wire under the No. 32 bolt.

26. Tighten the crankcase bolts in the ascending order of the numbers cast into the lower crankcase (**Figure 161**). Tighten in 2-3 stages until you reach the final torque specification listed in **Table 2**.

27. Install the engine as described in this chapter.

28. Install all exterior components removed as described in this and other related chapters.

29. On 1989-1990 models, install the left-hand rear cover and gasket. Install the screws and tighten securely.

CRANKSHAFT

Removal/Installation

1. Disassemble the crankcase as described in this chapter.

2. Remove both transmission assemblies from the upper crankcase half. Remove the transmission locating C-rings (**Figure 165**).

3. Remove the starter clutch assembly as described in this chapter.

4. Remove the crankshaft/connecting rod assembly and camshaft chain (**Figure 172**) from the upper crankcase half.

NOTE
In Step 5, the No. 1 mark is for the left-hand No. 1 cylinder. The No. 1-5 marks go from left to right across the

engine. The left-hand side of the engine refers to the engine as it sits in the bike frame—not as it sits on your bench upside down.

5. If the bearing inserts are going to be removed for cleaning, perform the following;

a. Remove the main bearing inserts from the upper and lower (**Figure 166**) crankcase half.

b. Mark the backside of the inserts with a 1, 2, 3, 4 or 5 and "U" (upper) or "L" (lower). Remember that the inserts with a hole go into the lower crankcase.

CAUTION
If the old bearings are reused, be sure that they are installed in their exact original locations.

6. Inspect the crankshaft and main bearings as described in this chapter.

7. Install the crankshaft/connecting rod assembly, Hy-Vo chain and camshaft chain (**Figure 173**) into the upper crankcase half.

8. After the crankshaft is installed, make sure the left-hand oil seal (**Figure 174**) and right-hand plug (**Figure 175**) are seated properly in the groove in the crankcase.

9. Install the starter clutch assembly as described in this chapter.

10. If removed, install the C-rings (**Figure 165**) in the upper crankcase.

11. Install both transmission assemblies into the upper crankcase half.

12. Assemble the crankcase as described in this chapter.

Inspection

1. Clean crankshaft thoroughly with solvent. Clean oil holes with rifle cleaning brushes; flush thoroughly and dry with compressed air. Lightly oil all bearing journal surfaces immediately to prevent rust.

2. Carefully inspect each main bearing journal (**Figure 176**) for scratches, ridges, scoring, nicks, etc. Very small nicks and scratches may be removed with crocus cloth. More serious damage must be removed by grinding; a job for a machine shop.

3. Inspect the camshaft chain sprocket teeth (A, **Figure 177**). If damaged, the crankshaft must be replaced.

4. Inspect the primary drive gear teeth (B, **Figure 177**). If damaged, the crankshaft must be replaced.

5. If the surface finish on all journals is satisfactory, measure the journals with a micrometer and check out-of-roundness, taper, and wear on the journals. Check against measurements given in **Table 1**.

Crankshaft Main Bearing Clearance Measurement

1. Check each main bearing insert for evidence of wear, abrasion, and scoring. If the bearings are good, they may be reused. If any insert is questionable, replace the entire set.

2. Clean the bearing surfaces of the crankshaft and the main bearing inserts.

3. Place the upper crankcase on a workbench upside down on a couple of 2 × 4 in. wood blocks. This is to protect the protruding connecting rod ends and the crankcase studs.

4. Install the existing main bearing inserts in the upper and the lower crankcase halves in their original positions. Remember that the inserts with a hole go into the lower crankcase.

5. Install the crankshaft into the upper crankcase (**Figure 172**).

6. Place a piece of Plastigage over each main bearing journal parallel to the crankshaft (**Figure 178**). Do not place the Plastigage material over an oil hole in the crankshaft.

> *CAUTION*
> *Do not rotate the crankshaft while the Plastigage is in place.*

7. Position the lower crankcase on the upper crankcase. Set the front portion down first and lower the rear. Join both halves and tap them together lightly with a plastic mallet—do not use a metal hammer as it will damage the case.

> *CAUTION*
> *Crankcase halves should fit together without force. If the crankcase halves do not fit together completely, do not attempt to pull them together with the crankcase bolts. Separate the crankcase halves and investigate the cause of the interference. If the transmission*

shafts were disassembled, recheck to make sure that a gear is not installed backwards. Do not risk damage by trying to force the cases together.

> *NOTE*
> *A number is cast into the lower crankcase next to each main bearing bolt hole.*

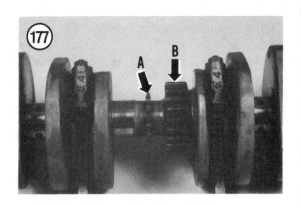

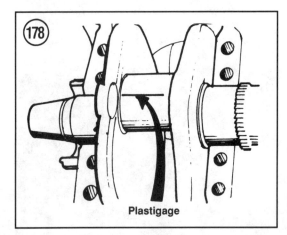

Plastigage

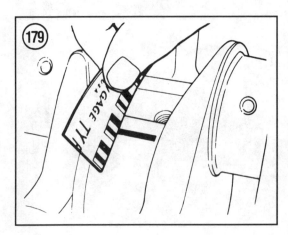

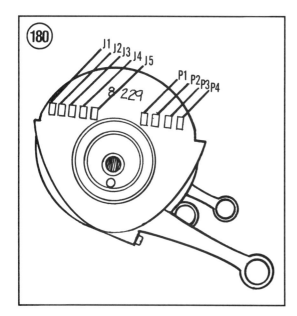

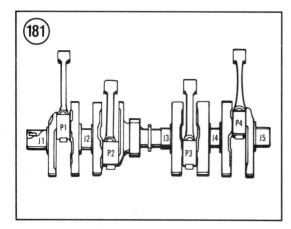

8. Apply a light coat of oil to the bolts prior to installation. Install the main bearing bolts and washers (Nos. 1-10, **Figure 163**).

9. Tighten the main bearing bolts in the ascending order of the numbers cast into the lower crankcase (**Figure 163**). Tighten in 2-3 steps to the final torque specification listed in **Table 2**.

10. Loosen each main bearing bolt in the descending order of the numbers cast into the lower crankcase. Remove the bolts and washers.

11. Carefully remove the lower crankcase half.

12. Measure the width of the flattened Plastigage according to manufacturer's instructions. Measure at both ends of Plastigage strip (**Figure 179**). A difference of 0.025 mm (0.001 in.) or more indicates a tapered journal. Confirm with a micrometer. Bearing clearances for new bearings are listed in **Table 1**.

13. Completely remove the Plastigage strips from the main bearing journals.

14. If the bearing clearance is greater than specified, select new bearings as described in this chapter.

Crankshaft-to-Crankcase Main Bearing Selection

> *NOTE*
> *The group of 4 numbers on the right-hand side of the crankweb relates to the crankshaft **connecting rod journals; do not** refer to these 4 numbers for this procedure.*

1. The crankshaft main bearing journals are marked with a "1," "2," "3," "4" or "5" (**Figure 180**), on the left-hand side of the left-hand crankweb. The first number on the left is for the No. 1 crankshaft journal; the numbers continue from left to right for journals 2-5. The stamped letters relate to the crankshaft main bearing journals (e.g. J4) as shown in **Figure 181**.

2. The crankcase journal I.D. code numbers "1," "2," "3," "4" or "5," (**Figure 180**) are stamped on the rear surface of the upper crankcase (**Figure 182**). The stamped numbers are in the same order as the journals are located within the crankcase.

3. To select the proper main bearing insert number, subtract the crankshaft bearing journal number from the crankcase bearing journal number. For example, if the crankcase journal is a No. 5 and the crankshaft journal is a No. 2, then subtract, 5 - 2 = 3. The new bearing insert is a No. 3.

4

NOTE
Determine the bearing insert number for all main bearing journals, then take the insert numbers to a Yamaha dealer for new bearing purchase.

4. After new bearing inserts have been installed, recheck the clearance by repeating the *Crankshaft Main Bearing Clearance Measurement* procedure in this chapter. If the clearance is still out of specifications, either the crankcase or the crankshaft is worn beyond the service limit and requires replacement.

CONNECTING RODS

Removal/Installation

1. Remove the crankshaft/connecting rod assembly and chain assembly as described in this chapter.

2. Measure the connecting rod big end side clearance. Insert a flat feeler gauge between a connecting rod big end and either crankshaft machined web. Record the clearance for each connecting rod and compare to the specifications listed in **Table 1**. If the clearance is greater than specified, the connecting rod is worn and must be replaced.

NOTE
Before disassembling the connecting rods, mark the rods and caps with a "1," "2," "3" and "4" starting from the left-hand side. The No. 1 cylinder is on the left-hand side. The No. 1-4 marks relate to the left- and right-hand side of the engine as it sits in the bike frame— not as it sits on your bench.

3. Remove the connecting rod cap nuts (**Figure 183**) and separate the rods from the crankshaft. Keep each cap with its original rod with the weight mark on the end of the cap matching the mark on the rod (**Figure 184**).

NOTE
Keep each bearing insert in its original place in the crankcase, rod or rod cap. If you are going to assemble the engine with the original inserts, they must be installed exactly as removed in order to prevent rapid wear.

4. Inspect the connecting rods and bearings as described in this chapter.

5. If new bearing inserts are going to be installed, check the bearing clearance as described in this chapter.

6. If the bearing inserts came off or new ones are installed, make sure they are locked in place correctly (**Figure 185**).

7. Apply a light even coat of molybdenum disulfide grease to the connecting rod bearing journals and to the connecting rod bearing inserts.

8. Install the connecting rod onto the crankshaft being careful not to damage the bearing surface of the crankshaft with the rod's threaded studs.

9. Match the weight mark on the end of the cap with the mark on the rod (**Figure 186**) and install the cap.

CAUTION
During the final tightening sequence, if a torque of 20 N•m (14.5 ft.-lb.) is reached, do not stop until the final torque value is achieved. If the tightening is interrupted between 20-25 N•m

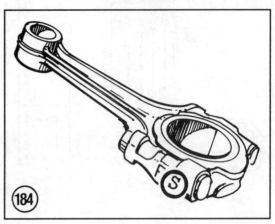

(14.5-18.0 ft.-lb.), loosen the nut to less than 20 N•m (14.5 ft.-lb.) and tighten to the final torque value in one step.

10. Apply a light coat of molybdenum disulfide grease to the connecting rod threaded studs and install the cap nuts (**Figure 183**). Tighten the cap nuts in 2-3 stages to the final torque listed in **Table 2**.

11. After the connecting rods are installed and the cap nuts tightened to the correct torque, rotate the crankshaft several times and check that the bearings are not too tight. Make sure there is no binding. If there is a problem, correct it at this time.

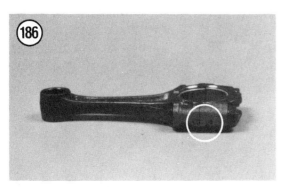

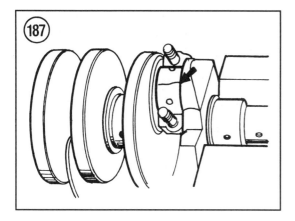

Connecting Rod Inspection

CAUTION
Never try to remove the connecting rod bolts. If loosened and retightened, the bearing cap will never fit properly.

1. Check each connecting rod for obvious damage such as cracks and burns.
2. Check the piston pin bushing for wear or scoring.
3. Take the connecting rods to a machine shop and check the alignment for twisting and bending.
4. Examine the bearing inserts for wear, scoring, or burning. They are reusable if in good condition. Make a note of the bearing color identification on the side of the insert if the bearing is to be discarded; a previous owner may have used undersize bearings.

Connecting Rod Bearing Clearance Measurement

1. Check each rod bearing insert for evidence of wear, abrasion, and scoring. If the bearings are good, they may be reused. If any insert is questionable, replace as a set.
2. Clean the bearing surfaces of the crankshaft and the connecting rod bearing inserts.
3. Install the rod bearing inserts in the connecting rod and bearing cap. Make sure they are locked in place correctly.
4. Install the connecting rod onto the crankshaft being careful not to damage the bearing surface of the crankshaft with the rod's threaded studs.
5. Place a piece of Plastigage over the rod bearing journal parallel to the crankshaft (**Figure 187**). Do not place the Plastigage material over an oil hole in the crankshaft.

CAUTION
Do not rotate the crankshaft while the Plastigage is in place.

6. Match the weight mark on the end of the cap with the mark on the rod and install the cap.

CAUTION
*During the final tightening sequence, if a torque of 20 N•m (14.5 ft.-lb.) is reached, **do not stop** until the final torque value is achieved. If the tightening is interrupted between 20-25 N•m (14.5-18.0 ft.-lb.), loosen the nut to less*

than 20 N•m (14.5 ft.-lb.) and tighten to the final torque value in one step.

7. Apply a light coat of molybdenum disulfide grease to the connecting rod threaded studs and install the cap nuts (**Figure 183**). Tighten the cap nuts in 2-3 stages to the final torque listed in **Table 2**.

8. Loosen the cap nuts and carefully remove the cap from the connecting rod.

9. Measure the width of the flattened Plastigage according to manufacturer's instructions. Measure at both ends of Plastigage strip (**Figure 188**). A difference of 0.025 mm (0.001 in.) or more indicates a tapered journal. Confirm with a micrometer. Bearing clearance for new connecting rod bearings are listed in **Table 1**.

10. Completely remove the Plastigage strips from the main bearing journals.

11. If the bearing clearance is greater than specified, select new bearings as described in this chapter.

Connecting Rod-to-Crankshaft Bearing Selection

> *NOTE*
> *The group of 5 numbers on the left-hand side of the crankweb relate to the crankshaft **main bearing journals**; **do not** refer to these 5 numbers for this procedure.*

1. The connecting rod bearing journals are marked with a "1," "2," "3" or "4" (**Figure 180**) on the right-hand side of the left-hand crankweb. The first number on the left is for the No. 1 connecting rod journal; the number continue from left to right for journals 2-4. The stamped letters relate to the crankshaft main bearing journals (e.g. P4) as shown in **Figure 181**.

2. The connecting rods are marked with a number "4" or "5" (**Figure 184**).

3. To select the proper connecting rod bearing insert number, subtract the connecting rod bearing journal number from the connecting rod and cap number. For example, if the connecting rod bearing journal is a No. 4 and the crankshaft journal is a No. 2, then subtract, 4 - 2 = 2. The new bearing insert is a No. 2.

> *NOTE*
> *Determine the bearing insert number for all connecting rod bearing journals, then take the insert numbers to a*

Yamaha dealer for new bearing purchase.

4. After new bearing inserts have been installed, recheck the clearance by repeating the *Connecting Rod Bearing Clearance Measurement* procedure in this chapter. If the clearance is still out of specifications, either the connecting rod or the crankshaft is

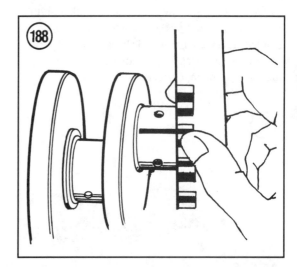

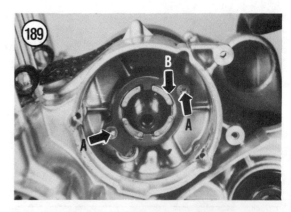

worn beyond the service limit and requires replacement.

STARTER CLUTCH ASSEMBLY

Removal

1. Remove the primary drive gear as described in this chapter.

2. Disassemble the crankcase as described in this chapter.

3. Remove both transmission assemblies from the upper crankcase half. Remove the transmission locating C-rings (**Figure 165**).

4. Remove the Torx bolts (A, **Figure 189**) securing the bearing cover plate (B, **Figure 189**) and remove the cover.

5. Remove the oil spray nozzle (**Figure 190**) from the side of the crankcase (**Figure 191**).

6. Gently tap on the right-hand end (primary drive gear side) of the starter gear shaft with a rubber or plastic mallet to break it loose from the crankcase.

7. Hold onto the starter clutch assembly and withdraw the shaft from the left-hand side of the crankcase (**Figure 192**).

8. Lift up on the Hy-Vo chain and lift the starter clutch assembly (**Figure 193**) up out of the upper crankcase.

9. Disengage the assembly from the Hy-Vo chain and remove the assembly. The chain will stay with the crankshaft.

10. Remove the screws (**Figure 194**) securing the bearing retainer and remove the retainer.

11. Hold onto the starter idler gear and withdraw the shaft (**Figure 195**) from the crankcase. Remove the starter idler gear (**Figure 196**).

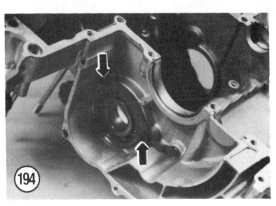

Disassembly/Inspection/Assembly

Refer to **Figure 197** for this procedure.

1. Remove bushing (A, **Figure 198**) and starter idle gear (B) from hub assembly (C).

2. Check the rollers (**Figure 199**) in the starter clutch for uneven or excessive wear, replace as a set if any are bad. If damaged, remove and replace the rollers, springs and plungers.

3. Check the Allen bolts (**Figure 200**) for tightness. If any of the bolts are loose, remove them and

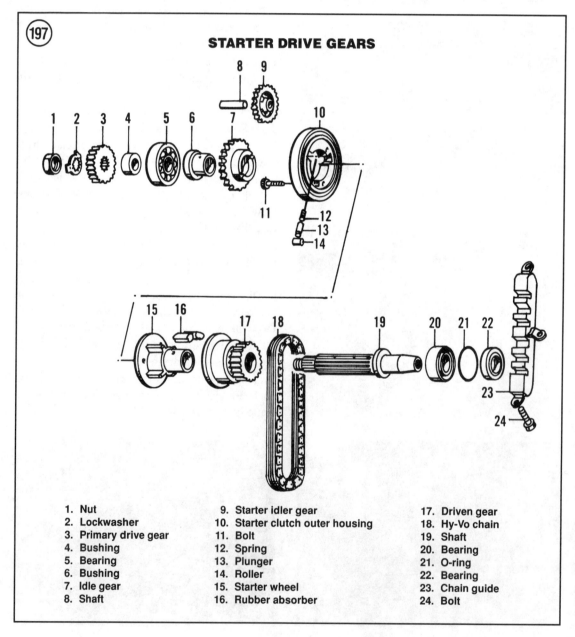

STARTER DRIVE GEARS

1. Nut
2. Lockwasher
3. Primary drive gear
4. Bushing
5. Bearing
6. Bushing
7. Idle gear
8. Shaft
9. Starter idler gear
10. Starter clutch outer housing
11. Bolt
12. Spring
13. Plunger
14. Roller
15. Starter wheel
16. Rubber absorber
17. Driven gear
18. Hy-Vo chain
19. Shaft
20. Bearing
21. O-ring
22. Bearing
23. Chain guide
24. Bolt

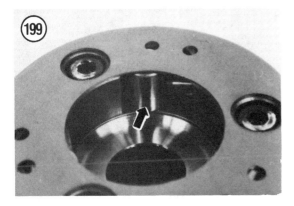

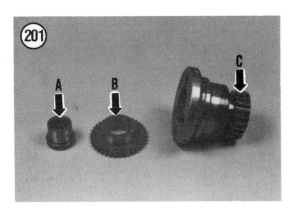

replace with new bolts. Apply Loctite Threadlocker to the threads prior to installation and tighten to the torque specification listed in **Table 2**.

4. Inspect the bushing (A, **Figure 201**) and the starter gear (B, **Figure 201**). Replace as a set if either is faulty.

5. Inspect the starter driven gear (C, **Figure 201**) for chipped or missing teeth. Look for uneven or excessive wear on the gear faces. If damaged, the starter driven gear, starter clutch and Hy-Vo chain must be replaced as a set.

6. Inspect the end oil seal (A, **Figure 202**) and replace if worn or damaged.

7. Inspect the shaft splines (B, **Figure 202**); replace the shaft if worn or damaged.

8. Inspect the bearing (C, **Figure 202**). Make sure it rotates smoothly with no signs of wear or damage. If the bearing requires replacement, have a Yamaha dealer press off the old bearing and install a new one.

9. Inspect the starter idle gear and shaft (**Figure 203**) for wear or damage. Replace both if either is damaged.

10. Inspect the roller riding surface of the starter driven gear for wear or abrasion. If damaged, both

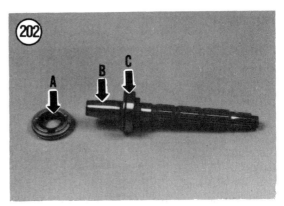

the starter driven gear and starter clutch must be replaced as a set.

> *NOTE*
> *Do not apply any grease to the rollers in the following step to hold them in place. If grease is applied, it will interfere with their movement during the normal engine starting sequence.*

11. If the rollers in the starter clutch were removed, perform the following:

   a. Install the spring into the plunger.

   b. Install the assembled spring and plunger into the receptacle in the starter clutch.

   c. Push the plunger into the receptacle and hold it in place with a small tool similar to a dental tool.

   d. Hold the plunger and spring in place and install the roller. Push the roller in until it bottoms out and stays in place.

   e. Repeat for the other 2 sets of rollers.

12. Install the starter idle gear and bushing onto the hub assembly.

Installation

1. Install the starter idler gear (**Figure 196**) and install the shaft (**Figure 195**) into the crankcase.

2. Install the bearing retainer and the screws. Tighten the screws securely.

3. Place the starter clutch assembly in the crankcase half and properly engage it with the Hy-Vo chain (**Figure 204**).

4. Lower the starter clutch assembly and engage it with the idler gear (**Figure 205**).

5. Install the shaft from the left-hand side of the crankcase (**Figure 192**).

6. Gently tap on the left-hand end of the starter gear shaft with a rubber or plastic mallet (**Figure 206**) to seat it in the crankcase correctly.

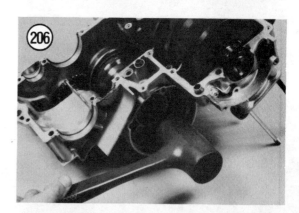

7. Use a suitable size piece of pipe (**Figure 207**) and tap the oil seal into place in the crankcase. Make sure the oil seal seats evenly around the housing bore.

> *CAUTION*
> *Always install a new O-ring seal on the oil spray nozzle. If an old O-ring is used, the oil volume sprayed will be insufficient, leading to engine damage.*

8. Install a *new* O-ring seal on the oil spray nozzle and install it in the crankcase (**Figure 208**). Make sure the end of the nozzle faces toward the bolt hole as shown in **Figure 209**.

9. Install the bearing cover plate (A, **Figure 210**) and the Torx screws (B, **Figure 210**). Tighten the screws securely.

10. Install the transmission locating C-rings (**Figure 165**). Install both transmission assemblies in the upper crankcase half.

11. Assemble the crankcase as described in this chapter.

12. Install the primary drive gear as described in this chapter.

BREAK-IN

Following cylinder servicing (boring, honing, new rings, etc.) and major lower end work, the engine should be broken in just as though it were new. The performance and service life of the engine depends greatly on a careful and sensible break-in.

For the first 800 km (500 miles), no more than one-third throttle should be used and speed should be varied as much as possible within the one-third throttle limit. Prolonged, steady running at one speed, no matter how moderate, is to be avoided, as is hard acceleration.

Following the 800 km (500 mile) service, increasingly more throttle can be used but full throttle should not be used until the motorcycle has covered at least 1,600 km (1,000 miles) and then it should be limited to short bursts until 2,410 km (1,500 miles) have been logged.

The mono-grade oils recommended for break-in and normal use provide a more superior bedding pattern for rings and cylinders than do multi-grade oils. As a result, piston ring and cylinder bore life are greatly increased. During this period, oil consumption will be higher than normal. It is therefore important to check and correct the oil level frequently. At no time, during break-in or later, should the oil level be allowed to drop below the bottom line on the dipstick; if the oil level is low, the oil will become overheated resulting in insufficient lubrication and increased wear.

800 km (500 Mile) Service

It is essential that the oil and filter be changed after the first 800 km (500 miles). In addition, it is a good idea to change the oil and filter at the completion of break-in (about 2,400 km/1,500 miles) to ensure that all of the particles produced during break-in are removed from the lubrication system. The small added expense should be considered a smart investment that will pay off in increased engine life.

Tables 1-3 are located on the following pages.

Table 1 ENGINE SPECIFICATIONS

Item	Specifications	Wear Limit
General		
Engine type	4-stroke, DOHC, inline 4	
Bore and stroke	58.5 × 55.7 mm (2.30 × 2.19 in.)	
Displacement	599 cm^2 (36.5 cu. in.)	
Compression ratio	10.0 to 1	
Lubrication	Wet sump	
Air filtration	Replaceable paper element type	
Cylinders		
Bore	58.505-58.545 mm (2.3033-2.3049 in.)	58.60 mm (2.307 in.)
Out of round	–	0.01 mm (0.0004 in.)
Taper	–	0.05 mm (0.002 in.)
Piston/cylinder clearance	0.025-0.045 mm (0.0010-0.0018 in.)	–
Pistons		
Diameter	58.47-58.51 mm (2.3020-2.3035 in.)	–
Piston rings		
Number per piston		
Compression	2	
Oil control	1	
Ring end gap		
Top and second	0.15-0.30 mm (0.0059-0.0118 in.)	0.7 mm (0.0276 in.)
Oil (side rail)	0.20-0.70 mm (0.0079-0.0276 in.)	–
Ring side clearance		
Top	0.03-0.07 mm (0.0012-0.0028 in.)	0.15 mm (0.0059 in.)
Second	0.02-0.06 mm (0.0008-0.0024 in.)	0.15 mm (0.0059 in.)
Connecting rod		
Oil clearance	0.016-0.040 mm (0.0006-0.0016 in.)	–
Crankshaft		
Runout	–	0.03 mm (0.001 in.)
Main bearing oil clearance	0.022-0.044 mm (0.0008-0.0017 in.)	–
Connecting rod big end side clearance	0.16-0.262 mm (0.006-0.010 in.)	0.5 mm (0.020 in.)
Camshaft		
Runout	–	0.5 mm (0.02 in.)
Oil clearance	0.020-0.054 mm (0.0008-0.0021 in.)	0.160 mm (0.006 in.)
Valves		
Valve stem outer diameter		
Intake	5.975-5.990 mm (0.2352-0.2358 in.)	5.945 mm (0.234 in.)
Exhaust	5.960-5.975 mm (0.2346-0.2352 in.)	5.920 mm (0.233 in.)
Valve guide inner diameter		
Intake	6.000-6.012 mm (0.2362-0.2367 in.)	6.045 mm (0.238 in.)
Exhaust	6.000-6.012 mm (0.2362-0.2367 in.)	6.020 mm (0.237 in.)

(continued)

Table 1 ENGINE SPECIFICATIONS (continued)

Item	Specifications	Wear Limit
Valve guide inner diameter (continued)		
Stem to guide clearance		
Intake	0.010-0.037 mm (0.0004-0.0015 in.)	0.10 mm (0.004 in.)
Exhaust	0.025-0.052 mm (0.0010-0.0020 in.)	0.10 mm (0.004 in.)
Valve seat width		
Intake and exhaust	0.9-1.1 mm (0.035-0.043 in.)	2.0 mm (0.08 in.)
Valve spring free length (intake and exhaust)		
Outer	37.2 mm (1.465 in.)	–
Inner	35.5 mm (1.398 in.)	–
Valve spring tilt (intake and exhaust)		
Inner and outer	–	2.5°/1.5 mm (0.063 in.)
Cylinder head warpage	–	0.03 mm (0.001 in.)
Oil pump		
Inner rotor tip to outer clearance	0.09-0.15 mm (0.0035-0.0059 in.)	–
Outer rotor to body clearance	0.03-0.08 mm (0.0012-0.0031 in.)	–

Table 2 ENGINE TIGHTENING TORQUES

Item	N·m	Ft.-lb.
Engine mounting bolts (Radian models)		
Front upper holding plate-to-engine bolt	42	30
Front upper holding plate-to-frame bolt	32	23
Front lower bolts	42	30
Rear through bolt	90	65
Engine mounting bolts (FZ600 models)		
Front middle through bolt	42	30
Front lower bolt	42	30
Sub-frame bolts		
Upper bolt	26	19
Lower rear	40	29
Rear through bolt	90	65
Camshaft bearing cap bolts	10	7.2
Cylinder head nuts		
Upper nuts (12)	22	16
Lower nuts (4)	10	7.2
Camshaft tensioner		
Mounting bolt and nut	10	7.2
Holding bolt	8	5.8
Holding bolt locknut	9	6.5
Camshaft sprocket bolts	24	18
Cylinder head cover bolts	10	7.2
Cylinder block front nut	20	14
Oil pump mounting bolts	7	5.1
Oil cooler adaptor		
large union bolt (FZ600)	50	36
Oil pickup strainer		
housing bolts	10	7.2
Oil pan bolts	10	7.2
(continued)		

4

Table 2 ENGINE TIGHTENING TORQUES (continued)

Item	N·m	Ft.-lb.
Hy-Vo chain tensioner mounting bolts	10	7.2
Crankcase bolts		
6 mm	12	8.7
8 mm	24	17
Connecting rod cap nuts	25	18
Primary drive gear nut	50	36

Table 3 CAMSHAFT LOBE HEIGHT

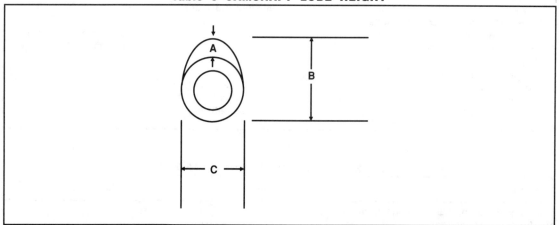

Dimension	Standard	Wear limit
Intake		
A	36.25-36.35 mm (1.427-1.431 in.)	36.2 mm (1.42 in.)
B	28.1-28.2 mm (1.106-1.11 in.)	28.05 mm (1.1 in.)
C	8.3 mm (0.327 in.)	8.1 mm (0.319 in.)
Exhaust		
A	35.75-35.85 mm (1.408-1.411 in.)	35.7 mm (1.40 in.)
B	28.05-28.15 mm (1.104-1.108 in.)	28.05 mm (1.1 in.)
C	7.8 mm (0.307 in.)	7.6 mm (0.299 in.)

CHAPTER FIVE

CLUTCH

This chapter provides complete service procedures for the clutch and clutch release mechanism.

The clutch is a wet multi-plate type which operates immersed in the engine oil. It is mounted on the right-hand end of the transmission main shaft. The inner clutch hub is splined to the main shaft and the outer housing can rotate freely on the main shaft. The outer housing is geared to the crankshaft.

The clutch release mechanism is mounted within the clutch outer cover and is operated by the clutch cable and hand lever mounted on the left-hand handlebar. This type of clutch requires routine adjustment as the cable will stretch with use, refer to Chapter Three.

Table 1 and **Table 2** are located at the end of this chapter.

CLUTCH

Removal/Disassembly

The clutch assembly can be removed with the engine in the frame. Refer to **Figure 1** for this procedure.

1A. On FZ600 models, perform the following:

    a. Remove the lower fairing on each side as described under *Lower Fairing Removal/In-*

stallation in Chapter Twelve. Remove the lower fairing mounting brackets.

    b. Remove the exhaust system as described under *Exhaust System Removal/Installation (FZ600 Models)* in Chapter Seven.

    c. Place wood block(s) under the engine to support the bike securely with the rear wheel off the ground.

1B. On Radian models, place wood block(s) under the engine or frame to support the bike securely with the rear wheel off the ground.

2. On Radian models, remove the rear brake lever (**Figure 2**) and right-hand foot peg assembly (**Figure 3**).

3. Drain the engine oil as described under *Engine Oil and Filter Change* in Chapter Three.

4. Slide back the rubber boot.

5. Shift the transmission into gear.

6. Loosen the clutch cable locknut (A, **Figure 4**) and loosen the adjuster (B, **Figure 4**) to allow maximum slack in the clutch cable.

7. Loosen the locknuts on the clutch cable lower adjuster (A, **Figure 5**) and disconnect the cable end from the clutch actuating lever (B, **Figure 5**).

8. Remove the bolts securing the clutch cover (C, **Figure 5**). Remove the clutch cover and gasket. Don't lose the locating dowels.

9. Have an assistant hold the rear brake on.

10. Using a crisscross pattern, loosen the clutch bolts (**Figure 6**).

11. Remove the bolts, washers and springs.

12. Remove the pressure plate. Note the alignment marks on the pressure place and the clutch boss (**Figure 7**).

13. Remove the clutch release bearing, washer and pushrod from inside the pressure plate (**Figure 8**).

14. Remove all friction discs (**Figure 9**) and clutch plates (**Figure 10**). Stack all of the plates and discs in the order in which they were removed.

15. Remove the clutch hub spring and spring seat.

16. Straighten the locking tab on the lockwasher.

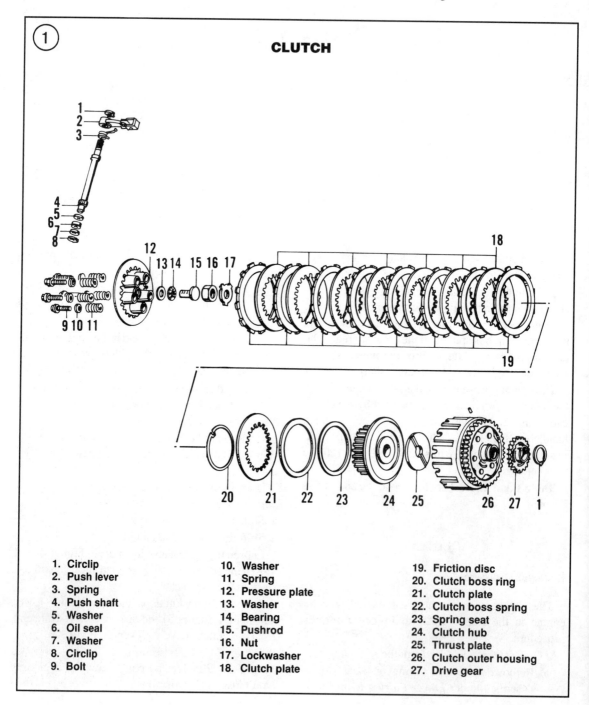

CLUTCH

1. Circlip	10. Washer	19. Friction disc
2. Push lever	11. Spring	20. Clutch boss ring
3. Spring	12. Pressure plate	21. Clutch plate
4. Push shaft	13. Washer	22. Clutch boss spring
5. Washer	14. Bearing	23. Spring seat
6. Oil seal	15. Pushrod	24. Clutch hub
7. Washer	16. Nut	25. Thrust plate
8. Circlip	17. Lockwasher	26. Clutch outer housing
9. Bolt	18. Clutch plate	27. Drive gear

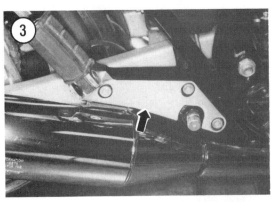

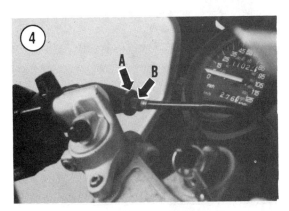

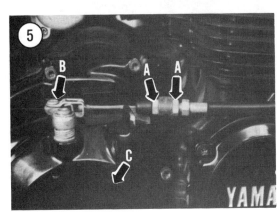

NOTE
The "Grabbit" tool can be obtained by order through Precision Manufacturing Sales Co., Inc., P.O. Box 149, Clearwater, Florida 34617.

CAUTION
Do not clamp the "Grabbit" on too tight as it may damage the grooves in the clutch hub.

17. To keep the clutch hub from turning in the next step, attach a special tool such as the "Grabbit" to it.
18. Loosen and then remove the clutch locknut (**Figure 11**) and lockwasher (A, **Figure 12**). Discard the lockwasher as a new one must be installed.
19. Remove the special tool from the clutch hub.
20. Remove the clutch hub (B, **Figure 12**).
21. Remove the thrust plate.
22. Slide the clutch outer housing off the transmission shaft.
23. Inspect all components as described in this chapter.

Inspection

Refer to **Table 1** for clutch specifications.
1. Clean all clutch parts in petroleum-based solvent such as a commercial solvent or kerosene and thoroughly dry with compressed air.
2. Measure the free length of each clutch spring as shown in **Figure 13**. Compare to the specifications listed in **Table 1**. Replace any springs that have sagged to the service limit or less.
3. Measure the thickness of each friction disc at several places around the disc as shown in **Figure 14**. Compare to the specifications listed in **Table 1**. Replace any disc that is worn to the service limit or less.

4. Measure the thickness of each clutch plate at several places around the plate. Compare to the specifications listed in **Table 1**. Replace any disc that is worn. Yamaha does not provide wear limit specifications for the clutch plates.

5. Check the clutch plates for warpage on a surface plate such as a piece of plate glass (**Figure 15**). Compare to the specifications listed in **Table 1**. Replace any plate that is warped to the service limit or more.

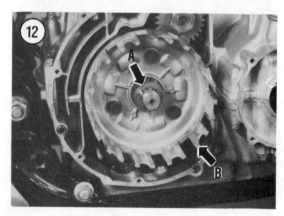

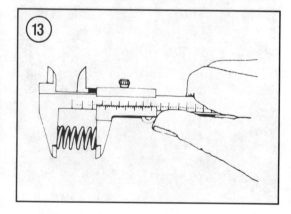

5

NOTE
If any of the friction discs, clutch plates or clutch springs require replacement, you should consider replacing all of

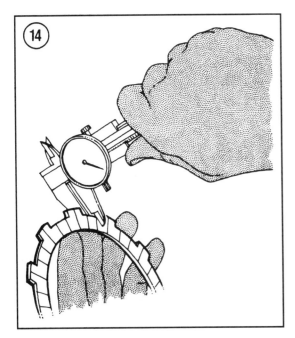

them as a set to retain maximum clutch performance.

6. Inspect the gear teeth on the primary drive gear (A, **Figure 16**) and the starter gear (B, **Figure 16**).

    a. If the starter gear is damaged, remove the snap ring (C, **Figure 16**) and replace the gear.

    b. While the starter gear is off, inspect the gear mating surface (**Figure 17**). If this surface is damaged or if the teeth on the primary driven gear are damaged, the clutch outer housing must be replaced.

    c. When installing the starter gear, install the dowel pin (**Figure 18**) into the clutch outer housing and then install the starter gear, aligning the slot in the gear with the dowel pin (**Figure 19**). Secure the gear with a new snap ring and make sure it is properly seated in the groove.

7. Inspect the gear teeth on the primary drive gear (A, **Figure 20**) and the oil pump gear (B, **Figure 20**). Replace if damaged.

8. Inspect the clutch outer housing (**Figure 21**) and clutch hub (**Figure 22**) for cracks, nicks or galling

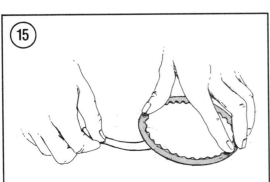

where they come in contact with the friction disc tabs. They must be smooth for chatter-free operation. If any severe damage is evident, the components must be replaced.

9. Inspect the inner splines of the clutch hub for damage. Remove any small nicks with an oilstone. If damage is severe, the clutch hub must be replaced.

10. Inspect the studs in the clutch hub. If they show signs of wear or galling, the clutch hub should be replaced.

11. Check the clutch release bearing (**Figure 23**). Make sure it rotates smoothly with no signs of wear or damage. Replace if necessary.

12. Inspect the pushrod (**Figure 24**) in the clutch cover. If damaged, remove the circlip (**Figure 25**) on the inside of the cover and pull the rod out. Reverse these steps to install.

Assembly/Installation

Refer to **Figure 1** for this procedure.

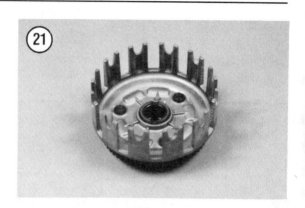

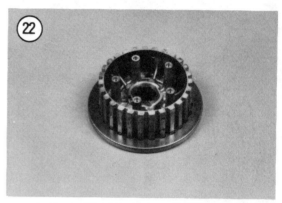

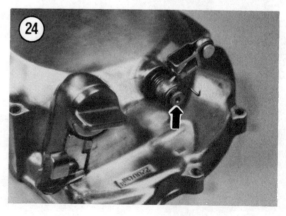

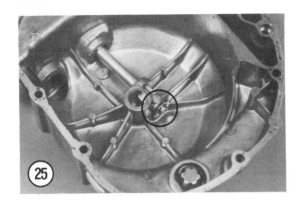

NOTE
When pushing the clutch housing on, slightly rotate it back and forth until all three gears mesh properly, then push in on it until it bottoms out.

1. Install the clutch outer housing assembly onto the transmission shaft. Make sure it meshes properly with both the primary drive gear (A, **Figure 20**) and the oil pump gear (B, **Figure 20**).
2. Install the thrust plate (**Figure 12**).
3. Install the clutch hub (**Figure 26**).
4. Install a *new* lockwasher (**Figure 27**). Make sure the locking tabs on the lockwasher engage the slots in the pressure plate.
5. Install the locknut (**Figure 28**).
6. Use the same special tool set-up (**Figure 29**) in Step 17 of *Removal/Disassembly* to hold the clutch hub for the following step.
7. Tighten the clutch locknut to the torque specification listed in **Table 2**.
8. Remove the special tool from the clutch hub.
9. Bend up one of the tabs of the lockwasher against one side of the clutch nut.

NOTE
If new friction discs and clutch plates are being installed, apply new engine oil to all surfaces to avoid having the clutch lock up when used for the first time.

10. Onto the clutch hub, install first a friction disc (**Figure 30**) then a clutch plate (**Figure 31**).

NOTE
*Each clutch plate has a raised outer tab (**Figure 32**). When installing the clutch plates, these tabs should be spaced 72°*

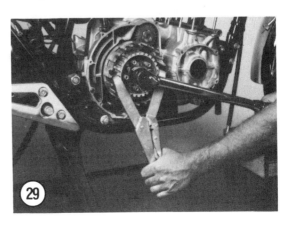

*apart from each other as shown in **Figure 33***.

11. Continue to install the friction discs and clutch plates, alternating them until all are installed. The last item installed is a friction disc (**Figure 31**).

12. Onto the release bearing pushrod (A, **Figure 34**), install the bearing (B, **Figure 34**) and the plate washer (C, **Figure 34**).

13. Install the release bearing pushrod assembly into the backside of the pressure plate (**Figure 35**).

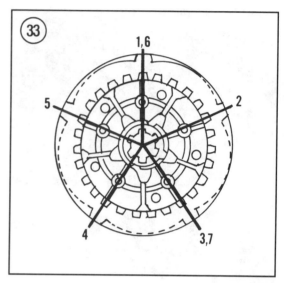

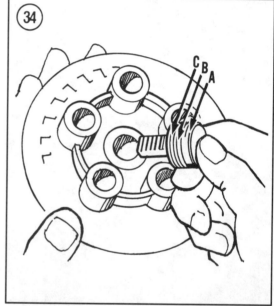

14. Align the dot on the pressure plate with the dot on the clutch hub and install the pressure plate (**Figure 36**).

15. Install the clutch springs, washers and bolts (**Figure 37**).

16. Make sure the transmission is still in gear. Have an assistant hold the rear brake on.

17. Using a crisscross pattern, tighten the clutch bolts to the torque specification listed in **Table 2**.

18. Turn the release bearing pushrod so the flat portion faces toward the rear of the engine (**Figure 38**).

19. Install a new gasket and make sure the locating dowels are in place.

20. Install the cover as follows:

  a. If the clutch lever is installed in the clutch cover, pull the clutch lever (**Figure 39**) until it is parallel to the clutch cover gasket surface. Hold it in this position and install the cover onto the crankcase.

  b. If the clutch lever has been removed from the clutch cover, install the cover without the lever. Then install the clutch lever and spring into the clutch lever shaft (A, **Figure 40**), aligning the punch mark on the lever with the mark on the clutch cover. Install the circlip.

21. Install the clutch cover bolts and tighten to the torque specification listed in **Table 2**.

22. Reconnect the clutch cable (B, **Figure 40**) to the clutch release lever.

23. On Radian models, install the brake lever and the right-hand footpeg assembly.

24. Refill the engine oil as described in Chapter Three.

25. Adjust the clutch as described in Chapter Three.

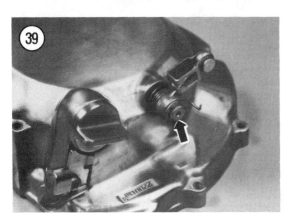

26. On FZ600 models, perform the following:

   a. Install the exhaust system as described in Chapter Seven.

   b. Install the lower fairing on each side as described in Chapter Twelve.

CLUTCH CABLE REPLACEMENT

In time, the clutch cable will stretch to the point where it is no longer useful and will have to be replaced.

1A. On FZ600 models, perform the following:

   a. Remove the lower fairing on each side as described under *Lower Fairing Removal/Installation* in Chapter Twelve. Remove the lower fairing mounting brackets.

   b. Remove the exhaust system as described under *Exhaust System Removal/Installation (FZ600 Models)* in Chapter Seven.

   c. Place wood block(s) under the engine to support the bike securely with the rear wheel off the ground.

1B. On Radian models, place wood block(s) under the engine or frame to support the bike securely with the rear wheel off the ground.

2. Slide back the rubber boot.

3. Loosen the clutch cable locknut (A, **Figure 41**) and loosen the adjuster (B, **Figure 41**) to allow maximum slack in the clutch cable.

4. Loosen the locknuts (C, **Figure 40**) on the clutch cable lower adjuster and disconnect the cable end from the clutch actuating lever (B, **Figure 40**).

NOTE
Prior to removing the cable, make a drawing of the cable routing through the frame. It is very easy to forget how it was, once it has been removed. Replace the cable exactly as it was, avoiding any sharp turns.

5. Pull the clutch cable out from behind the steering head area and out of the retaining loop and clips on the frame.

6. Remove the cable and replace it with a new cable.

7. Install by reversing these removal steps while noting the following.

8. Adjust the clutch as described in Chapter Three.

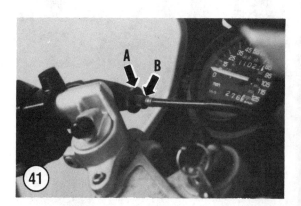

Table 1 CLUTCH SPECIFICATIONS

Item	Standard	Wear limit
Friction disc thickness	2.9-3.10 mm (0.114-0.122 in.)	2.7 mm (0.106 in.)
Clutch plate thickness	1.5-1.7 mm (0.059-0.067 in.)	–
Clutch plate warpage	–	0.15 mm (0.006 in.)
Clutch spring height	42.8 mm (1.690 in.)	41.8 mm (1.646 in.)

Table 2 CLUTCH TIGHTENING TORQUES

Item	N·m	ft.-lb.
Clutch locknut	70	50
Clutch spring bolts	8	5.8
Right-hand crankcase cover bolts	10	7.2

CHAPTER SIX

TRANSMISSION AND GEARSHIFT MECHANISMS

This chapter provides complete service procedures for the transmission and the external and the internal shift mechanism.

Yamaha does not provide any service specifications for any of the components covered in this chapter.

EXTERNAL GEARSHIFT MECHANISM

The gearshift mechanism is located on the same side of the crankcase as the clutch assembly. To remove the internal shift mechanism (shift drum and shift forks), it is necessary to remove the engine and split the crankcase. This procedure is covered in this chapter.

> *CAUTION*
> *The gearshift lever is subject to a lot of abuse. If the bike has been in a hard spill, the gearshift lever may have been hit and the gearshift shaft bent. It is very hard to straighten the shaft without subjecting the crankcase halves to abnormal stress where the shaft enters the crankcase. If the shaft is bent enough to prevent it from being withdrawn from the crankcase, there is little recourse but to cut the shaft off with a hacksaw very close to the crankcase. It is much cheaper in the long run to replace the shaft than risk damaging a very expensive crankcase assembly.*

Removal

Refer to **Figure 1** for this procedure.

1. Remove the clutch assembly as described under *Clutch Removal/Disassembly* in Chapter Five.

2A. On Radian models, remove the shift lever (A, **Figure 2**) from the shift shaft, then remove the left-hand crankcase cover (B, **Figure 2**).

2B. On FZ600 models, remove the shift lever arm (A, **Figure 3**) from the shift shaft, then remove the left-hand crankcase cover (B, **Figure 3**).

3. Slide the collar (**Figure 4**) and washer (**Figure 5**) off of the shift shaft.

4. Disengage the shift shaft arm (**Figure 6**) and the shift stopper lever (**Figure 7**) from the shift drum.

5. Slowly withdraw the shift shaft assembly (**Figure 8**) from the crankcase. See preceding CAUTION regarding a bent shaft.

Inspection

1. Inspect the shift shaft assembly for bending, wear or other damage; replace if necessary.

2. Inspect the return spring on the shift shaft assembly. If broken or weak, remove the circlip (**Figure 9**) and disassemble the shift shaft arm. Replace the parts that are worn or damaged.

3. If the shift stopper lever was replaced, assemble the new lever and spring as shown in **Figure 10**.

4. Assemble the shift shaft assembly as shown in (**Figure 1**).

Installation

1. Apply clean engine oil to the shift shaft and install it into the crankcase (**Figure 8**).

2. Pull the shift stopper lever down to engage the shift drum (**Figure 7**).

3. Pull the shift shaft lever arm down (**Figure 6**) and engage the shift drum.

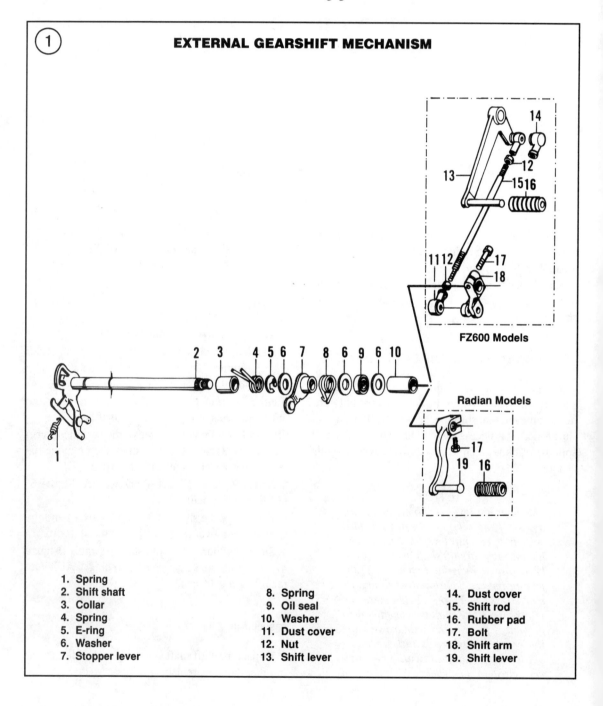

① EXTERNAL GEARSHIFT MECHANISM

FZ600 Models

Radian Models

1. Spring
2. Shift shaft
3. Collar
4. Spring
5. E-ring
6. Washer
7. Stopper lever
8. Spring
9. Oil seal
10. Washer
11. Dust cover
12. Nut
13. Shift lever
14. Dust cover
15. Shift rod
16. Rubber pad
17. Bolt
18. Shift arm
19. Shift lever

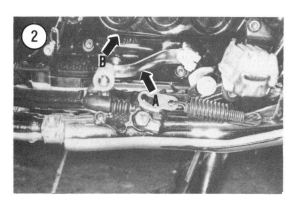

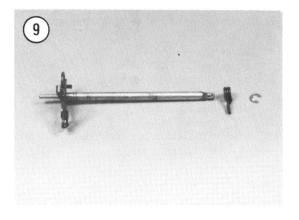

4. Push the shift shaft in until it bottoms out. After the shift lever arm and the shift stopper lever are engaged with the shift drum, check to make sure that the return spring is engaged properly with the pin in the crankcase (**Figure 11**).

5. Install the shift lever onto the left-hand end of the shift shaft and shift the transmission through all 6 gears to make sure it operates smoothly and correctly. Remove the shift lever.

6. Slide the washer (**Figure 5**) and collar (**Figure 4**) onto the shift shaft.

7. Install the left-hand crankcase cover and the shift lever.

8. Install the clutch assembly as described in Chapter Five.

TRANSMISSION

To gain access to the transmission and internal shift mechanism, it is necessary to remove the engine and split the crankcase as described in Chapter Four.

Preliminary Inspection

After the transmission shaft assemblies have been removed from the crankcase, clean and inspect the assemblies prior to disassembling them. Place the assembled shaft into a large can or plastic bucket and thoroughly clean with a petroleum based solvent such as kerosene and a stiff brush. Dry with compressed air or let it sit on rags to drip dry. Repeat for the other shaft assembly.

1. After they have been cleaned, visually inspect the components of the assemblies for excessive wear. Any burrs, pitting or roughness on the teeth of a gear will cause wear on the mating gear. Minor roughness can be cleaned up with an oilstone but there's little point in attempting to remove deep scars.

NOTE
Defective gears should be replaced. It's a good idea to replace the mating gear on the other shaft even though it may not show as much wear or damage.

2. Carefully check the engagement dogs. If any are chipped, worn, rounded or missing, the affected gear must be replaced.

3. Rotate the transmission bearings on the transmission shafts by hand. Check for roughness, noise and

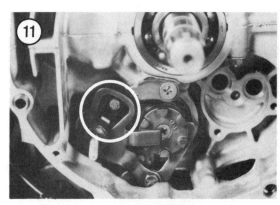

radial play. Any bearing that is suspect should be replaced as described in this chapter.

4. If the transmission shafts are satisfactory and are not going to be disassembled, apply assembly oil or engine oil to all components and reinstall them in the crankcase as described in this chapter.

NOTE
If disassembling a used, well run-in (high mileage) transmission for the first time by yourself, pay particular atten-

tion to any additional shims that may have been added by a previous owner. These may have been added to take up the tolerance of worn components and must be reinstalled in the same position since the shims have developed a wear pattern. If new parts are going to be installed, these shims may be eliminated. This is something you will have to determine upon reassembly.

Removal/Installation

1. Remove the engine and split the crankcase as described under *Crankcase Disassembly* in Chapter Four.

2. Remove the countershaft assembly (**Figure 12**) and mainshaft assembly (**Figure 13**).

NOTE
*After the transmission shaft assemblies are removed, the bearing circlips will usually stay in the crankcase (**Figure 14**). These circlips should be removed and placed in a plastic bag to avoid misplacing them.*

3. Inspect the transmission shaft assemblies as described under *Preliminary Inspection* in this chapter.

NOTE
Prior to installation, coat all bearing surfaces with assembly oil.

4. Install the bearing circlips (**Figure 14**) into the upper crankcase. Make sure they are properly seated in their respective grooves.

5. Move the shift forks into their UP positions so they will mesh properly with the transmission gear grooves.

6. Install the mainshaft and countershaft assemblies into the upper crankcase and check the following:

   a. Make sure the bearings are properly indexed into the circlips in the crankcase.

   b. Make sure the shift forks fit correctly into the grooves in the sliding gears (**Figure 15**).

   c. Check that the countershaft oil seal is seated correctly in the upper crankcase (**Figure 16**).

7. Reassemble the crankcase as described under *Crankcase Assembly* and install the engine as described in Chapter Four.

Mainshaft
Disassembly/Inspection

Refer to **Figure 17** for this procedure.

NOTE
A helpful "tool" that should be used for transmission disassembly is a large egg flat (the type that restaurants get their eggs in). As you remove a part from the shaft, set it in one of the depressions in the same position from which it was removed. This is an easy way to remember the correct relationship of all parts.

1. If not cleaned in the *Preliminary Inspection* sequence, place the assembled shaft into a large can or plastic bucket and thoroughly clean with solvent and a stiff brush. Dry with compressed air or let it sit on rags to dry.

2. If necessary, press off the bearing (A, **Figure 18**).

3. Remove the oil nozzle and the needle bearing (B, **Figure 18**).

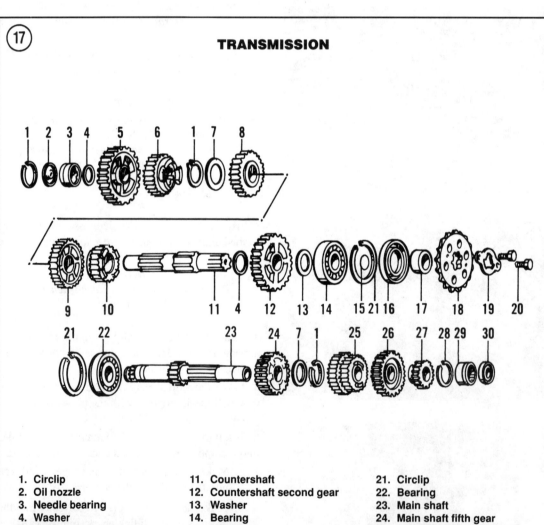

TRANSMISSION

1. Circlip	11. Countershaft	21. Circlip
2. Oil nozzle	12. Countershaft second gear	22. Bearing
3. Needle bearing	13. Washer	23. Main shaft
4. Washer	14. Bearing	24. Main shaft fifth gear
5. Countershaft first gear	15. O-ring	25. Main shaft third/forth gear
6. Countershaft fifth gear	16. Oil seal	26. Main shaft sixth gear
7. Washer	17. Collar	27. Main shaft second gear
8. Countershaft fourth gear	18. Drive sprocket	28. Circlip
9. Countershaft third gear	19. Locking plate	29. Needle bearing
10. Countershaft sixth gear	20. Bolt	30. Oil nozzle

4. Remove the circlip, then slide off the second gear, sixth gear and the third/fourth combination gear.

5. Remove the circlip and washer.

6. Slide off the fifth gear.

7. Check each gear for excessive wear, burrs, pitting, or chipped or missing teeth. Make sure the lugs on the gears are in good condition.

> *NOTE*
> *Defective gears should be replaced. It is a good idea to replace the mating gear on the countershaft even though it may not show as much wear or damage.*

8. Make sure that all gears slide smoothly on the mainshaft splines.

> *NOTE*
> *It is recommended that all circlips be replaced every time the transmission is disassembled to ensure proper gear alignment. Do not expand a circlip more than necessary to slide it over the shaft.*

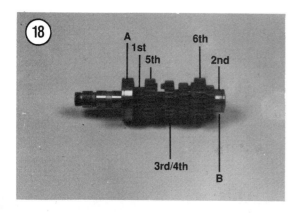

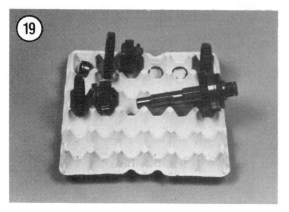

9. Inspect the splines and circlip grooves of the mainshaft. If any are damaged, the shaft must be replaced.

10. Check the needle bearing. Make sure the needles rotate smoothly with no signs of wear or damage. Replace as necessary.

Mainshaft Assembly

1. Apply a light coat of clean engine oil to all sliding surfaces prior to installing any parts.

2. Slide on the fifth gear and slide on the washer.

3. Install the circlip.

4. Position the third/fourth combination gear with the larger diameter fourth gear going on first and slide the gear onto the shaft.

5. Slide on the sixth gear and the second gear.

6. Install the circlip and slide on the needle bearing.

7. If removed, install the ball bearing onto the other end of the shaft.

8. Make sure each gear engages properly to the adjoining gear where applicable.

9. Refer to **Figure 18** for correct location of all gears.

Countershaft
Disassembly/Inspection

Refer to **Figure 17** for this procedure.

> *NOTE*
> *Use the same large egg flat (used on the mainshaft disassembly) during the mainshaft disassembly (**Figure 19**). This is an easy way to remember the correct relationship of all parts.*

1. If not cleaned in the *Preliminary Inspection* sequence, place the assembled shaft into a large can or plastic bucket and thoroughly clean with solvent and a stiff brush. Dry with compressed air or let it sit on rags to dry.

2. Remove the circlip and the oil nozzle then slide off the needle bearing and washer.

3. Slide off the first gear and the fifth gear.

4. Remove the circlip and slide off the washer.

5. Slide off the fourth gear, third gear and the sixth gear.

6. From the other end of the shaft, remove the collar, O-ring, oil seal, ball bearing, washer, second gear and washer.

7. Check each gear for excessive wear, burrs, pitting or chipped or missing teeth. Make sure the lugs on the gears are in good condition.

> *NOTE*
> *Defective gears should be replaced. It is a good idea to replace the mating gear on the mainshaft even though it may not show as much wear or damage.*

> *NOTE*
> *The first gear is part of the countershaft. If the gear is defective, the countershaft must be replaced.*

8. Make sure that all gears slide smoothly on the countershaft splines.

> *NOTE*
> *It is recommended that all circlips be replaced every time the transmission is disassembled to ensure proper gear alignment. Do not expand a circlip more than necessary to slide it over the shaft.*

9. Inspect the splines and circlip grooves of the countershaft. If any are damaged, the shaft must be replaced.
10. Check the needle bearing. Make sure the needles rotate smoothly with no signs of wear or damage. Replace as necessary.

Countershaft Assembly

1. Apply a light coat of clean engine oil to all sliding surfaces prior to installing any parts.
2. Onto the sprocket end of the countershaft, install the following components while referring to **Figure 20**:

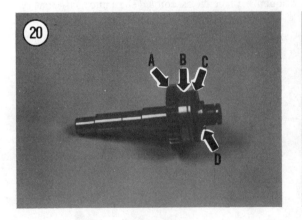

a. The washer and second gear (A).

b. The washer and the ball bearing (B).

c. The oil seal and O-ring (C)

d. The collar (D).

3. Position the sixth gear with the shift fork groove going on last and slide it onto the shaft (**Figure 21**).

4. Slide on the third gear (**Figure 22**).

5. Slide on the fourth gear (**Figure 23**).

6. Slide on the washer and install the circlip.

7. Slide on the fifth gear (**Figure 24**).

8. Slide on the first gear (**Figure 25**).

9. Slide on the washer, needle bearing and the oil nozzle.

10. Install the circlip.

11. Refer to **Figure 26** for correct location of all gears.

12. Make sure each gear engages properly to the adjoining gear where applicable.

INTERNAL GEARSHIFT MECHANISM

Refer to **Figure 27** for this procedure.

25

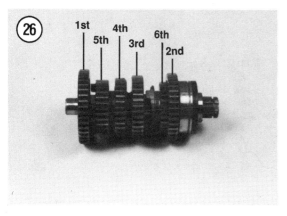

26

1st 4th 6th
5th 3rd 2nd

Removal

1. Remove the engine and split the crankcase as described under *Crankcase Disassembly* in Chapter Four.

2. Remove the transmission assemblies as described in this chapter.

3. Bend down the lockwasher tab (A, **Figure 28**) and remove the stopper bolt.

4. Remove the screw (B, **Figure 28**) securing the shift fork shaft stopper and remove the stopper.

5. Remove the screw securing the bearing cover plate and remove the cover plate.

6. Withdraw the shift fork shaft (**Figure 29**) and remove all 3 shift forks.

7. Carefully withdraw the gearshift drum and bearing assembly (**Figure 30**) from the crankcase.

8. Thoroughly clean all parts in solvent and dry with compressed air.

Inspection

1. Inspect each shift fork for signs of wear or cracking (**Figure 31**). Check for bending and make sure each fork slides smoothly on the shaft. Replace any worn or damaged forks.

2. Check for any arc-shaped wear or burned marks on the shift forks. This indicates that the shift fork has come in contact with the gear. The fork fingers have become excessively worn and the fork must be replaced.

3. Check the grooves in the shift drum (**Figure 32**) for wear or roughness. If any of the groove profiles have excessive wear or damage, replace the shift drum.

4. Check the cam pin followers (**Figure 33**) on each shift fork that rides in the shift drum for wear or damage. Replace the shift fork(s) as necessary.

5. Make sure the shift forks slide smoothly on the shift fork shaft (**Figure 34**). Replace if necessary.

6. Check the neutral switch contact plunger and spring for wear or damage. If the spring has sagged, replace it.

7. Check the shift drum bearing. Make sure it operates smoothly with no signs of wear or damage, replace if necessary.

8. Roll the shift fork shaft on a flat surface such as a piece of plate glass and check for any bends. If the shaft is bent, it must be replaced.

6

Installation

1. Apply a light coat of oil to the shift fork shafts and the inside bores of the shift forks prior to installation.

2. Apply oil to the gearshift drum bearing and install the gearshift drum (**Figure 30**) into the crankcase.

NOTE
After installing the shift drum, make sure it rotates smoothly with no binding.

3. Install the shift fork shaft through all 3 shift forks.

4. Install the bearing cover plate and screw. Apply a small amount of Loctite Threadlocker to the screw threads prior to installation. Tighten the screw to 10 N•m (7.2 ft.-lb).

5. Install the shift fork shaft stopper and the screw (B, **Figure 28**). Apply a small amount of Loctite Threadlocker to the screw threads prior to installation. Tighten the screw to 10 N•m (7.2 ft.-lb).

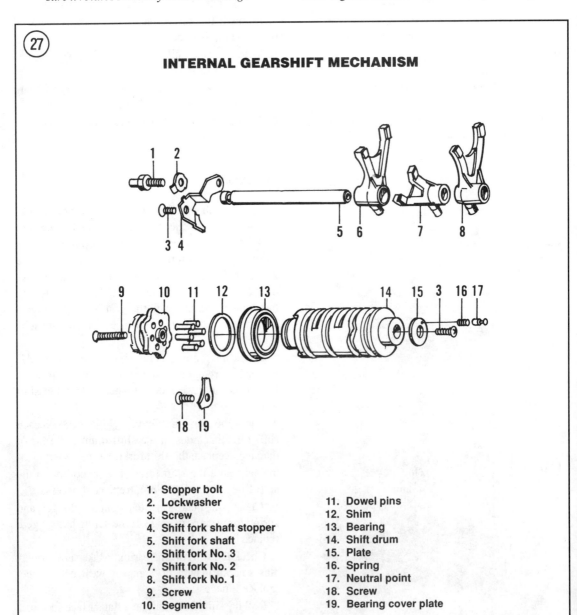

(27)

INTERNAL GEARSHIFT MECHANISM

1. Stopper bolt
2. Lockwasher
3. Screw
4. Shift fork shaft stopper
5. Shift fork shaft
6. Shift fork No. 3
7. Shift fork No. 2
8. Shift fork No. 1
9. Screw
10. Segment
11. Dowel pins
12. Shim
13. Bearing
14. Shift drum
15. Plate
16. Spring
17. Neutral point
18. Screw
19. Bearing cover plate

6. Install the stopper bolt. Apply a small amount of Loctite Threadlocker to the bolt threads prior to installation. Tighten the bolt to 22 N•m (16 ft.-lb).

7. Bend down the lockwasher tab (A, **Figure 28**) against one of the flats on the stopper bolt.

8. Install the transmission assemblies as described in this chapter.

9. Assemble the crankcase and install the engine as described under *Crankcase Disassembly* in Chapter Four.

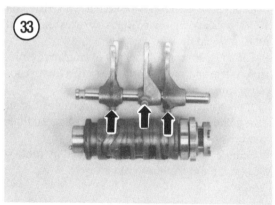

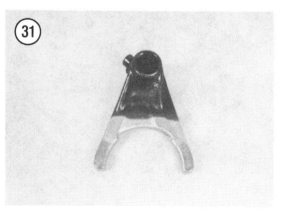

CHAPTER SEVEN

FUEL, EMISSION CONTROL AND EXHAUST SYSTEMS

The fuel system consists of the fuel tank, the shutoff valve, 4 carburetors and an air filter. The exhaust system consists of 4 exhaust pipes, a crossover pipe and 2 mufflers on Radian models or on FZ600 models, a 4-into-2-into-1 exhaust pipe and muffler assembly.

The emission controls consist of crankcase emission system and, on California models, a fuel evaporative emission control system.

This chapter includes service procedures for all parts of the fuel system and exhaust system. Air filter service is covered in Chapter Three.

Carburetor specifications are covered in **Table 1** located at the end of this chapter.

> *NOTE*
> *Where differences occur relating to the United Kingdom (UK) models they are identified. If there is no (UK) designation relating to a procedure, photo or illustration, it is identical to the United States (U.S.) models.*

CARBURETOR OPERATION

For proper operation, a gasoline engine must be supplied with fuel and air mixed in proper proportions by weight. A mixture in which there is an excess of fuel is said to be rich. A lean mixture is one which contains insufficient fuel. A properly adjusted carburetor supplies the proper mixture to the engine under all operating conditions.

Each carburetor consists of several major systems. A float and float valve mechanism maintain a constant fuel level in the float bowls. The pilot system supplies fuel at low speeds. The main fuel system supplies fuel at medium and high speeds. A starter (choke) system supplies the very rich mixture needed to start a cold engine.

CARBURETOR SERVICE

Major carburetor service (removal and cleaning) should be performed at the intervals indicated in **Table 2** in Chapter Three or when poor engine

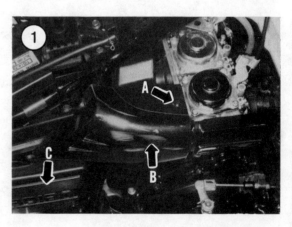

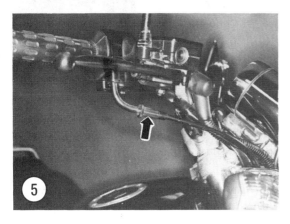

performance, hesitation and little or no response to mixture adjustment is observed. Alterations in jet size, throttle slide cutaway, and changes in jet needle position, etc., should be attempted only if you're experienced in this type of "tuning" work; a bad guess could result in costly engine damage or, at least, poor performance. If, after servicing the carburetor and making the adjustments described in this chapter, the bike does not perform correctly (and assuming that other factors affecting performance are correct, such as ignition component condition, etc.), the bike should be checked by a dealer or a qualified performance tuning specialist.

CARBURETOR ASSEMBLY

Removal/Installation
(Radian Models)

Remove all 4 carburetors as an assembled unit.

1. Remove the seat as described under *Seat Removal/Installation* in Chapter Twelve.

2. Disconnect the battery negative lead. See Chapter Three.

3. Remove the screws (A, **Figure 1**) securing the carburetor cover on each side and remove both covers (B, **Figure 1**).

4. Remove the fuel tank as described in this chapter.

5. Remove both frame side covers (C, **Figure 1**).

6. Remove the battery as described under *Battery Removal and Installation* in Chapter Three.

7. Loosen the screws on the 4 clamping bands on the front intake tubes (A, **Figure 2**) and slide the clamping bands away from the carburetors.

8. Loosen the screws on the 4 clamping bands on the rear intake tubes (B, **Figure 2**) and slide the clamping bands away from the carburetors.

9. Remove the tool kit and remove the screw located in the tool kit tray (**Figure 3**).

10. Remove the bolts securing the top of the air filter case (**Figure 4**) to the frame.

11. Loosen the locknut and turn the throttle cable adjuster (**Figure 5**) at the throttle lever to allow slack in the cable.

12. Loosen the choke cable clamp screw (A, **Figure 6**) and remove the cable end from the choke lever on the No. 4 carburetor.

13. Pull the air filter air case and battery case toward the rear and disengage it from all 4 carburetors.

7

14. Pull the carburetor assembly toward the rear and free the assembly from the intake tubes on the cylinder head.

15. Partially pull the carburetor assembly toward the right-hand side.

16. Pull the throttle cable from its holder (**Figure 7**) on the carburetor assembly.

17. At the carburetor, hold the lever up with one hand and disengage the throttle cable end (B, **Figure 6**). Slip the cable out through the carburetor bracket.

18. Carefully remove the carburetor from the engine and frame and take it to a workbench for disassembly and cleaning.

> *NOTE*
> *Drain most of the gasoline from the carburetor assembly and place the assembly in a clean heavy-duty plastic bag to keep it clean until it is worked on or reinstalled.*

19. While the carburetor assembly is removed, examine the intake manifolds on the cylinder head and the rubber carburetor boots on the air filter box for any cracks or damage that would allow unfiltered air to enter the engine. Replace any damaged parts.

20. Place lint-free cloths into the 4 intake tubes in the cylinder head to prevent the entry of foreign matter.

21. Install by reversing these removal steps while noting the following:

    a. Make sure the carburetors are fully seated forward in the rubber holders in the cylinder head. You should feel a solid "bottoming out" when they are correctly seated.

    b. Make sure the screws on the clamping bands are tight to avoid a vacuum loss and possible valve damage due to a lean fuel mixture.

    c. Adjust the throttle cable as described under *Throttle Cable Adjustment* in Chapter Three.

Removal/Installation (FZ600 Models)

Remove all 4 carburetors as an assembled unit.

1. Remove the ride and passenger seats as described under *Seat Removal/Installation* in Chapter Twelve.

2. Remove the lower fairing on each side as described under *Lower Fairing Removal/Installation* in Chapter Twelve. Remove the lower fairing stays.

3. Remove the exhaust system as described under *Exhaust System Removal/Installation (FZ600 Models)* in this chapter.

4. Place wood block(s) under the engine to support the bike securely.

5. Disconnect the battery negative lead. See Chapter Three.

6. Remove the fuel tank as described in this chapter.

7. Remove both frame side covers as described under *Side Cover Removal/Installation* in Chapter Twelve.

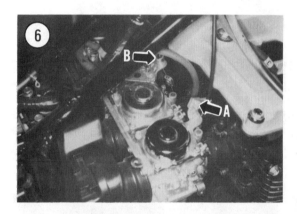

8. Remove the battery as described under *Battery Removal and Installation* in Chapter Three.

9. Remove the bolts securing the battery case and remove the case from the frame.

10. Remove the bolts securing the air filter case to the frame.

11. Loosen the screws on the 4 clamping bands on the front intake tubes (**Figure 8**) and slide the clamping bands away from the carburetors.

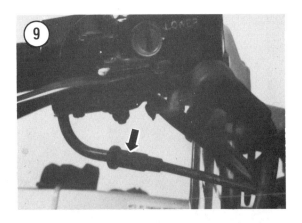

12. Loosen the screws on the 4 clamping bands on the rear intake tubes and slide the clamping bands away from the carburetors.

13. Loosen the locknut and turn the throttle cable adjuster at the throttle lever (**Figure 9**) to allow slack in the cable.

14. Pull the air filter air case and battery case toward the rear and disengage it from all 4 carburetors.

15. Pull the carburetor assembly toward the rear and free the assembly from the intake tubes on the cylinder head.

16. Pull the throttle cable from its holder (**Figure 10**) on the carburetor assembly.

17. At the carburetor, hold the lever up with one hand and disengage the throttle cable end. Slip the cable out through the carburetor bracket.

18. Remove the upper fairing mounting brackets on each side (**Figure 11**).

19. Carefully remove the carburetor from the engine and frame and take it to a workbench for disassembly and cleaning.

7

> *NOTE*
> *Drain most of the gasoline from the carburetor assembly and place the assembly in a clean heavy-duty plastic bag to keep it clean until it is worked on or reinstalled.*

20. While the carburetor assembly is removed, examine the intake manifolds on the cylinder head and the rubber carburetor boots on the air filter box for any cracks or damage that would allow unfiltered air to enter the engine. Replace any damaged parts.

21. Place lint-free cloths into the 4 intake tubes in the cylinder head to prevent the entry of foreign matter.

22. Install by reversing these removal steps while noting the following:

    a. Make sure the carburetors are fully seated forward in the rubber holders in the cylinder head. You should feel a solid "bottoming out" when they are correctly seated.

    b. Make sure the screws on the clamping bands are tight to avoid a vacuum loss and possible valve damage due to a lean fuel mixture.

    c. Adjust the throttle cable as described under *Throttle Cable Adjustment* in Chapter Three.

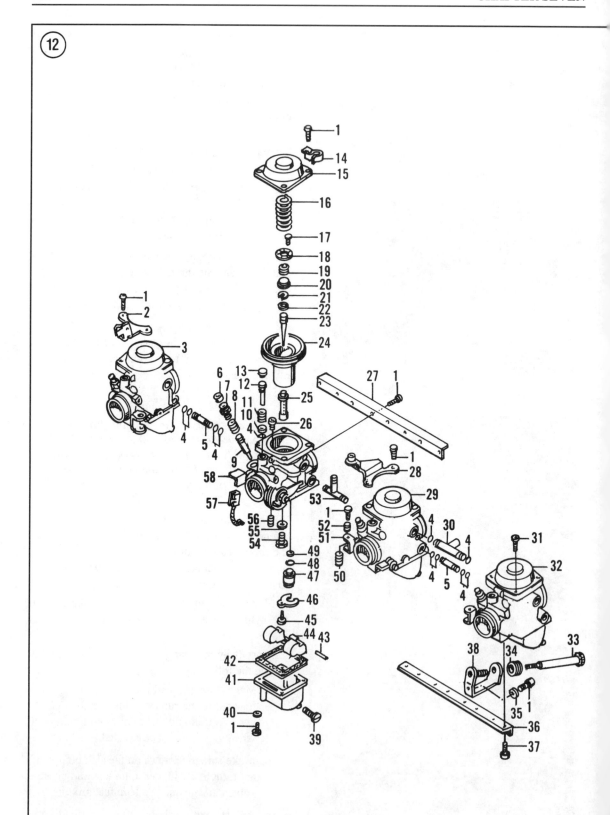

CARBURETOR

1. Screw
2. Cable clamp
3. No. 4 carburetor
4. O-rings
5. Connecting pipe
6. Plunger cap
7. Plunger cap cover
8. Spring
9. Starter plunger
10. O-ring
11. Spring
12. Pilot screw
13. Cap
14. Cable clamp
15. Diaphragm cover
16. Spring
17. Screw
18. Spring seat
19. Spring
20. Washer
21. Clip
22. Ring
23. Jet needle
24. Diaphragm assembly
25. Main jet nozzle
26. Pilot air jet
27. Mounting plate
28. Connecting plate
29. No. 2 carburetor
30. Connecting "T"
31. Screw
32. No. 1 carburetor
33. Throttle adjust screw
34. Spring
35. Washer
36. Mounting plate
37. Screw
38. Bracket
39. Drain screw
40. Washer
41. Float bowl
42. Gasket
43. Pivot pin
44. Float
45. Screw
46. Plate
47. Needle jet
48. O-ring
49. Filter
50. Spring
51. Bracket
52. Spring
53. Connecting "T"
54. Main jet
55. Washer
56. Pilot jet
57. Cable
58. No. 3 carburetor

CARBURETOR

Disassembly/Assembly

Refer to **Figure 12** for this procedure. It is recommended that one carburetor be disassembled at a time. This will prevent a mixup of parts.

All components that require cleaning can be removed from the carburetor body without removing the carburetors from the mounting plates. *Do not separate the carburetors as misalignment will occur on reassembly.*

CAUTION
When cleaning the carburetor assembly, do not turn the pilot screw, as it has been preset at the factory. Changing the basic setting will actually decrease engine performance. Carburetor adjustments which can be performed are described in Chapter Three.

NOTE
The carburetors are numbered in the same sequence as the engine cylinders. The No. 1 carburetor is on the left-hand side and the No. 2, 3, and 4 continue from left to right. Remember, the left-hand side refers to the carburetor assembly as it sits in the bike's frame, not as it sits on your workbench.

1. Loosen the screws on the choke lever shaft (**Figure 13**) and remove the shaft from all four carburetors.

2. Remove the screws securing the diaphragm cover and remove the cover (**Figure 14**).

3. Remove the spring and diaphragm (**Figure 15**).

NOTE
*To remove the diaphragm cover on the No. 2, 3 and 4 carburetors, you must remove the throttle cable and clutch cable supports and the fuel line guide (**Figure 16**). After removing these parts, store them in a separate plastic bag to prevent interchanging parts.*

4. Remove the screws securing the float bowl and remove the float bowl and gasket.

5. Remove the float pivot pin (**Figure 17**).

6. Remove the float and the float valve needle (**Figure 18**).

7. Remove the screw (**Figure 19**) securing the needle valve seat and remove the needle seat (**Figure 20**).

8. Use a small screwdriver and loosen the pilot jet, then remove it (**Figure 21**).

9. Unscrew the main jet (**Figure 22**) and remove the main jet washer (**Figure 23**).

10. Remove the needle jet (**Figure 24**).

11. Remove the pilot air jet (**Figure 25**).

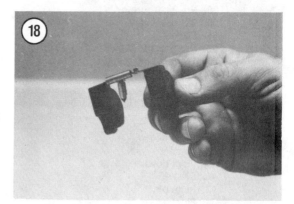

12. Remove the screws securing the diaphragm assembly and disassemble it (**Figure 26**). Replace any parts that appear to be worn or damaged.

NOTE
Further disassembly is neither necessary nor recommended. If throttle or choke shafts or butterflies are damaged,

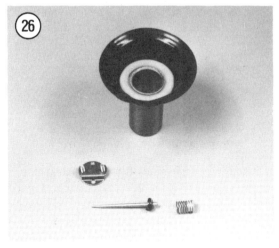

7

take the carburetor body to a dealer for replacement.

13. Clean and inspect all parts as described under *Cleaning and Inspection* in this chapter.

14. Assembly is the reverse of these disassembly steps while noting the following:

    a. After installing the needle jet, make sure the notch in the bottom of the needle jet aligns with the pin in the carburetor (**Figure 27**).

    b. When installing the diaphragm, position the tab on the diaphragm (**Figure 28**) into the recess in the carburetor body.

15. Repeat Steps 2-14 for the remaining three carburetors. Do not interchange parts—keep them separate.

16. After the carburetors have been disassembled, the idle speed should be adjusted and the carburetors synchronized as described in Chapter Three.

Cleaning and Inspection

1. Clean all parts, except rubber or plastic parts, in a good grade of carburetor cleaner. This solution is available at most automotive or motorcycle supply stores in a small, resealable tank with a dip basket for just a few dollars. If it is tightly sealed when not in use, the solution will last for several cleanings. Follow the manufacturer's instructions for correct soak time (usually about 1/2 hour).

2. Remove all parts from the cleaner and blow dry with compressed air. Blow out the jets and needle jet holder with compressed air.

> *CAUTION*
> *If compressed air is not available, allow the parts to air dry or use a clean lint-free cloth. Do **not** use a paper towel to dry carburetor parts, as small paper particles may plug openings in the carburetor body or jets.*

> *CAUTION*
> *Do **not** use a piece of wire to clean them as minor gouges in the jet can alter flow rate and upset the fuel/air mixture.*

3. Remove the drain screw from the float bowl.

4. Inspect the end of the float valve needle (**Figure 29**) for wear or damage. Also check the inside of the needle valve body. If either part is damaged, replace as a set. A damaged needle valve or a particle of dirt

or grit in the needle valve assembly will cause the carburetor to flood and overflow fuel.

5. Inspect all O-ring seals. O-ring seals tend to become hardened after prolonged use and heat and therefore lose their ability to seal properly.

6. Make sure the holes in the needle jet are clear. Clean out if they are plugged in any way. Replace the needle jet if you cannot unplug the holes.

7. Make sure all openings in the carburetor body are clear. Clean out if they are plugged in any way.

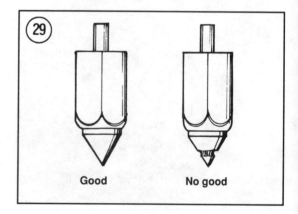

Good   No good

CARBURETOR ADJUSTMENTS

Fuel Level Measurement

The fuel level in the carburetor float bowls is critical to proper performance. The fuel flow rate from the bowl up to the carburetor bore depends not only on the vacuum in the throttle bore and the size of the jets, but also on the fuel level.

The measurement is more useful than a simple float height measurement because the actual fuel level can vary from bike to bike even when their floats are set at the same height. The bike must be *exactly level* for this procedure to be accurate. Place pieces of wood or shims under the centerstand or place a suitable jack under the engine to position the bike so that the carburetor assembly is level from side to side.

Fuel level inspection requires a special Yamaha Fuel Level Gauge (U.S. part No. YM-01312, UK part No. 90890-01312) and the Yamaha Fuel Level Gauge adapter (U.S. part No. YM-01329, UK part No. 90890-01329) that is shown in **Figure 30**. A substitute for the special tool is a piece of clear vinyl tubing with an inside diameter of 6 mm (0.24 in.) and must be long enough to reach from side of the carburetor assembly to the to the other.

> *WARNING*
> *Before starting any procedure involving gasoline, have a class B fire extinguisher rated for gasoline or chemical fires within reach. Do not smoke, allow anyone to smoke or work in an area where there is an open flame. The work area must be well ventilated—preferably outdoors.*

1A. On FZ600 models, remove the lower fairing on each side as described under *Lower Fairing Removal/Installation* in Chapter Twelve.

1B. On Radian models, remove the screws securing the carburetor cover on each side and remove both covers (**Figure 31**).

2. Place the bike in a vertical position on the centerstand or have an assistant hold it in this position.

3. Turn the fuel shutoff valve to the ON or RES position (**Figure 32**).

4. Start with the No. 1 carburetor (left-hand side). Place a small container under the carburetor to catch any fuel that may drip from the float bowl.

> *NOTE*
> ***Figure 33** is shown with the carburetor assembly removed for clarity and shows the fuel level gauge adapter holes for each carburetor. Do not remove the carburetor assembly for this procedure.*

5. Install the adapter into the drain hole in the carburetor float bowl (**Figure 33**). Connect the fuel level gauge tube to the adapter.

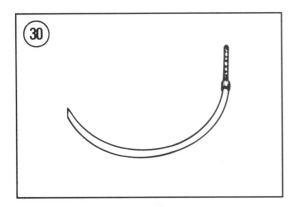

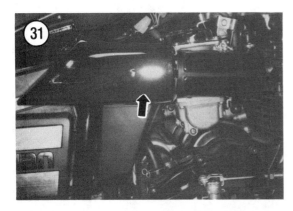

6. Hold the loose end of the tube up above the float bowl level (**Figure 34**) and loosen the drain screw. When the drain screw is loosened, fuel will flow into the gauge tube. Make sure to hold the loose end of the tube up or the fuel will flow out of the tube and onto the engine.

7. Start the engine and let it idle for 2-3 minutes. This is necessary to make sure the fuel level is at normal operating level in the float bowl. Shut the engine off.

8. Hold the loose end of the tube up against the No. 1 carburetor body (**Figure 34**). Mark the fuel level in relation to the top of the float bowl on the tube with a piece of masking tape or with a grease pencil.

9. Insert a golf tee into the open end of the tube so that fuel will not drain out when moving the hose from side to side.

NOTE
Always insert a golf tee in the fuel-filled tube whenever moving the tube from side to side.

10. Move the tube to the other side of the bike and remove the golf tee. Repeat Step 7, holding the tube up against the No. 4 carburetor body (right-hand). The fuel level in the tube should be the same; if not, the bike and the carburetor assembly are not level. Readjust the shims or jack until the carburetor assembly is exactly level—*this is necessary to obtain correct measurements*. Repeat Steps 5-8 until the bike and carburetor assembly are exactly level.

11. After the carburetor assembly is level, hold the loose end of the tube up against the No. 1 carburetor body. Check the fuel level in the tube. It should be 2 ±1mm (0.079 ±0.039 in.) below the top surface of the float bowl (**Figure 34**).

12. Tighten the drain screw (**Figure 35**) and hold both ends of the tube at the same height so the fuel will not drain out.

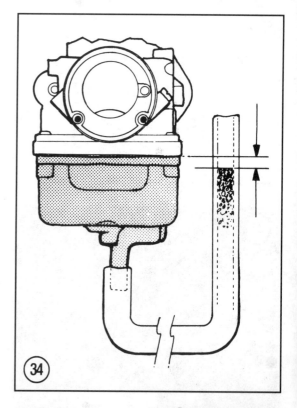

WARNING
Do not let any fuel spill on the hot exhaust system.

13. Remove the tube from the adapter, then remove the adapter. Immediately wipe up any spilled fuel from the engine.

14. Repeat this procedure for the No. 2, 3 and 4 carburetors. Record the measurements for all 4 carburetors.

15. If the fuel level is incorrect on any of the carburetors, remove the carburetor assembly and adjust the float tang on the affected carburetor(s).

16. Remove the carburetor assembly as described in this chapter.

17. Remove the screws securing the float bowls and remove them.

NOTE
*If the fuel level is correct on one or more of the carburetors, measure the installed float height (**Figure 36**) and use the measurement as a guide for correct float height.*

18. Adjust by carefully bending the tang (**Figure 37**) on the float arm. Bend the tang upward very slightly to lower the fuel level; bend the tang downward to raise the fuel level. If the float level is too high, the result will be a rich fuel/air mixture. If it is too low, the mixture will be too lean.

NOTE
The floats on all carburetors must be adjusted at the same height to maintain the same fuel/air mixture.

19. Reassemble and install the carburetors as described in this chapter.

Rejetting The Carburetors

Do not try to solve a poor running engine problem by rejetting the carburetors if all of the following conditions hold true:

   a. The engine has held a good tune in the past with the standard jetting.

   b. The engine has not been modified.

   c. The motorcycle is being operated in the same geographical region under the same general climatic conditions as in the past.

   d. The motorcycle was and is being ridden at average highway speeds.

If those conditions all hold true, the chances are that the problem is due to a malfunction in the carburetor or in another component that needs to be adjusted or repaired. Changing carburetor jet size probably won't solve the problem. Rejetting the carburetors may be necessary if any of the following conditions hold true:

   a. A non-standard type of air filter element is being used.

   b. A non-standard exhaust system is installed on the motorcycle.

   c. Any of the top end components in the engine (pistons, camshafts, valves, compression ratio, etc.) have been modified.

   d. The motorcycle is in use at considerably higher or lower altitudes or in a considerably hotter or colder climate than in the past.

   e. The motorcycle is being operated at considerably higher speeds than before and changing to colder spark plugs does not solve the problem.

   f. Someone has previously changed the carburetor jetting.

   g. The motorcycle has never held a satisfactory engine tune.

If it is necessary to rejet the carburetors, check with a dealer or motorcycle performance tuner for recommendations as to the size of jets to install for your specific situation.

If you do change the jets, do so only one size at a time. After rejetting, test ride the bike and perform a spark plug test; refer to *Reading Spark Plugs* in Chapter Three.

7

Aftermarket Air Filters

If you modify the intake system and install individual aftermarket air filters there will be a void left where the stock air filter air case was located. The stock air filter air case is the holding fixture for the ignition system's ignitor unit which is a very expensive piece of electronic gear. The air case not only holds the ignitor unit in place but it also positions it between the top of the air case and the bottom of the seat in a location which helps keep it dry.

If you have performed this intake system modification, secure the ignitor unit so it will not bounce around within this void and also waterproof the electrical connectors by packing them with a dielectric compound or place the unit within a waterproof envelope to keep it out of the rain or moisture.

If the electrical connectors become wet it will make the bike either impossible to start, difficult to start or will cause the ignition system to cut out at any rpm while the engine is running.

THROTTLE CABLE REPLACEMENT

1. Remove the seat as described under *Seat Removal/Installation* in Chapter Twelve.
2. On FZ600 models, remove the lower fairing on each side as described under *Lower Fairing Removal/Installation* in Chapter Twelve. Remove the lower fairing mounting brackets.
3. Place wood block(s) under the engine to support the bike securely.
4. Remove the fuel tank as described in this chapter.
5. Loosen the locknut and turn the throttle cable adjuster (**Figure 38**) at the throttle lever to allow slack in the cable.
6. Remove the screws securing the right-hand switch assembly (**Figure 39**) together, then disengage the throttle cable from the throttle grip.
7. At the carburetor assembly, hold the lever up with one hand and disengage the cable end from the lever. Slip the throttle cable out through the carburetor bracket (**Figure 40**).

> *NOTE*
> *The piece of string attached in the next step will be used to pull the new throttle cable back through the frame so it will be routed in exactly the same position as the old one was.*

8. Tie a piece of heavy string or cord (approximately 7 ft./2 m long) to the carburetor end of the throttle cable. Wrap this end with masking or duct tape. Do not use an excessive amount of tape as it must be pulled through the frame during removal. Tie the other end of the string to the frame or air box.

9. At the throttle grip end of the cable, carefully pull the cable (and attached string) out through the frame. Make sure the attached string follows the same path as the cable through the frame.

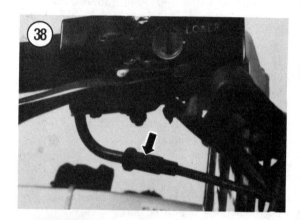

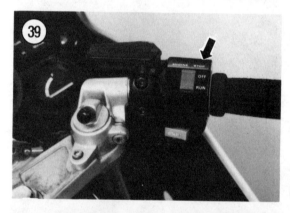

CHOKE LEVER (RADIAN)

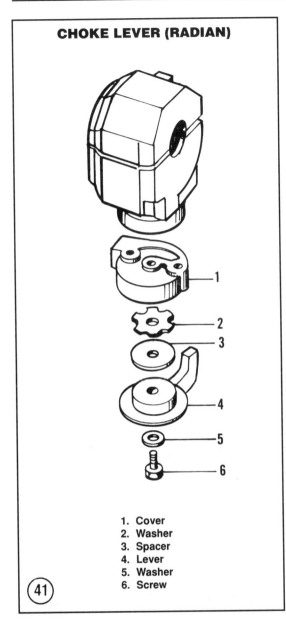

1. Cover
2. Washer
3. Spacer
4. Lever
5. Washer
6. Screw

(41)

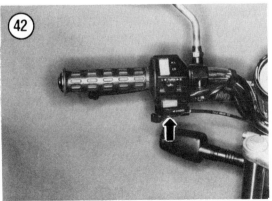

(42)

10. Remove the tape and untie the string from the old cable.

11. Lubricate the new cable as described under *Control Cable* in Chapter Three.

12. Tie the string to the new throttle cable and wrap it with tape.

13. Carefully pull the string back through the frame routing the new cable through the same path as the old cable.

14. Remove the tape and untie the string from the cable and the frame.

15. Slip the cable through the carburetor bracket. Hold the lever up with one hand and attach the cable end into the lever.

16. Install the right-hand switch housing. Tighten the forward screws first, then the rear screws. Tighten them securely.

17. Operate the throttle grip and make sure the carburetor throttle linkage is operating correctly, with no binding. If operation is incorrect or there is binding, carefully check that the cable is attached correctly and there are no tight bends in the cable.

18. Install the fuel tank and seat.

19. Adjust the throttle cable as described under *Throttle Cable Adjustment* Chapter Three.

20. On FZ600 models, install the lower fairing on each side as described in Chapter Twelve.

21. Test ride the bike slowly at first and make sure the throttle is operating correctly.

CHOKE CABLE
(RADIAN MODELS)

Replacement

> *NOTE*
> *The FZ600 model is not equipped with*
> *a choke cable.*

1. Remove the seat as described under *Seat Removal/Installation* in Chapter Twelve.

2. Remove the fuel tank as described in this chapter.

3. Refer to **Figure 41** and remove the choke lever as follows:

    a. Remove the screw and washer securing the choke lever at the handlebar (**Figure 42**).

    b. Remove the lever, spacer and star washer.

    c. Remove the cover and disengage the choke cable from it.

7

4. At the carburetor assembly, loosen the cable clamp screw (A, **Figure 43**) and remove the cable from the choke lever (B, **Figure 43**).

> *NOTE*
> *The piece of string attached in the next step will be used to pull the new choke cable back through the frame so it will be routed in exactly the same position as the old one was.*

5. Tie a piece of heavy string or cord (approximately 7 ft./2 m long) to the carburetor end of the choke cable. Wrap this end with masking or duct tape. Do not use an excessive amount of tape as it must be pulled through the frame during removal. Tie the other end of the string to the frame or air box.

6. At the grip end of the cable, carefully pull the cable (and attached string) out through the frame. Make sure the attached string follows the same path as the cable through the frame.

7. Remove the tape and untie the string from the old cable.

8. Lubricate the new cable as described under *Control Cable* in Chapter Three.

9. Tie the string to the new choke cable and wrap it with tape.

10. Carefully pull the string back through the frame routing the new cable through the same path as the old cable.

11. Remove the tape and untie the string from the cable and the frame.

12. Attach the new cable to the choke linkage and tighten the cable clamp screw.

13. Attach the new choke cable to the choke lever. Install the choke lever and cable to the left-hand switch housing.

14. Operate the choke lever and make sure the choke linkage is operating correctly with no binding. If operation is incorrect or there is binding, carefully check that the cable is attached correctly and there are no tight bends in the cable.

15. Install the fuel tank and seat.

16. Adjust the throttle cable as described in this chapter.

Adjustment

1. Operate the choke arm on the handlebar switch and check for smooth operation of the cable and choke mechanism.

2. Slide the choke lever at the carburetor assembly all the way to the closed position. Then pull the choke arm at the handlebar to make sure it is at the end of its travel. If you can still move the choke lever an additional amount, there is slack in the cable. It must be adjusted as follows:

   a. Loosen the cable clamp screw (A, **Figure 43**) and move the cable sheath *up* until the choke lever is fully closed. Hold the choke lever in this position and tighten the cable clamp screw securely.

   b. Slide the choke lever all the way to the fully open position.

3. If proper adjustment cannot be achieved using this procedure, the cable has stretched and must be replaced as described in this chapter.

FUEL SHUTOFF VALVE

Troubleshooting

The fuel shutoff valve has 3 positions. They are:

   a. ON: Fuel flows when the engine is running but stops when the engine is not running.

b. RES (reserve): Fuel flows when the engine is running but stops when the engine is not running. The RES position should only be used when there is not a sufficient supply of fuel in the tank to operate in the ON position. If the engine runs out of fuel when in the ON posi-

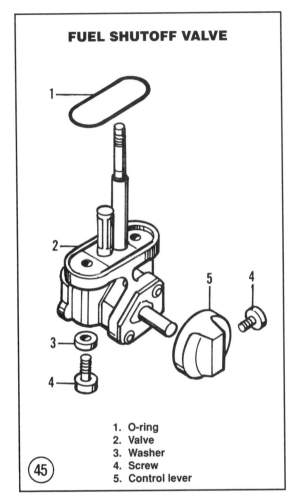

FUEL SHUTOFF VALVE

1. O-ring
2. Valve
3. Washer
4. Screw
5. Control lever

(45)

tion, turn the shutoff valve to the PRI (prime) to allow fuel to flow to the carburetors. Then start the engine and turn the shutoff valve to the RES position. Refill the tank as soon as possible, then switch back to the ON position.

c. PRI (prime): In this position, the fuel flows whether the engine is running or not. The PRI position should be used when the fuel tank has become empty. First fill the tank with fresh gasoline. Then turn the shutoff valve to the PRI position to allow the carburetors to fill with fuel. Start the engine and turn the valve to the ON position.

WARNING
Never leave the valve in the PRI position.

The shutoff valve has no OFF position. Fuel will not flow through the shutoff valve in the ON or RES position without the engine running, creating vacuum, to open the shutoff valve. If there is fuel in the tank but it will not flow in the ON or RES positions with the engine running, check the vacuum line (**Figure 44**) from the shutoff valve to the engine intake manifold. If this line is not connected properly or is leaking vacuum, the fuel shutoff valve will not operate correctly. If the vacuum line is okay, the valve may be damaged. Remove and clean it as described in this chapter; replace the valve if any damage is found.

Removal/Cleaning/Installation

The fuel filter is built into the shutoff valve and removes particles which might otherwise enter into the carburetors and may cause a float needle(s) to remain in the open position.

Refer to **Figure 45** for this procedure.

1. Remove the fuel tank as described in this chapter.
2. If necessary, drain the fuel from the fuel tank into a clean sealable metal container. If the fuel is kept clean, it can be reused.
3. Place an old blanket or several shop cloths on the workbench to protect the fuel tank's painted surface. Place the fuel tank on its side on these protective items.
4. On Radian models, remove the screw securing the knob and remove the knob (A, **Figure 46**).
5. Remove the screws and washers (B, **Figure 46**) securing the fuel shutoff valve to the fuel tank.

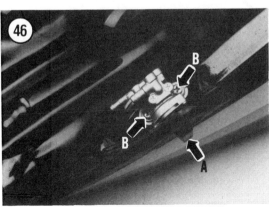

6. Remove the valve from the fuel tank. Don't lose the O-ring seal between the fuel tank and the valve.

7. After removing the valve from the fuel tank, insert a corner of a lint-free cloth into the opening in the tank to prevent the entry of foreign matter.

8. Clean the filter with a medium soft toothbrush and blow out with compressed air. Replace the filter if it is broken in any area.

9. Install by reversing these removal steps while noting the following:

   a. Be sure to install the O-ring seal between the shutoff valve and the fuel tank. Tighten the screws securely.

   b. Install the fuel tank as described in this chapter.

   c. Start the engine and check for fuel leaks.

FUEL TANK

Removal/Installation

Refer to **Figure 47** for Radian models or **Figure 48** for FZ600 models for this procedure.

1. Remove the seat(s) as described under *Seat Removal/Installation* in Chapter Twelve.

2. On FZ600 models, perform the following:

   a. Remove the lower fairing on each side as described under *Lower Fairing Removal/Installation* in Chapter Twelve.

   b. Remove the side cover (A, **Figure 49**) on each side as described under *Side Cover Removal/Installation* in Chapter Twelve.

3. Disconnect the battery negative lead. See Chapter Three.

4. Turn the fuel shutoff valve to the ON or RES position. Refer to **Figure 50** for Radian models or B, **Figure 49** for FZ600 models.

5. Remove the bolt, plate and rubber damper securing the rear of the fuel tank to the frame. Refer to **Figure 51** for Radian models or **Figure 52** for FZ600 models.

6. On Radian models, disconnect the breather hose at the rear of the tank (**Figure 53**).

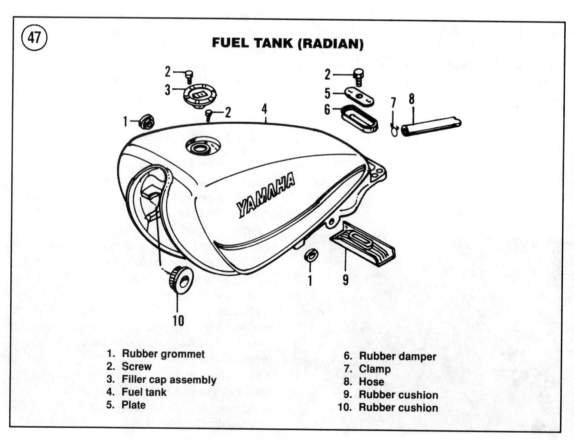

(47)   FUEL TANK (RADIAN)

1. Rubber grommet
2. Screw
3. Filler cap assembly
4. Fuel tank
5. Plate
6. Rubber damper
7. Clamp
8. Hose
9. Rubber cushion
10. Rubber cushion

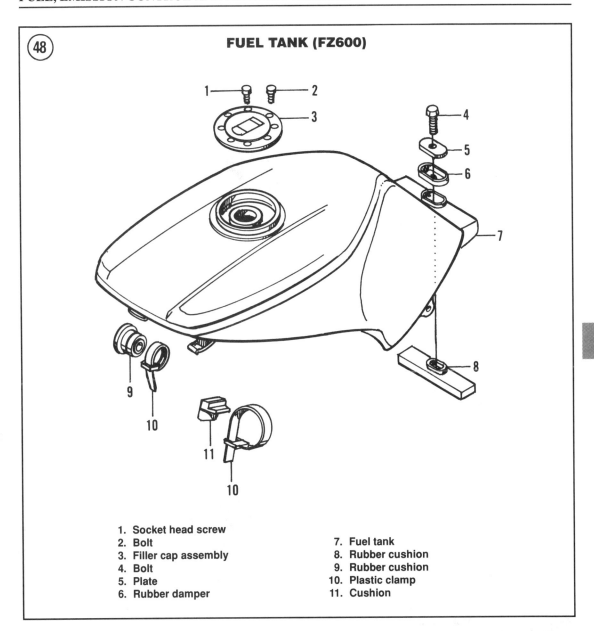

FUEL TANK (FZ600)

1. Socket head screw
2. Bolt
3. Filler cap assembly
4. Bolt
5. Plate
6. Rubber damper
7. Fuel tank
8. Rubber cushion
9. Rubber cushion
10. Plastic clamp
11. Cushion

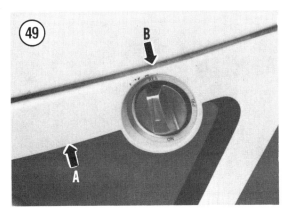

NOTE
In Step 7, the smaller diameter hose is
the vacuum hose.

7. Pull the fuel tank partially up and disconnect the fuel line and vacuum line from the fuel shutoff valve. Refer to **Figure 54** for Radian models or **Figure 55** for FZ600 models.

8. Install a golf tee (**Figure 56**) into the ends of both lines to prevent the entry of foreign matter.

9. On FZ600 models, disconnect the electrical connector for the fuel gauge.

10. On California models, disconnect the evaporative emission system vent line from the fuel tank (**Figure 57**).

11. Lift up and pull the tank to the rear.

12. On FZ600 models, disconnect the breather hose from the front of the tank.

13. Remove the fuel tank from the frame.

14. Install by reversing these removal steps while noting the following:

NOTE
The number of rubber cushions varies
between the two different models.

  a. Inspect the rubber cushions at the front (**Figure 58**) and rear where the fuel tank attaches to the frame. Replace the cushion(s) if they are damaged or starting to deteriorate.

  b. Start the engine and check for fuel leaks.

GASOLINE/ALCOHOL BLEND TEST

Gasoline blended with alcohol is available in many areas. Most states and most fuel suppliers require labeling of gasoline pumps that dispense gasoline containing a certain percentage of alcohol (methyl or wood). If in doubt, ask the service station operator if their fuel contains any alcohol. A gasoline/alcohol blend, even if it contains co-solvents and corrosion inhibitors for methanol, may be damaging to the fuel system. It may also cause poor performance, hot engine restart or hot-engine running problems.

If you are not sure if the fuel you purchased contains alcohol, run this simple and effective test. A blended fuel doesn't look any different from straight gasoline so it must be tested.

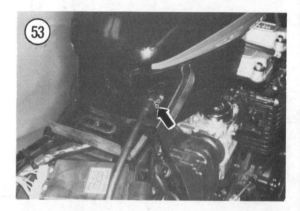

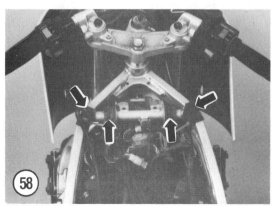

WARNING
Gasoline is very volatile and presents an extreme fire hazard. Be sure to work in a well-ventilated area away from any open flames (including pilot lights on household appliances). Do not allow anyone to smoke in the area and have a fire extinguisher rated for gasoline fires handy.

During this test keep the following facts in mind:

a. Alcohol and gasoline mix together.

b. Alcohol mixes *easier* with water.

c. Gasoline and water do *not* mix.

NOTE
If co-solvents have been used in the gasoline, this test may not work with water. Repeat this test using automotive antifreeze instead of water.

Use an 8 oz. transparent baby bottle with a sealable cap.

1. Set the baby bottle on a level surface and add water up to the 1.5 oz. mark. Mark this line on the bottle with a fine-line permanent marking pen. This will be the reference line used later in this test.

2. Add the suspect fuel into the baby bottle up to the 8 oz. mark.

3. Install the sealable cap and shake the bottle vigorously for about 10 seconds.

4. Set the baby bottle upright on the level surface used in Step 1 and wait for a few minutes for the mixture to settle down.

5. If there is *no* alcohol in the fuel the gasoline/water separation line will be exactly on the 1.5 oz. reference line made in Step 1.

6. If there *is* alcohol in the fuel the gasoline/water separation line will be *above* the 1.5 oz. reference line made in Step 1. The alcohol has separated from the gasoline and mixed in with the water (remember it is easier for the alcohol to mix with water than gasoline).

WARNING
*After the test, discard the baby bottle or place it out of reach of small children. There will always be a gasoline and alcohol residue in it and should **not** be used to drink out of.*

CRANKCASE BREATHER SYSTEM
(U.S. ONLY)

To comply with air pollution standards, all models are equipped with a closed crankcase breather system (**Figure 59**). The system routes the engine combustion gases into the air filter air box where they are burned in the engine.

Make sure the hose clamps at each end of the hose (**Figure 60**) are tight. Check the hose for deterioration and replace as necessary.

EVAPORATIVE EMISSION
CONTROL SYSTEM
(CALIFORNIA MODELS ONLY)

Fuel vapor from the fuel tank is routed into a charcoal canister (**Figure 61**). This vapor is stored when the engine is not running. When the ignition switch is turned to the ON position, and the engine started, the air vent control valve opens and these vapors are drawn into the carburetors to be burned.

A roll-over contol valve (**Figure 62**) is installed in line with the fuel tank and the charcoal canister. If the bike is rolled or turned over, the internal weight in the valve automatically moves to block off the passage. This prevents fuel from flowing freely into the charcoal canister and onto the ground.

Make sure all hose clamps are tight. Check all hoses for deterioration and replace as necessary.

When removing the hoses from any component in the system, mark the hose and the fitting with a piece of masking tape and identify where the hose goes. There are so many vacuum hoses on these models that reconnecting the hoses can be very confusing.

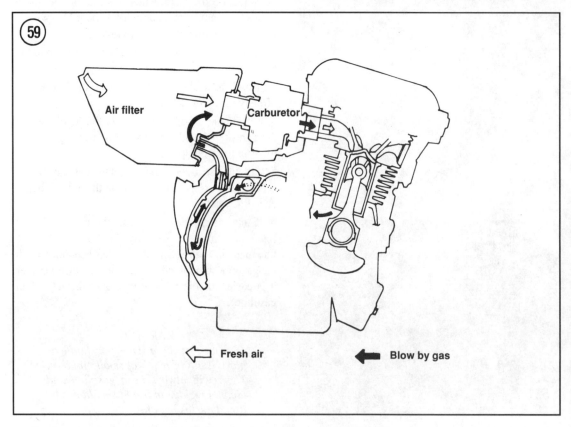

Air filter

Carburetor

Fresh air

Blow by gas

Service to the emission control system is limited to replacement of the damaged parts. No attempt should be made to modify or remove the emission control system.

EXHAUST SYSTEM

The exhaust system is a vital performance component and frequently, because of its design, it is a vulnerable piece of equipment. Check the exhaust system for deep dents and fractures and repair or replace them immediately. Check the muffler frame mounting flanges for fractures and loose bolts. Check the cylinder head mounting flanges for tightness. A loose exhaust pipe connection can rob the engine of power.

The exhaust system consists of 4 exhaust pipes, a crossover pipe and two mufflers on Radian models

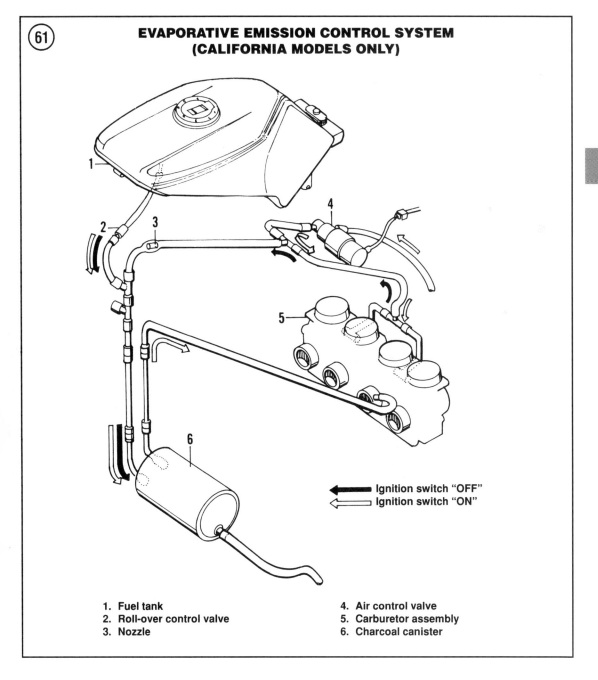

EVAPORATIVE EMISSION CONTROL SYSTEM (CALIFORNIA MODELS ONLY)

◀━ Ignition switch "OFF"
◁━ Ignition switch "ON"

1. Fuel tank
2. Roll-over control valve
3. Nozzle
4. Air control valve
5. Carburetor assembly
6. Charcoal canister

and on FZ600 models a 4-into-2-into-1 exhaust pipe
and muffler assembly.

Removal/Installation
(Radian Models)

Refer to **Figure 63** for this procedure.

> *WARNING*
> *If the bike has been run recently the*
> *entire exhaust system is HOT, allow it*
> *to cool down prior to working on any*
> *portion of the exhaust system.*

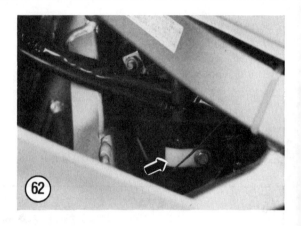

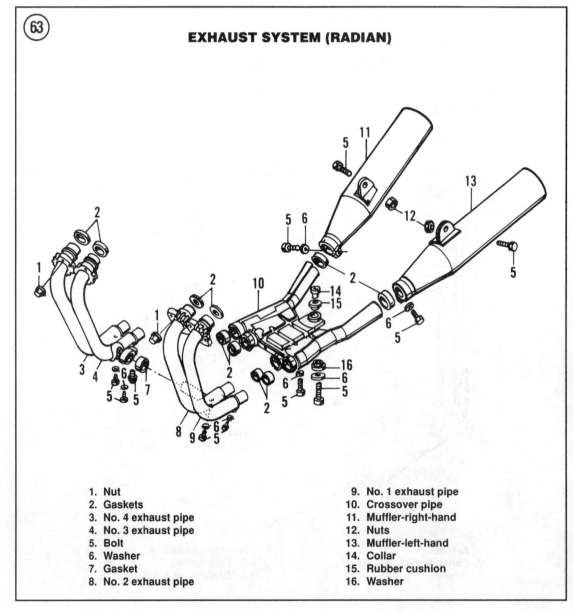

EXHAUST SYSTEM (RADIAN)

1. Nut
2. Gaskets
3. No. 4 exhaust pipe
4. No. 3 exhaust pipe
5. Bolt
6. Washer
7. Gasket
8. No. 2 exhaust pipe
9. No. 1 exhaust pipe
10. Crossover pipe
11. Muffler-right-hand
12. Nuts
13. Muffler-left-hand
14. Collar
15. Rubber cushion
16. Washer

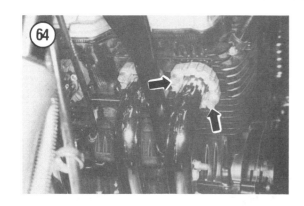

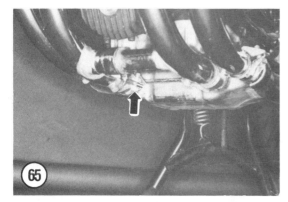

1. Place the bike on the centerstand.

2. Loosen the bolt securing the clamp on the crossover pipe.

3. Remove the nuts (**Figure 64**) securing each exhaust pipe clamp to the cylinder head.

NOTE
Don't lose the gasket at each exhaust port when the exhaust pipe is removed from the cylinder head.

4. Loosen the inboard exhaust pipe-to-exhaust pipe clamp bolt (**Figure 65**).

5. Loosen each clamp bolt (**Figure 66**) securing the outboard and inboard exhaust pipes to the front portion of the crossover pipe assembly.

6. Remove the 4 exhaust pipes from the threaded studs on the cylinder head and the crossover pipe.

7. Loosen the crossover pipe-to-exhaust pipe clamp bolts (**Figure 67**).

8. Remove the bolt and nut (**Figure 68**) securing the muffler to the footpeg bracket.

9. Remove both mufflers.

10. Remove the bolt, lockwasher and washer securing the rear portion of the crossover pipe assembly to the frame.

11. Remove the crossover pipe assembly from the frame.

12. Inspect the gaskets at all joints; replace as necessary.

13. Be sure to install a new gasket in each exhaust port in the cylinder head and each joint throughout the exhaust system.

14. Install all of the exhaust system components and tighten the fasteners only finger-tight at this time. Make sure the exhaust pipe inlets are correctly seated in the cylinder head exhaust ports.

7

15. Securely tighten the nuts securing each exhaust pipe clamp to the cylinder head then work your way back through the exhaust system and tighten the rest of the exhaust system bolts securely. This will minimize exhaust leakage at the cylinder head.

16. After installation is complete, start the engine and make sure there are no exhaust leaks. Correct any leak prior to riding the bike.

Removal/Installation (FZ600 Models)

Refer to **Figure 69** for this procedure.

WARNING
If the bike has been run recently the entire exhaust system is HOT, allow it

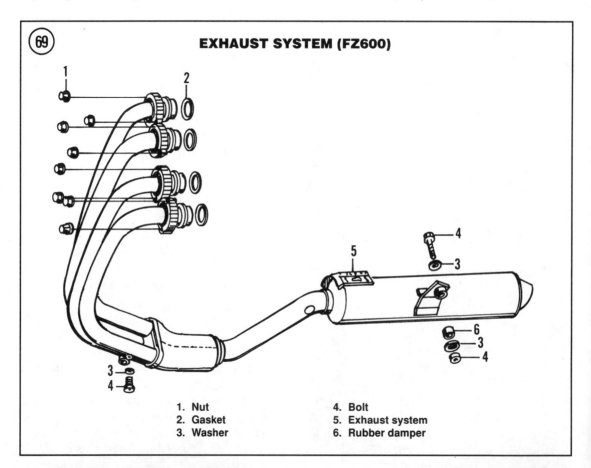

(69) EXHAUST SYSTEM (FZ600)

1. Nut
2. Gasket
3. Washer
4. Bolt
5. Exhaust system
6. Rubber damper

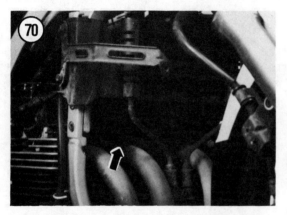

to cool down prior to working on any portion of the exhaust system.

1. Remove the lower fairing on each side as described under *Lower Fairing Removal/Installation* in Chapter Twelve.
2. Place the bike on the side stand.
3. Remove the nuts securing each exhaust pipe clamp to the cylinder head (**Figure 70**).

NOTE
Don't lose the gasket at each exhaust port when the exhaust pipe is removed from the cylinder head.

NOTE
Figure 71 *is shown with an aftermarket exhaust system. Removal and installation of the factory-equipped and the aftermarket exhaust system is the same.*

4. Remove the bolt, washers and nut (**Figure 71**) securing the rear portion of the exhaust system to the frame. Don't lose the rubber damper within the mounting bracket.

5. Carefully move the exhaust system forward to clear the threaded studs on the cylinder head exhaust ports and remove the exhaust system.

6. Inspect the gaskets at the entrance of the exhaust pipes; replace as necessary.

7. Be sure to install a new gasket in each exhaust port in the cylinder head.

8. Install all of the exhaust system and tighten the fasteners only finger-tight at this time. Make sure the exhaust pipe inlets are correctly seated in the cylinder head exhaust ports.

9. Securely tighten the nuts securing each exhaust pipe clamp to the cylinder head then tighten the bolt and nut securing the exhaust system to the frame. This will minimize exhaust leakage at the cylinder head.

10. After installation is complete, start the engine and make sure there are no exhaust leaks. Correct any leak prior to riding the bike.

11. Install the upper fairing on each side as described in Chapter Twelve.

Table 1 is on the following page.

7

Table 1 CARBURETOR SPECIFICATIONS

Radian	
Carburetor model No.	BS30 Mikuni
I.D. mark	
49-state	1UJ00
California	1UL00
Main jet number	97.5
Main air jet number	140
Jet needle clip setting	
No. 1 and No. 4	4CHP2
No. 2 and No. 3	4CHP4
Needle jet	0-6
Pilot jet	No. 30
Pilot air jet	No. 135
Pilot screw	preset
Starter jet	No. 25
Float level	20 ± 1.0 mm (0.8 ± 0.04 in.)
Fuel level	2.0 ± 0.5 mm (0.08 ± 0.02 in.)
Idle speed	1,250-1,350 rpm

FZ600 (U.S.)	
Carburetor model No.	BS30 Mikuni
I.D. mark	
49-state	2AX00
California	2AY00
Main jet number	107.5
Main air jet number	140
Jet needle clip setting	4CHP2
Needle jet	0-6
Pilot jet	No. 30
Pilot air jet	No. 135
Pilot screw	preset
Starter jet	No. 22.5
Float level	20 ± 1.0 mm (0.8 ± 0.04 in.)
Fuel level	2.0 ± 0.5 mm (0.08 ± 0.02 in.)
Idle speed	1,150-1,250 rpm

FZ600 (UK)	
Carburetor model No.	BS30 Mikuni
I.D. mark	2EW00
Main jet number	107.5
Main air jet number	140
Jet needle clip setting	4CHP3-3
Needle jet	0-6
Pilot jet	No. 30
Pilot air jet	No. 125
Pilot screw	2 1/2 turns out
Starter jet	No. 22.5
Float level	20 ± 1.0 mm (0.8 ± 0.04 in.)
Fuel level	2.0 ± 0.5 mm (0.08 ± 0.02 in.)
Idle speed	1,150-1,250 rpm

ELECTRICAL SYSTEM

This chapter contains operating principles and service and test procedures for all electrical and ignition components that are available from Yamaha. Information regarding the battery and spark plug are covered in Chapter Three.

The electrical system includes the following systems:

a. Charging system.

b. Ignition system.

c. Lighting system.

Electrical specifications are listed in **Table 1. Tables 1-5** are at the end of this chapter.

> *NOTE*
> *Where differences occur relating to the United Kingdom (UK) models they are identified. If there is no (UK) designation relating to a procedure, photo or illustration, it is identical to the United States (U.S.) models.*

CHARGING SYSTEM

The charging system consists of the battery, alternator and a solid-state voltage regulator/rectifier.

Alternating current generated by the alternator is rectified to direct current. The voltage regulator maintains the voltage to the electrical load (lights, ignition, etc.) at a constant voltage regardless of variations in engine speed and load.

Charging System Test

Whenever charging system trouble is suspected, make sure the battery is fully charged and in good condition before going any further. Clean and test the battery as described in Chapter Three. Make sure all electrical connectors are tight and free of corrosion.

1. Start the engine and let it reach normal operating temperature; shut off the engine.

2. Remove the seat(s) as described under *Seat Removal/Installation* in Chapter Twelve.

3. Remove the right-hand side cover.

4. Start the engine and let it idle.

> *NOTE*
> *Do not disconnect either the positive or negative battery cables; they are to remain in the circuit as is.*

5. Connect a 0-20 DC voltmeter positive (+) test lead to the battery positive (+) terminal and the negative (−) test lead to ground (**Figure 1**).

6. Increase engine speed to 5,000 rpm. The voltage reading should be between 14-15 volts. If the voltage is less than specified, inspect the alternator and

the voltage regulator/rectifier as described in this chapter.

7. If the charging voltage is too high, the voltage regulator/rectifier is probably at fault.

8. After the test is completed, disconnect the voltmeter and shut off the engine.

9. Install the right-hand side cover.

10. Install the seat.

ALTERNATOR (1986-1988 MODELS)

The alternator is a form of electrical generator in which a magnetized field called a rotor revolves within a set of stationary coils called a stator. As the rotor revolves, alternating current is induced in the stator. The current is then rectified to direct current and is used to operate the electrical accessories on the bike and to charge the battery.

The rotor is an electro-magnet.

Testing

1. Remove the right-hand side cover.

2. To test the stator coils, refer to **Figure 2** and perform the following:

 a. Disconnect the white electrical connector (containing 3 white wires).

 b. Use an ohmmeter set at R × 1 and check the resistance between terminals No. 1 and No. 2, then between terminals No. 2 and No. 3. Each reading should be between 0.5-0.6 ohms at 20° C (68° F).

3. To test the stator coils, refer to **Figure 3** and perform the following:

 a. Disconnect the white electrical connector (containing 2 wires-one green and one brown).

 b. Use an ohmmeter set at R × 1 and check the resistance between the green and brown wire terminals. The reading should be between 2.7-3.3 ohms at 20° C (68° F).

4. If the resistance values are not within the specificated range, check the electrical wires to and within the connectors. If they are okay, remove and inspect the stator and rotor as described in this chapter. Replace the rotor or stator if necessary.

5. If the tests are okay, reconnect the electrical connectors and reinstall the right-hand side cover.

6. Make sure all electrical connectors are free of corrosion and are tight.

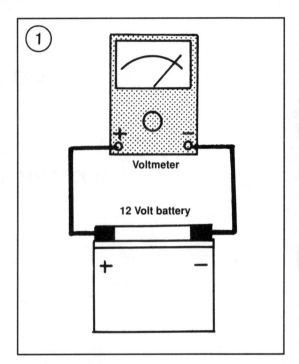

Voltmeter

12 Volt battery

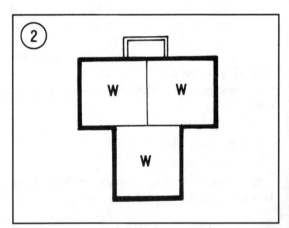

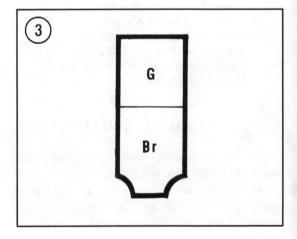

Removal/Installation

Refer to **Figure 4** for this procedure.

NOTE
This procedure is shown with the engine
partially disassembled. It is not neces-

sary to remove any components other
than those described in this procedure.

1. Place the bike on the sidestand (FZ600 models)
or centerstand (Radian models).

2. Remove the right-hand side cover.

3. On FZ600 models, remove the right-hand lower
fairing as described under *Lower Fairing Re-
moval/Installation (FZ600 Models)* in Chapter
Twelve.

4. Disconnect the battery negative cable, see Chapter
Three.

5. Disconnect the 2 alternator white electrical connectors. One contains 3 white wires and the other
one contains 2 wires (one green and one brown).

6. Remove the Allen screws (**Figure 5**) securing the
alternator cover/coil assembly.

7. Straighten the wire clamps (**Figure 6**) securing the
electrical cables to the crankcase. Move the cables
out of the clamps.

8. Remove the alternator cover/coil assembly, gasket
and electrical cables from the engine (**Figure 7**).

9. To remove the stator coil assembly from the cover,
pull it out of the cover. When installing a new stator
coil, align the 3 bolt grooves with the bolt holes in
the cover (**Figure 8**).

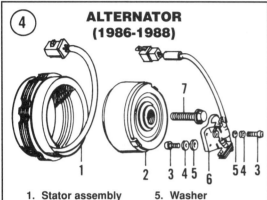

ALTERNATOR
(1986-1988)

1. Stator assembly
2. Rotor assembly
3. Screw
4. Lockwasher
5. Washer
6. Brush holder
   assembly
7. Bolt

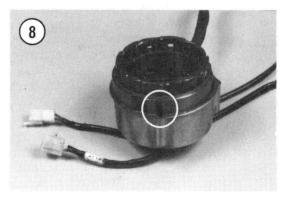

8

10. To remove the rotor, perform the following:

NOTE
Use a strap wrench or similar tool to keep the rotor from turning while removing the bolt.

a. Remove the bolt and washer securing the rotor.

b. Screw in a flywheel puller (**Figure 9**) until it stops. Use Yamaha special tool Rotor Puller (U.S. part No. YM-01080, UK part No. 90890-01080), and Pin (U.S. part No. YM-04052, UK part No. 90890-04052), or equivalent.

c. Use a wrench on the puller (**Figure 10**) and tap on the end of it with a plastic mallet until the rotor disengages.

d. Remove the rotor and remove the puller from the rotor.

11. Inspect the components as described in this chapter.

12. Install by reversing these removal steps while noting the following:

a. Tighten the rotor bolt to the torque specification listed in **Table 2**.

b. Install a new cover gasket.

c. Make sure all electrical connectors are free of corrosion and are tight.

Inspection

1. Inspect the alternator cover/coil assembly for wear or cracks (**Figure 7**).

2. Inspect both brushes within the cover (A, **Figure 11**). The brushes must be replaced if worn to the scribe line. Always replace both brushes as a set.

3. If brush replacement is necessary, perform the following:

a. Remove the Phillips screws (B, **Figure 11**) securing the brush holder.

b. Remove the small screw securing each brush to the holder and remove the brushes from the holders.

c. Install new brushes and tighten the small screw securely.

d. Install the Phillips screws and tighten to the torque specification listed in **Table 2**.

4. Inspect the stator assembly for any opens or poor electrical connections. Also check the stator's insulating material for cracking. If the stator appears

damaged in any way, test the coil resistance as described in this chapter.

5. Carefully clean the brush contact slip rings on the rotor with aerosol electrical contact cleaner.

6. Connect an ohmmeter between the 2 slip rings (**Figure 12**). There should be an indicated low resistance (continuity). If the resistance reading is high, replace the rotor. Yamaha does not provide exact resistance values.

7. Check the resistance between either brush slip ring contact surface and the body. There should be

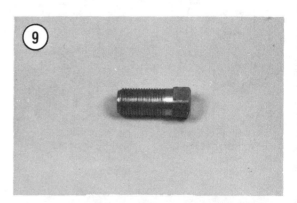

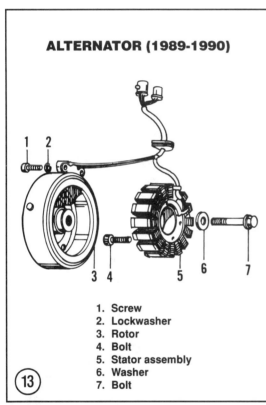

ALTERNATOR (1989-1990)

1. Screw
2. Lockwasher
3. Rotor
4. Bolt
5. Stator assembly
6. Washer
7. Bolt

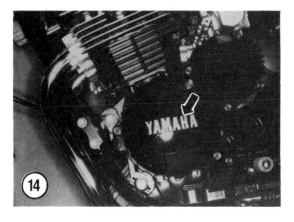

infinite resistance (no continuity). If not, the rotor winding is shorted and the rotor must be replaced.

ALTERNATOR (1989-1990 MODELS)

The alternator is a form of electrical generator in which a magnetized field called a rotor revolves within a set of stationary coils called a stator. As the rotor revolves, alternating current is induced in the stator. The current is then rectified to direct current and is used to operate the electrical accessories on the bike and to charge the battery.

The rotor is a permanent magnet type.

Testing

Yamaha does not provide any test procedures or specifications for these models.

Removal/Installation

Refer to **Figure 13** for this procedure.
1. Place the bike on the sidestand.
2. Remove the right-hand side cover.
3. Disconnect the battery negative cable, see Chapter Three.
4. Disconnect the 2 alternator electrical connectors. One contains 3 white wires and the other contains 2 wires (one white/red and one white/black wire).
5. Remove the bolts securing the alternator cover/coil assembly (**Figure 14**).
6. Remove the alternator cover/coil assembly, gasket and electrical cables from the engine. Don't lose the locating dowels.
7. To remove the stator coil assembly from the cover, perform the following:
   a. Remove the gasket from the cover.
   b. Remove the bolts (A, **Figure 15**) securing the stator coil assembly and the ignition pickup coil assembly (B, **Figure 15**) to the cover.
   c. Carefully slide the electrical cable rubber grommet from the groove in the cover and remove the coil assembly.
8. To remove the rotor, perform the following:

NOTE
Use a strap wrench or similar tool to keep the rotor from turning while removing the bolt.

a. Remove the bolt and washer (**Figure 16**) securing the rotor.

b. Screw in a flywheel puller until it stops.

c. Use a wrench on the puller and tap on the end of it with a plastic mallet until the rotor disengages from the crankshaft.

d. Remove the rotor and remove the puller from the rotor.

e. Don't lose the Woodruff key on the crankshaft.

9. Inspect the components as described in this chapter.

10. Install by reversing these removal steps while noting the following:

a. Make sure the Woodruff key is in place on the crankshaft.

b. Align the rotor keyway with the Woodruff key and install the rotor.

c. Tighten the rotor bolt to the torque specification listed in **Table 2**.

d. Make sure the locating dowels (A, **Figure 17**) are in place and install a new cover gasket (B, **Figure 17**).

e. Make sure all electrical connectors are free of corrosion and are tight.

Inspection

1. Inspect the alternator cover/coil assembly (C, **Figure 15**) for wear or cracks.

2. Inspect the stator assembly for any opens or poor electrical connections. Also check the stator's insulating material for cracking. If the stator appears damaged in any way, have it tested by a Yamaha dealer.

3. Inspect the inside of the rotor for small bolts, washers or other metal "trash" that may have been picked up by the magnets. These small metal bits can cause severe damage to the stator assembly components.

4. The rotor can lose magnetism from old age or a sharp blow. If defective, the rotor must be replaced; it cannot be serviced.

VOLTAGE REGULATOR/RECTIFIER

The rectifier converts the alternator's AC output to DC. It is a solid state unit that is an integral unit along with the voltage regulator.

Testing

Yamaha does not provide any test procedures or specifications for these models.

Replacement
(Radian Models)

1. Place the bike on the centerstand.

2. Remove the seat as described under *Seat Removal/Installation* in Chapter Twelve.

3. Remove the right-hand side cover.

4. Disconnect the battery negative cable, see Chapter Three.

5. Disconnect the voltage regulator/rectifier electrical connector (contains 7 wires—one brown, one red, one black, one green and three white).

6A. On1986-1988 models, remove the screws securing the voltage regulator/rectifier to the side of the battery case.

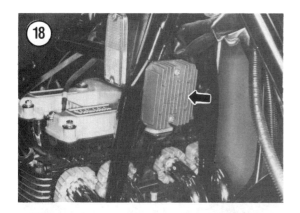

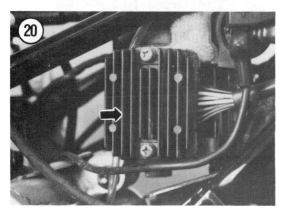

6B. On 1989-1990 models, remove the screws securing the voltage regulator/rectifier to the front frame down tube (**Figure 18**).

7. Remove the voltage regulator/rectifier and install a new one.

8. Make sure all electrical connectors are free of corrosion and are tight.

Replacement
(FZ600 Models)

1. Place the bike on the side stand.

2. Remove the seat as described under *Seat Removal/Installation* in Chapter Twelve.

3. Remove the left-hand side cover as described under *Side Cover Removal/Installation (FZ600 Models)* in Chapter Twelve.

4. Disconnect the battery negative cable, see Chapter Three.

5. Disconnect the voltage regulator/rectifier electrical connector (contains 7 wires—one brown, one red, one black, one green and three white) (**Figure 19**).

6. Remove the screws securing the voltage regulator/rectifier to the side of the battery case (**Figure 20**).

7. Remove the voltage regulator/rectifier and install a new one.

8. Make sure all electrical connectors are free of corrosion and are tight.

TRANSISTORIZED IGNITION

All models are equipped with a transistorized ignition system, a solid-state system that uses no breaker points. The ignition system on the 1986-1988 models is different from the one used on the 1989-1990 models. Where differences occur, they are identified in this section.

On 1986-1988 models, the ignition pickup coils are mounted on the left-hand end of the crankcase adjacent to the end of the crankshaft. As the projection on the timing plate, attached to the crankshaft, passes a pickup coil a signal is sent to the ignitor unit. This signal turns the ignitor unit transistor alternately ON and OFF. As the transistor is turned ON and OFF, the current passing through the primary windings of the ignition coil, is also turned ON and OFF. Thus it induces the secondary current on the

8

ignition coils secondary windings and produces the current necessary to fire the spark plugs.

On 1989-1990 models, the ignition pickup coil is mounted inside the alternator stator cover on the left-hand end of the crankcase. As the raised ignition tab on the alternator rotor passes the pickup coil, a signal is sent to the digital ignitor unit. This signal turns the ignitor unit transistor alternately ON and OFF. As the transistor is turned ON and OFF, the current passing through the primary windings of the ignition coil, is also turned ON and OFF. Thus it induces the secondary current on the ignition coils secondary windings and produces the current necessary to fire the spark plugs.

Ignition System Precautions

Certain measures must be taken to protect the ignition system. Instantaneous damage to the semi-conductors in the system will occur if the following precautions are not observed.

1. Never disconnect any of the electrical connections while the engine is running.

2. Keep all connections between the various units clean and tight. Be sure that the wiring connectors are pushed together firmly to help keep out moisture.

3. Do not substitute another type of ignition coil.

Troubleshooting

Problems with the transistorized ignition system fall into one of the following categories. See **Table 3**.

   a. Weak spark.

   b. No spark.

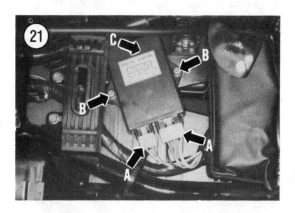

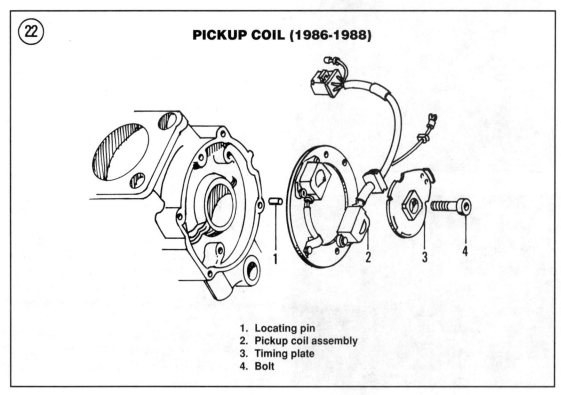

PICKUP COIL (1986-1988)

1. Locating pin
2. Pickup coil assembly
3. Timing plate
4. Bolt

IGNITOR UNIT

Testing

Complete testing of the ignitor unit requires 2 pieces of special Yamaha test equipment. The tests should be performed by a Yamaha dealer as this equipment is expensive.

The dealer will either test the ignitor unit with the test equipment or perform a "remove and replace" test to see if the ignitor unit is faulty. This type of test is expensive if performed by yourself. Remember if you purchase a new ignitor unit and it does *not* solve your particular ignition system problem, you cannot return the ignitor unit for refund. Most motorcycle dealers will *not* accept returns on any electrical component since the component could be damaged internally even though it looks okay externally.

Make sure all connections between the various components are clean and tight. Be sure that the wiring connectors are pushed together firmly to help keep out moisture.

Removal/Installation

1. Remove the seat as described under *Seat Removal/Installation* in Chapter Twelve.
2. Disconnect the 2 electrical connectors from the ignitor unit (A, **Figure 21**).
3. Remove the screws (B, **Figure 21**) securing the ignitor unit (C, **Figure 21**) and remove it.
4. Install by reversing these removal steps. Make sure all electrical connectors are free of corrosion and are tight.

PICK-UP COIL

Removal/Installation
(1986-1988 Models)

Refer to **Figure 22** for this procedure.
1. Place the bike on the sidestand (FZ600 models) or centerstand (Radian models).
2. On FZ600 models, remove the right-hand lower fairing as described under *Lower Fairing Removal/Installation (FZ600 Models)* in Chapter Twelve.
3. Disconnect the battery negative cable, see Chapter Three.
4. Remove the ignition cover and gasket from the right-hand side of the crankcase.
5. Carefully pull the pick-up coil wire harness and rubber grommet from the slot in the crankcase (**Figure 23**).
6. Disconnect the pick-up coil electrical connectors.
7. Remove the Allen bolt (**Figure 24**) securing the timing plate to the crankshaft.
8. Remove the 2 screws (A, **Figure 25**) securing the base plate to the crankcase and remove it. Do not remove the ignition timing pointer screw (B, **Figure 25**).

9. Install by reversing these removal steps while noting the following:

a. Align the slot in the back of the timing plate with the locating pin (**Figure 26**) in the end of the crankshaft.

b. Tighten the timing plate screw to the torque specification listed in **Table 2**.

c. Check the ignition timing as described in Chapter Three.

Removal/Installation
(1989-1990 Models)

The pick-up coil is an integral part of the alternator stator assembly. If it is faulty, the entire assembly must be replaced (pick-up coil and stator assembly). Refer to *Alternator Removal/Installation (1989-1990 Models)* in this chapter.

Testing
(1986-1988 Models)

If the pick-up coil condition is doubtful, perform this test.

1. Disconnect the pick-up coil electrical connector (containing 3 wires—one black, one orange, one gray) from the ignitor unit (**Figure 27**).

2. Use an ohmmeter set at R × 100 and check the resistance between the following terminals (**Figure 28**):

a. Positive (+) test lead to the orange terminal and the negative (–) test lead to the black terminal.

b. Positive (+) test lead to the gray terminal and the negative (–) test lead to the black terminal.

The specified resistance in each case is 108-132 ohms at 20° C (68° F).

3. If either pick-up coil fails this test, replace the pick-up coil assembly as described in this chapter.

IGNITION COIL

There are 2 ignition coils; the left-hand coil fires the No. 1 and No. 4 cylinders and the right-hand coil fires the No. 2 and No. 3 cylinders.

Preliminary Spark Test

The ignition coil is a form of transformer which develops the high voltage required to jump the spark plug gap. The only maintenance required is that of keeping the electrical connections clean and tight and occasionally checking to see that the coils are mounted securely.

If the condition of the coil(s) is doubtful, there are several checks which may be made.

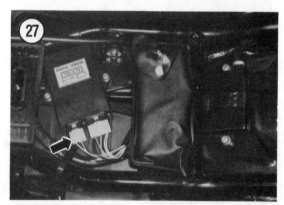

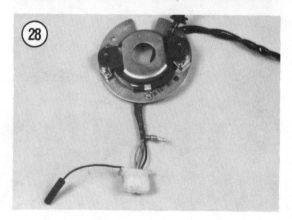

NOTE
The spark plug must be grounded against a piece of bare metal on the engine or frame. If necessary, carefully scrape away some of the engine paint.

First, as a quick check of coil condition, disconnect the high voltage lead from the spark plug. Remove one of the spark plugs from the cylinder head (refer to Chapter Three). Connect a new or known good spark plug to the high voltage lead and place the spark plug base on a good ground like the engine cylinder head (**Figure 29**). Position the spark plug so you can see the electrodes.

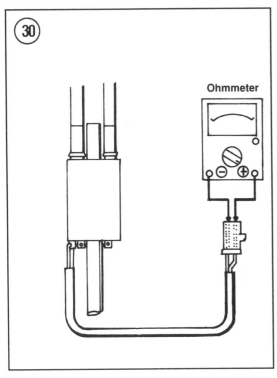

Ohmmeter

WARNING
If it is necessary to hold the high voltage lead, do so with an insulated pair of pliers. The high voltage generated by the signal generator could produce serious or fatal shocks.

Turn the engine over with the starter. If a fat blue spark occurs, the coil is in good condition; if not proceed as follows. Make sure that you are using a known good spark plug for this test. If the spark plug used is defective, the test results will be incorrect.

Reinstall the spark plug in the cylinder head and connect the high voltage lead.

Testing

NOTE
In order to get accurate resistance measurements, the coil must be warm (minimum temperature is 20° C/68° F). If necessary, start the engine and let it warm up to normal operating temperature.

1. Remove the fuel tank as described under *Fuel Tank Removal/Installation* in Chapter Seven.
2. Disconnect all ignition coil wires (including the spark plug leads from the spark plugs) before testing.
3. Use an ohmmeter set at R × 1 and measure the primary coil resistance between the positive (+) and the negative (–) terminals on the ignition coil (**Figure 30**). The specified resistance value is 2.43-2.97 ohms.
4. Use an ohmmeter set at R × 1,000 to measure the secondary coil resistance between the 2 spark plug leads (with the spark plug caps attached) (**Figure 31**). The specified resistance value is 10,560-15,840 ohms.
5. If the coil resistance does not meet either of these specifications, the coil must be replaced. If the coil exhibits visible damage, it should be replaced.
6. Reconnect all ignition coil wires to the ignition coil.
7. Repeat this procedure for the other ignition coil.

Removal/Installation

1. On FZ600 models, remove the lower fairing on each side as described under *Lower Fairing Re-*

moval/Installation (FZ600 Models) in Chapter Twelve.

2. Remove the seat as described under *Seat Removal/Installation* in Chapter Twelve.

3. Disconnect the battery negative lead, see Chapter Three.

4. Remove the fuel tank as described under *Fuel Tank Removal/Installation* in Chapter Seven.

NOTE
On the original equipment ignition coil and high voltage leads, the spark plug cylinder number is marked on each lead. If these marks are no longer legible or are missing, mark each lead as to which cylinder it is attached to. The No. 1 cylinder is on the left-hand side and working across from left to right are the No. 2, No. 3 and No. 4 cylinders. These marks will make it easier during installation and it will make sure that the correct leads go to the correct cylinders.

5. Disconnect the high voltage lead (A, **Figure 32**) from each spark plug.

6. Remove the screws securing the ignition coil (B, **Figure 32**) to the frame.

7. Carefully pull the ignition coil away from the frame and disconnect the primary electrical wires from the coil.

8. If necessary, repeat Steps 5-7 for the other ignition coil.

9. Install by reversing these removal steps. Make sure all electrical connections are free of corrosion and are tight.

STARTING SYSTEM

The starting system includes a starter switch, starter solenoid, neutral switch, clutch switch, sidestand switch, cut-off relay coil, battery and starter motor.

When the starter button is pressed under the correct conditions, current flows through the starter solenoid coil. The starter solenoid contacts close and current flows directly from the battery to the starter motor. Current flow through the starter solenoid coil is controlled by the cut-off relay. Current cannot reach the starter solenoid coil unless the cut-off relay contacts are closed. The cut-off relay contacts close only when current flows through the cut-off relay

coil. Current flow through the cut-off relay coil is controlled by the neutral switch, the clutch switch and the sidestand switch.

Current will flow through the cut-off relay coil only when the neutral switch is closed (transmission in NEUTRAL) *or* when both the clutch switch and the sidestand switch are closed (clutch lever pulled in and the sidestand is up).

CAUTION
Do not operate the starter for more than five seconds at a time. Let it rest approximately ten seconds, then use it again.

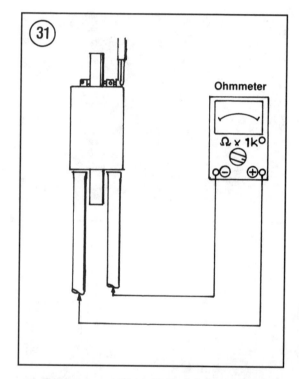

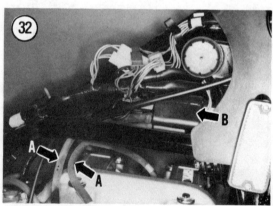

Service to the starter gears is covered in Chapter Four.

Table 4 lists possible starter problems, probable causes and most common remedies. Before checking any circuit component, make sure the battery is fully charged (see Chapter Three) and that all starting system electrical wiring is in good condition and all electrical connectors are tight and free of corrosion.

ELECTRIC STARTER

Removal/Installation

1. On FZ600 models, remove the left-hand lower fairing as described under *Lower Fairing Removal/Installation* in Chapter Twelve.

2. Disconnect the battery negative lead, see Chapter Three.

3. Remove the bolt securing the gearshift lever (A, **Figure 33**) and remove the lever.

4. Remove the bolts securing the drive sprocket cover (B, **Figure 33**) and remove the cover.

5. Slide back the rubber boot on the electrical cable connector.

6. Disconnect the starter electrical cable (A, **Figure 34**) from the starter.

7. Remove the bolts securing the starter (B, **Figure 34**) to the crankcase.

8. Withdraw the starter from the top of the crankcase.

9. Install by reversing these removal steps while noting the following:

    a. Make sure the O-ring seal (A, **Figure 35**) is in good condition and is in place. Replace if necessary.

    b. Tighten the bolts to the torque specifications listed in **Table 2**.

Preliminary Inspection

The overhaul of a starter motor is best left to an expert. This procedure shows how to detect a defective starter.

Inspect the O-ring seal (A, **Figure 35**). O-ring seals tend to harden after prolonged use and heat and therefore lose their ability to seal properly. Replace as necessary.

Inspect the gear (B, **Figure 35**) for chipped or missing teeth. If damaged, the starter assembly must be replaced.

Disassembly

Refer to **Figure 36** for this procedure.

1. Remove the case screws and washers (**Figure 37**), then separate the front and rear covers from the case.

NOTE
Write down the number of shims used on the shaft next to the commutator and next to the rear cover. Be sure to install the same number when reassembling the starter.

2. Remove the shims from the front cover end of the shaft and the shims from the armature end of the shaft.

3. Withdraw the armature coil assembly from the front end of the case.

4. If necessary, remove the brush holder assembly from the end of the case.

NOTE
Before removing the nuts and washers,
write down their description and order.
They must be reinstalled in the same
order to insulate this set of brushes from
the case.

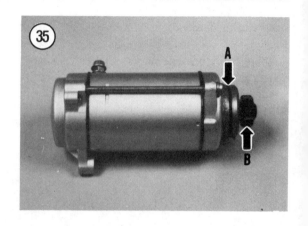

5. Remove the nuts, washers and O-ring securing the brush terminal set. Remove the brush terminal set.

CAUTION
Do not immerse the wire windings in the
case or the armature coil in solvent as

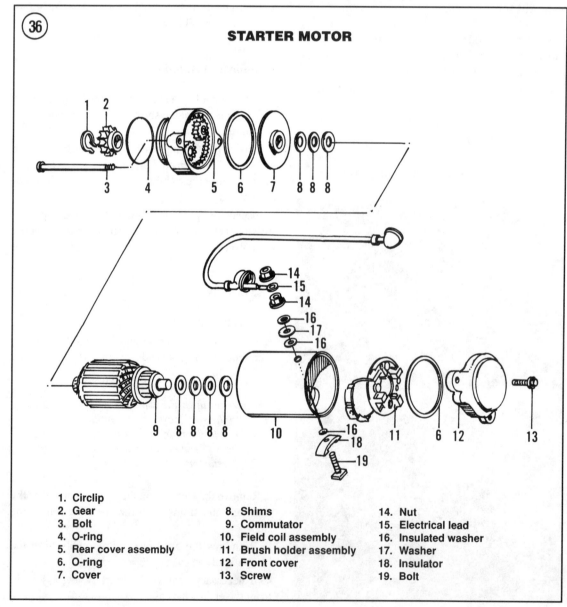

STARTER MOTOR

1. Circlip
2. Gear
3. Bolt
4. O-ring
5. Rear cover assembly
6. O-ring
7. Cover
8. Shims
9. Commutator
10. Field coil assembly
11. Brush holder assembly
12. Front cover
13. Screw
14. Nut
15. Electrical lead
16. Insulated washer
17. Washer
18. Insulator
19. Bolt

the insulation may be damaged. Wipe the windings with a cloth lightly moistened with solvent and thoroughly dry.

6. Clean all grease, dirt and carbon from all components.
7. Inspect the components as described in this chapter.

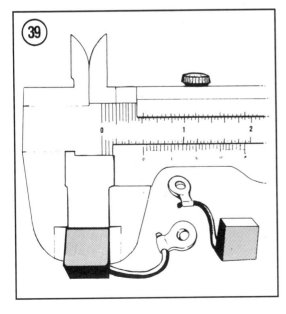

Inspection

1. Pull back the spring from behind the brushes and remove the brushes from their guides (**Figure 38**).
2. Measure the length of each brush (**Figure 39**) with a vernier caliper. If the length is 5.0 mm (0.20 in.) or less for any one of the brushes, the brush holder assembly and brush terminal set must be replaced. The brushes cannot be replaced individually.
3. Inspect the commutator (**Figure 40**). The mica in a good commutator is below the surface of the copper bars. On a worn commutator the mica and copper bars may be worn to the same level (**Figure 41**). If necessary, have the commutator serviced by a dealer or electrical repair shop.
4. Inspect the commutator copper bars for discoloration. If a pair of bars are discolored, grounded armature coils are indicated.
5. Use an ohmmeter and perform the following:

    a. Check for continuity between the commutator bars (**Figure 42**); there should be continuity (indicated resistance) between pairs of bars.

    b. Check for continuity between the commutator bars and the shaft (**Figure 43**); there should be *no* continuity (infinite resistance).

8

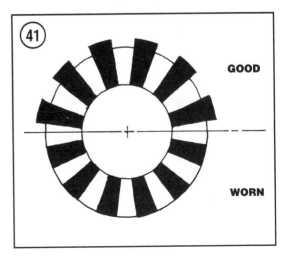

c. If the unit fails either of these tests, the starter assembly must be replaced. The armature cannot be replaced individually.

6. Use an ohmmeter and perform the following:
   a. Check for continuity between the starter cable terminal and the starter case; there should be continuity (indicated resistance).
   b. Check for continuity between the starter cable terminal and the brush wire terminal; there should be *no* continuity (infinite resistance).
   c. If the unit fails either of these tests, the starter assembly must be replaced. The case/field coil assembly cannot be replaced individually.

7. Inspect the oil seal and bushing (**Figure 44**) in the front cover for wear or damage. If either is damaged, replace the starter assembly as these parts are not available separately.

8. Remove the cover on the gear housing and inspect the gears (**Figure 45**). If they are chipped or worn, replace the starter motor. The rear cover and gears are not sold as a separate assembly.

Assembly

1. If the gears were inspected, perform the following:
   a. Install the cover, making sure to align the case screw grooves in both parts (**Figure 46**).
   b. Install the O-ring (**Figure 47**).

2. If removed, install the brush holder assembly.

3. Make sure the correct number of shims is installed on the ends of the armature shaft (**Figure 48**) and insert the armature coil assembly into the front end of the case. Do not damage the brushes during this step and make sure each of the 4 brushes (**Figure 49**) contact the commutator evenly.

4. Align the raised marks (**Figure 50**) on the rear cover with the case.

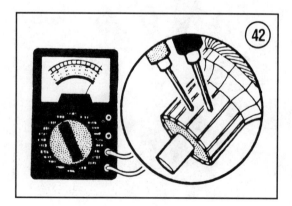

5. Install the front cover, then the case screws and washers. Tighten the screws to the torque specifications listed in **Table 2**.

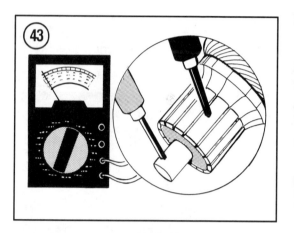

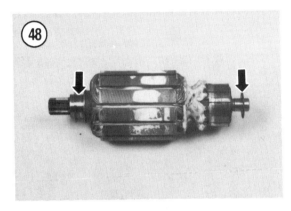

STARTER SOLENOID

Testing

1. Place the bike on the sidestand.

2. Shift the transmission into NEUTRAL.

3. Remove the seat(s) as described under *Seat Removal/Installation* in Chapter Twelve.

4A. On Radian models, remove the right-hand side cover.

4B. On FZ600 models, remove the left-hand side cover as described under *Side Cover Removal/Installation (FZ600 Models)* in Chapter Twelve.

5. Make sure the battery is fully charged, refer to Chapter Three.

6. Turn the main (ignition) switch to the ON position.

> *CAUTION*
> *This test should be performed within a few seconds to prevent further damage to any component in the starting system.*

7. Connect a heavy duty jumper cable from the battery positive (+) terminal (A, **Figure 51**) on the starter solenoid to the starter motor terminal (B, **Figure 51**). The starter motor should run. Immediately disconnect the jumper cable from the solenoid terminals.

8. If the starter motor does not run, inspect and/or replace the starter motor.

9A. On Radian models, if the starter motor runs, check the starter cut-off relay as follows:

    a. Remove the fuel tank as described under *Fuel Tank Removal/Installation* in Chapter Seven.

    b. Disconnect the electrical connector (A, **Figure 52**) from the cut-off relay (B, **Figure 52**).

8

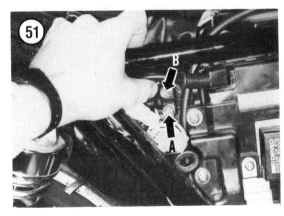

c. Connect a jumper wire from the blue/white terminal in the connector to the battery negative terminal.

d. If the starter motor runs, the cut-off relay is faulty and must be replaced.

e. If the starter motor does not run, the starter relay is faulty and must be replaced.

9B. On FZ600 models, if the starter motor runs, check the starter cut-off relay as follows:

a. Disconnect the electrical connector (A, **Figure 53**) from the cut-off relay (B, **Figure 53**).

b. Connect a jumper wire from the blue/white terminal in the connector to the battery negative terminal.

c. If the starter motor runs, the cut-off relay is faulty and must be replaced.

d. If the starter motor does not run, the starter relay is faulty and must be replaced.

10. Reconnect the electrical connector to the cut-off relay. Make sure the electrical connection is free of corrosion and is tight.

11. Install the side cover and seat as described in Chapter Twelve.

Removal/Installation

The starter solenoid is located behind the battery. On Radian models it is on the right-hand side and on FZ600 models it is on the left-hand side.

1. Remove the seat(s) as described under *Seat Removal/Installation* in Chapter Twelve.

2A. On Radian models, remove the right-hand side cover.

2B. On FZ600 models, remove the left-hand side cover as described under *Side Cover Removal/Installation (FZ600 Models)* in Chapter Twelve.

3. Slide off the rubber protective boots from the solenoid.

4. Remove the nuts and lockwashers and disconnect the large electrical wires from the top terminals of the solenoid (A, **Figure 54**).

5. Disconnect the 2 small electrical wires from the side of the solenoid.

6. Remove the solenoid's rubber mount from the frame and remove the solenoid.

7. Replace by reversing these removal steps while noting the following.

8. Install all electrical wires to the solenoid and onto the large terminals, tighten the nuts securely. Make sure the electrical connectors are on tight and that

the rubber boot (B, **Figure 54**) is properly installed to keep out moisture.

9. Install the side cover and seat as described in Chapter Twelve.

LIGHTING SYSTEM

The lighting system consists of a headlight, taillight/brakelight, directional lights, indicator lights and a speedometer illumination light. **Table 5** lists replacement bulbs for these components.

Always use the correct wattage bulb as indicated in this section. The use of a larger wattage bulb will

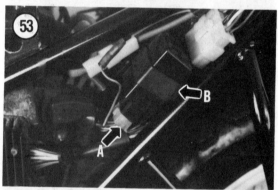

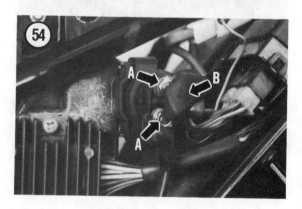

give a dim light and a smaller wattage bulb will burn out prematurely.

Headlight Bulb Replacement
(Radian Models)

Refer to **Figure 55** for this procedure.

1. Remove the screw (**Figure 56**) on each lower corner of the headlight case.

2. Pull out on the bottom of the headlight lens assembly and unhook it from the retainer on the top of the case.

3. Partially pull the lens assembly out of the case and disconnect the electrical connector on the backside. Remove the lens assembly.

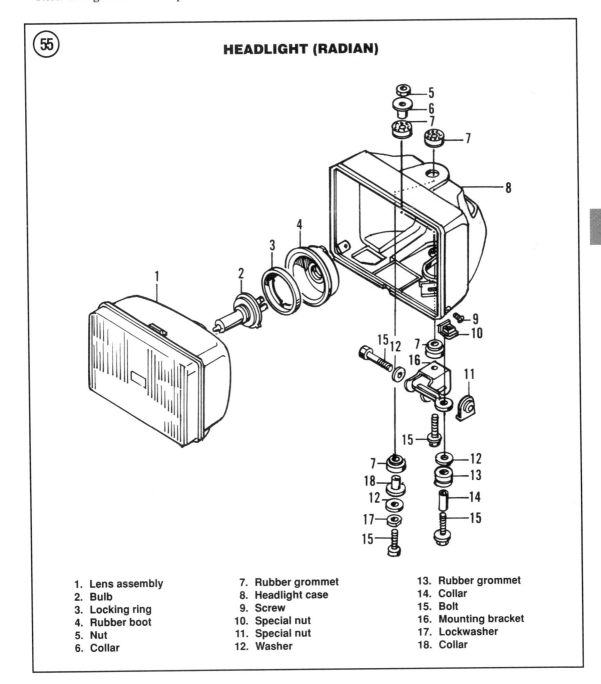

HEADLIGHT (RADIAN)

1. Lens assembly	7. Rubber grommet	13. Rubber grommet
2. Bulb	8. Headlight case	14. Collar
3. Locking ring	9. Screw	15. Bolt
4. Rubber boot	10. Special nut	16. Mounting bracket
5. Nut	11. Special nut	17. Lockwasher
6. Collar	12. Washer	18. Collar

4. Remove the dust boot (**Figure 57**) from the back of the lens assembly.

5. Rotate the bulb locking ring *counterclockwise* (A, **Figure 58**) and remove it from the lens assembly.

6. Remove the bulb (B, **Figure 58**) from the lens assembly.

CAUTION
Carefully read all instructions shipped with the replacement quartz bulb. Do not touch the bulb glass with your fin-

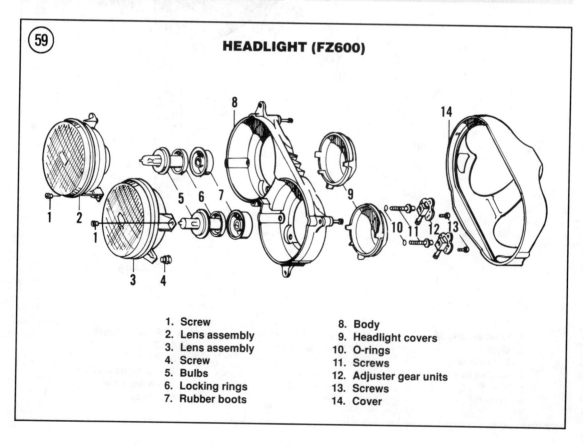

HEADLIGHT (FZ600)

1. Screw
2. Lens assembly
3. Lens assembly
4. Screw
5. Bulbs
6. Locking rings
7. Rubber boots
8. Body
9. Headlight covers
10. O-rings
11. Screws
12. Adjuster gear units
13. Screws
14. Cover

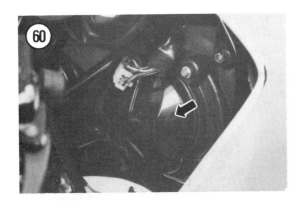

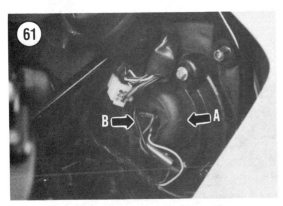

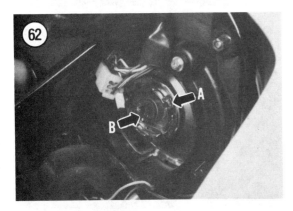

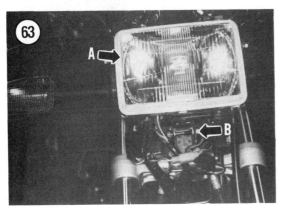

gers because any traces of skin oil on the quartz halogen bulb will drastically reduce bulb life. Clean any traces of oil from the bulb with a cloth moistened in alcohol or lacquer thinner.

7. Install by reversing these removal steps.

Headlight Bulb Replacement (FZ600 Models)

Refer to **Figure 59** for this procedure.
1. Turn the handlebar to the opposite side of the bulb that is to be replaced. This will allow additional work room within the front fairing.
2. Remove the headlight cover (**Figure 60**) from the backside of the headlight body.
3. Remove the dust boot (A, **Figure 61**) and disconnect the electrical connector (B, **Figure 61**) from the backside of the headlight.
4. Rotate the bulb locking ring *counterclockwise* (A, **Figure 62**) and remove it from the lens assembly.
5. Remove the bulb (B, **Figure 62**) from the lens assembly.

CAUTION
Carefully read all instructions shipped with the replacement quartz bulb. Do not touch the bulb glass with your fingers because any traces of skin oil on the quartz halogen bulb will drastically reduce bulb life. Clean any traces of oil from the bulb with a cloth moistened in alcohol or lacquer thinner.

6. Install by reversing these removal steps.
7. Repeat for the other bulb if necessary.

Headlight Case Removal/Installation (Radian Models)

Refer to **Figure 55** for this procedure.
1. Remove the screw on each side securing the front cover below the headlight and remove the cover.
2. Remove the headlight bulb and lens assembly (A, **Figure 63**) as described in this chapter.
3. Disconnect all of the electrical connectors (A, **Figure 64**) within and below the headlight case.
4. Remove the bolt washer and special nut (B, **Figure 63**) securing the headlight case to the lower mounting bracket.

5. Remove the bolt, lockwasher and washer (B, **Figure 64**) securing the upper portion of the headlight case. Don't lose the collar and rubber grommets in the upper mount.

6. Carefully pull the electrical connectors and cables out through the base of the headlight case.

7. Remove the headlight case from the steering head.

8. Install by reversing these removal steps while noting the following:

   a. Make sure the rubber grommets and collars are in place in the mounting holes where applicable. These grommets help prevent the plastic from fracturing at the attachment points.

   b. Tighten the bolts and nuts securely. Do not overtighten as the plastic parts may fracture.

   c. Adjust the headlight as described in this chapter.

Headlight Lens and Housing Removal/Installation (FZ600 Models)

Refer to **Figure 59** for this procedure.

1. Remove the front fairing as described under *Front Fairing Removal/Installation* in Chapter Twelve.

2. Remove the headlight bulb as described in this chapter.

3. Remove the nuts securing the headlight lens and housing to the body and remove it.

4. Install by reversing these removal steps.

5. Adjust the headlight as described in this chapter.

Headlight Adjustment (Radian Models)

Adjust the headlight horizontally and vertically according to Department of Motor Vehicle regulations in your area.

1. Remove the screw on each side securing the front cover below the headlight and remove the cover.

2. To adjust the headlight horizontally, perform the following:

   a. Loosen the bolt (A, **Figure 65**).

   b. Move the headlight case in either direction sideways until the vertical aim is correct.

   c. Tighten the bolt securely.

3. To adjust the headlight vertically, perform the following:

   a. Loosen the bolt (B, **Figure 65**).

   b. Move the headlight case up or down until the horizontal aim is correct.

   c. Tighten the bolt securely.

4. Install the front cover and tighten the screws securely.

Headlight Adjustment (FZ600 Models)

Adjust the headlight horizontally and vertically according to Department of Motor Vehicle regulations in your area.

1. To adjust the headlight horizontally, turn the lower screw adjust (A, **Figure 66**). Turn the screw clockwise or counterclockwise until the aim is correct.

2. For vertical adjustment, turn the upper adjust screw (B, **Figure 66**). Turn the upper adjust screw either clockwise or counterclockwise until the aim is correct.

Taillight/Brakelight Bulb Replacement

Refer to **Figure 67** for this procedure.

1A. On Radian models, remove the seat as described under *Seat Removal/Installation* in Chapter Twelve.

1B. On FZ600 models, remove only the passenger seat as described under *Seat Removal/Installation* in Chapter Twelve.

2. Remove the cover from the taillight assembly.

3. Push in on the bulb socket (**Figure 68**), turn it *counterclockwise* about 30°, then withdraw it from the taillight assembly.

4. Remove the bulb (**Figure 69**) and install a new one.

5. Install the bulb and socket and reinstall the cover.

6. Install the seat.

Taillight/Brakelight Lens and Housing Removal/Installation

Refer to **Figure 67** for this procedure.

1A. On Radian models, remove the seat as described under *Seat Removal/Installation* in Chapter Twelve.

1B. On FZ600 models, remove only the passenger seat as described under *Seat Removal/Installation* in Chapter Twelve.

2. Remove the cover from the taillight assembly.

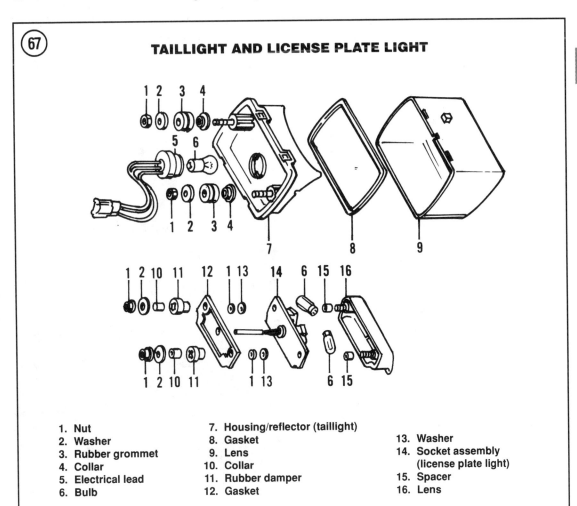

TAILLIGHT AND LICENSE PLATE LIGHT

8

1. Nut	7. Housing/reflector (taillight)	
2. Washer	8. Gasket	13. Washer
3. Rubber grommet	9. Lens	14. Socket assembly
4. Collar	10. Collar	(license plate light)
5. Electrical lead	11. Rubber damper	15. Spacer
6. Bulb	12. Gasket	16. Lens

3. Push in on the bulb socket (A, **Figure 70**), turn it *counterclockwise* about 30°, then withdraw it from the taillight assembly.

4. Remove the nut and washer (B, **Figure 70**) on each side securing the taillight/brakelight assembly.

5. Withdraw the taillight/brakelight assembly (**Figure 71**) out through the rear of the housing. Don't lose the collar located within each rubber grommet on the mounting brackets.

6. Unsnap the lens from the housing/reflector and remove the lens and gasket.

7. Wash out the inside and outside of the lens and the reflector surface with a mild detergent and wipe dry.

8. Inspect the gasket for deterioration or damage, replace if necessary.

9. Install by reversing these removal steps.

Directional Signal Light Replacement

Refer to **Figure 72** for this procedure.

1. Remove the screw (**Figure 73**) securing the lens and remove the lens.

2. Wash out the inside and outside of the lens with a mild detergent and wipe dry.

3. Replace the bulb (**Figure 74**) and install the lens; do not overtighten the screws as the lens may crack.

Speedometer and Tachometer Illumination Light Replacement (Radian Models)

1. Remove the instrument cluster as described in this chapter.

2. Remove the screws securing the cover to the instrument and remove the cover.

3. Carefully pull the defective lamp holder/electrical wire assembly from the backside of the meter housing.

4. Remove and replace the defective bulb.

> *NOTE*
> *If a new bulb will not work, check the wire connections for loose or broken wires. Also check the bulb socket for corrosion. Clean or replace as necessary.*

5. Push the lamp socket/electrical wire assembly back into the housing. Make sure it is completely seated to prevent the entry of water and moisture.

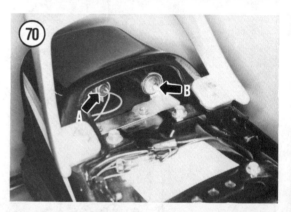

6. Install the instrument cluster as described in Chapter Twelve.

Speedometer and Tachometer Illumination Light Replacement (FZ600 Models)

1. Reach under the meter and carefully pull the defective lamp holder/electrical wire assembly from the backside of the meter housing.

2. Remove and replace the defective bulb.

NOTE
If a new bulb will not work, check the wire connections for loose or broken wires. Also check the bulb socket for corrosion. Clean or replace as necessary.

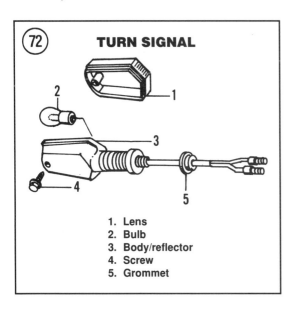

72 **TURN SIGNAL**

1. Lens
2. Bulb
3. Body/reflector
4. Screw
5. Grommet

3. Push the lamp socket/electrical wire assembly back into the housing. Make sure it is completely seated to prevent the entry of water and moisture.

Indicator Light Replacement (Radian Models)

1. Remove the screws securing the indicator lens assembly (**Figure 75**).
2. Carefully pull the assembly up and away from the handlebar area.
3. Carefully pull the defective lamp holder/electrical wire assembly from the backside of the indicator lens assembly.
4. Remove and replace the defective bulb.

NOTE
If a new bulb will not work, check the wire connections for loose or broken wires. Also check the bulb socket for corrosion. Replace as necessary.

5. Push the lamp socket/electrical wire assembly back into the indicator lens assembly. Make sure it

8

74

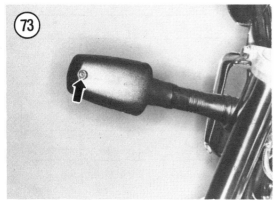

73

75

is completely seated to prevent the entry of water and moisture.

6. Move the indicator lens assembly back into place and install the screws. Tighten the screws securely.

Indicator Light Replacement
(FZ600 Models)

1. Reach under the indicator lens assembly and carefully pull the defective lamp holder/electrical wire assembly from the backside of the indicator lens assembly.

2. Remove and replace the defective bulb.

> *NOTE*
> *If a new bulb will not work, check the wire connections for loose or broken wires. Also check the bulb socket for corrosion. Clean or replace as necessary.*

3. Push the lamp socket/electrical wire assembly back into the indicator lens assembly. Make sure it is completely seated to prevent the entry of water and moisture.

SWITCHES

Switches can be tested with an ohmmeter or a battery operated test light. Follow the manufacturer's instructions when using the test equipment.

Test the switch by operating the switch in each of its operating positions and comparing the results with the switch operation. For example, **Figure 76** shows a continuity diagram for a typical horn button. It shows which terminals should show continuity when the horn button is in a given position.

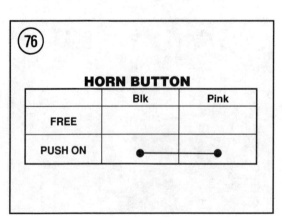

When the horn button is pushed, there should be continuity between the black and pink terminals. This is indicated by the line on the continuity diagram (**Figure 76**). An ohmmeter connected between these 2 terminals should indicate continuity (low resistance) or a test lamp should light. When

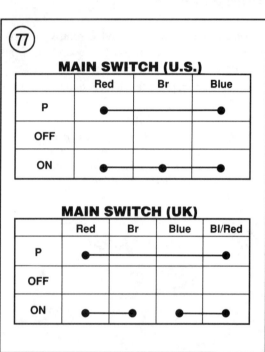

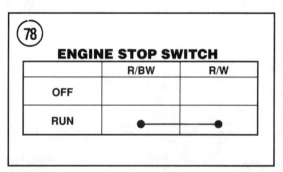

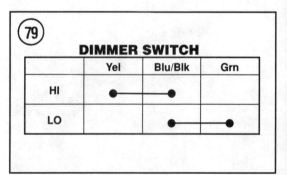

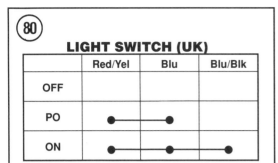

LIGHT SWITCH (UK) — Figure 80

	Red/Yel	Blu	Blu/Blk
OFF			
PO	●————————●		
ON	●————————●————————●		

FRONT BRAKE SWITCH — Figure 82

	Br	G/Y
Brake lever free		
Brake lever depressed	●————————●	

REAR BRAKE SWITCH — Figure 83

	Br	Yel
Brake pedal free		
Brake pedal depressed	●————————●	

the horn button is free, there should be no continuity (infinite resistance) between the same set of terminals, or the test lamp should not light.

If the switch or button doesn't perform properly, replace it. Refer to the following figures when testing the switches:

  a. Horn button: **Figure 76**.
  b. Main switch (U.S.): **Figure 77**. Main switch (UK): **Figure 77**.
  c. Engine stop switch: **Figure 78**.
  d. Dimmer switch: **Figure 79**.
  e. Light switch (UK): **Figure 80**.
  f. Turn switch: **Figure 81**.
  g. Front brake switch: **Figure 82**.
  h. Rear brake switch: **Figure 83**.
  i. Starter switch (U.S.): **Figure 84**. Starter switch (UK): **Figure 84**.
  j. Clutch switch: **Figure 85**.

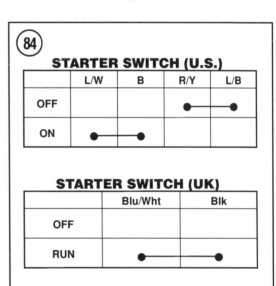

STARTER SWITCH (U.S.) — Figure 84

	L/W	B	R/Y	L/B
OFF			●————————●	
ON	●————————●			

STARTER SWITCH (UK)

	Blu/Wht	Blk
OFF		
RUN	●————————●	

8

TURN SWITCH — Figure 81

		Ch	Brn/White	Dk. Grn	Yel/Red	Blk
L		●————————●			●————————●	
N	L	●————————●				
	N					
	R		●————————●			
R			●————————●		●————————●	

When testing these switches for continuity, note the following:

a. First check any applicable fuse in that specific circuit as described under *Fuses* in this chapter.

b. Check the condition of the battery to make sure it is fully charged, recharge if necessary. Refer to *Battery* in Chapter Three.

CAUTION
If the battery is left connected in the circuit and the switch is turned ON during testing, the test equipment will be damaged.

c. Disconnect the battery negative (–) cable if the switch connectors are not disconnected from the circuit being tested.

CAUTION
Do not attempt to start the engine with the battery negative (–) cable disconnected as you will damage the wiring and electrical components in the circuit.

d. When separating 2 electrical connectors, pull on the connector housings—not on the wires.

e. After locating a defective circuit, check the electrical connectors to make sure they are clean, free of corrosion and are properly connected. Check all wires going into an electrical connector housing to make sure each wire is properly positioned and that the wire end is not loose.

f. To connect electrical connectors properly, push them together until they click into place.

g. When replacing handlebar switch assemblies, make sure the cables are routed correctly so that they do not get crimped when the handlebar is turned from side-to-side.

Use the wiring diagrams at the end of this book to help in locating and identifying the following switch wiring and terminal connectors.

Main Switch
Removal/Installation
(Radian Models)

1. Remove the seat as described under *Seat Removal/Installation* in Chapter Twelve.

2. Remove the fuel tank as described under *Fuel Tank Removal/Installation* in Chapter Seven.

3. Remove the screws securing the indicator lens assembly (A, **Figure 86**).

4. Carefully pull the assembly up and away from the handlebar area.

5. On the right-hand side of the frame rail, locate and disconnect the 3-pin electrical connector (containing 3 wires—one red, one brown and one blue) at the base of the main (ignition) switch.

6. Remove the mounting screws and washers securing the main (ignition) switch (B, **Figure 86**) to the upper fork bridge.

7. Remove the switch assembly from the upper fork bridge.

8. Install the new main (ignition) switch onto the upper fork bridge and tighten the screws securely.

9. Reconnect the 3-pin electrical connector. Make sure the electrical connector is free of corrosion and is tight.

10. Install the indicator panel and screws. Tighten the screws securely.

11. Install the fuel tank as described in Chapter Seven.

12. Install the seat as described in Chapter Twelve.

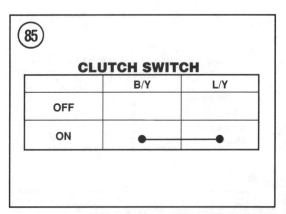

CLUTCH SWITCH

	B/Y	L/Y
OFF		
ON	●———————●

Main Switch
Removal/Installation
(FZ600 Models)

1. Remove the seat as described under *Seat Removal/Installation* in Chapter Twelve.

2. Remove the fuel tank as described under *Fuel Tank Removal/Installation* in Chapter Seven.

3A. On U.S. models, locate and disconnect the 3-pin electrical connector (containing 3 wires—1 red, 1 brown and 1 blue) just behind the steering head.

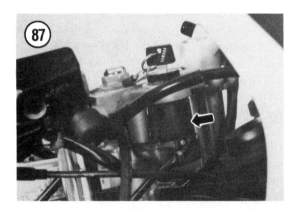

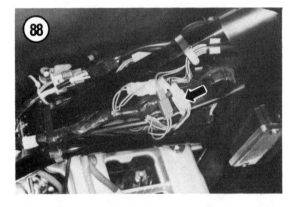

3B. On UK models, locate and disconnect the 4-pin electrical connector (containing 4 wires—1 red, 1 brown, 1 blue and 1 blue/red) just behind the steering head.

4. Remove the mounting screws and washers securing the main (ignition) switch (**Figure 87**) to the upper fork bridge.

5. Remove the switch assembly from the upper fork bridge.

6. Install the new main (ignition) switch onto the upper fork bridge and tighten the screws securely.

7. Reconnect the 3-pin (U.S.), or 4-pin (UK), electrical connector. Make sure the electrical connector is free of corrosion and is tight.

8. Install the fuel tank as described in Chapter Seven.

9. Install the seat and the front fairing as described in Chapter Twelve.

Right-hand Combination Switch
Engine Start and Stop Switch—Radian models
or Engine Start, Stop Switch, Front Brake
Light Switch [FZ600] and Light Switch [UK]

The right-hand combination switch assembly contains both the engine start and engine stop switch. On FZ600 models, the front brake light switch is also incorporated in the switch. If either switch is faulty, the entire switch assembly must be replaced.

1. Remove the seat as described under *Seat Removal/Installation* in Chapter Twelve.

2. Remove the fuel tank as described under *Fuel Tank Removal/Installation* in Chapter Seven.

3A. On Radian models, on the right-hand side of the frame rail locate the engine start and stop switch 6-pin electrical connector (containing 6 wires—1 red/yellow, 1 blue/black, 1 blue/white, 1 black and 2 red/white). Disconnect this electrical connector (**Figure 88**).

3B. On FZ600 U.S. models, between the upper frame rails, locate the engine start and stop switch (also included are the front brake light wires) 10-pin electrical connector (containing 8 wires—1 brown, 1 green/yellow, 2 red/white, 1 blue/white, 1 black, 1 red/yellow and 1 blue/black). Disconnect this electrical connector (A, **Figure 89**).

3C. On FZ600 UK models, between the upper frame rails, locate the engine start and stop switch (also included are the front brake light wires) 10-pin electrical connector (containing 9 wires—1 brown, 1 green/yellow, 2 red/white, 1 blue/white, 1 black, 1 red/yellow, 1 blue and 1 blue/black). Disconnect this electrical connector.

4. Remove the electrical wire harness from any clips on the frame and carefully pull the harness out from the frame.

5. Remove the electrical wire harness from any clips on the handlebar (A, **Figure 90**).

6. Remove the screws securing the right-hand combination switch together and remove the switch assembly (B, **Figure 90**).

7. Install a new switch and tighten the screws securely. Do not overtighten the screws or the plastic switch housing may crack.

8. Make sure the electrical connector is free of corrosion. Reconnect the electrical connector and make sure it is tight. Install the tie wrap to hold the electrical wires to the handlebar and to the frame. The wires must be retained in this manner to allow room for the fuel tank.

9. Install the fuel tank as described in Chapter Seven.

10. Install the seat as described in Chapter Twelve.

Left-hand Combination Switch (Clutch Switch, Headlight Dimmer Switch, Turn Signal Switch, Horn Switch and Pass Switch [UK]) Removal/Installation

The left-hand combination switch assembly contains the clutch switch, headlight dimmer switch, turn signal switch and horn switch. If any of the switches are faulty, the entire switch assembly must be replaced.

1. Remove the seat as described under *Seat Removal/Installation* in Chapter Twelve.

2. Remove the fuel tank as described under *Fuel Tank Removal/Installation* in Chapter Seven.

3A. On Radian models, on each side of the frame rail locate and disconnect the following electrical connectors:

  a. The clutch switch and turn signal switch: 6-pin electrical connector (containing 6 wires—1 chocolate, 1 brown/white, 1 yellow/red, 1 dark green, 1 black/yellow and 1 blue/yellow).

  b. Headlight dimmer switch: 3-pin electrical connector (containing 1 yellow, 1 blue/black and 1 green).

  c. Horn switch: 2-pin electrical connector (containing 2 wires—1 pink and 1 black).

3B. On FZ600 models, between the upper frame rails, locate and disconnect the following electrical connectors:

  a. Clutch switch, turn switch, horn and dimmer switch (partial): 9-pin electrical connector (containing 8 wires—1 yellow/red, 1 pink, 1 blue/yellow, 1 blue/black, 1 brown/white, 1 dark green, 1 chocolate, 1 yellow/black and 1 black) (B, **Figure 89**).

  b. Remainder of dimmer switch: 2-pin electrical connector (containing 2 wires—1 yellow and 1 green) (C, **Figure 89**).

  c. Pass switch (UK models): 2-pin electrical connector (containing 2 wires—1 black/yellow and 1 blue/yellow).

4. Remove the electrical wire harness from any clips on the frame and carefully pull the harness out from the frame.

5. Remove the electrical wire harness from any clips (**Figure 91**) on the handlebar.

6. Remove the screws securing the left-hand combination switch together and remove the switch assembly (**Figure 92**).

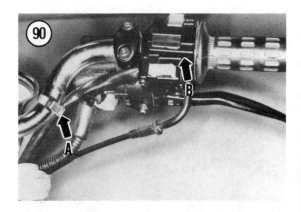

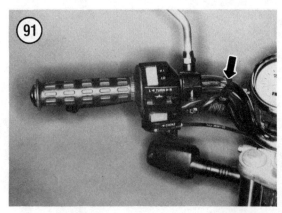

7. Install a new switch and tighten the screws securely. Do not overtighten the screws or the plastic switch housing may crack.

8. Reconnect the two electrical connectors.

9. Make sure the electrical connectors are free of corrosion. Reconnect the electrical connectors and make sure they are tight. Install the tie wrap to hold the electrical wires to the handlebar and to the frame. The wires must be retained in this manner to allow room for the fuel tank.

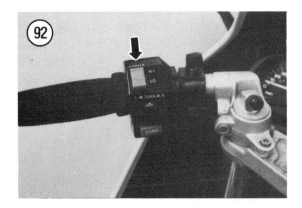

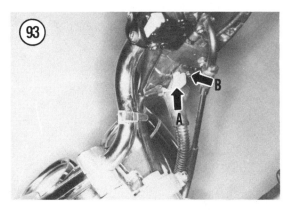

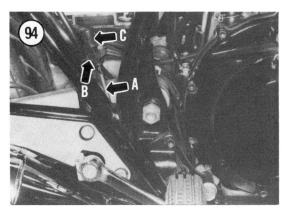

10. Install the fuel tank as described in Chapter Seven.

11. Install the seat as described in Chapter Twelve.

Front Brake Light Switch
(Radian Models)
Removal/Installation

NOTE
On FZ600 models, the front brake light switch is an integral part of the right-hand switch assembly.

1. Disconnect the electrical connector (A, **Figure 93**) from the brake switch.

2. Remove the screw and lockwasher (B, **Figure 93**) securing the front brake light switch to the front brake lever housing and remove the switch assembly.

3. Install a new switch and tighten the screw securely. Do not overtighten as the switch may be damaged.

4. Reconnect the electrical connector.

5. Make sure the electrical connector is free of corrosion and is tight.

Rear Brake Light Switch Replacement
(Radian Models)

1. Disconnect the 2-pin electrical connector containing 2 wires (1 brown and 1 yellow).

2. Disconnect the spring (A, **Figure 94**) from the brake pedal pivot shaft.

3. Remove the brake switch (C, **Figure 94**) from the mounting lug on the frame.

4. Install the brake switch by reversing these removal steps and noting the following:

    a. Make sure the electrical connector is free of corrosion and is tight.

    b. Adjust the rear brake switch as described in this chapter.

Rear Brake Light Switch Replacement
(FZ600 Models)

1. Remove the bolts (A, **Figure 95**) securing the trim plate and remove the trim plate (B, **Figure 95**).

2. Disconnect the 2-pin electrical connector containing 2 wires (1 brown and 1 yellow).

3. Disconnect the spring from the brake pedal tab.

8

4. Remove the brake switch from the mounting lug on the frame.

5. Install the brake switch by reversing these removal steps while noting the following:

    a. Make sure the electrical connector is free of corrosion and is tight.

    b. Adjust the rear brake switch as described in this chapter.

Rear Brake Light Switch Adjustment

1. Turn the main (ignition) switch to the ON position.

2. Depress the brake pedal. The brake light should come on just as the brake begins to work.

3. To make the brake light come on earlier, hold the brake light switch body (C, **Figure 94**) and turn the adjusting nut (B, **Figure 94**) *clockwise* as viewed from the top. Turn the adjusting nut *counterclockwise* to delay the light coming on.

> *NOTE*
> *Some riders prefer the brake light to come on a little early. This way, they can tap the pedal without braking to warn drivers who are following too closely.*

Side Stand Check Switch Testing

> *NOTE*
> *The 1986 FZ600 UK models are not equipped with this switch. It was added to the 1987 models.*

1. Remove the shift lever and sprocket cover.

2. Locate and disconnect the side stand check switch 2-pin electrical connector (containing 2 wires—1 blue/yellow wire and 1 black) (**Figure 96**).

3. Use an ohmmeter and check for continuity. Connect the test leads to the side stand check switch side of the electrical connectors as follows:

    a. Place the side stand in the down position: there should be continuity (low resistance).

    b. Have an assistant hold the bike in the upright position, raise the side stand and check for continuity: there should be no continuity (infinite resistance).

4. If the side stand check switch fails either one of these tests, the switch must be replaced as described in this chapter.

5. If necessary, remove the switch as described in this chapter.

6. Reconnect the 2-pin electrical connector.

7. Make sure the electrical connector is free of corrosion and is tight. Install the tie wrap to hold the electrical wires to the frame.

8. Install the left-hand side cover.

Side Stand Check Switch Removal/Installation

> *NOTE*
> *The 1986 FZ600 UK models are not equipped with this switch. It was added to the 1987 models.*

1. Remove the shift lever and sprocket cover (A, **Figure 97**).

2. Unhook the wire wrap (A, **Figure 98**) securing the electrical wires to the crankcase.

> *NOTE*
> *The side stand switch electrical cable is made up of 2 separate wire assemblies.*

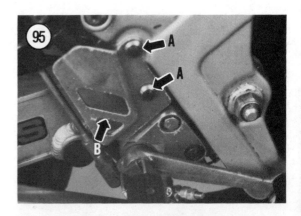

There are 2 lower short individual wires that are connected directly to the switch. These 2 wires are connected to the upper electrical wire that terminates with a 2-pin electrical connector as shown in **Figure 96**.

3. Disconnect the side stand check switch 2-pin electrical connectors (B, **Figure 98**) (1 blue/yellow wire and 1 black).

4. Have an assistant hold the bike in the upright position.

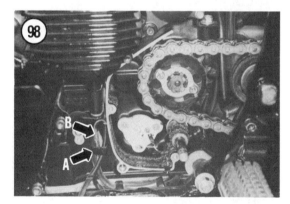

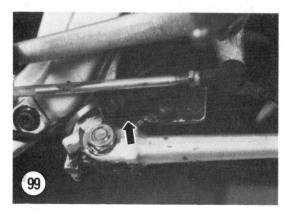

5. Remove the screws securing the side stand check switch to the frame and remove the switch. Refer to B, **Figure 97** for Radian models or **Figure 99** for FZ600 models.

6. Install a new side stand check switch and tighten the screws securely.

7. Route the electrical wire harness through the frame and install the tie wraps securing the harness to the frame.

8. Reconnect the 2-pin electrical connector.

9. Make sure the electrical connector is free of corrosion and is tight. Install the tie wrap to hold the electrical wires to the frame.

10. Install the sprocket cover and the left-hand side cover.

Oil Level Switch Removal and Testing

1. Drain the engine oil as described under *Engine Oil and Filter Change* in Chapter Three.

2. Remove the exhaust system as described under *Exhaust System Removal/Installation* in Chapter Seven.

3. Disconnect the oil pressure switch individual black/red wire electrical connector.

4. Remove the bolts securing the oil level switch to the bottom left-hand side of the oil pan. Remove the switch assembly.

5. Use an ohmmeter and check for continuity. Connect one of the test leads to the black/red electrical connector and the other test lead to the switch mounting tab and perform the following:

    a. Hold the switch in the normal position with the mounting flange down. There should be no continuity (infinite resistance).

    b. Hold the switch upside down with the mounting flange up. There should be continuity (low or 0 resistance).

6. If the switch fails either one of these tests, the switch must be replaced.

7. Install the oil level switch and tighten the bolts securely.

8. Reconnect the individual electrical connector.

9. Make sure the electrical connector is free of corrosion and is tight. Install the tie wrap to hold the electrical wires to the frame.

10. Install the left-hand side cover.

11. Install the exhaust system as described in Chapter Seven.

8

12. Fill the engine with oil as described in Chapter Three.

Fuel Gauge Test (FZ600 Models)

1. Remove the fuel tank as described under *Fuel Tank Removal/Installation* in Chapter Seven.

2. Turn the fuel tank on its side and remove the screws securing the fuel gauge to the base of the fuel tank. Remove the fuel gauge from the tank.

3. Use an ohmmeter set at R × 1 and check for resistance values.

4. Connect one of the test leads to the black wire terminal and the other to the green wire terminal in the electrical connector.

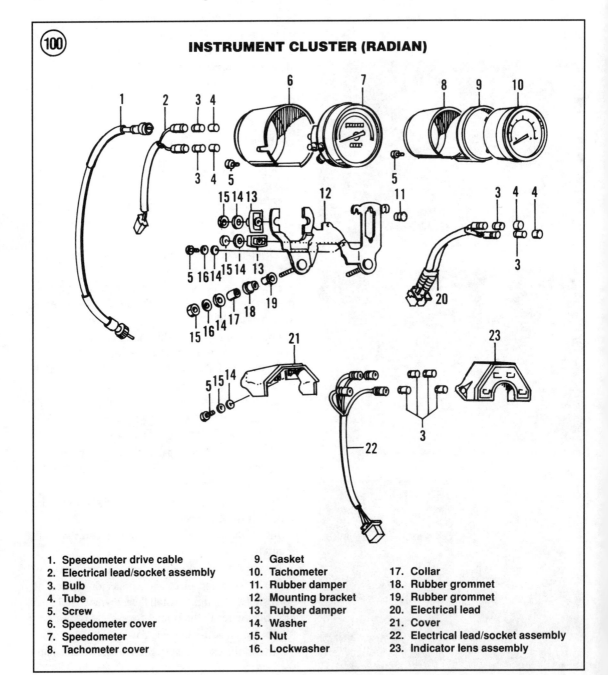

INSTRUMENT CLUSTER (RADIAN)

1. Speedometer drive cable
2. Electrical lead/socket assembly
3. Bulb
4. Tube
5. Screw
6. Speedometer cover
7. Speedometer
8. Tachometer cover
9. Gasket
10. Tachometer
11. Rubber damper
12. Mounting bracket
13. Rubber damper
14. Washer
15. Nut
16. Lockwasher
17. Collar
18. Rubber grommet
19. Rubber grommet
20. Electrical lead
21. Cover
22. Electrical lead/socket assembly
23. Indicator lens assembly

5. Hold the gauge in the correct position (as installed in the fuel tank).

6. Raise the float up to the full fuel tank position. The resistance value should be 8.7-14.7 ohms at 20° C (68° F).

7. Lower the float to the empty fuel tank position. The resistance value should be 125-145 ohms at 20° C (68° F).

8. If the fuel gauge fails either one of these tests, the gauge must be replaced.

9. Install the fuel gauge and gasket in the base of the fuel tank and tighten the screws securely.

10. Install the fuel tank as described in Chapter Seven. Check for fuel leaks.

ELECTRICAL COMPONENTS

This section contains information on all electrical components except switches and relays.

Instrument Cluster Removal/Installation (Radian Models)

Refer to **Figure 100** for this procedure.

1. Disconnect the battery negative lead, see Chapter Three.

2. Unscrew the speedometer drive cable (**Figure 101**) from the back of the speedometer.

3. Remove the screw (A, **Figure 102**) on each side securing the front cover (B, **Figure 102**) and remove the cover.

4. Remove the headlight bulb and lens assembly as described in this chapter.

5. Disconnect all of the electrical connectors relating to the instrument cluster and indicator panel within the headlight case and in the area below the case (**Figure 103**).

6. Remove the nuts, washers and lockwashers securing the instrument cluster mounting bracket to the upper fork bridge.

7. Remove the instrument cluster assembly, carefully working the electrical cables out of the headlight case.

8. Install by reversing these removal steps. Make sure the electrical connectors are free of corrosion and are tight.

Instrument Cluster Removal/Installation (FZ600 Models)

Refer to **Figure 104** for this procedure.

1. Remove the front fairing (A, **Figure 105**) as described under *Front Fairing Removal/Installation* in Chapter Twelve.

2. Disconnect the battery negative lead, see Chapter Three.

8

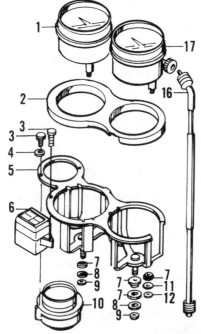

(104) INSTRUMENT CLUSTER (FZ600)

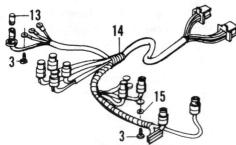

1. Tachometer
2. Rubber damper
3. Bolt
4. Washer
5. Mounting bracket
6. Indicator lamp lens assembly
7. Rubber damper
8. Washer
9. Nut
10. Fuel meter
11. Washer
12. Nut
13. Bulb
14. Electrical lead/socket assembly
15. Washer
16. Speedometer drive cable
17. Speedometer

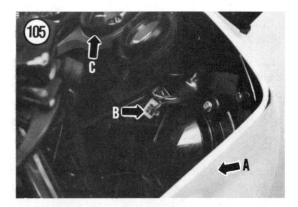

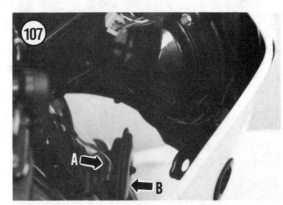

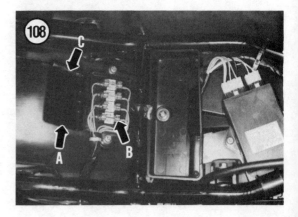

3. Unscrew the speedometer drive cable from the back of the speedometer.

4. In back of the instrument cluster, disconnect the instrument cluster electrical connectors (B, **Figure 105**).

5. Remove the nuts, washers and lockwashers securing the instrument cluster (C, **Figure 105**) to the mounting bracket.

6. Remove the instrument cluster assembly from the bracket.

7. If necessary, remove the bolts and lockwashers securing the instrument cluster mounting bracket (**Figure 106**) to the steering head.

8. Install by reversing these removal steps. Make sure the electrical connectors are free of corrosion and are tight.

Horn Testing

1. Disconnect horn wires from harness.
2. Connect a 12 volt battery to the horn.
3. If the horn is good, it will sound. If not, replace it.

Horn
Removal/Installation

1. Disconnect the electrical connectors (A, **Figure 107**) from the horn.

2. Remove the screw and washers securing the horn (B, **Figure 107**) to the bracket. Remove the horn.

3. Install by reversing these removal steps. Note the following.

4. Make sure the electrical connector is free of corrosion and is tight.

FUSES

The fuse panel is located under the seat on top of the rear fender.

Whenever the fuse blows, find out the reason for the failure before replacing the fuse. Usually, the trouble is a short circuit in the wiring. This may be caused by worn-through insulation or a disconnected wire shorted to ground.

CAUTION
Never substitute metal foil or wire for a fuse. Never use a higher amperage fuse than specified. An overload could result in a fire and complete loss of the bike.

CAUTION
When replacing a fuse, make sure the main (ignition) switch is in the OFF position. This will lessen the chance of a short circuit.

Fuse Replacement

1. Remove the seat as described under *Seat Removal/Installation* in Chapter Twelve.

2. Flip up the fuel panel cover (A, **Figure 108**).

3. Remove the fuse (B, **Figure 108**) and install a new one. There are spare fuses on the inside of the cover (C, **Figure 108**).

4. Push the cover down until it clicks into place.

5. Install the seat.

WIRING DIAGRAMS

Wiring diagrams for all models are located at the end of this book.

Tables 1-5 are on the following pages.

Table 1 ELECTRICAL SYSTEM SPECIFICATIONS

Item	Specification
Ignition coil	
Primary coil resistance	2.43-2.97 ohms
Secondary coil resistance	10.56-15.84K ohms
Pickup coil resistance	108-132 ohms
Alternator coil resistance	
White to white terminals	0.5-0.6 ohms
Starter	
Armature coil resistance	0.012 ohms
Brush length (minimum)	5 mm (0.2 in.)
Armature mica undercut	1.6 mm (0.06 in.)
Battery type	12 volt, 12 amp hour

Table 2 TIGHTENING TORQUES

Item	N·m	ft.-lb.
Alternator rotor bolt		
1986-1988	35	25
1989-1990	NA	NA
Alternator brush holder		
screw (1986-1988)	8	5.8
Pickup coil timing plate screw	8	5.8
(1986-1988 models)		
Starter motor case screws	10	7.2
Starter motor mounting screws	10	7.2

NA = Information not available from Yamaha. Tighten securely.

Table 3 IGNITION TROUBLESHOOTING

Symptoms	Probable cause (remedy)
Weak spark	Poor connections in circuit (clean and retighten all connections)
	High voltage leak (replace defective wire)
	Defective ignition coil (replace coil)
No spark	Broken wire (replace wire)
	Faulty engine stop switch (replace switch)
	Defective ignition coil (replace coil)
	Defective signal generator (replace signal generator assembly)
	Defective ignitor unit (replace ignitor unit)

Table 4 STARTER TROUBLESHOOTING

Symptom	Probable Cause	Remedy
Starter does not work	Low battery	Recharge battery
	Worn brushes	Replace brushes
	Defective solenoid	Replace solenoid
	Defective clutch switch, NEUTRAL switch or side stand switch	Replace switches
Starter action is weak	Low battery	Recharge battery
	Pitted solenoid contacts	Replace solenoid
	Worn brushes	Replace brushes
	Defective connection	Clean and tighten
	Short circuit in commutator	Replace armature
Starter runs continuously	Stuck solenoid	Replace solenoid
Starter turns; engine does not turn over	Defective starter clutch	Replace starter clutch

Table 5 REPLACEMENT BULBS

Item	Wattage
U.S. Models	
Headlight	Quartz Halogen
Radian	12V 60/55W (single)
FZ600	12V 35/35W (dual)
Tail/brakelight	12V 8/27W
Turn signals	12V 27W
License plate	12V 3.8 W
Instruments lights	12V 3.4W
Indicator lights	12V 3W
UK Models	
Headlight	Quartz Halogen
High beam	12V 60W
Low beam	12V 50W
Tail/brakelight	12V 5/21W
Turn signals	12V 21W
License plate	12V 5W
Instruments lights	12V 3.4W
Indicator lights	12V 3W

8

FRONT SUSPENSION AND STEERING

This chapter describes procedures for the repair and maintenance of the front wheel, front forks and steering components.

Front suspension torque specifications are covered in **Table 1**. **Table 1** and **Table 2** are at the end of this chapter.

> *NOTE*
> *Where differences occur relating to the United Kingdom (UK) models, they are identified. If there is no (UK) designation relating to a procedure, photo or illustration, it is identical to the United States (U.S.) models.*

FRONT WHEEL

Removal
(Radian Models)

1. Place wood block(s) under the crankcase to support the bike securely with the front wheel off the ground.

2. Disconnect the speedometer cable from the speedometer gear box (**Figure 1**).

3. Loosen the front axle pinch bolt and nut (A, **Figure 2**) on the right-hand side.

4. Unscrew the front axle (B, **Figure 2**) from the left-hand fork leg.

5. Pull the wheel down and forward and remove it. This allows the brake discs to slide out of the caliper assemblies.

6. Remove the wheel. Don't lose the collar on the right-hand side.

> *CAUTION*
> *Do not set the wheel down on the disc surface as it may get scratched or warped. Set the sidewalls on 2 wood blocks.*

> *NOTE*
> *Insert a piece of vinyl tubing or wood in each caliper in place of the brake disc. That way, if the brake lever is inadver-*

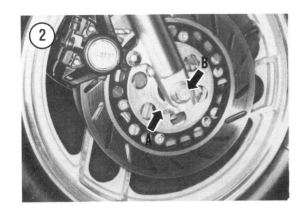

tently squeezed, the piston will not be forced out of the cylinder. If this does happen, the caliper may have to be disassembled to reseat the piston and the system will have to be bled. By using the wood, bleeding the brake is not necessary when installing the wheel.

Installation
(Radian Models)

1. Make sure the axle bearing surfaces of the fork sliders and axle are free from burrs and nicks.

2. Apply a light coat of lithium based grease to the lips of both oil seals (A, **Figure 3**) and to the seal in the speedometer housing (B, **Figure 3**). Install the speedometer housing (**Figure 4**).

3. If removed, install the wheel collar (**Figure 5**) on the right-hand side.

4. Remove the vinyl tubing or pieces of wood from the brake calipers.

5. Position the wheel in place and carefully insert the brake discs between the brake pads in the caliper assemblies.

> *NOTE*
> *Make sure the speedometer gear box seats completely. If the speedometer components do not mesh properly, the hub components of the wheel will be too wide for installation.*

6. Properly index the locating boss on the fork tube so that it is engaged with the locating slot on the speedometer gear box (**Figure 6**).

7. Apply a light coat of grease to the front axle. Insert the front axle from the right-hand side through the wheel hub and the speedometer gear box. Screw the

axle into the left-hand fork leg but don't tighten at this time.

8. Slowly rotate the wheel and install the speedometer cable (A, **Figure 7**) into the speedometer housing (B, **Figure 7**). Position the speedometer housing and cable so that the cable does not have a sharp bend in it.

9. Tighten the front axle to the torque specification listed in **Table 1**.

10. Remove the wood block(s) from under the crankcase.

11. With the front brake applied, push down hard on the handlebars and pump the forks several times to seat the front axle within the front forks.

12. Tighten the front axle pinch bolt and nut to the torque specification listed in **Table 1**.

13. After the wheel is completely installed, rotate it several times to make sure that it rotates freely. Apply the front brake as many times as necessary to make sure all brake pads are against both brake discs correctly.

Removal
(FZ600 Models)

1. Remove the lower fairing on each side as described under *Lower Fairing Removal/Installation* in Chapter Twelve. Remove the lower fairing mounting brackets.

2. Remove the exhaust system as described under *Exhaust System Removal/Installation (FZ600 Models)* in Chapter Seven.

3. Place wood block(s) under the crankcase to support the bike securely with the front wheel off the ground.

4. Disconnect the speedometer cable from the speedometer gear box (**Figure 8**).

> *NOTE*
> *Insert a piece of vinyl tubing or wood in each caliper in place of the brake disc. That way if the brake lever is inadvertently squeezed, the piston will not be forced out of the cylinder. If this does happen, the caliper may have to be disassembled to reseat the piston and the system will have to be bled. By using the wood, bleeding the brake is not necessary when installing the wheel.*

5. Remove the right- and left-hand brake calipers (A, **Figure 9**) as described under *Front Brake Caliper Removal/Installation (FZ600 Models)* in Chapter Eleven.

6. Loosen the front axle pinch bolt (B, **Figure 9**) on the right-hand side.

7. Unscrew the front axle from the left-hand fork leg (C, **Figure 9**).

8. Pull the wheel down and forward and remove it.

9. Remove the collar (**Figure 5**) on the right-hand side.

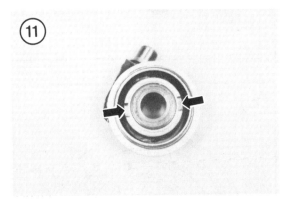

CAUTION
Do not set the wheel down on the disc surface as it may get scratched or warped. Set the sidewalls on 2 wood blocks.

Installation (FZ600 Models)

1. Make sure the axle bearing surfaces of the fork sliders and axle are free from burrs and nicks.

2. Apply a light coat of lithium based grease to the lips of both oil seals (**Figure 10**) and to the seal in the speedometer housing

3. Install the wheel collar on the right-hand side.

4. If removed, align the slots (**Figure 11**) with the 2 speedometer drive tabs (**Figure 12**) in the front wheel hub, then install the speedometer housing.

5. Position the wheel in place within the fork legs.

NOTE
Make sure the speedometer gear box seats completely. If the speedometer components do not mesh properly, the hub components of the wheel will be too wide for installation.

6. Properly index the locating boss on the fork tube so that it is engaged with the locating slot on the speedometer gear box (**Figure 13**).

7. Apply a light coat of grease to the front axle. Insert the front axle from the right-hand side through the wheel hub and the speedometer gear box. Screw the axle into the left-hand fork leg but don't tighten at this time.

8. Slowly rotate the wheel and install the speedometer cable into the speedometer housing. Position the speedometer housing and cable so that the cable does not have a sharp bend in it.

9. Tighten the front axle to the torque specification listed in **Table 1**.

10. Remove the vinyl tubing or pieces of wood from the brake calipers.

11. Install the right- and left-hand brake calipers as described in Chapter Eleven.

12. Remove the wood block(s) from under the crankcase.

13. With the front brake applied, push down hard on the handlebars and pump the forks several times to seat the front axle within the front forks.

14. Tighten the front axle, then the pinch bolt and nut to the torque specification listed in **Table 1**.

15. After the wheel is completely installed, rotate it several times to make sure that it rotates freely. Apply the front brake as many times as necessary to make sure all brake pads are against both brake discs correctly.

16. Install the exhaust system as described in Chapter Seven.

17. Install the lower fairing on each side as described in Chapter Twelve.

WHEEL INSPECTION

Measure the axial (end play) and radial (side play) runout of the wheel with a dial indicator as shown in **Figure 14**. The maximum runout is as follows:

    a. Radian and UK FZ600 models: vertical and lateral runout are 2.0 mm (0.08 in.).

    b. U.S. FZ600 models: vertical runout is 1.0 mm (0.039 in.) and lateral runout 0.5 mm (0.020 in.).

If the runout exceeds this dimension, check the wheel bearing condition. If the wheel bearings are in good condition and no other cause can be found, the wheel will have to be replaced as it cannot be serviced.

Check the wheel for signs of cracks, fractures, dents or bends. If it is damaged in any way, it must be replaced.

> *WARNING*
> *Do not try to repair any damage to the wheel as it will result in an unsafe riding condition.*

Check the front axle runout as described under *Front Hub* in this chapter.

FRONT HUB

Inspection

Inspect each wheel bearing prior to removing it from the wheel hub.

> *CAUTION*
> *Do not remove the wheel bearings for inspection purposes as they will be damaged during the removal process. Remove wheel bearings only if they are to be replaced.*

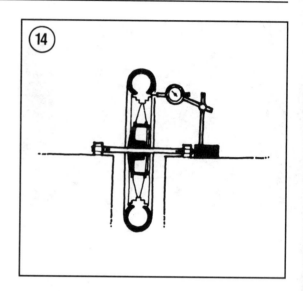

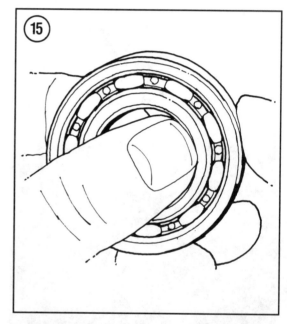

1. Perform Steps 1-4 of *Disassembly* in this chapter.

2. Turn each bearing by hand (**Figure 15**). Make sure bearings turn smoothly.

3. Inspect the play of the inner race (**Figure 16**) of each wheel bearing. Check for excessive axial (side play) and radial (end play) play. Replace the bearing if it has an excess amount of free play.

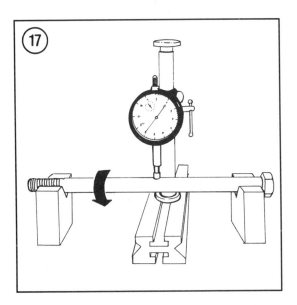

4. On non-sealed bearings, check the balls for evidence of wear, pitting or excessive heat (bluish tint). Replace the bearings if necessary; always replace as a complete set. When replacing the bearings, be sure to take your old bearings along to ensure a perfect matchup.

NOTE
Fully sealed bearings are available from many bearing specialty shops. Fully sealed bearings provide better protection from dirt and moisture that may get into the hub.

5. Check the axle for wear and straightness. Use V-blocks and a dial indicator as shown in **Figure 17**. If the runout is 0.2 mm (0.01 in.) or greater, the axle should be replaced. *Never* try to straighten a front axle.

Disassembly

Refer to **Figure 18** for this procedure.

1. Remove the front wheel as described in this chapter.

9

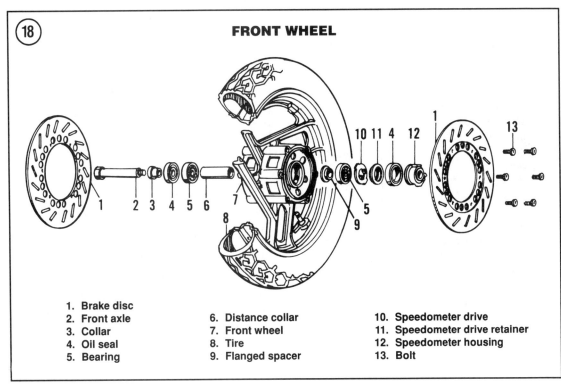

FRONT WHEEL

1. Brake disc
2. Front axle
3. Collar
4. Oil seal
5. Bearing
6. Distance collar
7. Front wheel
8. Tire
9. Flanged spacer
10. Speedometer drive
11. Speedometer drive retainer
12. Speedometer housing
13. Bolt

2. Remove the speedometer gear box (A, **Figure 19**) from the left-hand side of the hub.

3. Remove the collar (A, **Figure 20**) and the oil seal (B, **Figure 20**) from the right-hand side.

4. Before proceeding further, inspect the wheel bearings as described in this chapter. If they must be replaced, proceed as follows.

5. Remove the oil seal (B, **Figure 19**) and the speedometer drive retainer and drive (C, **Figure 19**).

6. To remove the right- and left-hand bearings and distance collar, insert a soft aluminum or brass drift into one side of the hub.

7. Push the distance collar over to one side and place the drift on the inner race of the lower bearing.

8. Tap the bearing out of the hub with a hammer, working around the perimeter of the inner race.

9. Remove the distance collar and the flanged spacer.

10. Repeat for the bearing on the other side.

11. Clean the inside and the outside of the hub with solvent. Dry with compressed air.

Assembly

1. On non-sealed bearings, pack the bearings with a good-quality bearing grease. Work the grease in between the balls thoroughly; turn the bearing by hand a couple of times to make sure the grease is distributed evenly inside the bearing.

2. Blow any dirt or foreign matter out of the hub prior to installing the bearings.

> *CAUTION*
> *Install non-sealed bearings with the single sealed side facing outward. Tap the bearings squarely into place and tap on the outer race only. Do not tap on the inner race or the bearing might be damaged. Be sure that the bearings are completely seated.*

3. Tap the left-hand bearing squarely into place and tap on the outer race only. Use a socket (**Figure 21**) that matches the outer race diameter. Do not tap on the inner race or the bearing might be damaged. Be sure that the bearing is completely seated.

4. Turn the wheel over (right-hand side up) on the workbench.

5. Position the flanged spacer with the flange toward the distance collar and install the flanged spacer and distance collar.

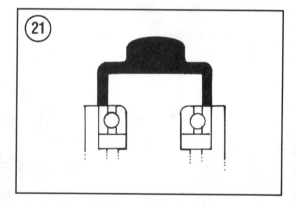

6. Use the same tool set-up and drive in the right-hand bearing.

7. Install the oil seal on the right-hand side.

8. Install the speedometer drive, retainer and oil seal in the left-hand side.

9. Disassemble the speedometer housing (**Figure 22**) and lubricate the gears and sliding surfaces with a lithium based grease. Reassemble the housing.

10. Align the tangs of the speedometer drive gear (C, **Figure 19**) with the speedometer drive in the front hub and install the speedometer housing.

NOTE
Make sure the speedometer gear box seats completely. If the speedometer components do not mesh properly, the wheel will be too wide for installation.

11. Install the front wheel as described in this chapter.

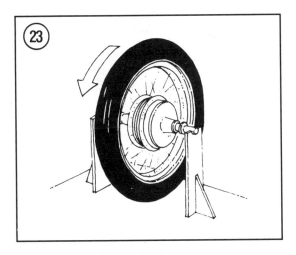

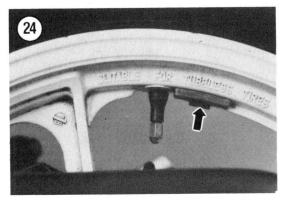

WHEELS

Wheel Balance

An unbalanced wheel is unsafe. Depending on the degree of unbalance and the speed of the motorcycle, the rider may experience anything from a mild vibration to a violent shimmy which may even result in loss of control.

The weights are attached to the rim. Weight kits are available from motorcycle dealers. These kits contain test weights and strips of adhesive-backed weights that can be cut to the desired length and attached directly to the rim.

Before you attempt to balance the wheel, check to be sure that the wheel bearings are in good condition and properly lubricated and that the brakes do not drag. The wheel must rotate freely.

NOTE
When balancing the wheels, do so with the brake discs attached and on the rear wheel with the driven sprocket assembly attached. These components rotate with the wheels and they affect the balance.

1. Remove the wheel as described in this chapter or Chapter Ten.

2. Mount the wheel on a fixture such as the one shown in **Figure 23** so it can rotate freely.

3. Give the wheel a spin and let it coast to a stop. Mark the tire at the lowest point.

4. Spin the wheel several more times. If the wheel keeps coming to rest at the same point, it is out of balance.

5. Tape a test weight to the upper (or light) side of the wheel.

6. Experiment with different weights until the wheel, when spun, comes to a rest at a different position each time.

7. Remove the test weight and install the correct size weight (**Figure 24**).

Wheel Alignment

Refer to **Figure 25** for this procedure.

1. Measure the tires at their widest point.

2. Subtract the small dimension from the larger dimension.

3. Make an alignment tool out of wood, approximately 7 feet long, with an offset equal to one-half of the dimension obtained in Step 2. Refer to (D).

4. If the wheels are not aligned as in (A) and (C), the rear wheel must be shifted to correct the alignment.

5. Remove the cotter pin and loosen the rear axle nut (A, **Figure 26**).

6. Loosen the drive chain adjuster locknut (B, **Figure 26**) on either side and move the rear wheel until the wheels align.

7. Adjust the drive chain as described under *Drive Chain Adjustment* in Chapter Three.

TIRE CHANGING

Removal

1. Mark the valve stem location on the tire, so the tire can be installed in the same position for easier balancing.

2. Remove the valve core to deflate the tire.

> *NOTE*
> *Removal of tubeless tires from their rims can be very difficult because of the exceptionally tight bead/rim seal.*

> *Breaking the bead seal may require the use of a special tool (**Figure 27**). If you are unable to break the seal loose, take the wheel to a motorcycle dealer and have them break it loose.*

> *CAUTION*
> *The inner rim and tire bead area are sealing surfaces on the tubeless tire. Do not scratch the inside of the rim or damage the tire bead.*

3. Press the entire bead on both sides of the tire into the center of the rim.

4. Lubricate the beads with soapy water.

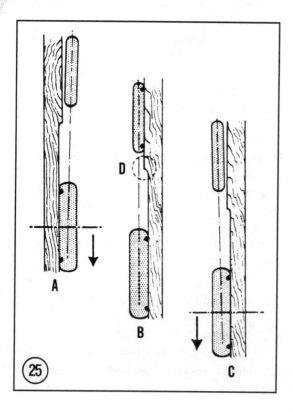

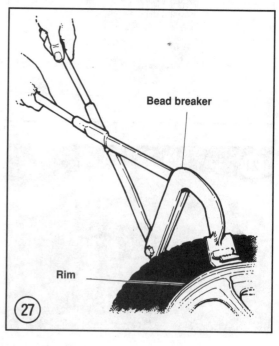

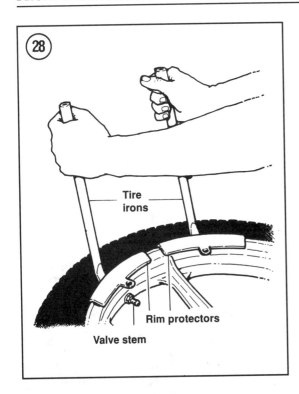

Tire
irons

Rim protectors

Valve stem

*Use rim protectors (**Figure 28**) or insert scraps of leather between the tire irons and the rim to protect the rim from damage.*

5. Insert the tire iron under the bead next to the valve (**Figure 29**). Force the bead on the opposite side of the tire into the center of the rim and pry the bead over the rim with the tire iron.

6. Insert a second tire iron next to the first to hold the bead over the rim. Then work around the tire with the first tire iron, prying the bead over the rim (**Figure 30**).

7. Turn the tire over. Insert the tire iron between the second bead and the side of the rim that the first bead was pried over (**Figure 31**). Force the bead on the opposite side from the tire iron into the center of the rim. Pry the second bead off the rim, working around as with the first.

8. Inspect the valve stem seal. Because rubber deteriorates with age, it is advisable to replace the valve stem when replacing the tire.

9. Remove the old valve stem and discard it. Inspect the valve stem hole in the rim. Remove any dirt or corrosion from the hole and wipe dry with a clean cloth.

9

Tire and Rim Inspection

1. Wipe off the inner surfaces of the wheel rim. Clean off any rubber residue or any oxidation.

2. If a can of pressurized tire sealant was used for a temporary fix of a flat, thoroughly clean off all

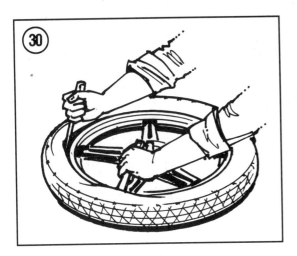

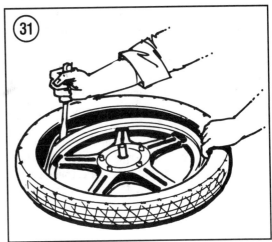

sealant residue. Any remaining residue will present a problem when reinstalling the tire and achieving a good seal of the tire bead against the rim.

3. If a tire is going to be patched, thoroughly inspect the tire. If any one of the following is observed, do *not* repair the tire; *replace it with a new one*:

    a. A puncture or split whose total length or diameter exceeds 6 mm (0.24 in.).

    b. A scratch or split on the side wall.

    c. Any type of ply separation.

    d. Tread separation or excessive abnormal wear pattern.

    e. Tread depth of less than 1.6 mm (0.06 in.) in the front tire or less than 2.0 mm (0.08 in.) in the rear tire on original equipment tires. Aftermarket tires' tread depth minimum may vary.

    f. Scratches on either sealing bead.

    g. The cord is cut in any place.

    h. Flat spots in the tread from skidding.

    i. Any abnormality in the inner liner.

Installation

1. Install a new valve stem as follows:

    a. Insert the new valve stem into the rim.

    b. Install the locknut and tighten to the torque specification listed in **Table 1**. Do not use pliers and overtighten the locknut as it may distort the rubber grommet that could cause an air leak.

2. Carefully inspect the tire for any damage, especially inside.

3. A new tire may have balancing rubbers inside. These are not patches and should not be disturbed or removed.

4. Lubricate both beads of the tire with soapy water.

5. When installing the tire onto the rim make sure the direction arrow (**Figure 32**) faces the direction of wheel rotation.

6. If remounting the old tire, align the mark made in Step 1, *Removal* with the valve stem. If a new tire is being installed, align the colored spot near the bead (indicating a lighter point on the tire) with the valve stem (**Figure 33**).

7. Place the backside of the tire into the center of the rim. The lower bead should go into the center of the rim and the upper bead outside. Work around the tire in both directions (**Figure 34**). Use a tire iron for the last few inches of bead (**Figure 35**).

8. Press the upper bead into the rim opposite the valve stem (**Figure 36**). Pry the bead into the rim on both sides of the initial point with a tire iron, working around the rim to the valve (**Figure 37**).

9. Check the bead on both sides of the tire for even fit around the rim.

10. Bounce the wheel several times, rotating it each time. This will force the tire beads against the rim flanges. After the tire beads are in contact with the rim evenly, inflate the tire to seat the beads.

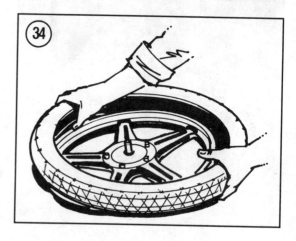

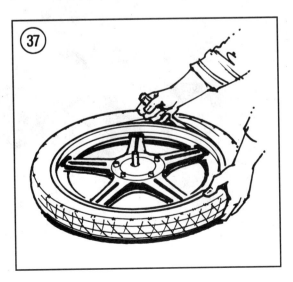

11. Place an inflatable band around the circumference of the tire. Slowly inflate the band until the tire beads are pressed against the rim. Inflate the tire enough to seat it, deflate the band and remove it.

WARNING
In the next step never exceed 56 psi (4.0 kg/cm²) inflation pressure as the tire could burst causing severe injury. Never stand directly over a tire while inflating it.

12. After inflating the tire, check to see that the beads are fully seated and that the tire rim lines are the same distance from the rim all the way around the tire. If the beads won't seat, deflate the tire and relubricate the rim and beads with soapy water.
13. Reinflate the tire to the required pressure. Install the valve stem cap.
14. Balance the wheel as described in this chapter.

WARNING
*If you have repaired a tire, do not ride the bike any faster than 30 mph (50 km/h) for the first 24 hours. It takes at least 24 hours for a patch to cure. Also **never** ride the bike faster than 80 mph (130 km/h) with a repaired tire.*

TIRE REPAIRS

Patching a tubeless tire on the road is very difficult. If both beads are still against the rim, a can of pressurized tire sealant may inflate the tire and seal the hole, although this is only a temporary fix. The beads must be against the rim for this method to work. Another solution is to carry a spare inner tube that could be installed and inflated. This will enable you to get to a service station where the tire can be correctly repaired. Be sure that the inner tube is designed for use with tubeless tires.

Yamaha (and the tire industry) recommends that the tubeless tire be patched from the inside. Use a combination plug/patch applied from the inside the tire (**Figure 38**). Do not patch the tire with an external type plug. If you find an external patch on the tire, it is recommended that it be patch-reinforced from the inside

Due to the variations of material supplied with different tubeless tire repair kits, follow the instructions and recommendations supplied with the repair kit.

HANDLEBAR

Removal/Installation
(Radian Models)

1. Unhook the straps securing the electrical cables to the handler on both sides.

2. Disconnect the brake light switch electrical connector (A, **Figure 39**) from the brake lever.

> *CAUTION*
> *Cover the frame and fuel tank with a heavy cloth or plastic tarp to protect it from accidental spilling of brake fluid. Wash any spilled brake fluid off any painted or plated surface immediately, as it will destroy the finish. Use soapy water and rinse thoroughly.*

3. Remove the bolts securing the brake master cylinder (B, **Figure 39**) and lay it on the fuel tank in the upright position. This is to minimize loss of brake fluid and to keep air from entering the brake system. It is not necessary to remove the hydraulic brake line.

4. Remove the screws securing the right-hand handlebar switch assembly (C, **Figure 39**) together.

5. Disconnect the throttle cable (D, **Figure 39**) from the twist grip and remove the right-hand switch assembly from the handlebar.

6. Slide back the rubber boot (A, **Figure 40**), loosen the locknut on the clutch cable adjuster and turn the adjuster to allow slack in the clutch cable.

7. Disconnect the clutch cable from the clutch hand lever.

8. Remove the screws securing the left-hand handlebar switch assembly (B, **Figure 40**) together and remove the switch assembly from the handlebar.

9. Remove the caps and remove the Allen bolts (A, **Figure 41**) securing the handlebar upper holders.

10. Remove the upper holders (B, **Figure 41**) and the handlebar (C, **Figure 41**).

11. Install by reversing these removal steps while noting the following:

    a. Install the handlebar into position and install the handlebar holders with the punch mark facing forward (**Figure 42**), then install the bolts.

    b. Correctly position the handlebar assembly and tighten the upper holder bolts to the torque specification listed in **Table 1**. Tighten the front bolts first, then the rear.

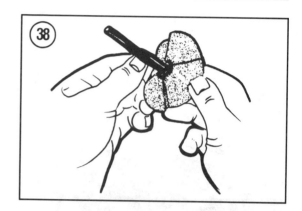

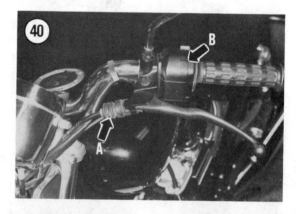

c. Install the brake master cylinder onto the handlebar. Tighten the upper bolt first and then the lower bolt. Tighten the bolts to the torque specification listed in **Table 1**.

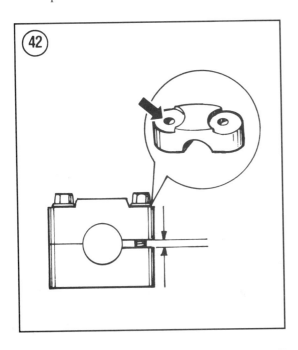

> *WARNING*
> *After installation is completed, make sure the brake lever does not come in contact with the throttle grip assembly when it is pulled on fully. If it does, the brake fluid may be low in the reservoir; refill as necessary. Refer to **Front Disc Brakes** in Chapter Eleven.*

d. Adjust the throttle operation as described in Chapter Three.

Removal/Installation (FZ600 Models)

These models use a separate handlebar assembly that slips over the top of the fork tube and bolts directly to the upper fork bridge.

> *NOTE*
> *If individual handlebar replacement is not required, proceed to Step 8.*

1. Disconnect the brake light switch electrical connector (**Figure 43**) from the brake lever.

> *CAUTION*
> *Cover the frame and fuel tank with a heavy cloth or plastic tarp to protect it from accidental spilling of brake fluid. Wash any spilled brake fluid off any painted or plated surface immediately, as it will destroy the finish. Use soapy water and rinse thoroughly.*

2. Remove the bolts securing the brake master cylinder (A, **Figure 44**) and lay it on the fuel tank in the upright position. This is to minimize loss of brake fluid and to keep air from entering the brake system. It is not necessary to remove the hydraulic brake line.

3. Remove the screws securing the right-hand handlebar switch assembly (B, **Figure 44**) together.

4. Disconnect the throttle cable from the twist grip and remove the right-hand switch assembly from the handlebar.

5. Loosen the locknut (A, **Figure 45**) on the clutch cable adjuster and turn the adjuster (B, **Figure 45**) to allow slack in the clutch cable.

6. Disconnect the clutch cable from the clutch hand lever.

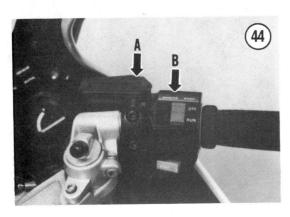

9

7. Remove the screws securing the left-hand handlebar switch assembly (A, **Figure 46**) together and remove the switch assembly from the handlebar.

8. Loosen the handlebar pinch bolt (B, **Figure 46**).

9. Remove the handlebar mounting bolt (C, **Figure 46**) and lift the handlebar straight up and off the fork tube.

10. Repeat Step 8 and Step 9 for the other handlebar.

11. Install by reversing these removal steps while noting the following:

NOTE
If the fork assembly(ies) have been removed, the alignment of the fork tube to the handlebar will have to be adjusted by moving the fork tube up or down within the fork bridges until alignment is achieved.

a. Install the handlebar into position on the fork tube and align the top surface of the handlebar with the top surface of the fork tube (**Figure 47**). Adjust the fork tube height if necessary.

b. Install the handlebar mounting bolt and tighten to the torque specification listed in **Table 1**.

c. Tighten the handlebar pinch bolt to the torque specification listed in **Table 1**.

d. Install the brake master cylinder onto the handlebar. Tighten the upper bolt first and then the lower bolt. Tighten the bolts to the torque specification listed in **Table 1**.

WARNING
*After installation is completed, make sure the brake lever does not come in contact with the throttle grip assembly when it is pulled on fully. If it does, the brake fluid may be low in the reservoir; refill as necessary. Refer to **Front Disc Brakes** in Chapter Eleven.*

e. Adjust the throttle operation as described in Chapter Three.

STEERING HEAD AND STEM

Disassembly

Refer to **Figure 48** for Radian models or **Figure 49** for FZ600 models for this procedure.

1. Remove the front wheel as described in this chapter.

2. On FZ600 models, remove the front fairing as described under *Front Fairing Removal/Installation* in Chapter Twelve.

3. Loosen the steering stem bolt or nut (A, **Figure 50**).

4. Remove the handlebars (B, **Figure 50**) as described in this chapter.

5. Remove the front forks (C, **Figure 50**) as described in this chapter.

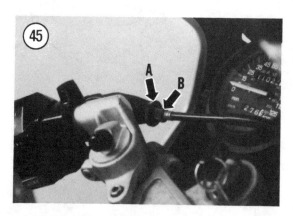

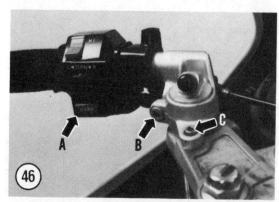

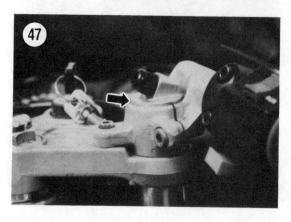

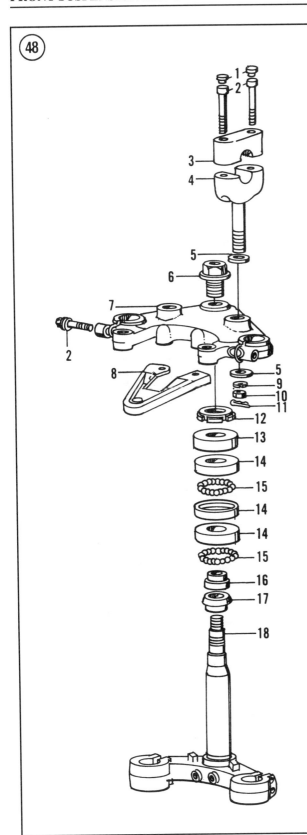

STEERING STEM (RADIAN)

1. Caps
2. Allen bolts
3. Handlebar upper holder
4. Handlebar lower holder
5. Washer
6. Steering stem bolt
7. Upper fork bridge
8. Bracket
9. Lockwasher
10. Nut
11. Pin
12. Locknut
13. Upper bearing cover
14. Bearing race (upper)
15. Ball bearings (1/4 in.)
16. Bearing race (lower)
17. Dust seal
18. Steering stem

9

6. Remove the fuel tank as described under *Fuel Tank Removal/Installation* in Chapter Seven.

7. Remove the bolts securing the front brake hydraulic hose 2-way joint. Move the 2-way joint and brake hose assembly out of the way. It is not necessary to disconnect any of the brake hoses from the 2-way joint.

8. On Radian models, perform the following:

    a. Remove the instrument cluster as described under *Instrument Cluster Removal/Installation* in Chapter Eight.

    b. Remove the headlight case and bracket as described under *Headlight Case and Bracket Removal/Installation* in Chapter Eight.

    c. Remove the turn signal assemblies as described under *Turn Signals Removal/Installation* in Chapter Eight.

    d. Remove the bolts securing the ignition switch and move the ignition switch out of the way.

9. Remove the steering stem bolt or nut (A, **Figure 50**).

10. Remove the upper fork bridge (D, **Figure 50**).

11. Loosen the steering stem locknut. To loosen the lock nut, use a large drift and hammer or use the easily improvised tool shown in **Figure 51**.

12. Hold onto the lower end of the steering stem assembly and remove the steering stem locknut.

13. Remove the upper bearing cover and the bearing race No. 1.

14. Lower the steering stem assembly down and out of the steering head (**Figure 52**). Be prepared to catch any loose steel balls that may fall out when the steering stem is withdrawn.

> *NOTE*
> *There are 38 steel ball bearings of the same size; 19 in the top bearing and 19 in the lower bearing. The bearings should not be intermixed because, if worn or damaged, they must be replaced as a set of 19.*

15. Remove the loose ball bearings from the top of the headset area of the frame and from the steering stem. Do not intermix the steel balls—keep them separated and place them in a small container.

Inspection

1. Clean the bearing races in the steering head and the steering stem and the steel ball bearings with solvent.

STEERING STEM (FZ600)

1. Steering stem cap nut
2. Upper fork bridge
3. Locknut
4. Upper bearing cover
5. Bearing race (upper)
6. Ball bearings (1/4 in.)
7. Bearing race (lower)
8. Dust seal
9. Steering stem
10. Bracket
11. Bolt
12. Washer
13. Wire clip
14. Allen bolt

2. Check the welds around the steering head for cracks and fractures. If any are found, have them repaired by a competent frame shop or welding

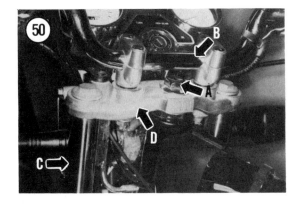

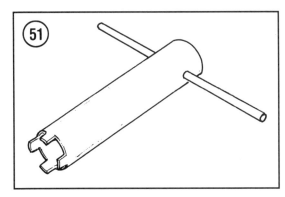

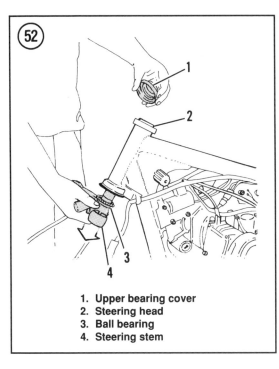

1. Upper bearing cover
2. Steering head
3. Ball bearing
4. Steering stem

service that is knowledgeable in the welding of aluminum.

3. Check the steel balls for pitting, scratches or discoloration indicating wear or corrosion. Replace them as a set of 19 if any are bad.

4. Check the races for pitting, galling and corrosion. If any of these conditions exist, replace the races as described in this chapter.

5. Check the steering stem for cracks, damage or wear. If damaged in any way, replace the steering stem.

Steering Stem Assembly

Refer to **Figure 48** for Radian models or **Figure 49** for FZ600 models for this procedure.

1. Make sure the steering head outer races are properly seated.

2. Apply an even complete coat of wheel bearing grease to the steering head outer races.

3. Apply a coat of cold wheel bearing grease to the lower bearing race cone and fit 19 steel ball bearings around it.

4. Apply a coat of cold wheel bearing grease to the upper bearing race cone and fit 19 steel ball bearings around it (**Figure 53**).

5. Install the steering stem into the head tube and hold it firmly in place.

6. Install the upper bearing race No. 1 onto the top of the headset, then install the upper bearing cover.

7. Install the steering stem locknut and tighten it to the torque specification listed in **Table 1**.

8. Turn the steering stem from lock-to-lock 5-6 times to seat the ball bearings.

9. Loosen the steering stem locknut 1/4 to 1/2 turn.

10. Retighten the steering stem locknut to the torque specification listed in **Table 1**.

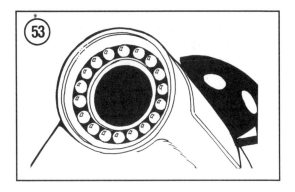

NOTE
If during Step 7 and Step 10 the locknut will not tighten, remove the nut and inspect both the nut and the steering stem threads for dirt and/or burrs. Clean both parts with a tap and die if necessary, then repeat Steps 6-10.

11. Install the upper fork bridge steering bolt only finger-tight at this time.

NOTE
Steps 12-14 must be performed in this order to assure proper upper and lower fork bridge to fork alignment.

12. Temporarily slide the fork tubes into position so the top surface of the fork tube aligns with the top surface of the upper fork bridge.

13. Tighten the *lower* fork bridge bolts to the torque specification listed in **Table 1**.

14. Tighten the steering stem bolt or nut to the torque specification listed in **Table 1**.

15. Loosen the lower fork bridge bolts and slide the front fork tubes down and out.

16. Move the 2-way joint and hose assembly into position and install the mounting bolts. Tighten the bolts securely.

17. On Radian models, perform the following:
  a. Move the ignition switch into position and install the mounting bolts. Tighten the bolts securely.
  b. Move the 2-way joint and hose assembly into position and install the mounting bolts. Tighten the bolts securely.
  c. Install the turn signal assemblies as described in Chapter Eight.
  d. Install the headlight case and bracket as described in Chapter Eight.
  e. Install the instrument cluster as described in Chapter Eight.

18. Install the front forks as described in this chapter.

19. Install the handlebars as described in this chapter.

20. On FZ600 models, install the front fairing as described in Chapter Twelve.

21. Install the front wheel as described in this chapter.

STEERING HEAD BEARING RACES

The headset and steering stem bearing races are pressed into place. Because they are easily bent, do

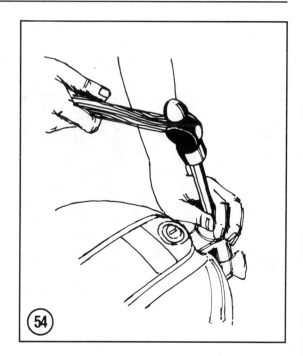

(54)

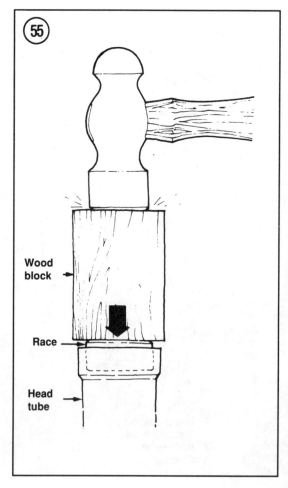

(55)

Wood block →

Race →

Head tube →

not remove them unless they are worn and require replacement.

Headset Bearing Race Removal/Installation

1. Remove the steering stem as described in this chapter.

2. To remove the headset race, insert a hardwood stick or soft punch into the head tube (**Figure 54**) and carefully tap the race out from the inside. After it is started, tap around the race so that neither the race nor the head tube is damaged.

3. To install the headset race, tap it in slowly with a block of wood, a suitable size socket or piece of pipe. Make sure that the race is squarely seated in the headset race bore before tapping it into place. Tap the race in until it is flush with the steering head surface (**Figure 55**).

Steering Stem Bearing Race Removal/Installation

1. Use a chisel and hammer and remove the bearing race from the steering stem (**Figure 56**). Work evenly around the bearing race with the chisel until the race is free from the shoulder on the steering stem. Remove the steering stem race from the steering stem.

2. Remove the dust seal and discard it.

3. Install a new dust seal and push it down all the way until it seats.

4. Apply a light coat of grease to the steering stem shoulder.

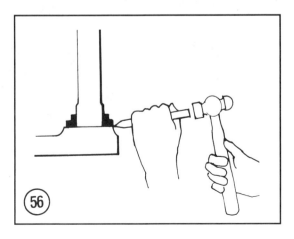

(56)

5. Install a new steering stem race onto the steering stem.

> *CAUTION*
> *While tapping the steering stem race into position, do **not** strike the bearing surface where the steel balls ride with the pipe or the race will be damaged.*

6. Use a long piece of pipe that matches the raised shoulder diameter of the race and carefully tap it down until it is completely seated against the dust seal. Make sure it is seated squarely and is all the way down.

FRONT FORKS

The front suspension on all models uses spring controlled, hydraulically damped, telescopic forks.

Front Fork Service

Before suspecting major trouble, drain the front fork oil and refill with the proper type and quantity; refer to *Front Fork Oil Change* in Chapter Three. If you still have trouble, such as poor damping, a tendency to bottom or top out or leakage around the rubber seals, follow the service procedures in this section.

To simplify fork service and to prevent the mixing of parts, the legs should be removed, serviced and installed individually.

Removal/Installation

1. Remove both front caliper assemblies as described under *Front Brake Caliper Removal/Installation* in Chapter Eleven.

2. Remove the front wheel as described in this chapter.

3. Remove the screws securing the front fork brace (A, **Figure 57**) and remove the brace.

4. Remove the screws securing the front fender (B, **Figure 57**) to the front forks and remove the front fender.

5. On FZ600 models, if the fork tube is going to be disassembled, perform the following:

    a. Remove the air valve dust cap (**Figure 58**) from the fork top cap bolt.

WARNING
Release the air pressure gradually. If it is released too fast, fork oil will spurt out with the air. Protect your eyes and clothing accordingly.

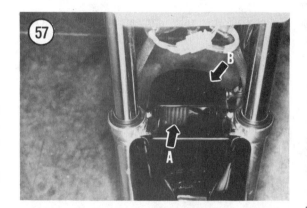

b. Depress the valve stem (**Figure 59**) with a small screwdriver and *bleed off all air pressure* within the fork tube. Remove the valve stem from the valve.

6. On FZ600 models, remove the handlebars as described in this chapter.

NOTE
*If the fork tube is going to be disassembled, loosen the fork cap bolt (**Figure 60**) after first loosening the upper fork bridge bolt.*

7. Loosen the upper (**Figure 61**) and lower (**Figure 62**) fork bridge bolts and slide the fork tube from the lower fork bridge. It may be necessary to rotate the fork tube slightly while pulling it down and out.

8. Install by reversing these removal steps while noting the following:

a. On Radian models, install the fork tubes so that the top of the fork tube aligns with the top surface of the upper fork bridge (**Figure 63**).

b. On FZ600 models, install the fork tubes so that the top of the fork tube aligns with the top surface of the handlebar (**Figure 64**).

c. Tighten the upper and lower fork bridge bolts to the torque specifications listed in **Table 1**.

d. On FZ600 models, tighten the handlebar bolts to the torque specification listed in **Table 1**.

Disassembly

Refer to **Figure 65** for Radian models or **Figure 66** for FZ600 models during the disassembly procedure.

1. Position the slider so that it is vertical and clamp it in a vise with soft jaws.

2. On FZ600 models, if the air pressure was not relieved prior to removal perform the following:

a. Remove the air valve dust cap (**Figure 58**) from the fork top cap bolt.

WARNING
Release the air pressure gradually. If it is released too fast, fork oil will spurt

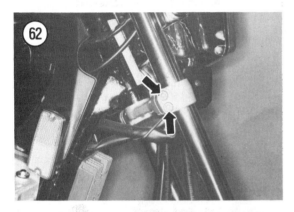

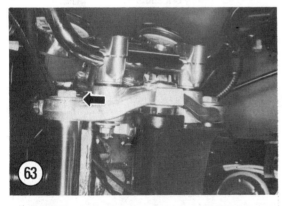

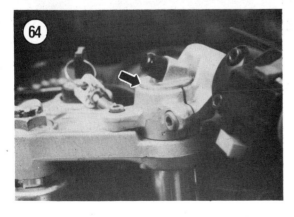

out with the air. Protect your eyes and clothing accordingly.

b. Depress the valve stem (**Figure 59**) with a small screwdriver and *bleed off all air pressure* within the fork tube. Remove the valve stem from the valve.

NOTE
The Allen bolt has been secured with a locking agent and is often very difficult to remove because the damper rod will turn inside the slider. It sometimes can be removed with an air impact driver. If you are unable to remove it, take the fork tubes to a dealer and have the bolts removed.

3. Loosen the Allen bolt (**Figure 67**) on the bottom of the slider. If you cannot loosen the Allen bolt, it can be loosened with the special tools in Step 9.
4. Remove the Allen bolt and gasket from the slider.
5. Hold the upper fork tube in a vise with soft jaws and loosen the fork cap bolt (if it was not loosened during the fork removal sequence).

WARNING
Be careful when removing the fork cap bolt as the spring is under pressure. Protect your eyes accordingly.

6. Remove the fork cap bolt from the fork tube.
7A. On Radian models, remove the spring seat and the fork spring.
7B. On FZ600 models, remove the spring seat, the fork spring and the variable damper.
8. Remove the fork from the vise, pour the fork oil out and discard it. Pump the fork several times by hand to expel most of the remaining oil.
9. If the Allen bolt was not loosened in Step 3, proceed as follows:
   a. To prevent the damper rod from turning, use the Yamaha special tool T-handle (U.S. part No. YM-01326, UK part No. 90890-01326) and damper rod holder (U.S. part No. YM-33298, UK part No. 90890-04104).
   b. Insert the T-handle into the fork tube so that the damper rod holder locks the damper (**Figure 68**) in place.
   c. Loosen then remove the Allen bolt.
10. Remove the dust seal from the slider.
11. Remove the retaining clip from the slider.

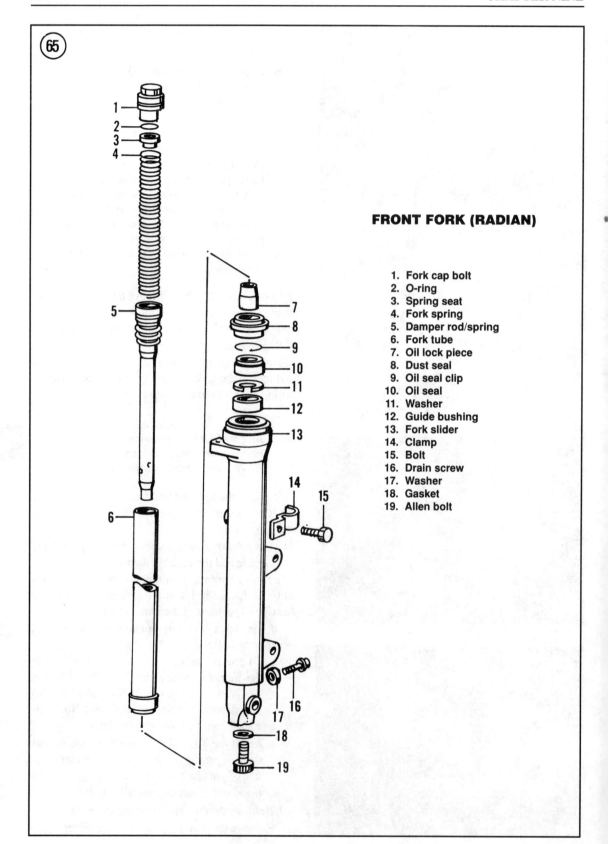

FRONT FORK (RADIAN)

1. Fork cap bolt
2. O-ring
3. Spring seat
4. Fork spring
5. Damper rod/spring
6. Fork tube
7. Oil lock piece
8. Dust seal
9. Oil seal clip
10. Oil seal
11. Washer
12. Guide bushing
13. Fork slider
14. Clamp
15. Bolt
16. Drain screw
17. Washer
18. Gasket
19. Allen bolt

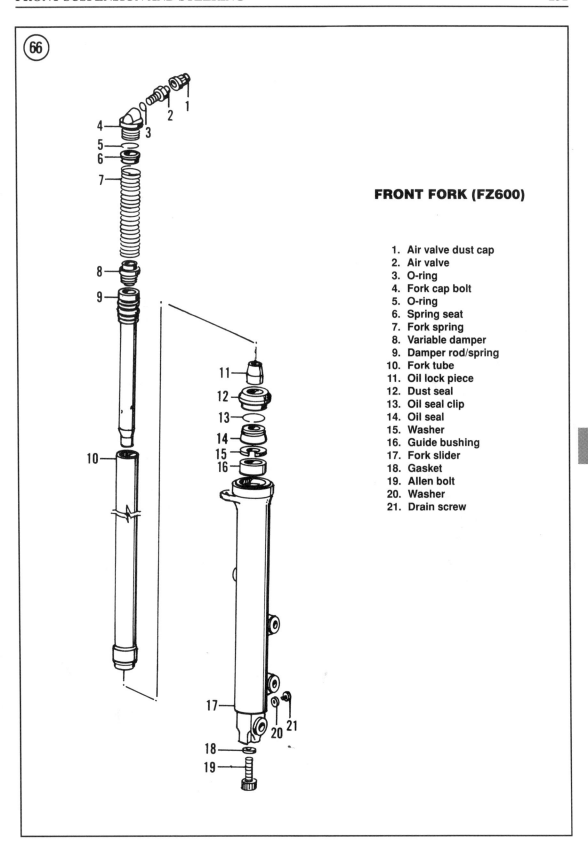

FRONT FORK (FZ600)

1. Air valve dust cap
2. Air valve
3. O-ring
4. Fork cap bolt
5. O-ring
6. Spring seat
7. Fork spring
8. Variable damper
9. Damper rod/spring
10. Fork tube
11. Oil lock piece
12. Dust seal
13. Oil seal clip
14. Oil seal
15. Washer
16. Guide bushing
17. Fork slider
18. Gasket
19. Allen bolt
20. Washer
21. Drain screw

9

NOTE
On this type of fork, force is needed to remove the fork tube from the slider.

12. Install the fork tube in a vise with soft jaws.

CAUTION
In the next step, do not allow the fork tube to bottom out in the slider as the oil lock piece will be damaged.

13. There is an interference fit between the guide bushing in the fork slider and the guide bushing on the fork tube. In order to remove the fork tube from the slider, pull hard on the fork tube using quick in-and-out strokes (**Figure 69**). Doing so will withdraw the guide bushing, washer and oil seal from the slider.

NOTE
It may be necessary to heat the area on the slider around the oil seal slightly prior to removal. Use a rag soaked in hot water; do not apply a flame directly to the fork slider.

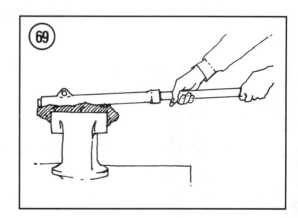

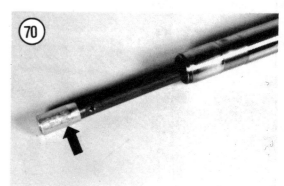

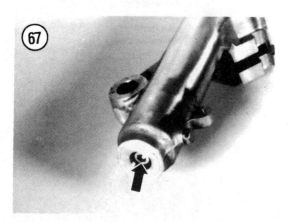

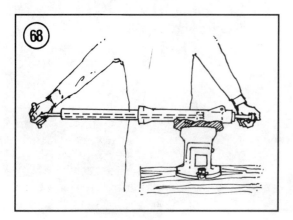

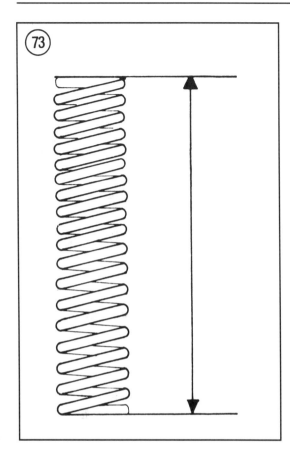

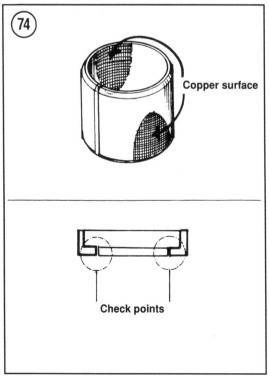

Copper surface

Check points

14. Withdraw the fork tube from the slider.

NOTE
Do not remove the fork tube guide bushing unless it is going to be replaced. Inspect it as described in this chapter.

15. Remove the oil lock piece from the damper rod (**Figure 70**).
16. Remove the damper rod and rebound spring from the slider.
17. Inspect the components as described in this chapter.

Inspection

1. Thoroughly clean all parts in solvent and dry them. Check the fork tube for signs of wear or scratches.
2. Check the damper rod for straightness (**Figure 71**). The damper rod should be replaced if the runout is 0.2 mm (0.008 in.) or greater.
3. Make sure the oil holes in the damper rod are clear. Clean out if necessary.
4. Inspect the damper rod and piston ring (**Figure 72**) for wear or damage. Replace as necessary.
5. Check the upper fork tube for straightness. If bent or severely scratched, it should be replaced.
6. Check the lower slider for dents or exterior damage that may cause the upper fork tube to hang up during riding. Replace if necessary.
7. Measure the uncompressed length of the fork spring (not rebound spring) as shown in **Figure 73**. If the spring has sagged to the service limit dimensions listed in **Table 2**, the spring must be replaced.
8. Inspect the slider and fork tube guide bushings. If either are scratched or scored they must be replaced. If the Teflon coating is worn off so that the copper base material is showing on approximately 3/4 of the total surface, the bushing must be replaced (**Figure 74**).
9. Inspect the gasket on the Allen bolt, replace if damaged.
10. On FZ600 models, check the variable damper as follows:
  a. Measure the height of the variable damper with a vernier caliper between the points indicated by Dimension "A" (**Figure 75**).
  b. The correct measurement is 42 mm (1.65 in.). If the height is incorrect, loosen the locknut (A, **Figure 75**) and turn the adjuster (B, **Fig-**

ure 75) in or out as required. Tighten the locknut and recheck the measurement.

c. Visually inspect the variable damper springs, spring seats and spool for cracks, breakage or other damage; replace the variable damper assembly if necessary (no replacement parts are available).

11. Any parts that are worn or damaged should be replaced. Simply cleaning and reinstalling unserviceable fork components will not improve performance of the front suspension.

Assembly

Refer to **Figure 65** for Radian models or **Figure 66** for FZ600 models during the disassembly procedure.

1. Coat all parts with fresh SAE 10W fork oil prior to installation.

2. Install the rebound spring onto the damper rod and insert this assembly into the fork tube (**Figure 76**).

3. On FZ600 models, position the variable damper with the locknut end facing up then install the variable damper into the fork tube.

4. Temporarily install the fork spring, spring seat and fork cap bolt to hold the damper rod in place. Tighten the fork cap bolt securely.

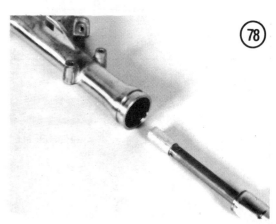

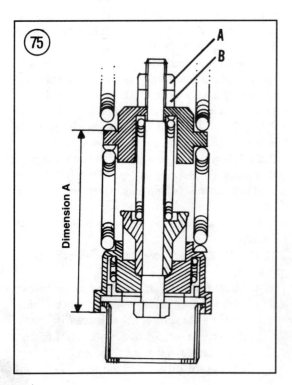

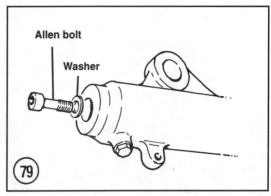

5. Install the oil lock piece onto the damper rod (**Figure 77**).

6. Install the upper fork assembly into the slider (**Figure 78**).

7. Make sure the washer is on the Allen bolt (**Figure 79**).

8. Apply Loctite Threadlocker to the threads of the Allen bolt prior to installation. Install it in the fork slider (**Figure 80**) and tighten to the torque specification listed in **Table 1**.

9. Slide the fork slider guide bushing and the washer down the fork tube and rest it on top of the fork slider.

10. Install the new oil seal as follows:

    a. Coat the new seal with ATF (automatic transmission fluid).

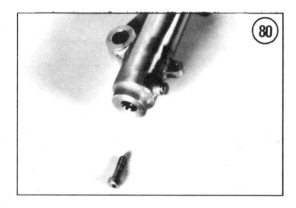

    b. Position the seal with the open groove facing upward and slide the oil seal down onto the fork tube.

    c. Drive the oil seal, washer and guide bushing into the slider with a piece of pipe of the appropriate size.

    d. Drive the oil seal in until the groove in the slider can be seen above the top surface of the upper washer.

11. Install the retaining clip and make sure it is completely seated in the groove in the fork slider.

12. Install the dust seal into the slider.

13. Remove the fork cap bolt, the spring seat and the fork spring.

14. Fill the fork tube with the correct quantity SAE 10W fork oil. Refer to **Table 2** for specified quantity.

15. Install the fork spring with the closer wound coils facing upward going in last.

16. Inspect the O-ring seal on the fork cap bolt; replace if necessary.

17. Install the spring seat and the fork cap bolt while pushing down on the spring. Start the bolt slowly, don't cross-thread it.

18. Place the slider in a vise with soft jaws and tighten the top fork cap bolt to the torque specifications listed in **Table 1**.

19. Repeat for the other fork assembly.

20. Install the fork assemblies as described in this chapter.

9

Tables 1 and 2 are on the following page.

Table 1 FRONT SUSPENSION TIGHTENING TORQUES

Item	N·m	ft.-lb.
Front axle nut	105	75
Front axle pinch bolt	20	14
Front fender brace bolts	8	5.8
Tire valve stem locknut	1.5	1.1
Handlebar (Radian)		
Upper holder Allen bolt	20	14
Handlebar (FZ600)		
Mounting bolts	10	7.2
Pinch bolt	20	14
Master cylinder clamp bolt	8	5.8
Steering stem		
Locknut	37	27
Stem bolt or nut	54	39
Fork bridge bolts		
Upper	20	14
Lower	23	17
Fork cap bolt	23	22
Fork slider Allen bolt	30	22

Table 2 FRONT SUSPENSION SPECIFICATIONS

Item	Standard	Service limit
Front axle runout	–	0.2 mm (0.01 in.)
Front wheel rim runout (radial and axial)	–	2.0 mm (0.08 in.)
Fork spring free length	542 mm (21.3 in.)	537 mm (21.1 in.)
Fork tube runout	–	0.2 mm (0.01 in.)
Front fork oil		
Capacity*	320 cc (10.8 oz.)	
Oil type	SAE 10W or equivalent	
Front fork air pressure (FZ600)		
Standard air pressure	39 kPa (5.7 psi)	
Minimum air pressure	0 kPa (0 psi)	
Maximum air pressure	98 kPa (14 psi)	
Differential between fork legs	9.8 kPa (1.4 psi) or less	

* Capacity for each leg.

CHAPTER TEN

REAR SUSPENSION

This chapter includes repair and replacement procedures for the rear wheel and rear suspension components. Tire changing and wheel balancing are covered in Chapter Nine.

Refer to **Table 1** for rear suspension torque specifications. **Table 1** is located at the end of this chapter.

NOTE
Where differences occur relating to the United Kingdom (UK) models, they are identified. If there is no (UK) designation relating to a procedure, photo or illustration it is identical to the United States (U.S.) models.

REAR WHEEL

**Removal/Installation
(Radian Models)**

1. Place the bike on the centerstand to support the bike securely with the rear wheel off the ground.

2. Completely unscrew the rear brake adjust nut (A, **Figure 1**). Depress the brake pedal and remove the brake rod from the brake lever on the brake panel.

3. Remove the pivot pin from the brake lever, install it on the brake rod and reinstall the adjust nut to avoid misplacing these small parts.

4. Remove the cotter pin on the rear brake torque link. Discard the cotter pin.

5. Remove the bolt, washer, lockwasher and nut (B, **Figure 1**) from the torque link. Let the torque link (C, **Figure 1**) pivot down to the ground.

6. Loosen the drive chain adjuster locknuts and nuts (A, **Figure 2**) on each side of the swing arm so the wheel can be moved forward for maximum chain slack.

7. Remove the cotter pin (B, **Figure 2**) on the rear axle nut. Discard the cotter pin.

8. Remove the rear axle nut and indicator plate (C, **Figure 2**) from the left-hand side.

9. Move the wheel forward, then rotate the rear wheel and derail the drive chain from the driven sprocket.

10. Withdraw the rear axle (A, **Figure 3**) and indicator plate (B, **Figure 3**) from the right-hand side.

11. Slide the wheel to the rear and remove it. Don't lose the collar (C, **Figure 3**) on each side of the wheel hub.

12. Inspect the rear hub and wheel as described in this chapter.

13. If the rear wheel is going to be left off for any length of time or if it is being taken to a shop for repair, install the collars and indicator plates onto the rear axle along with the axle nut to avoid misplacing any parts.

14. Install by reversing these removal steps while noting the following:

a. Apply a light coat of lithium base grease to the oil seal lips on each side of the wheel hub.

b. Position the left-hand collar with the shoulder side facing away from the bearing. The smaller diameter side of the collar must be against the bearing inner race or the bearing will not spin properly. Install the left-hand spacer.

c. Install the right-hand collar (**Figure 4**) against the brake panel.

d. Install the rear axle in from the right-hand side and don't forget to install the indicator plate (B, **Figure 3**) on each side.

e. Adjust the drive chain as described in Chapter Three.

f. Tighten the rear axle nut to the torque specification listed in **Table 1**.

g. Tighten the rear brake torque link nut to the torque specification listed in **Table 1**.

h. Install a new cotter pin on the axle nut and the brake torque link. Bend the ends over completely.

i. After the wheel is completely installed, rotate it several times to make sure that it rotates freely. Apply the rear brake and make sure it operates properly.

j. Adjust the rear brake pedal free play as described in Chapter Three.

**Removal/Installation
(FZ600 Models)**

1A. Place a suitable size aftermarket swing arm stand under the rear swing arm and support the bike with the rear wheel off the ground.

1B. If a swing arm stand is unavailable, perform the following:

a. Remove both lower fairings as described under *Lower Fairing Removal/Installation (FZ600 Models)* in Chapter Twelve. Remove the fairing mounting brackets.

b. Remove the exhaust system as described under *Exhaust System Removal/Installation (FZ600 Models)* in Chapter Seven.

c. Place wood block(s) under the engine to support the bike securely with the rear wheel off the ground.

2. Remove the rear brake caliper as described under *Rear Brake Caliper Removal/Installation* in Chapter Eleven.

3. Loosen the drive chain adjuster locknuts and nuts (A, **Figure 5**) on each side of the swing arm so the

wheel can be moved forward for maximum chain slack.

4. Remove the cotter pin (B, **Figure 5**) on the rear axle nut. Discard the cotter pin.

5. Remove the rear axle nut and washer from the left-hand side.

6. Move the wheel forward, then rotate the rear wheel and derail the drive chain from the driven sprocket.

7. Withdraw the rear axle from the right-hand side. Catch the brake caliper bracket when the rear axle is withdrawn from it.

8. Slide the wheel to the rear and remove it. Don't lose the collar on each side of the wheel hub.

CAUTION
Do not set the wheel down on the disc surface as it may be scratched or bent. Either lean the wheel against a wall or place the tire portion on a couple of wood blocks.

9. Inspect the rear hub and wheel as described in this chapter.

10. If the rear wheel is going to be left off for any length of time or if it is being taken to a shop for repair, install the collars onto the rear axle along with the axle nut and washer to avoid misplacing any parts.

11. Install by reversing these removal steps while noting the following:

   a. Apply a light coat of lithium base grease to the oil seal lips on each side of the wheel hub.

   b. Position the left-hand collar with the shoulder side facing away from the bearing. The smaller diameter side of the collar must be against the bearing inner race or the bearing will not spin properly. Install the left-hand collar.

   c. Install the right-hand collar onto the hub.

   d. Install the rear axle in from the right-hand side and don't forget to install the brake caliper bracket between the rear hub and the swing arm.

   e. Adjust the drive chain as described in Chapter Three.

   f. Tighten the rear axle nut to the torque specification listed in **Table 1**.

   g. After the wheel is completely installed, rotate it several times to make sure that it rotates freely. Apply the rear brake as many times as necessary to make sure the brake pads are against the brake disc correctly.

WHEEL INSPECTION

Measure the axial (end play) and radial (side play) runout of the wheel with a dial indicator as shown in **Figure 6**. The maximum axial and radial runout is as follows:

   a. Radian and UK FZ600 models: vertical and lateral runout is 2.0 mm (0.08 in.).

   b. U.S. FZ600 models: vertical runout is 1.0 mm (0.039 in.) and lateral runout 0.5 mm (0.020 in.).

If the runout exceeds this dimension, check the wheel bearing condition. If the wheel bearings are in good condition and no other cause can be found, the wheel will have to be replaced as it cannot be serviced.

Check the wheel for signs of cracks, fractures, dents or bends. If it is damaged in any way, it must be replaced.

WARNING
Do not try to repair any damage to the wheel as it will result in an unsafe riding condition.

Check the rear axle runout as described under *Rear Hub* in this chapter.

REAR HUB

Inspection

Inspect each wheel bearing prior to removing it from the wheel hub.

CAUTION
Do not remove the wheel bearings for inspection purposes as they will be damaged during the removal process. Remove wheel bearings only if they are to be replaced.

1. Perform Steps 1-6 of *Disassembly* in this chapter.

2. Turn each bearing by hand. Make sure the bearings turn smoothly.

3. On non-sealed bearings, check the balls for evidence of wear, pitting or excessive heat (bluish tint). Replace the bearings if necessary; always replace as a complete set. When replacing the bearings, be sure to take your old bearings along to ensure a perfect matchup.

NOTE
Fully sealed bearings are available from many bearing specialty shops. Fully sealed bearings provide better protection from dirt and moisture that may get into the hub.

4. Check the axle for wear and straightness. Use V-blocks and a dial indicator as shown in **Figure 7**. If the runout is 0.2 mm (0.01 in.) or greater, the axle should be replaced.

5. Inspect the raised webs where the rubber dampers fit. Check for cracks or wear. If any damage is visible, replace the wheel.

6. On Radian models, check the brake drum (**Figure 8**) for any scoring or damage. If any damage is apparent, refer to Chapter Eleven for service procedures.

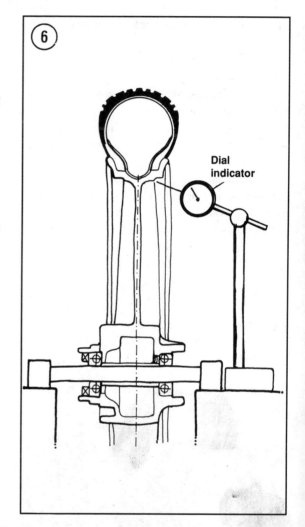

Dial indicator

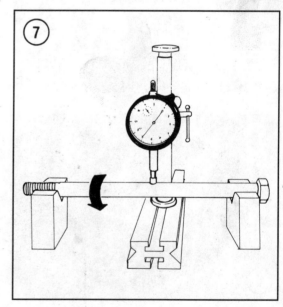

Disassembly

Refer to **Figure 9** for Radian models or **Figure 10** for FZ600 models for this procedure.

1. Remove the rear wheel as described in this chapter.

2. If not already removed, remove the collar from each side.

3. On Radian models, pull the rear brake assembly up and out of the wheel hub.

4. Remove the driven sprocket and drum assembly (**Figure 11**) from the rear wheel hub.

5. Remove the rubber dampers (**Figure 12**) from the rear hub.

6. Before proceeding further, inspect the wheel bearings as described in this chapter. If they must be replaced, proceed as follows.

7. On FZ600 models, use a long flat-bladed screwdriver and pry the oil seal from the right-hand side of the hub.

8. To remove the right- and left-hand bearings and distance collar, insert a soft aluminum or brass drift into one side of the hub.

9. Push the distance collar over to one side and place the drift on the inner race of the lower bearing.

10. Tap the bearing out of the hub with a hammer, working around the perimeter of the inner race (**Figure 13**).

11. Remove the distance collar and flanged spacer.

12. Repeat for the other bearing.

13. Clean the inside and the outside of the hub with solvent. Dry with compressed air.

Assembly

Refer to **Figure 9** for Radian models or **Figure 10** for FZ600 models for this procedure.

1. On non-sealed bearings, pack the bearings with a good quality bearing grease. Work the grease in between the balls thoroughly; turn the bearing by hand a couple of times to make sure the grease is distributed evenly inside the bearing.

2. Blow any dirt or foreign matter out of the hub prior to installing the bearings.

CAUTION
*Install non-sealed bearings with the single sealed side facing outward (**Figure 14**). Tap the bearings squarely into place and tap on the outer race only. Do not tap on the inner race or the bearing might be damaged. Be sure that the bearings are completely seated.*

3. Tap the right-hand bearing squarely into place and tap on the outer race only (**Figure 15**). Use a socket (**Figure 16**) that matches the outer race diameter. Do *not* tap on the inner race or the bearing might be damaged. Be sure that the bearing is completely seated.

4. Turn the wheel over (left-hand side up) on the workbench and install the distance collar.

5. Position the flanged spacer with the flange toward the distance collar and install the flanged spacer and distance collar.

6. Use the same tool set-up and drive in the left-hand bearing.

7. Install the rubber dampers (**Figure 12**) into the rear hub.

8. If removed, install the collar (**Figure 17**) into the driven sprocket.

9. Install the driven sprocket (**Figure 11**).

10. Position the right-hand collar with the smaller diameter portion of the collar facing in toward the bearing. This shoulder must be against the bearing inner race or the bearing will not spin properly. Install the right-hand collar.

11. On Radian models, install the rear brake assembly into the wheel hub.

12. Install the left-hand collar (A, **Figure 18**) into the grease seal (B, **Figure 18**) in the hub.

13. Install the rear wheel as described in this chapter.

10

REAR WHEEL (RADIAN)

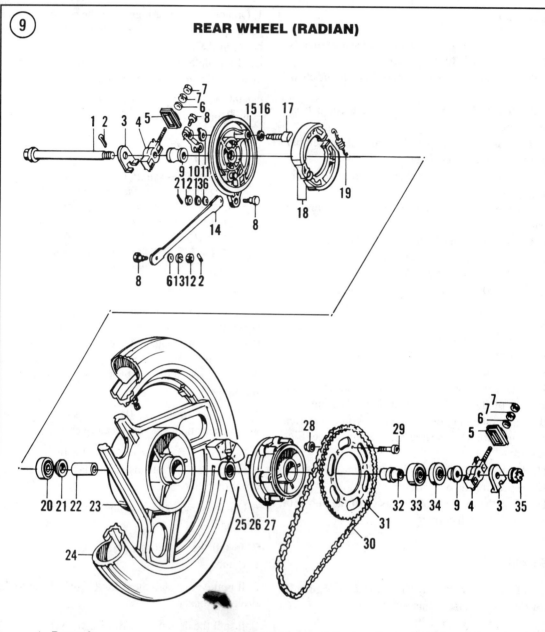

1. Rear axle
2. Cotter pin
3. Indicator plate
4. Drive chain adjuster
5. End plate
6. Washer
7. Nut
8. Bolt
9. Collar
10. Brake arm
11. Wear indicator plate
12. Nut
13. Washer
14. Torque arm
15. Brake backing plate
16. Oil seal
17. Camshaft
18. Brake shoes
19. Return spring
20. Bearing
21. Flanged spacer
22. Distance collar
23. Wheel
24. Tire
25. Bearing
26. Rubber damper
27. Driven sprocket hub
28. Nut
29. Allen bolt
30. Drive chain
31. Driven sprocket
32. Spacer
33. Bearing
34. Oil seal
35. Rear axle nut

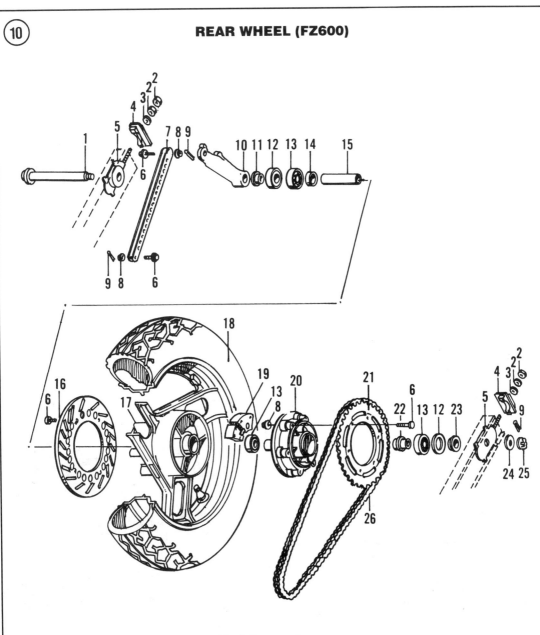

REAR WHEEL (FZ600)

1. Rear axle
2. Nut
3. Washer
4. End plate
5. Drive chain adjuster
6. Bolt
7. Torque arm
8. Nut
9. Cotter pin
10. Caliper carrier
11. Collar
12. Oil seal
13. Bearing
14. Flanged spacer
15. Distance collar
16. Brake disc
17. Wheel
18. Tire
19. Rubber damper
20. Driven sprocket hub
21. Driven sprocket
22. Spacer
23. Collar
24. Washer
25. Rear axle nut
26. Drive chain

10

DRIVEN SPROCKET AND
FLANGE ASSEMBLY

Disassembly/Assembly

Refer to **Figure 9** for Radian models or **Figure 10** for FZ600 models for this procedure.

1. Remove the rear wheel as described in this chapter.

2. Remove the driven sprocket and flange assembly (**Figure 11**) straight up and out of the rear hub.

> *NOTE*
> *If the driven sprocket and flange assembly is difficult to remove, tap on the backside of the sprocket (from the opposite side of the wheel through the wheel spokes) with a wooden handle of a hammer. Tap evenly around the perimeter of the sprocket until the assembly is free.*

3. Remove the spacer (A, **Figure 19**) from the inside of the driven sprocket and flange assembly.

4. Remove the driven sprocket bolts and nuts (B, **Figure 19**) and separate the driven sprocket from the flange assembly.

5. Install by reversing these removal steps while noting the following.

6. If the driven sprocket was removed, tighten the bolts and nuts to the torque specification listed in **Table 1**.

Inspection

1. Visually inspect the rubber dampers (**Figure 12**) for signs of damage or deterioration. Replace as a complete set.

2. Inspect the driven sprocket flange assembly for cracks or damage, replace if necessary.

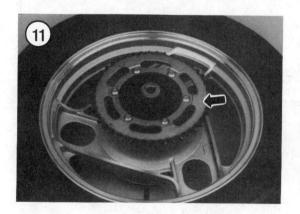

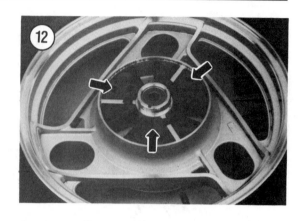

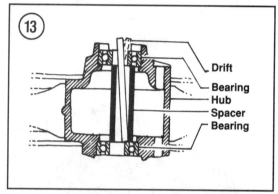

Drift
Bearing
Hub
Spacer
Bearing

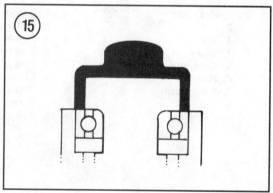

3. Inspect the teeth of the driven sprocket. If the teeth are visibly worn (**Figure 20**), remove bolts and nuts and replace the sprocket.

4. If the sprocket requires replacement, also inspect the drive chain and the drive sprocket on the engine. They also may be worn and need replacing.

5. Inspect the bearing, turn each bearing by hand. Make sure it turns smoothly. Replace if necessary.

6. On non-sealed bearings, check the balls for evidence of wear, pitting or excessive heat (bluish tint). Replace the bearings if necessary; always replace as a complete set. When replacing the bearings, be sure to take your old bearings along to ensure a perfect matchup.

NOTE
Fully sealed bearings are available from many bearing specialty shops. Fully sealed bearings provide better protection from dirt and moisture that may get into the hub.

Bearing Replacement

1. Remove the grease seal (A, **Figure 21**) from the flange assembly.

2. Remove the spacer (**Figure 17**) from the flange assembly.

3. To remove the bearing (B, **Figure 21**), insert a soft aluminum or brass drift into one side of the drum.

4. Place the drift on the inner race of the bearing.

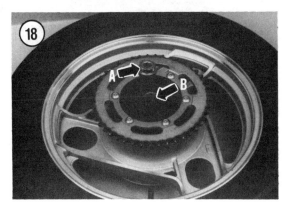

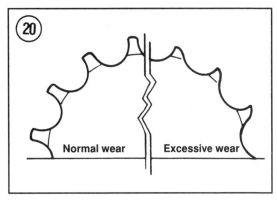

5. Tap the bearing out of the drum with a hammer, working around the perimeter of the inner race.

6. On a non-sealed bearing, pack the bearing with a good quality bearing grease. Work the grease in between the balls thoroughly; turn the bearing by hand a couple of times to make sure the grease is distributed evenly inside the bearing.

7. Blow any dirt or foreign matter out of the drum prior to installing the bearing.

8. Tap the bearing squarely into place and tap on the outer race only. Use a socket (**Figure 15**) that matches the outer race diameter. Do not tap on the inner race or the bearing might be damaged. Be sure that the bearing is completely seated.

9. Install a new grease seal.

DRIVE CHAIN

Removal/Installation

> *WARNING*
> *The original equipment Yamaha drive chain is manufactured as a continuous closed loop with no master link. Do **not** cut it with a chain cutter as this will result in future chain failure and possible loss of control under riding conditions.*

> *NOTE*
> *If an aftermarket drive chain has been installed, it may be equipped with a master link. Follow manufacturer's instructions for removal.*

1. Remove the bolt securing the gearshift lever (A, **Figure 22**) to the shift shaft and remove the gearshift lever assembly.

2. Remove the bolts securing the drive sprocket cover (B, **Figure 22**) and remove the cover.

3. Have an assistant apply the rear brake. Remove the drive sprocket bolts (A, **Figure 23**).

4. Remove the rear wheel as described in this chapter.

5. Rotate the sprocket holder plate (B, **Figure 23**) until it clears the splines on the transmission shaft. Remove the holder plate.

6. Slide the drive sprocket and drive chain (C, **Figure 23**) off of the transmission shaft.

7. Remove the swing arm as described in this chapter. The drive chain will come off with the swing arm.

8. Inspect the drive chain as described under *Drive Chain Cleaning, Inspection, Lubrication* in Chapter Three.

9. Install the drive chain by reversing these removal steps while noting the following:

    a. Feed the drive chain through the swing arm and the frame. Install the swing arm as described in this chapter.

    b. Tighten the sprocket bolts to the torque specification in **Table 1**.

c. Adjust the drive chain as described under *Drive Chain Adjustment* in Chapter Three.

SWING ARM

In time, the needle bearings will wear and will have to be replaced. The condition of the bearings can greatly affect handling performance and if worn parts are not replaced they can produce erratic and dangerous handling. Common symptoms are wheel

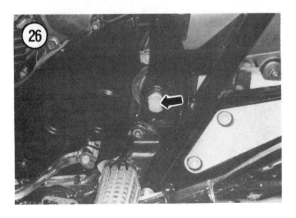

hop, pulling to one side during acceleration and pulling to the other side during braking.

Removal
(Radian Models)

1. Remove the mufflers as described under *Exhaust System Removal/Installation* in Chapter Seven.
2. Remove the rear wheel as described in this chapter.
3. Remove both shock absorbers (A, **Figure 24**) as described in this chapter.
4. Remove the bolts securing the drive chain cover and remove the cover.
5. Grasp the rear end of the swing arm and try to move it from side to side in a horizontal arc. There should be no noticeable side play. If play is evident and the pivot bolt and nut is tightened correctly, the needle bearings should be replaced.
6. Remove the self-locking nut (**Figure 25**) and withdraw the pivot bolt (**Figure 26**) from the left-hand side.
7. Pull back on the swing arm (B, **Figure 24**), free it from the drive chain (C, **Figure 24**) and remove the swing arm from the frame.
8. Inspect the swing arm as described in this chapter.

NOTE
Don't lose the dust seal cap and shim on each side of the pivot points; they will usually fall off when the swing arm is removed.

Installation
(Radian Models)

1. Position the drive chain over the left-hand side of the swing arm.
2. Make sure the shim and dust seal cap are correctly installed at each side of the swing arm.
3. Position the swing arm in the mounting area of the frame. Align the holes in the swing arm with the holes in the frame. To help align the holes, insert an appropriate size drift in from the right-hand side.
4. Apply a light coat of molybdenum disulfide grease to the pivot bolt and install the pivot bolt from the left-hand side.
5. Install the self-locking nut and tighten to the torque specification listed in **Table 1**.

10

6. Move the swing arm up and down several times to make sure all components are properly seated. Correct any problems that may exist at this time.

7. Install the drive chain cover and tighten the bolts securely.

8. Install both shock absorbers as described in this chapter.

9. Install the rear wheel as described in this chapter.

10. Install the mufflers as described in Chapter Seven.

Removal
(FZ600 Models)

1. Remove the rear wheel as described in this chapter.

2. Remove the shock absorber as described in this chapter.

3. Grasp the rear end of the swing arm and try to move it from side to side in a horizontal arc (**Figure 27**). There should be no noticeable side play. If play is evident and the pivot bolt and nut is tightened correctly, the needle bearings should be replaced.

4. Remove the self-locking nut (**Figure 28**) and withdraw the pivot bolt (**Figure 29**) from the left-hand side.

5. Pull back on the swing arm, free it from the drive chain and remove the swing arm from the frame (**Figure 30**).

6. Inspect the swing arm as described in this chapter.

NOTE
*Don't lose the thrust cover and washer (**Figure 31**) on each side of the pivot points; they will usually fall off when the swing arm is removed.*

Installation
(FZ600 Models)

1. Position the drive chain over the left-hand side of the swing arm.

2. Make sure the thrust cover and washer are correctly installed at each side of the swing arm pivot points.

3. Position the swing arm in the mounting area of the frame. Align the holes in the swing arm with the holes in the frame. To help align the holes, insert an appropriate size drift in from the right-hand side.

4. Apply a light coat of molybdenum disulfide grease to the pivot bolt and install the pivot bolt from the left-hand side.

5. Install the self-locking nut and tighten to the torque specification listed in **Table 1**.

6. Move the swing arm up and down several times to make sure all components are properly seated. Correct any problems that may exist at this time.

7. Install the shock absorber as described in this chapter.

8. Install the rear wheel as described in this chapter.

Disassembly/Inspection/Assembly
(All Models)

Refer to **Figure 32** for Radian models or **Figure 33** for FZ600 models for this procedure.

1. Remove the swing arm as described in this chapter.

2. Remove the bolts securing the drive chain cover and remove the cover (A, **Figure 34**).

3A. On Radian models, remove both dust seal caps and shims if they have not already fallen off during the removal sequence.

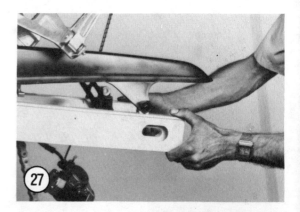

3B. On FZ600 models, remove both thrust covers and washers (**Figure 31**) if they have not already fallen off during the removal sequence.

4. Remove the bolt and nut securing the brake torque link (B, **Figure 34**) to the swing arm and remove it.

5. If necessary, remove the bolt(s) and collar(s) securing the drive chain slider (C, **Figure 34**) and remove it.

6. Withdraw the pivot collar from the swing arm.

7. If necessary, remove the drive chain adjuster assemblies from the rear of the swing arm.

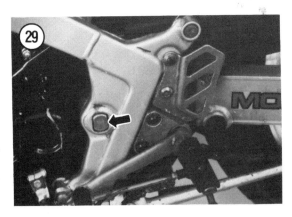

8. Clean all parts in solvent and thoroughly dry.

NOTE
There are no factory specifications for the outside diameter of the pivot collar.

9. Inspect the shims, washers and the pivot collar for abnormal wear, scratches or score marks. Replace if necessary.

NOTE
If the pivot collar is replaced, the needle bearing at each end of the swing arm must also be replaced at the same time.

10. Inspect the pivot needle bearings as follows:
   a. Wipe off any excess grease from the needle bearing at each end of the swing arm (**Figure 35**).
   b. Turn each bearing with your fingers; make sure they rotate smoothly. The needle bearings wear very slowly and wear is very difficult to measure.
   c. Check the rollers for evidence of wear, pitting or color change (bluish tint) indicating heat from lack of lubrication.

NOTE
If damaged, always replace both needle bearings even though only one may be worn.

11. Check the welded sections on the swing arm for cracks or fractures.

12. Inspect the drive chain adjuster assemblies for wear or damage, replace if necessary.

13. Prior to installing the pivot collar, coat it and both bearings with molybdenum disulfide grease.

14. Insert the pivot collar.

NOTE
Be sure to install the shim between the pivot collar and the dust seal cap. This shim must be reinstalled to maintain the proper clearance between the 2 parts.

15A. On Radian models, perform the following:
   a. Install the shim onto each end.
   b. Coat the inside of both dust seal caps with molybdenum disulfide grease and install them onto the ends of the swing arm.

15B. On FZ600 model, perform the following:
   a. Install the washer onto each end.

10

b. Coat the inside of both thrust covers with molybdenum disulfide grease and install them onto the ends of the swing arm.

16. If removed, install the drive chain slider, collar(s) and bolt(s). Tighten the bolt securely.

17. Install the swing arm as described in this chapter.

Pivot Point Bearing Replacement

The swing arm is equipped with a bearing at each end. The bearing is pressed in place and has to be removed with force. The bearing will get distorted when removed, so don't remove it unless absolutely necessary.

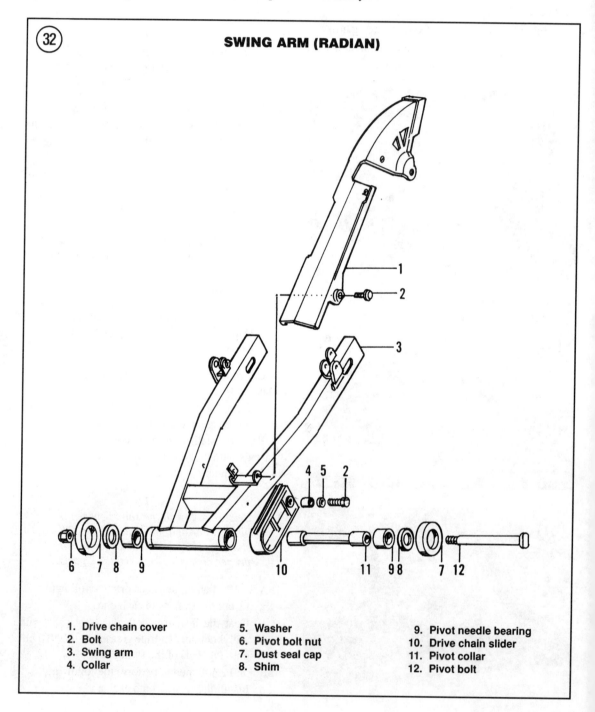

SWING ARM (RADIAN)

1. Drive chain cover
2. Bolt
3. Swing arm
4. Collar
5. Washer
6. Pivot bolt nut
7. Dust seal cap
8. Shim
9. Pivot needle bearing
10. Drive chain slider
11. Pivot collar
12. Pivot bolt

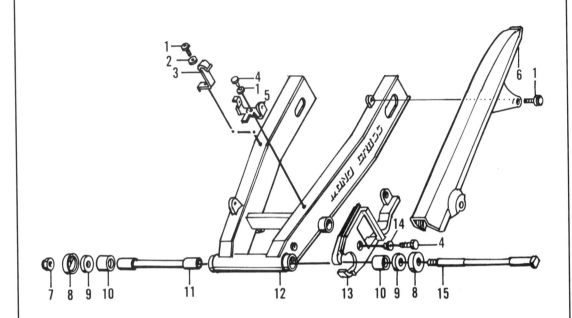

33 **SWING ARM (FZ600)**

1. Screw
2. Washer
3. Brake hose clamp
4. Bolt
5. Bracket
6. Drive chain cover
7. Pivot bolt nut
8. Dust seal cap
9. Shim
10. Pivot needle bearing
11. Pivot collar
12. Swing arm
13. Drive chain slider
14. Collar
15. Pivot bolt

10

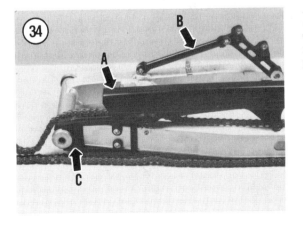

34

35

1. Remove the swing arm as described in this chapter.

2A. On Radian models, remove both dust seal caps and shims if they have not already fallen off during the removal sequence.

2B. On FZ600 models, remove both thrust covers and washers (**Figure 31**) if they have not already fallen off during the removal sequence.

3. Withdraw the pivot collar from the swing arm.

4. Either the right- or left-hand bearing can be removed first.

5. Install the swing arm in a vise with soft jaws.

6. Insert a soft aluminum or brass drift from the opposite end (**Figure 36**).

7. Tap on the drift with a hammer working around the perimeter of the bearing until it is completely driven out.

8. Turn the swing arm over in the vise and repeat Step 6 and Step 7 for the other bearing.

9. Thoroughly clean out the inside of the swing arm with solvent and dry with compressed air.

10. Apply a light coat of molybdenum disulfide grease to all parts prior to installation.

> *NOTE*
> *Either the right- or left-hand bearing can be installed first.*

> *CAUTION*
> *Never reinstall a bearing that has been removed. During removal, it becomes slightly damaged and is no longer true to alignment. If installed, it will damage the pivot collar and create an unsafe riding condition.*

> *CAUTION*
> *The new bearings must be pressed into place. Do not try to drive them into the swing arm as they will be damaged. If you do not have access to a hydraulic press, take the swing arm to a dealer or machine shop and have them install the bearings for you.*

11. Position the new bearing onto the end of the swing arm and press it into place until it is flush with the outer surface of the pivot portion of the swing arm.

12A. On Radian models, perform the following:

a. Install the shim onto each end.

b. Coat the inside of both dust seal caps with molybdenum disulfide grease and install them onto the ends of the swing arm.

12B. On FZ600 models, perform the following:

a. Install the washer onto each end.

b. Coat the inside of both thrust covers with molybdenum disulfide grease and install them onto the ends of the swing arm.

13. Install the swing arm as described in this chapter.

RELAY ARM ASSEMBLY (FZ600 MODELS)

Removal

Refer to **Figure 37** for this procedure.

1. Remove the swing arm as described in this chapter.

> *NOTE*
> *Remember that right-hand side refers to the swing arm as it is installed in the bike's frame, not as it sits on your workbench. Right-hand side refers to a rider sitting on the bike facing forward.*

2. Mark each pivot arm (right- and left-hand side) so it will be reinstalled on the correct side. The parts are asymmetrical and must be reinstalled on the correct

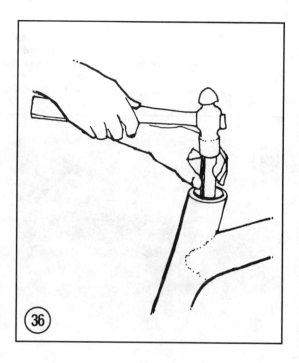

side or there will be interference with the shock absorber when it is installed.

3. Remove the bolt and lockwasher holding both pivot arms together.

4. Swing the pivot arms apart, then remove each of them from the pivot receptacles in the swing arm.

NOTE
The relay arm is not symmetrical. Note its relation to the frame prior to removal

and mark it so it will be reinstalled correctly.

5. Mark the shock absorber relay arm (right- and left-hand side) so it will be reinstalled correctly. See NOTE preceding Step 2 regarding right- and left-hand side of components.

6. Remove the pivot bolt, nut and washer securing the shock absorber relay arm to the frame and remove it.

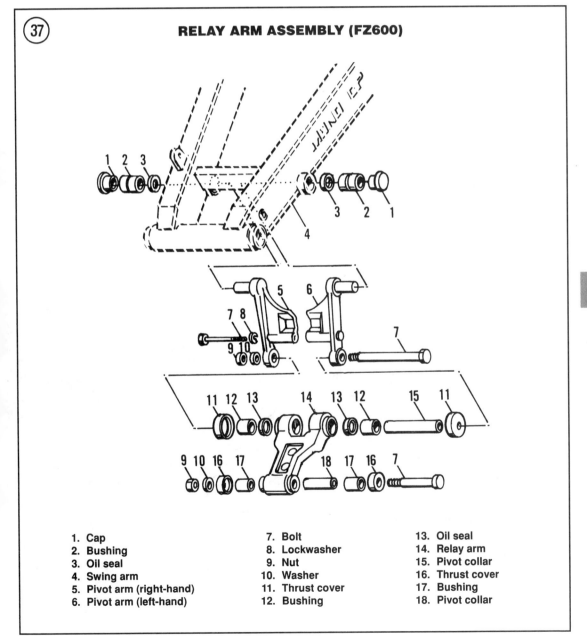

RELAY ARM ASSEMBLY (FZ600)

1. Cap
2. Bushing
3. Oil seal
4. Swing arm
5. Pivot arm (right-hand)
6. Pivot arm (left-hand)
7. Bolt
8. Lockwasher
9. Nut
10. Washer
11. Thrust cover
12. Bushing
13. Oil seal
14. Relay arm
15. Pivot collar
16. Thrust cover
17. Bushing
18. Pivot collar

10

Disassembly/Inspection/Assembly

1. Remove the thrust covers from both pivot points on the relay arm.
2. Withdraw the pivot collars from both pivot points on the relay arm.
3. Clean all parts in solvent and thoroughly dry.
4. Inspect the pivot bolts for abnormal wear, scratches or score marks. Replace if necessary.

NOTE
If the pivot collar is replaced, the bushing at each end of the pivot point must also be replaced at the same time.

5. Inspect the pivot bushings as follows:
   a. Wipe off any excess grease from the bushing at each end of the pivot point.
   b. Check the bushings for evidence of wear, pitting or color change (bluish tint) indicating heat from lack of lubrication.
   c. If the bushings are damaged, have them replaced by a dealer or machine shop as a press is required.

NOTE
If damaged, always replace both bushings even though only one may be worn.

6. Check the relay arm and both pivot arms for cracks or fractures. Replace if necessary.
7. Apply a light coat of molybdenum disulfide grease to all parts prior to installation.
8. Install the pivot collars into both pivot points on the relay arm.
9. Install the thrust covers onto both pivot points on the relay arm.

Installation

CAUTION
These parts are asymmetrical and must be reinstalled on the correct side or there will be interference with the shock absorber when it is installed.

1. Refer to marks made prior to removal, then correctly position and install the shock absorber relay arm onto the pivot point on the frame.
2. Install the bolt from the left-hand side and install the washer and nut. Tighten to the torque specification listed in **Table 1**.

3. Refer to marks made prior to removal, then correctly position and install the pivot arms onto the pivot receptacles on the swing arm.
4. Swing the pivot arms together, then install the bolt and lockwasher holding both pivot arms together. Tighten to the torque specification listed in **Table 1**.
5. Install the swing arm as described in this chapter.

SHOCK ABSORBERS (RADIAN MODELS)

The shock absorbers are spring controlled and hydraulically dampened. The spring preload can be adjusted for different ride and road conditions.

Spring Preload Adjustment

The spring preload can be adjusted to 5 different settings. Position 1 is the softest setting and position 5 is the stiffest setting. The adjuster is located at the base of the shock absorber (A, **Figure 38**).

Make sure that the adjuster is located into one of the detentes and not in between any 2 settings. Both

shocks must set on the same preload number or it will result in an unsafe riding condition.

Removal/Installation

Removal and installation of the shock absorbers is easier if done separately. The remaining shock will support the rear of the bike and maintain the correct relationship between the top and bottom mounts.

If both shock absorbers must be removed at the same time, cut a piece of wood a few inches longer than the shock absorber and drill two holes in the wood the same distance apart as the bolt holes in the shock absorbers. Install the piece of wood after the first shock has been removed. This will allow the bike to be easily moved around until the shock absorbers are reinstalled or replaced.

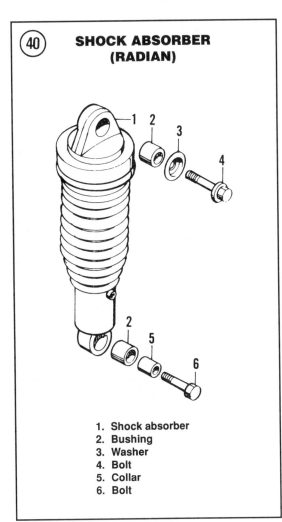

SHOCK ABSORBER (RADIAN)

1. **Shock absorber**
2. **Bushing**
3. **Washer**
4. **Bolt**
5. **Collar**
6. **Bolt**

1. Place the bike on the centerstand.
2. Remove the upper mounting bolt and washer (**Figure 39**) and the lower mounting bolt and collar (B, **Figure 38**).
3. Remove the shock absorber from the frame and swing arm.
4. Inspect the shock absorber as described in this chapter.
5. Install by reversing these removal steps while noting the following:

    a. Apply a light coat of molybdenum disulfide paste grease to the shoulder portion of each mounting bolt.

    b. Make sure the bushing is in place in each mounting hole in the shock absorber.

    c. Make sure the collar is in place in the lower bushing.

NOTE
*The torque specifications on the upper and lower bolt are different, please note this in **Table 1** and tighten accordingly.*

    d. Tighten the mounting bolts to the torque specification listed in **Table 1**.

Inspection

Refer to **Figure 40** for this procedure.

The shock absorber should not be disassembled as it cannot be serviced, there are *no* replacement parts available.

Check the damper unit for dents, oil leakage or other damage. Make sure the damper rod is straight.

Inspect the mounting receptacles at each end of the shock absorber for wear or damage. If damaged, replace the shock absorber.

SHOCK ABSORBER (FZ600 MODELS)

The shock absorber is spring controlled and hydraulically dampened. The spring preload can be adjusted for different ride and road conditions.

Spring Preload Adjustment

The spring preload can be adjusted to 5 different settings. Position 1 is the softest setting and position 5 is the stiffest setting.

10

1. Remove the rider and passenger seats as described under *Seat Removal/Installation* in Chapter Twelve.

2. Remove the right-hand side cover as described under *Side Cover Removal/Installation (FZ600 Models)* in Chapter Twelve.

3. Rotate the remote pulley (**Figure 41**), attached to the frame mounting bracket, until it aligns with the fixed mark on the mounting bracket. Make sure that the adjuster is located in one of the detents and not in between any 2 settings.

4. Install the right-hand side cover and both seats as described in Chapter Twelve.

Removal/Installation

1. Remove the seats as described under *Seat Removal/Installation* in Chapter Twelve.

2. Remove the lower fairing on each side as described under *Lower Fairing Removal/Installation* in Chapter Twelve. Remove the lower faring mounting brackets.

3. Remove the exhaust system as described under *Exhaust System Removal/Installation (FZ600 Models)* in Chapter Seven.

4. Place wood block(s) under the engine to support the bike securely.

5. Remove both side covers as described under *Side Cover Removal/Installation (FZ600 Models)* in Chapter Twelve.

6A. On 1986-1987 models, remove the lower mounting bolt and nut securing the shock to the relay arm and the pivot arms. Move both arms out of the way.

6B. On 1988 models, perform the following:

   a. Remove the mounting bolt and nut (A, **Figure 42**) securing pivot arms to the relay arm. Move the pivot arms toward the rear.

   b. Remove the lower mounting bolt and nut (B, **Figure 42**) securing the shock to the relay arm.

7. Remove the bolts securing the pulley bracket (A, **Figure 43**) to the frame.

8. Disengage the drive belt from the pulley and remove the pulley and bracket.

9. Remove the upper mounting bolt and nut (B, **Figure 43**) securing the shock to the frame.

10. Lower the shock absorber and remove the drive belt from it. Don't lose the washer on each side of the upper mount on the shock absorber.

11. Carefully lower the shock and remove it from the frame and swing arm. Don't lose the dust cover on each side of the lower mount on the shock absorber.

12. Inspect the shock absorber as described in this chapter.

13. Install by reversing these removal steps while noting the following:

   a. Apply a light coat of molybdenum disulfide paste grease to the shoulder portion of each mounting bolt and to all pivot points on the shock absorber and frame.

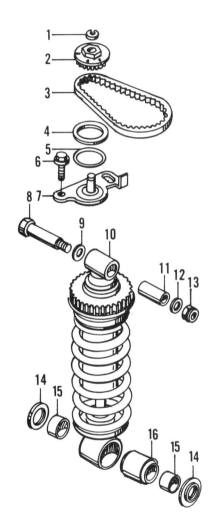

(44)

SHOCK ABSORBER
(FZ600)

1. Circlip	9. Washer
2. Pulley	10. Shock absorber
3. Drive belt	11. Collar
4. Washer	12. Washer
5. O-ring	13. Nut
6. Bolt	14. Dust cover
7. Mounting bracket	15. Collar
8. Bolt	16. Bushing

b. Make sure the washer is in place on each side of the upper mount on the shock absorber.

c. Make sure the dust cover is in place on each side of the lower mount on the shock absorber.

d. Make sure the drive belt is in place prior to moving the upper portion of the shock absorber into place on the frame.

NOTE
*The torque specifications on the upper and lower bolt are different, please note this in **Table 1** and tighten accordingly.*

e. Tighten the mounting bolts to the torque specification listed in **Table 1**.

Inspection

Refer to **Figure 44** for this procedure.

The shock absorber should not be disassembled as it cannot be serviced, there are *no* replacement parts available except those mentioned in this procedure.

WARNING
The shock absorber contains highly compressed nitrogen gas. Do not tamper with or attempt to open the cylinder. Do not place it near an open flame or other extreme heat. Do not weld on the frame near it. Do not dispose of the shock absorber yourself, take it to a Yamaha dealer where it can be deactivated and disposed of properly.

1. Check the damper unit for dents, oil leakage or other damage. Make sure the damper rod is straight, if damaged, replace the shock absorber.

2. Remove the pivot collars from each end of the shock.

3. Inspect the lower pivot bushing for wear or damage, replace if necessary.

4. Inspect the mounting receptacles at each end of the shock absorber for wear or damage. If damaged, replace the shock absorber.

5. Check the spring for cracks, damage or sagging. Replace the shock if any defects are found.

6. Inspect the drive belt for wear or damage, replace if necessary.

Table 1 is on the following page.

Table 1 REAR SUSPENSION TIGHTENING TORQUES

Item	N·m	ft.-lb.
Rear axle nut	105	75
Brake torque link nut	20	14
Driven sprocket bolts and nuts	32	23
Drive sprocket bolts	10	7.2
Swing arm pivot bolt nut	90	65
Shock absorber mounting bolts		
Radian		
Upper	20	14
Lower	30	22
FZ600		
Upper	40	29
Lower	70	50
Shock absorber linkage bolts (FZ600)		
Relay arm-to-frame	70	50
Relay arm-to-pivot arm	70	50
Pivot arm	20	14

CHAPTER ELEVEN

BRAKES

The brake system consists of a dual disc on the front wheel on all models with a drum brake on the rear on Radian models or a single rear disc on the FZ600 models. This chapter describes repair and replacement procedures for all brake components.

Table 1 contains the brake system torque specifications and **Table 2** contains brake system specifications. **Table 1** and **Table 2** are located at the end of this chapter.

DISC BRAKES

The front disc brakes are actuated by hydraulic fluid and are controlled by a hand lever on the master cylinder on the right-hand side of the handlebar. The rear disc brake is actuated by hydraulic fluid and is controlled by a foot pedal attached to the master cylinder on the right-hand side of the frame. As the brake pads wear, the brake fluid level drops in the master cylinder reservoir and automatically adjusts for wear.

When working on hydraulic brake systems, it is necessary that the work area and all tools be absolutely clean. Any tiny particles of foreign matter and grit in the caliper assembly or the master cylinder can damage the components. Also, sharp tools must not be used inside the calipers or on the piston. If there is any doubt about your ability to correctly and safely carry out major service on the brake components, take the job to a Yamaha dealer or brake specialist.

When adding brake fluid, use only a brake fluid clearly marked DOT 3 or DOT 4 from a sealed container. Other types may vaporize and cause brake failure. Always use the same brand name; do not intermix as many brands are not compatible. Brake fluid will draw moisture which greatly reduces its ability to perform correctly, so it is a good idea to purchase brake fluid in small containers.

> *WARNING*
> *Do not intermix silicone based (DOT 5) brake fluid as it can cause brake component damage leading to brake system failure.*

Whenever *any* component has been removed from the brake system the system is considered "opened" and must be bled to remove air bubbles. Also if the brake feels "spongy," this usually means there are air bubbles in the system and it must be bled. For safe operation, refer to *Bleeding the System* in this chapter.

CAUTION
Disc brake components rarely require disassembly, so do not disassemble them unless necessary. Do not use solvents of any kind on the brake system's internal components. Solvents will cause the seals to swell and distort and require replacement. When disassembling and cleaning brake components (except brake pads), use new brake fluid.

FRONT BRAKE PAD REPLACEMENT

There is no recommended mileage interval for changing the friction pads in the disc brakes. Pad wear depends greatly on riding habits and conditions. The pads should be checked for wear every 6 months and replaced when the wear indicator reaches the edge of the brake disc. To maintain an even brake pressure on the disc always replace both

pads in the caliper at the same time. Also replace the pads in both calipers at the same time.

Disconnecting the hydraulic brake hose from the brake caliper is not necessary for brake pad replacement. Disconnect the hose only if the caliper assembly is going to be removed.

CAUTION
Check the pads more frequently when the wear line approaches the disc. On some pads the wear line is very close to the metal backing plate. If pad wear happens to be uneven for some reason, the backing plate may come in contact with the disc and cause damage.

Refer to **Figure 1** and **Figure 2** for this procedure.

It is not necessary to remove the caliper from the front fork and disc in order to replace the brake pads. In this procedure it is removed for clarity only.

1. Remove the dust cover from the brake caliper.
2. Remove the clips securing the pad pins.

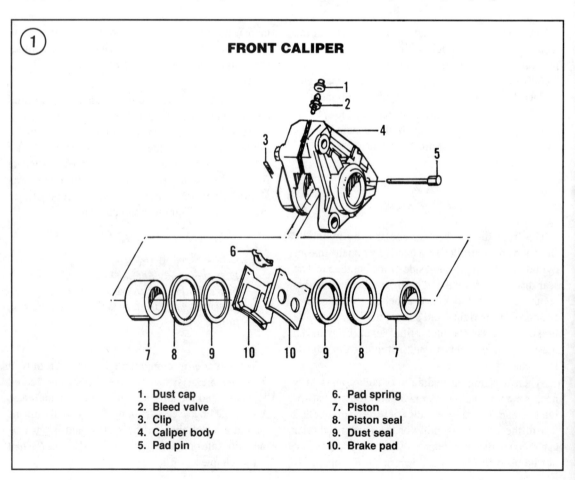

FRONT CALIPER

1. Dust cap
2. Bleed valve
3. Clip
4. Caliper body
5. Pad pin
6. Pad spring
7. Piston
8. Piston seal
9. Dust seal
10. Brake pad

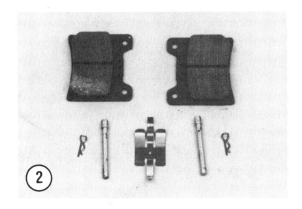

3. Withdraw both pad pins and remove the pad spring.

4. Withdraw both brake pads (**Figure 3**) from the caliper assembly.

5. Clean the pad recess and the end of the pistons with a soft brush. Do not use solvent, a wire brush or any hard tool which would damage the cylinders or pistons.

6. Carefully remove any rust or corrosion from the disc.

7. Lightly coat the end of the pistons and the backs of the new pads (*not* the friction material) with disc brake lubricant.

NOTE
When purchasing new pads, check with your dealer to make sure the friction compound of the new pad is compatible with the disc material. Remove any roughness from the backs of the new pads with a fine-cut file; blow them clean with compressed air.

8. When new pads are installed in the caliper, the master cylinder brake fluid level will rise as the caliper pistons are repositioned. Perform the following:

　a. Clean the top of the master cylinder of all dirt and foreign matter.

　b. Remove the screws securing the cover (**Figure 4**). Remove the cover and the diaphragm from the master cylinder and slowly push the caliper pistons into the caliper. Constantly check the reservoir to make sure brake fluid does not overflow. Remove fluid, if necessary, prior to it overflowing.

　c. The pistons should move freely. If they don't and there is evidence of them sticking in the cylinder, the caliper should be removed and serviced as described in this chapter.

9. Push the caliper pistons in all the way to allow room for the new pads.

10. Install the inboard brake pad (**Figure 5**) then the outboard brake pad into the caliper.

11. Partially install the pad pins (A, **Figure 6**) through the holes in the caliper.

12. Position the pad spring with the longer tangs facing toward the normal disc rotation (**Figure 7**) and install the pad spring (B, **Figure 6**).

11

13. Push one of the pad pins through the holes in one of the pads and the spring, then push in the other pad pin. Push the pad pins in until they stop.

14. Install the clip (C, **Figure 6**) into the hole in each pad pin. Push the clips in until they seat completely on the pad pin.

15. Install the dust cover (**Figure 8**). Make sure it snaps into place otherwise it will fly off when you hit the first bump in the road.

16. Repeat Steps 1-15 for the other caliper assembly.

17. Roll the bike back and forth and activate the front brake lever as many times as it takes to refill the cylinders in each caliper and correctly locate both sets of pads.

> *WARNING*
> *Use brake fluid clearly marked DOT 3 or DOT 4 from a sealed container. Other types may vaporize and cause brake failure. Always use the same brand name; do not intermix as many brands are not compatible. Do not intermix silicone based (DOT 5) brake fluid as it can cause brake component damage leading to brake system failure.*

18. Refill the master cylinder reservoir, if necessary, to maintain the correct fluid level as seen through the viewing port on the side. Install the diaphragm and cover. Tighten the screws securely.

> *WARNING*
> *Do not ride the motorcycle until you are sure the brakes are operating correctly with full hydraulic advantage. If necessary, bleed the brake as described under **Bleeding the System** in this chapter.*

19. Bed the pads in gradually for the first 5-10 days of riding by using only light pressure as much as possible. Immediate hard application will glaze the new friction pads and greatly reduce the effectiveness of the brake.

FRONT MASTER CYLINDER

Removal/Installation

> *CAUTION*
> *Cover the fuel tank, front fender and instrument cluster with a heavy cloth or plastic tarp to protect them from acci-*

dental brake fluid spills. Wash brake fluid off any painted or plated surfaces or plastic parts immediately, as it will destroy the finish. Use soapy water and rinse completely.

1. Disconnect the brakelight switch electrical connector (A, **Figure 9**) from the master cylinder.

2. On Radian models, remove the rear view mirror (B, **Figure 9**) from the master cylinder.

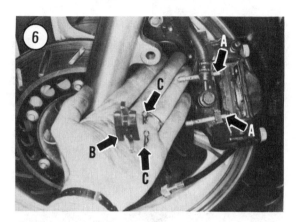

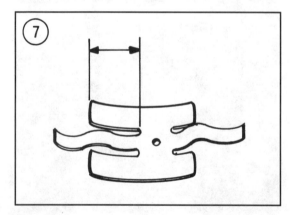

3. Pull back the rubber boot (C, **Figure 9**) on the master cylinder union bolt.

4. Place a shop cloth under the union bolt to catch any spilled brake fluid that will leak out.

5. Unscrew the union bolt (**Figure 10**) securing the upper brake hose to the master cylinder. Don't lose the sealing washer on each side of the hose fitting. Tie the loose end of the hose up to the handlebar and cover the end to prevent the entry of moisture and foreign matter.

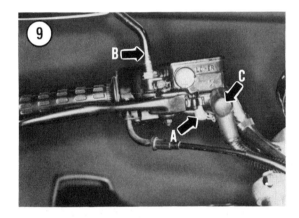

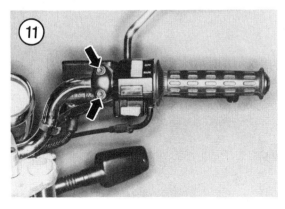

6. Remove the clamping bolts (**Figure 11**) and clamp securing the master cylinder to the handlebar and remove the master cylinder.

7. Install by reversing these removal steps while noting the following:

   a. Tighten the upper clamp bolt first, then the lower bolt to the torque specification listed in **Table 1**.

   b. Place a sealing washer on each side of the brake hose fitting and install the union bolt.

   c. Tighten the union bolt to the torque specification listed in **Table 1**.

   d. Bleed the front brakes as described under *Bleeding the System* in this chapter.

Disassembly

Refer to **Figure 12** for this procedure.

1. Remove the master cylinder as described in this chapter.

NOTE
Do not intermix used brake fluid with motor oil that is going to be recycled. The oil will be considered contaminated and will not be accepted at most oil recycling centers.

2. Remove the screws (**Figure 13**) securing the top cover and remove the top cover and the diaphragm. Pour out any remaining brake fluid and discard it according to local regulations. *Never* re-use hydraulic fluid.

3. Remove the screw and washer securing the brake-light switch to the master cylinder and remove the switch assembly.

4. Remove the screw, collar and nut (A, **Figure 14**) securing the brake lever to the master cylinder and remove the lever (B, **Figure 14**) and the *small* return spring (**Figure 15**).

5. Remove the rubber boot (**Figure 16**) from the area where the hand lever actuates the piston assembly.

6. Using circlip pliers, remove the internal circlip (A, **Figure 17**) from the body.

7. Remove the piston assembly (A, **Figure 18**) and the spring (**Figure 19**).

8. Remove the seat (B, **Figure 18**) from the piston.

9. Remove the primary cup (A, **Figure 20**) from the piston.

11

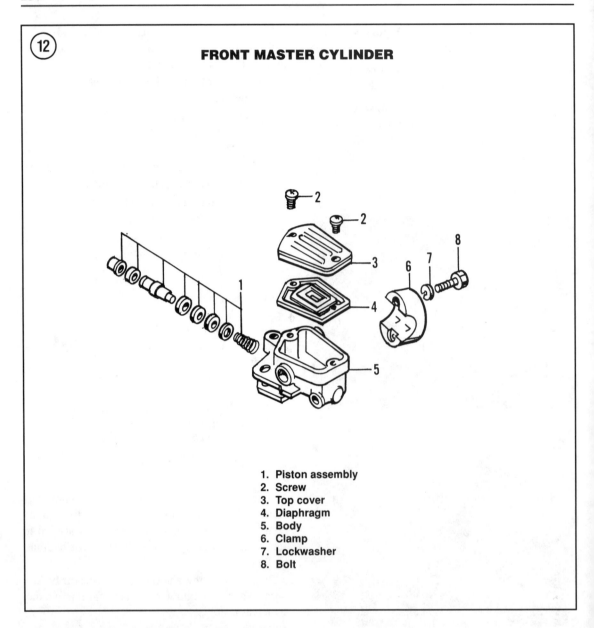

FRONT MASTER CYLINDER

1. Piston assembly
2. Screw
3. Top cover
4. Diaphragm
5. Body
6. Clamp
7. Lockwasher
8. Bolt

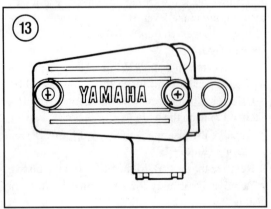

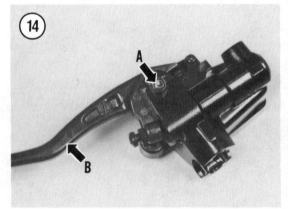

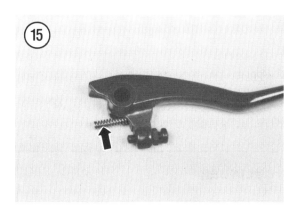

CAUTION
*Do not remove the secondary cup (**B**, **Figure 20**) from the piston or damage to the secondary cup will occur.*

10. Remove the baffle plate from the base of the reservoir (**Figure 21**).

Inspection

1. Clean all parts (**Figure 22**) in denatured alcohol or fresh hydraulic fluid.

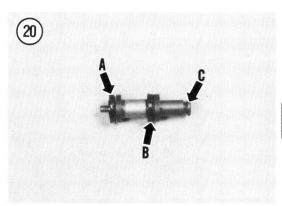

11

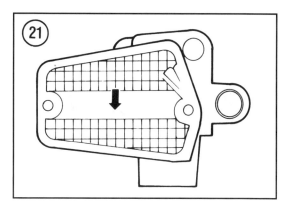

2. Inspect the body cylinder bore surface for signs of wear and damage. If less than perfect, replace the master cylinder assembly. The body cannot be replaced separately.

3. Inspect the piston contact surfaces for signs of wear and damage. If less than perfect, replace the piston assembly.

4. Check the end of the piston (C, **Figure 20**) for wear caused by the hand lever. If worn, replace the piston assembly.

5. Replace the piston assembly if either the primary or secondary cup requires replacement.

6. Inspect the hand lever pivot hole (**Figure 23**). If worn or elongated, it must be replaced.

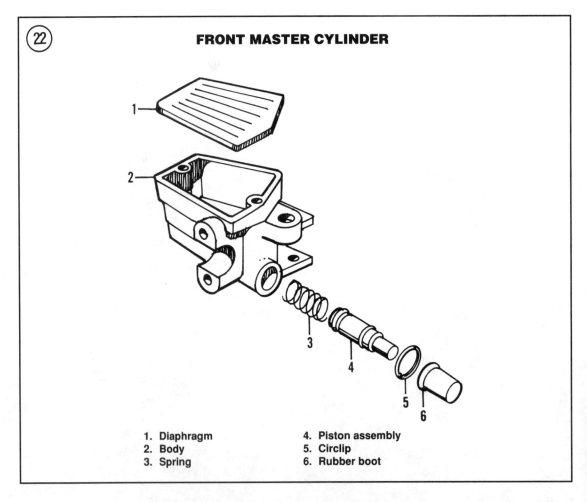

FRONT MASTER CYLINDER

1. Diaphragm
2. Body
3. Spring
4. Piston assembly
5. Circlip
6. Rubber boot

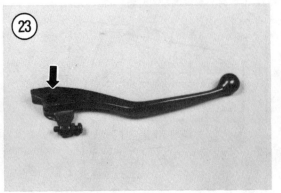

7. Make sure the passages in the bottom of the master cylinder reservoir are clear (**Figure 24**).

8. Check the reservoir diaphragm (A, **Figure 25**) and top cover (B, **Figure 25**) for damage and deterioration. Replace as necessary.

9. Inspect the threads in the bore of the reservoir for the union bolt. If worn or damaged, clean out with a thread tap or replace the master cylinder assembly.

10. Check the hand lever pivot lugs on the master cylinder body for cracks. If damaged, replace the master cylinder assembly.

Assembly

1. Soak the new cups in fresh brake fluid for at least 15 minutes to make them pliable. Coat the inside of the cylinder bore with fresh hydraulic fluid prior to the assembly of parts.

> *CAUTION*
> *When installing the piston assembly, do not allow the cups to turn inside out as they will be damaged and allow brake fluid leakage within the cylinder bore.*

2. Position the primary cup so that the larger seal lip will face into the master cylinder bore first. Slide the primary cup (A, **Figure 20**) onto the piston assembly.

3. Install the piston seat (B, **Figure 18**) onto the piston.

4. Position the spring so the small end of the spring faces the piston (**Figure 19**). Install the spring and piston assembly into the cylinder as an assembly.

5. Install the circlip (A, **Figure 17**) and slide on the rubber boot (B, **Figure 17**). Make sure the boot is firmly seated in the reservoir.

6. Install the baffle plate into the bottom of the reservoir.

7. Install the diaphragm and top cover. Do not tighten the cover screws at this time as hydraulic fluid will have to be added later when the system is bled.

8. Apply a light coat of multipurpose grease to the bolt pivot point of the brake lever and to the bolt pivot point on the body.

9. Install the spring into the brake lever (**Figure 15**) and install the brake lever (B, **Figure 14**) onto the master cylinder. Install the pivot bolt, collar and nut (A, **Figure 14**) and tighten the nut securely.

10. Install the brakelight switch, washer and screw onto the master cylinder. Tighten the screw securely.

11. Install the master cylinder as described in this chapter.

FRONT CALIPER

Removal/Installation

Refer to **Figure 26** for this procedure.

It is not necessary to remove the front wheel in order to remove the caliper assembly.

> *CAUTION*
> *Do not spill any brake fluid on the front fork or front wheel. Wash off any spilled brake fluid immediately, as it will destroy the finish. Use soapy water and rinse completely.*

1. Clean the top of the master cylinder of all dirt and foreign matter.

2. Loosen the screws securing the master cylinder top cover(**Figure 27**). Pull up and loosen the cover and the diaphragm. This will allow air to enter the reservoir and allow the brake fluid to drain out more quickly in the next step.

3. Place a container under the brake line at the caliper.

4. Loosen then remove the union bolt and sealing washers from the caliper (A, **Figure 28**).

> *NOTE*
> *Do not intermix used brake fluid with motor oil that is going to be recycled. The oil will be considered contaminated and will not be accepted at most oil recycling centers.*

5. Remove the brake hose (B, **Figure 28**) and let the brake fluid drain out into the container. Dispose of

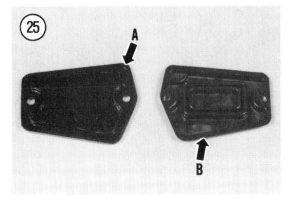

11

this brake fluid according to local regulations—never reuse brake fluid.

6. Remove the clamp bolt (C, **Figure 28**) and clamp securing the brake hose to the fork leg.

7. To prevent the entry of moisture and dirt, cap the end of the brake hose and tie the loose end up to the forks.

> *CAUTION*
> *In the following step, do not push or pull too hard on the caliper as the rotor is relatively thin in order to dissipate heat and to minimize unsprung weight. The rotor is designed to withstand tremendous rotational loads but can be damaged when subjected to side loads.*

8. Loosen the bolts (D, **Figure 28**) securing the brake caliper assembly to the front fork. Push in, then pull out on the caliper while loosening the bolts to push the pistons back into the caliper bores.

9. Remove the bolts (D, **Figure 28**) securing the brake caliper assembly to the front fork.

10. Remove the caliper assembly from the brake disc.

11. Install by reversing these removal steps while noting the following:

    a. Carefully install the caliper assembly onto the disc being careful not to damage the leading edge of the brake pads.

    b. Install the bolts securing the brake caliper assembly to the front fork and tighten to the torque specifications listed in **Table 1**.

    c. Install a new sealing washer on each side of the fitting and install the brake hose onto the caliper.

    d. Install the union bolt and tighten to the torque specifications listed in **Table 1**.

12. If necessary, repeat Steps 3-11 for the other caliper assembly.

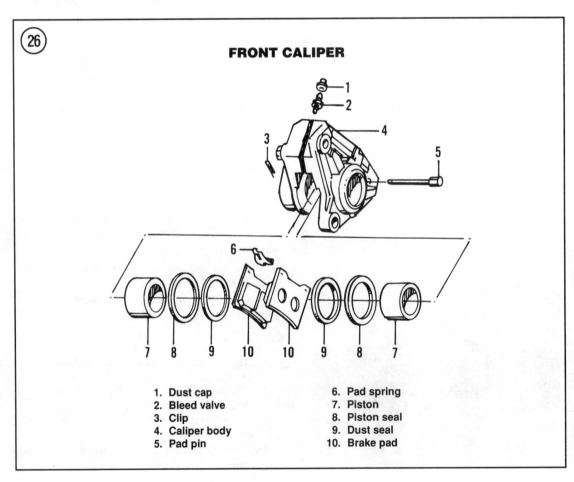

FRONT CALIPER

1. Dust cap
2. Bleed valve
3. Clip
4. Caliper body
5. Pad pin
6. Pad spring
7. Piston
8. Piston seal
9. Dust seal
10. Brake pad

13. Remove the master cylinder top cover and diaphragm.

> *WARNING*
> *Use brake fluid clearly marked DOT 3 or DOT 4 from a sealed container. Other types may vaporize and cause brake failure. Always use the same brand name; do not intermix as many brands are not compatible. Do not intermix silicone-based (DOT 5) brake fluid as it can cause brake component damage leading to brake system failure.*

14. Roll the bike back and forth and activate the front brake lever as many times as it takes to refill the cylinders in the caliper(s) and correctly locate the pads.

15. Refill the master cylinder reservoir. Install the diaphragm and cover. Do not tighten the screws at this time.

16. Bleed the brake as described under *Bleeding the System* in this chapter.

> *WARNING*
> *Do not ride the motorcycle until you are sure that the brakes are operating properly.*

Caliper Rebuilding
(Front and Rear Calipers)

Refer to **Figure 26** for the front caliper or **Figure 29** for the rear caliper for this procedure.

> *CAUTION*
> *The caliper assembly is a two-part assembly—but do **not** remove the bolts **Figure 30** securing the two halves together. The pistons and seals can be removed without separating the caliper halves.*

1. Remove the caliper and brake pads as described in this chapter.

2. Place a folded-over shop rag up against the inboard piston and hold the cloth in place with a pair of channel-lock pliers. Apply pressure and hold the inner piston in place.

3. Perform this step over and close down to a workbench top. Hold the caliper body with the piston facing away from you.

> *WARNING*
> *In the next step, the piston may shoot out of the caliper body like a bullet. Keep your fingers out of the way. Wear shop gloves and apply air pressure gradually. Do **not** use high pressure air or place the air hose nozzle directly against the hydraulic line fitting inlet in the caliper body. Hold the air nozzle away from the inlet allowing some of the air to escape.*

4. Apply the air pressure in short spurts to the union bolt hole in the caliper and force the outboard piston out. Use a service station air hose if you don't have an air compressor.

5. Remove the shop cloth and channel-lock pliers.

6. Remove the outboard piston.

7. Place a folded-over shop rag up against the outboard piston and hold the cloth in place.

8. Perform this step over and close down to a workbench top. Hold the caliper body with the piston facing away from you.

11

WARNING
*In the next step, the piston may shoot out of the caliper body like a bullet. Keep your fingers out of the way. Wear shop gloves and apply air pressure gradually. Do **not** use high pressure air or place the air hose nozzle directly against the hydraulic line fitting inlet in the caliper body. Hold the air nozzle away from the inlet allowing some of the air to escape.*

9. Apply the air pressure in short spurts to the union bolt hole in the caliper and force the inboard piston out. Use a service station air hose if you don't have an air compressor.

10. Remove the shop cloth and the inboard piston.

CAUTION
In the following step, do not use a sharp tool to remove the dust and piston seals

from the caliper cylinder. Do not damage the cylinder surface.

11. Use a piece of plastic or wood and carefully push the dust seal and the piston seal in toward the caliper cylinder and out of their grooves. Remove the dust and piston seals from the cylinder and discard both seals. Repeat for the other set of seals.

12. Inspect the seal grooves in the caliper body for damage. If damaged or corroded, replace the caliper assembly.

13. Inspect the cylinder walls and the pistons for scratches, scoring or other damage. If either is rusty or corroded, replace either the piston or the caliper assembly.

14. Inspect the caliper body for damage, replace the caliper body if necessary.

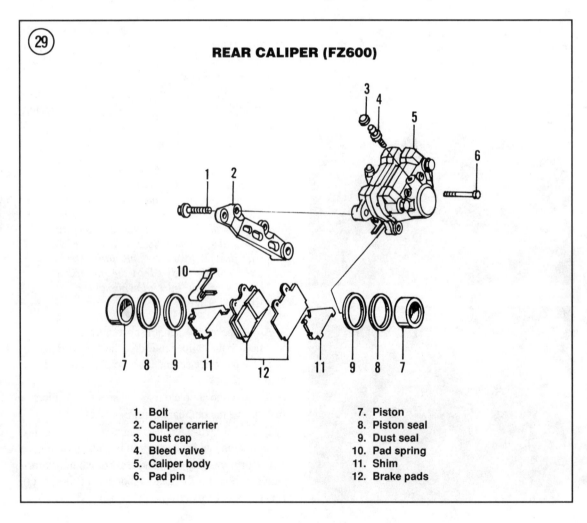

29

REAR CALIPER (FZ600)

1. Bolt
2. Caliper carrier
3. Dust cap
4. Bleed valve
5. Caliper body
6. Pad pin
7. Piston
8. Piston seal
9. Dust seal
10. Pad spring
11. Shim
12. Brake pads

15. Inspect the caliper mounting bolt holes on the caliper body. If worn or damaged, replace the caliper assembly.

16. Remove the bleed screw and make sure it is clean and open. Apply compressed air to the opening and make sure it is clear. Clean out if necessary with fresh brake fluid.

17. If serviceable, clean the caliper body with rubbing alcohol and rinse with clean brake fluid.

NOTE
Never reuse the old dust seals or piston seals. Very minor damage or age deterioration can make the seals useless.

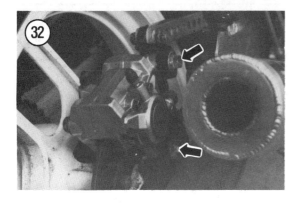

18. Coat the new dust seal and piston seal with fresh DOT 3 or DOT 4 brake fluid.

19. Carefully install the new dust seal and piston seal in the grooves in the caliper cylinders. Make sure the seals are properly seated in their respective grooves.

20. Coat the piston and caliper cylinder with fresh DOT 3 or DOT 4 brake fluid.

21. Position the piston with the open end facing out toward the brake pads and install the piston into the caliper cylinder. Push the piston in until it bottoms out. Repeat for the other piston.

22. Install the caliper and brake pads as described in this chapter.

REAR BRAKE PAD REPLACEMENT (FZ600 MODELS)

There is no recommended mileage interval for changing the friction pads in the disc brakes. Pad wear depends greatly on riding habits and conditions. The pads should be checked for wear every 6 months and replaced when the wear indicator reaches the edge of the brake disc. To maintain an even brake pressure on the disc, always replace both pads in the caliper at the same time.

Disconnecting the hydraulic brake hose from the brake caliper is not necessary for brake pad replacement. Disconnect the hose only if the caliper assembly is going to be removed.

CAUTION
Check the pads more frequently when the wear line approaches the disc. On some pads, the wear line is very close to the metal backing plate. If pad wear happens to be uneven for some reason, the backing plate may come in contact with the disc and cause damage.

Refer to **Figure 29** for this procedure.

1. Loosen the pad pins (**Figure 31**).

NOTE
It is not necessary to remove the bolt and nut securing the rear caliper to the torque link on the swing arm.

2. Remove the bolts (**Figure 32**) securing the caliper to the caliper carrier. Pivot the caliper up and off of the rear disc.

3. Remove both pad pins (**Figure 31**).

11

4. Withdraw both brake pads and shims from the lower part of the caliper assembly.

5. Remove the brake pad spring from the caliper.

6. Clean the pad recess and the end of the pistons with a soft brush. Do not use solvent, a wire brush or any hard tool which would damage the cylinders or pistons.

7. Carefully remove any rust or corrosion from the disc.

8. Lightly coat the end of the pistons and the backs of the new pads (*not* the friction material) with disc brake lubricant.

NOTE
When purchasing new pads, check with your dealer to make sure the friction compound of the new pad is compatible with the disc material. Remove any roughness from the backs of the new pads with a fine-cut file; blow them clean with compressed air.

9. When new pads are installed in the caliper, the master cylinder brake fluid level will rise as the caliper pistons are repositioned. Perform the following:

   a. Remove the right-hand side cover as described under *Side Cover Removal/Installation (FZ600 Models)* in Chapter Twelve.

   b. Clean the top of the master cylinder of all dirt and foreign matter.

   c. Unscrew cover (**Figure 33**). Remove the cover, seal and the diaphragm from the master cylinder.

   d. Slowly push the caliper pistons into the caliper. Constantly check the reservoir to make sure brake fluid does not overflow. Remove fluid, if necessary, prior to it overflowing.

   e. The pistons should move freely. If they don't and there is evidence of them sticking in the cylinder, the caliper should be removed and serviced as described in this chapter.

10. Push the caliper pistons in all the way to allow room for the new pads.

11. Position the brake pad spring with the closed end of the spring facing toward the front of the bike and install the spring into the caliper.

12. Install the shims onto the brake pads as shown in **Figure 34**.

13. Install both brake pads and shims into the caliper.

14. Push up on the brake pads and partially install the pad pins through the holes in the caliper and both brake pads.

15. Screw both pad pins into the caliper. Do not tighten at this time as it is easier after the caliper is reinstalled on the carrier.

16. Pivot the caliper assembly down onto the brake disc. Be careful not to damage the leading edge of the brake pads when installing the caliper onto the disc.

17. Install the bolts securing the caliper to the caliper carrier. Tighten the bolts to the torque specification listed in **Table 1**.

18. Tighten the pad pins securely.

19A. Place a suitable size aftermarket swing arm stand under the rear swing arm and support the bike with the rear wheel off the ground.

19B. If a swing arm stand is unavailable, roll the bike back and forth and activate the rear brake pedal as many times as it takes to refill the cylinders in the caliper and correctly locate the pads.

WARNING
Use brake fluid clearly marked DOT 3 or DOT 4 from a sealed container.

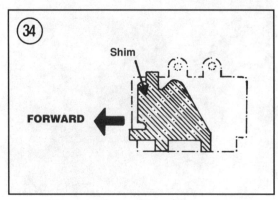

Other types may vaporize and cause brake failure. Always use the same brand name; do not intermix as many brands are not compatible. Do not intermix silicone based (DOT 5) brake fluid as it can cause brake component damage leading to brake system failure.

20. Refill the master cylinder reservoir, if necessary, to maintain the correct fluid level as seen through the side of the transparent reservoir. Install the diaphragm, seal and cover. Tighten the cover securely.

WARNING
Do not ride the motorcycle until you are sure the brakes are operating correctly with full hydraulic advantage. If necessary, bleed the brake as described under **Bleeding the System** *in this chapter.*

21. Bed the pads in gradually for the first 10 days of riding by using only light pressure as much as possible. Immediate hard application will glaze the new friction pads and greatly reduce the effectiveness of the brake.

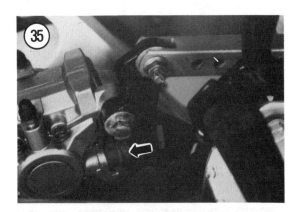

REAR MASTER CYLINDER

Removal/Installation

1. Remove the seats as described under *Seat Removal/Installation (FZ600 Models)* in Chapter Twelve.
2. Remove the right-hand side cover as described under *Side Cover Removal/Installation (FZ600 Models)* in Chapter Twelve.
3. Clean the top of the master cylinder of all dirt and foreign matter.
4. Unscrew the master cylinder top cover (**Figure 33**). Pull up and loosen the top cover and the diaphragm. This will allow air to enter the reservoir and allow the brake fluid to drain out more quickly in the next steps.
5. Place a container under the brake line at the rear caliper.
6. Loosen, then remove, the union bolt and sealing washers from the rear caliper (**Figure 35**).

NOTE
Do not intermix used brake fluid with motor oil that is going to be recycled. The oil will be considered contaminated and will not be accepted at most oil recycling centers.

7. Remove the brake hose and let the brake fluid drain out into the container. Apply the rear brake pedal as many times as necessary to pump the fluid out of the hydraulic brake lines. Dispose of this brake fluid according to local regulations—never reuse brake fluid.
8. Loosen the locknut (A, **Figure 36**) on the master cylinder pushrod.
9. Unscrew the pushrod from the joint holder (B, **Figure 36**) on the brake pedal.
10. Loosen the hose clamp (A, **Figure 37**) securing the brake hose to the fitting on the master cylinder.
11. Remove the reservoir brake hose from the master cylinder and plug the end of the hose to prevent the entry of foreign matter.
12. Loosen the union bolt securing the caliper brake hose to the rear of the master cylinder.
13. Remove the bolts and nuts (B, **Figure 37**) securing the master cylinder to the frame.
14. Pull the master cylinder away from the frame and remove the union bolt and sealing washers securing the caliper brake hose to the master cylinder. Don't

11

lose the sealing washer on each side of the hose fitting.

15. Remove the master cylinder.

16. Install new hoses, sealing washers and union bolts in the reverse order of removal. Be sure to install new sealing washers in their correct positions.

17. Tighten the union bolts to the torque specifications listed in **Table 1**. Tighten the master cylinder mounting bolts and nuts securely.

18. Refill the master cylinder reservoir to maintain the correct fluid level as seen through the transparent side of the reservoir (**Figure 38**). Install the diaphragm and screw on the top cover. Do not tighten at this time.

> *WARNING*
> *Use brake fluid clearly marked DOT 3 or DOT 4 from a sealed container. Other types may vaporize and cause brake failure. Always use the same brand name; do not intermix as many brands are not compatible. Do not intermix silicone-based (DOT 5) brake fluid as it can cause brake component damage leading to brake system failure.*

> *WARNING*
> *Do not ride the motorcycle until you are sure that the brakes are operating properly.*

19. Bleed the brake as described under *Bleeding the System* in this chapter.

20. Adjust the rear brake pedal height as described in Chapter Three.

21. Install the right-hand side covers and seats as described in Chapter Twelve.

Reservoir Removal/Installation

Refer to **Figure 39** for this procedure.

1. Remove the seats as described under *Seat Removal/Installation (FZ600 Models)* in Chapter Twelve.

2. Remove the right-hand side cover as described under *Side Cover Removal/Installation (FZ600 Models)* in Chapter Twelve.

3. Clean the top of the master cylinder of all dirt and foreign matter.

4. Unscrew the master cylinder top cover (A, **Figure 40**) and remove the top cover, seal and the diaphragm.

5. Siphon off the brake fluid from the reservoir.

6. Place a clean shop cloth under the reservoir to catch any residual fluid in the reservoir.

7. Loosen the hose clamp (B, **Figure 40**) securing the brake hose to the fitting on the base of the reservoir.

8. Remove the brake hose and plug the end to prevent the entry of foreign matter.

9. Tie the hose up to the frame to prevent the loss of brake fluid from the hose.

10. Remove the bolt (C, **Figure 40**) securing the reservoir to the frame and remove the reservoir.

11. Install by reversing these removal steps while noting the following:

    a. Refill the master cylinder reservoir to maintain the correct fluid level as seen through the transparent side of the reservoir (**Figure 38**). Install the diaphragm and screw on the top cover. Do not tighten at this time.

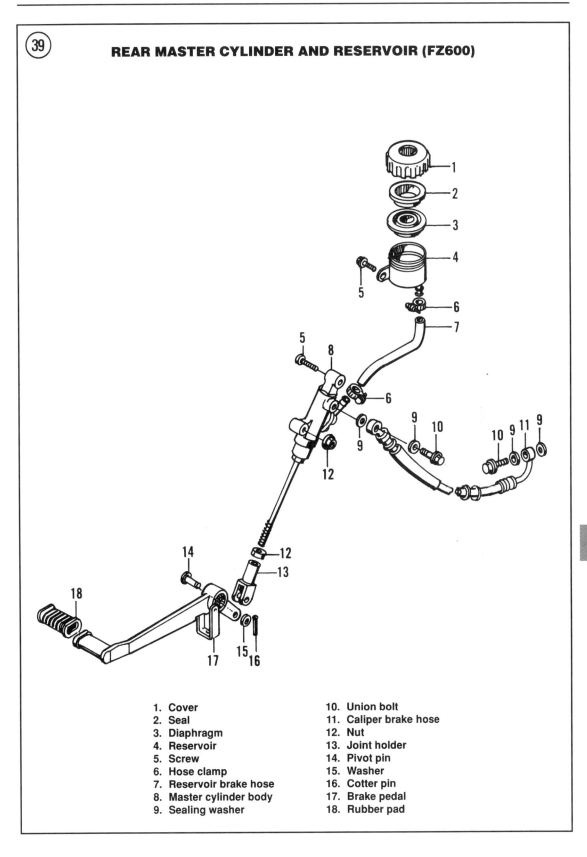

39

REAR MASTER CYLINDER AND RESERVOIR (FZ600)

1. Cover
2. Seal
3. Diaphragm
4. Reservoir
5. Screw
6. Hose clamp
7. Reservoir brake hose
8. Master cylinder body
9. Sealing washer
10. Union bolt
11. Caliper brake hose
12. Nut
13. Joint holder
14. Pivot pin
15. Washer
16. Cotter pin
17. Brake pedal
18. Rubber pad

11

WARNING
Use brake fluid clearly marked DOT 3 or DOT 4 from a sealed container. Other types may vaporize and cause brake failure. Always use the same brand name; do not intermix as many brands are not compatible. Do not intermix silicone-based (DOT 5) brake fluid as it can cause brake component damage leading to brake system failure.

WARNING
Do not ride the motorcycle until you are sure that the brakes are operating properly.

b. If necessary, bleed the brake as described under *Bleeding the System* in this chapter.

Disassembly

Refer to **Figure 41** for this procedure.

1. Remove the rear master cylinder as described in this chapter.

NOTE
Do not intermix used brake fluid with motor oil that is going to be recycled. The oil will be considered contaminated and will not be accepted at most oil recycling centers.

2. If not already removed, unscrew the master cylinder top cover and remove the top cover, seal and the diaphragm. Pour out any remaining brake fluid and discard it. *Never* re-use hydraulic fluid.
3. Unscrew the pushrod assembly from the base of the body.
4. Remove the piston assembly, seat and the spring.

CAUTION
Do not remove the primary cup from the piston or damage to the primary cup will occur.

Inspection

If any internal parts are damaged, they must be replaced as a set. The repair kit contains the pushrod assembly, the piston assembly and the spring.

1. Clean all parts in denatured alcohol or fresh hydraulic fluid.

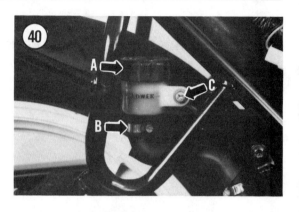

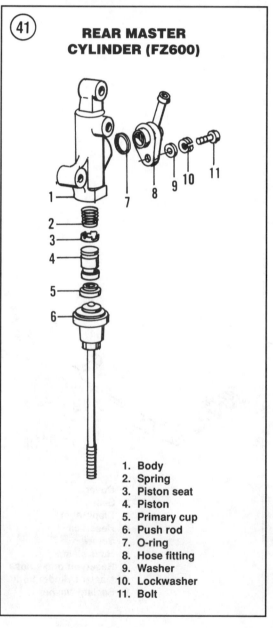

REAR MASTER CYLINDER (FZ600)

1. Body
2. Spring
3. Piston seat
4. Piston
5. Primary cup
6. Push rod
7. O-ring
8. Hose fitting
9. Washer
10. Lockwasher
11. Bolt

2. Inspect the body cylinder bore surface for signs of wear and damage. If less than perfect, replace the master cylinder assembly. The body cannot be replaced separately.

3. Inspect the piston contact surfaces for signs of wear and damage. If less than perfect, replace the piston assembly.

4. Check the end of the piston for wear caused by the pushrod. If worn, replace the piston assembly.

5. Replace the piston assembly if the primary cup requires replacement.

6. Inspect the threads on the piston assembly and the ones in the body for wear or damage. If worn, they must be replaced.

7. Check the reservoir diaphragm and top cover for damage and deterioration. Replace as necessary.

Assembly

1. Soak the new piston assembly and cup in fresh brake fluid for at least 15 minutes to make the cup pliable. Coat the inside of the cylinder bore with fresh hydraulic fluid prior to the assembly of parts.

> *CAUTION*
> *When installing the piston assembly, do not allow the cup to turn inside out as it will be damaged and allow brake fluid leakage within the cylinder bore.*

2. Install the piston seat onto the piston.

3. Position the spring so the small end of the spring faces the piston. Install the spring and piston assembly into the cylinder as an assembly.

4. Install the pushrod assembly and tighten it securely into the body.

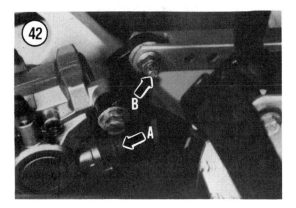

5. Install the diaphragm and top cover. Do not tighten the cover at this time as hydraulic fluid will have to be added later when the system is bled.

6. Install the master cylinder as described in this chapter.

REAR CALIPER

Removal/Installation

> *CAUTION*
> *Do not spill any brake fluid on the frame or rear wheel. Wash off any spilled brake fluid immediately, as it will destroy the finish. Use soapy water and rinse completely.*

1. Remove the right-hand side cover as described under *Side Cover Removal/Installation (FZ600 Models)* in Chapter Twelve.

2. Clean the top of the master cylinder of all dirt and foreign matter.

3. Unscrew cover (**Figure 33**) and loosen the cover and the diaphragm. This will allow air to enter the reservoir and allow the brake fluid to drain out more quickly in the next step.

4. Place a container under the brake line at the caliper.

> *NOTE*
> *Do not intermix used brake fluid with motor oil that is going to be recycled. The oil will be considered contaminated and will not be accepted at most oil recycling centers.*

5. Loosen then remove the union bolt and sealing washers (A, **Figure 42**) from the caliper.

6. Remove the brake hose and let the brake fluid drain out into the container. Dispose of this brake fluid according to local regulations—never reuse brake fluid.

7. To prevent the entry of moisture and dirt, cap the end of the brake hose and tie the loose end up to the frame.

8. Remove the bolt and nut (B, **Figure 42**) securing the rear caliper to the torque link on the swing arm.

> *CAUTION*
> *In the following step, do not push or pull too hard on the caliper as the rotor is relatively thin in order to dissipate heat*

11

FRONT BRAKE HOSE (RADIAN)

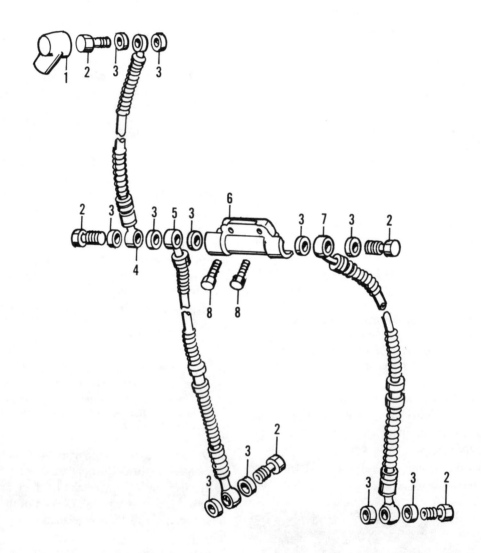

1. Rubber boot
2. Union bolt
3. Sealing washer
4. Upper hose
5. Right-hand lower hose
6. 2-way joint
7. Left-hand lower hose
8. Bolt

and to minimize unsprung weight. The rotor is designed to withstand tremendous rotational loads but can be damaged when subjected to side loads.

9. Loosen the bolts (**Figure 32**) securing the caliper to the caliper carrier. Push in, then pull out on the caliper while loosening the bolts to push the pistons back into the caliper cylinders.

10. Remove the bolts securing the brake caliper assembly to the caliper carrier.

11. Pivot the caliper up and off of the rear disc.

12. Install the caliper onto the disc by reversing these removal steps. Note the following:

   a. Carefully install the caliper assembly onto the disc being careful not to damage the leading edge of the brake pads.

   b. Install the bolts securing the brake caliper assembly to the caliper carrier and tighten to the torque specifications listed in **Table 1**.

   c. Install the bolt and nut securing the torque link to the caliper and tighten securely. Install a new cotter pin and bend the ends over completely.

   d. Install a new sealing washer on each side of the fitting and install the brake hose onto the caliper assembly.

   e. Install the union bolt and tighten to the torque specifications listed in **Table 1**.

13. Remove the right-hand side cover as described under *Side Cover Removal/Installation (FZ600 Models)* in Chapter Twelve.

14. Clean the top of the master cylinder of all dirt and foreign matter.

15. Unscrew cover (**Figure 33**). Remove the cover, seal and the diaphragm from the master cylinder.

16A. Place a suitable size aftermarket swing arm stand under the rear swing arm and support the bike with the rear wheel off the ground. Spin the rear wheel and activate the rear brake pedal as many times as it takes to refill the cylinders in the caliper and correctly locate the pads.

16B. If a swing arm stand is unavailable, roll the bike back and forth and activate the rear brake pedal as many times as it takes to refill the cylinders in the caliper and correctly locate the pads.

> *WARNING*
> *Use brake fluid clearly marked DOT 3 or DOT 4 from a sealed container. Other types may vaporize and cause*

brake failure. Always use the same brand name; do not intermix as many brands are not compatible. Do not intermix silicone based (DOT 5) brake fluid as it can cause brake component damage leading to brake system failure.

17. Refill the master cylinder reservoir, if necessary, to maintain the correct fluid level (**Figure 38**) as seen through the side of the transparent reservoir. Install the diaphragm, seal and cover. Tighten the cover securely.

> *WARNING*
> *Do not ride the motorcycle until you are sure the brakes are operating correctly with full hydraulic advantage. If necessary, bleed the brake as described under **Bleeding the System** in this chapter.*

18. Bleed the brake as described under *Bleeding the System* in this chapter.

FRONT BRAKE HOSE REPLACEMENT

Radian Models

Yamaha recommends replacing all brake hoses every four years or when they show signs of cracking or damage.

Refer to **Figure 43** for this procedure.

> *CAUTION*
> *Cover the fuel tank, front fender and instrument cluster with a heavy cloth or plastic tarp to protect them from accidental brake fluid spills. Wash brake fluid off any painted or plated surfaces or plastic parts immediately, as it will destroy the finish. Use soapy water and rinse completely.*

1. Remove the screw on each side securing the front cover (**Figure 44**) below the headlight and remove the cover.

2. Clean the top of the master cylinder of all dirt and foreign matter.

3. Loosen the screws securing the master cylinder top cover (A, **Figure 45**). Pull up and loosen the top cover and the diaphragm. This will allow air to enter the reservoir and allow the brake fluid to drain out more quickly in the next step.

11

4. Place a container under the brake line at the left-hand caliper.

5. Loosen, then remove the union bolt and sealing washers from the left-hand caliper (A, **Figure 46**).

NOTE
Do not intermix used brake fluid with motor oil that is going to be recycled. The oil will be considered contaminated and will not be accepted at most oil recycling centers.

6. Remove the brake hose and let the brake fluid drain out into the container. Apply the brake lever as many times as necessary to pump the fluid out of the hydraulic brake lines. Dispose of this brake fluid according to local regulations—never reuse brake fluid.

7. Remove the clamp bolt (B, **Figure 46**) and clamp securing the brake hose to the left-hand fork leg.

8. Remove the union bolt (A, **Figure 47**) and sealing washers securing the left-hand lower hose to the 2-way joint.

9. Remove the left-hand lower hose (B, **Figure 47**).

10. Pull back the rubber boot (B, **Figure 45**) on the union bolt on the master cylinder.

11. Place a shop cloth under the union bolt to catch any spilled brake fluid that will leak out.

12. Unscrew the union bolt securing the upper brake hose to the master cylinder. Don't lose the sealing washer on each side of the hose fitting.

13. Unscrew the union bolt (A, **Figure 48**) securing the upper brake hose and the upper end of the right-hand lower hose to the 2-way joint. Don't lose the sealing washer on each side of each brake hose fitting.

14. Remove the upper brake hose (B, **Figure 48**) from the frame.

15. Remove the union bolt (A, **Figure 49**) and sealing washers securing the right-hand lower hose to the right-hand caliper.

16. Remove the clamp bolt (B, **Figure 49**) and clamp securing the brake hose to the right-hand fork leg.

17. Remove the right-hand lower hose (C, **Figure 49**).

18. If necessary, remove the mounting bolts securing the 2-way joint to the lower fork bridge and remove the 2-way joint.

19. Install new hoses, sealing washers and union bolts in the reverse order of removal. Be sure to install new sealing washers in their correct positions.

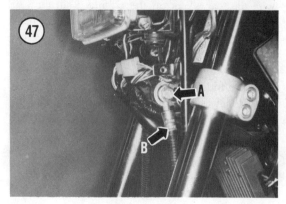

20. Tighten the union bolts to the torque specifications listed in **Table 1**.

21. Refill the master cylinder reservoir to maintain the correct fluid level as seen through the viewing port on the side (**Figure 50**). Install the diaphragm and top cover. Do not tighten the screws at this time.

WARNING
Use brake fluid clearly marked DOT 3 or DOT 4 from a sealed container. Other types may vaporize and cause brake failure. Always use the same

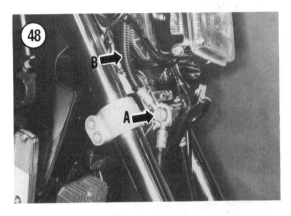

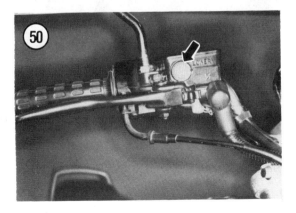

brand name; do not intermix as many brands are not compatible. Do not intermix silicone-based (DOT 5) brake fluid as it can cause brake component damage leading to brake system failure.

WARNING
Do not ride the motorcycle until you are sure that the brakes are operating properly.

22. Bleed the brake as described under *Bleeding the System* in this chapter.

23. Install the front cover and screws. Tighten the screws securely.

FZ600 Models

Yamaha recommends replacing all brake hoses every four years or when they show signs of cracking or damage.

Refer to **Figure 51** for this procedure.

CAUTION
Cover the fuel tank, front fender and instrument cluster with a heavy cloth or plastic tarp to protect them from accidental brake fluid spills. Wash brake fluid off any painted or plated surfaces or plastic parts immediately, as it will destroy the finish. Use soapy water and rinse completely.

1. Remove both lower fairings as described under *Lower Fairing Removal/Installation (FZ600 Models)* in Chapter Twelve.

2. Clean the top of the master cylinder of all dirt and foreign matter.

3. Loosen the screws securing the master cylinder top cover (A, **Figure 52**). Pull up and loosen the top cover and the diaphragm. This will allow air to enter the reservoir and allow the brake fluid to drain out more quickly in the next step.

4. Pull back the rubber boot (B, **Figure 52**) on the union bolt on the master cylinder.

5. Place a container under the brake line at the left-hand caliper.

6. Loosen then remove the union bolt and sealing washers from the right-hand caliper (**Figure 53**).

NOTE
Do not intermix used brake fluid with motor oil that is going to be recycled.

11

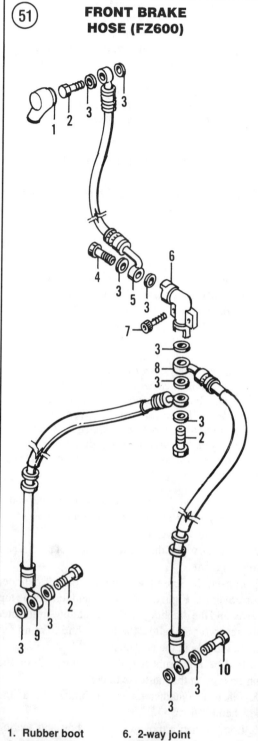

FRONT BRAKE HOSE (FZ600)

1. Rubber boot
2. Union bolt
3. Sealing washer
4. Union bolt
5. Upper hose
6. 2-way joint
7. Bolt
8. Left-hand lower hose
9. Right-hand lower hose
10. Union bolt

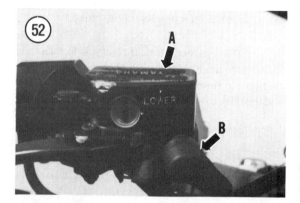

The oil will be considered contaminated and will not be accepted at most oil recycling centers.

7. Remove the brake hose and let the brake fluid drain out into the container. Apply the brake lever as many times as necessary to pump the fluid out of the hydraulic brake lines. Dispose of this brake fluid according to local regulations—never reuse brake fluid.

8. Remove the clamp bolt and clamp (A, **Figure 54**) securing the brake hose to the right-hand fork leg.

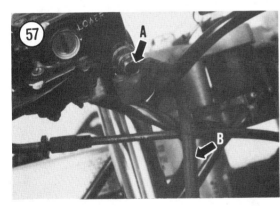

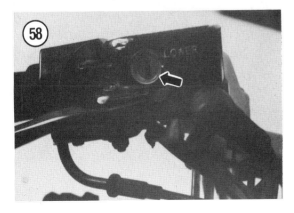

9. Remove the union bolt (A, **Figure 55**) and sealing washers securing the right-hand and left-hand lower hoses to the 2-way joint.

10. Remove the right-hand lower hose (B, **Figure 54**).

11. Remove the union bolt (A, **Figure 56**) and sealing washers securing the left-hand lower hose to the left-hand caliper.

12. Remove the clamp bolt and clamp (B, **Figure 56**) securing the brake hose to the left-hand fork leg.

13. Remove the left-hand lower hose (B, **Figure 55**).

14. Place a shop cloth under the union bolt to catch any spilled brake fluid that will leak out.

15. Unscrew the union bolt (A, **Figure 57**) securing the upper brake hose to the master cylinder. Don't lose the sealing washer on each side of the hose fitting.

16. Unscrew the union bolt securing the upper brake hose to the 2-way joint. Don't lose the sealing washer on each side of the brake hose fitting.

17. Remove the upper brake hose (B, **Figure 57**) from the frame.

18. If necessary, remove the mounting bolts securing the 2-way joint to the lower fork bridge and remove the 2-way joint.

19. Install new hoses, sealing washers and union bolts in the reverse order of removal. Be sure to install new sealing washers in their correct positions.

20. Tighten the union bolts to the torque specifications listed in **Table 1**.

21. Refill the master cylinder reservoir to maintain the correct fluid level as seen through the viewing port on the side (**Figure 58**). Install the diaphragm and top cover. Do not tighten the screws at this time.

11

> *WARNING*
> *Use brake fluid clearly marked DOT 3 or DOT 4 from a sealed container. Other types may vaporize and cause brake failure. Always use the same brand name; do not intermix as many brands are not compatible. Do not intermix silicone-based (DOT 5) brake fluid as it can cause brake component damage leading to brake system failure.*

> *WARNING*
> *Do not ride the motorcycle until you are sure that the brakes are operating properly.*

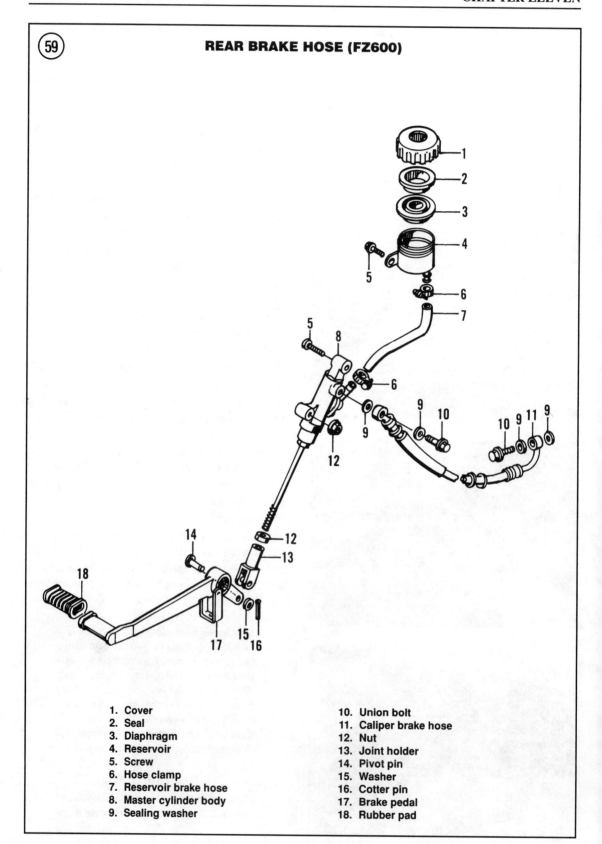

59

REAR BRAKE HOSE (FZ600)

1. Cover
2. Seal
3. Diaphragm
4. Reservoir
5. Screw
6. Hose clamp
7. Reservoir brake hose
8. Master cylinder body
9. Sealing washer
10. Union bolt
11. Caliper brake hose
12. Nut
13. Joint holder
14. Pivot pin
15. Washer
16. Cotter pin
17. Brake pedal
18. Rubber pad

22. Bleed the brake as described under *Bleeding the System* in this chapter.

23. Install both lower fairings as described in Chapter Twelve.

REAR BRAKE HOSE REPLACEMENT (FZ600 MODELS)

Yamaha recommends replacing all brake hoses every four years or when they show signs of cracking or damage.

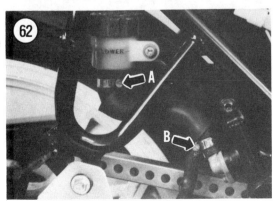

Refer to **Figure 59** for this procedure.

> *CAUTION*
> *Cover the swing arm and rear wheel with a heavy cloth or plastic tarp to protect them from accidental brake fluid spills. Wash brake fluid off any painted or plated surfaces or plastic parts immediately, as it will destroy the finish. Use soapy water and rinse completely.*

1. Remove both seats as described under *Seat Removal/Installation (FZ600 Models)* in Chapter Twelve.

2. Remove the right-hand side cover as described under *Side Cover Removal/Installation (FZ600 Models)* in Chapter Twelve.

3. Clean the top of the master cylinder of all dirt and foreign matter.

4. Unscrew the master cylinder top cover (**Figure 60**). Pull up and loosen the top cover and the diaphragm. This will allow air to enter the reservoir and allow the brake fluid to drain out more quickly in the next steps.

5. Place a container under the brake line at the rear caliper.

6. Loosen then remove the union bolt and sealing washers from the rear caliper (**Figure 61**).

> *NOTE*
> *Do not intermix used brake fluid with motor oil that is going to be recycled. The oil will be considered contaminated and will not be accepted at most oil recycling centers.*

7. Remove the brake hose and let the brake fluid drain out into the container. Apply the rear brake pedal as many times as necessary to pump the fluid out of the hydraulic brake lines. Dispose of this brake fluid according to local regulations—never reuse brake fluid.

8. To remove the reservoir hose, perform the following:

    a. Loosen the hose clamp (A, **Figure 62**) securing the brake hose to the fitting on the base of the reservoir and remove the hose from it.

    b. Loosen the hose clamp (B, **Figure 62**) securing the brake hose to the fitting on the master cylinder and remove the hose from it.

    c. Remove the reservoir brake hose.

11

9. To remove the caliper brake hose, perform the following:

    a. Loosen the union bolt securing the caliper brake hose to the rear of the master cylinder.

    b. Remove the union bolt and sealing washers securing the caliper brake hose (**Figure 63**) to the rear of the master cylinder. Don't lose the sealing washer on each side of the hose fitting.

    c. Remove the bolt and clamp securing the brake hose to the swing arm.

    d. Remove the caliper brake hose from the frame.

10. Install new hoses, sealing washers and union bolts in the reverse order of removal. Be sure to install new sealing washers in their correct positions.

11. Tighten the union bolts to the torque specifications listed in **Table 1**. Tighten the master cylinder mounting bolts and nuts securely.

12. Refill the master cylinder reservoir to maintain the correct fluid level as seen through the transparent side of the reservoir (**Figure 64**). Install the diaphragm and screw on the top cover. Do not tighten at this time.

> *WARNING*
> *Use brake fluid clearly marked DOT 3 or DOT 4 from a sealed container. Other types may vaporize and cause brake failure. Always use the same brand name; do not intermix as many brands are not compatible. Do not intermix silicone-based (DOT 5) brake fluid as it can cause brake component damage leading to brake system failure.*

> *WARNING*
> *Do not ride the motorcycle until you are sure that the brakes are operating properly.*

13. Bleed the brake as described under *Bleeding the System* in this chapter.

14. Install the right-hand side covers and seats as described in Chapter Twelve.

BRAKE DISC—FRONT AND REAR

Removal/Installation

1. Remove the front wheel or rear wheel as described in Chapter Nine or Chapter Ten.

> *NOTE*
> *Place a piece of wood or vinyl tube in the caliper in place of the disc. This way, if the brake lever is inadvertently squeezed, the pistons will not be forced out of the cylinders. If this does happen, the caliper might have to be disassembled to reseat the pistons and the system will have to be bled. By using the wood or vinyl tube, bleeding the system is not necessary when installing the wheel.*

> *CAUTION*
> *Do not set the wheel down on the disc surface, as it may get scratched or*

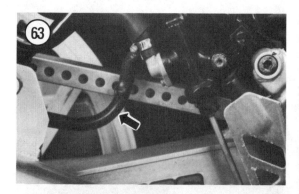

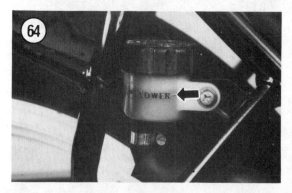

warped. Set the wheel on 2 blocks of wood.

2. Remove the bolts (**Figure 65**) securing the brake disc to the hub and remove the disc.

3. If necessary, repeat Step 2 for the brake disc on the other side.

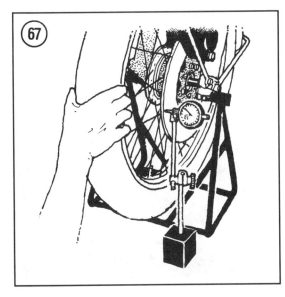

4. Install by reversing these removal steps while noting the following.

5. Apply Loctite Threadlocker to the disc mounting bolt threads prior to installation. Tighten the disc mounting bolts to the torque specifications listed in **Table 1**.

Inspection

It is not necessary to remove the disc(s) from the wheel to inspect it. Small marks on the disc are not important, but radial scratches deep enough to snag a fingernail reduce braking effectiveness and increase brake pad wear. If these grooves are found, the disc should be replaced.

1. Measure the thickness of the disc at several locations around the disc with a micrometer (**Figure 66**) or vernier caliper. The disc must be replaced if the thickness in any area is less than that specified in **Table 2**.

2. Make sure the disc mounting bolts are tight prior to running this check. Check the disc runout with a dial indicator as shown in **Figure 67**.

3. Slowly rotate the wheel and watch the dial indicator. If the runout exceeds that listed in **Table 2** the disc must be replaced.

4. Clean the disc of any rust or corrosion and wipe clean with lacquer thinner. Never use an oil-based solvent that may leave an oil residue on the disc.

BLEEDING THE SYSTEM

This procedure is not necessary unless the brakes feel spongy, there has been a leak in the system, a component has been replaced or the brake fluid has been replaced.

Brake Bleeder Process

This procedure uses a brake bleeder that is available from motorcycle or automotive supply stores or from mail order outlets.

1. Remove the dust cap from the bleed valve on the caliper assembly. Refer to **Figure 68** for the front caliper or **Figure 69** for the rear caliper (FZ600 models).

11

NOTE
On the rear caliper, bleed the outer portion of the caliper first, then the inner portion.

2. Connect the brake bleeder to the bleed valve on the caliper assembly.

CAUTION
Cover the front wheel and rear wheel with a heavy cloth or plastic tarp to protect it from the accidental spilling of brake fluid. Wash any brake fluid off of any plastic, painted or plated surface immediately; as it will destroy the finish. Use soapy water and rinse completely.

3. Clean the top of the master cylinder of all dirt and foreign matter.

4A. For the front brakes, remove the screws securing the reservoir top cover (**Figure 70**) and remove the reservoir cover and diaphragm.

4B. For the rear brake, unscrew the master cylinder top cover (**Figure 60**). Remove the top cover and the diaphragm.

5. Fill the reservoir almost to the top lip; insert the diaphragm and the cover loosely. Leave the cover in place during this procedure to prevent the entry of dirt.

WARNING
Use brake fluid from a sealed container marked DOT 3 or DOT 4 only (specified for disc brakes). Other types may vaporize and cause brake failure. Do not intermix different brands or types as they may not be compatible. Do not intermix a silicone based (DOT 5) brake fluid as it can cause brake component damage leading to brake system failure.

6. Open the bleed valve about one-half turn and pump the brake bleeder.

NOTE
If air is entering the brake bleeder hose from around the bleed valve, apply several layers of Teflon tape to the bleed valve. This should make a good seal between the bleed valve and the brake bleeder hose.

7. As the fluid enters the system and exits into the brake bleeder the level will drop in the reservoir.

Maintain the level at about 3/8 inch (9.5 mm) from the top of the reservoir to prevent air from being drawn into the system.

8. Continue to pump the lever on the brake bleeder until the fluid emerging from the hose is completely free of bubbles. At this point, tighten the bleed valve.

NOTE
Do not allow the reservoir to empty during the bleeding operation or more air will enter the system. If this occurs, the entire procedure must be repeated.

9. When the brake fluid is free of bubbles, tighten the bleed valve, remove the brake bleeder tube and install the bleed valve dust cap.

10. If necessary, add fluid to correct the level in the reservoir. It should be to the upper level line.

11A. On front brakes, repeat Step 2 and Steps 6-9 for the other caliper.

11B. On rear brake, repeat Step 2 and Steps 6-9 for the other half of the caliper.

12. Install the diaphragm and the reservoir cover. Tighten the screws (front brake) or cap (rear brake) securely.

13. Test the feel of the brake lever and/or pedal. It should be firm and should offer the same resistance each time it's operated. If it feels spongy, it is likely that there is still air in the system and it must be bled again. When all air has been bled from the system and the fluid level is correct in the reservoir, double-check for leaks and tighten all fittings and connections.

> *WARNING*
> *Before riding the bike, make certain that the brake is operating correctly by operating the lever several times.*

14. Test ride the bike slowly at first to make sure that the brakes are operating properly.

Without a Brake Bleeder

1. Remove the dust cap from the bleed valve on the caliper assembly. Refer to **Figure 68** for the front caliper or **Figure 69** for the rear caliper (FZ600 models).

> *NOTE*
> *On the rear caliper, bleed the outer portion of the caliper first, then the inner portion.*

2. Connect the bleed hose to the bleed valve on the caliper assembly (**Figure 71**).
3. Place the other end of the tube into a clean container. Fill the container with enough fresh brake

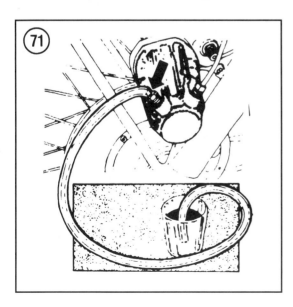

fluid to keep the end submerged. The tube should be long enough so that a loop can be made higher than the bleed valve to prevent air from being drawn into the caliper during bleeding.

> *CAUTION*
> *Cover the front fender and front wheel with a heavy cloth or plastic tarp to protect it from the accidental spilling of brake fluid. Wash any brake fluid off of any plastic, painted or plated surface immediately; as it will destroy the finish. Use soapy water and rinse completely.*

4. Clean the top of the master cylinder of all dirt and foreign matter.
5A. For the front brakes, remove the screws securing the reservoir top cover (**Figure 70**) and remove the reservoir cover and diaphragm.
5B. For the rear brake, unscrew the master cylinder top cover (**Figure 60**). Remove the top cover and the diaphragm.
6. Fill the reservoir almost to the cover lip; insert the diaphragm and the cover loosely. Leave the cover in place during this procedure to prevent the entry of dirt.

> *WARNING*
> *Use brake fluid from a sealed container marked DOT 3 or DOT 4 only (specified for disc brakes). Other types may vaporize and cause brake failure. Do not intermix different brands or types as they may not be compatible. Do not intermix a silicone based (DOT 5) brake fluid as it can cause brake component damage leading to brake system failure.*

7A. On front brakes, slowly apply the brake lever several times as follows:
    a. Pull the lever in and hold the lever in the applied position.
    b. Open the bleed valve about one-half turn. Allow the lever to travel to its limit.
    c. When this limit is reached, tighten the bleed screw.
7B. On rear brake, slowly apply the brake pedal several times as follows:
    a. Depress the rear brake pedal and hold the pedal in the applied position.

11

b. Open the bleed valve about one-half turn. Allow the pedal to travel to its limit.

c. When this limit is reached, tighten the bleed screw.

8. As the fluid enters the system, the level will drop in the reservoir. Maintain the level at about 3/8 inch (9.5 mm) from the cover of the reservoir to prevent air from being drawn into the system.

9. Continue to pump the lever or pedal and fill the reservoir until the fluid emerging from the hose is completely free of bubbles.

NOTE
Do not allow the reservoir to empty during the bleeding operation or more air will enter the system. If this occurs, the entire procedure must be repeated.

10. Hold the lever in or the pedal down, tighten the bleed valve, remove the bleed tube and install the bleed valve dust cap.

11. If necessary, add fluid to correct the level in the reservoir. It should be to the upper level line.

12A. On front brakes, repeat Step 2 and Steps 7-11 for the other caliper.

12B. On rear brake, repeat Step 2 and Steps 7-11 for the other half of the caliper.

13. Install the diaphragm and the reservoir cover. Tighten the screws (front brake) or cap (rear brake) securely.

14. Test the feel of the brake lever and/or pedal. It should be firm and should offer the same resistance each time it's operated. If it feels spongy, it is likely that there is still air in the system and it must be bled again. When all air has been bled from the system and the fluid level is correct in the reservoir, double-check for leaks and tighten all fittings and connections.

WARNING
Before riding the bike, make certain that the brakes are operating correctly

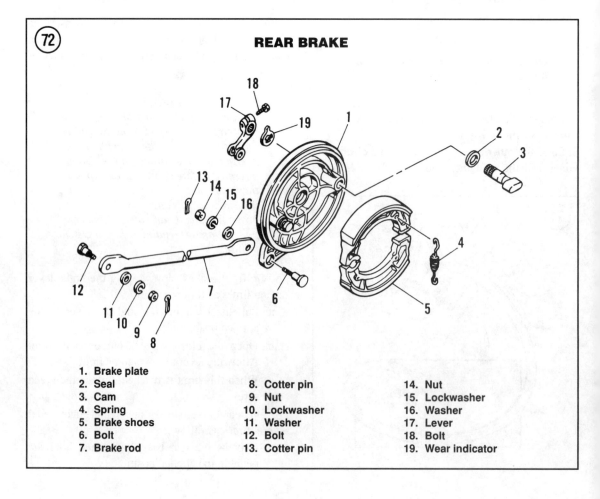

REAR BRAKE

1. Brake plate		
2. Seal	8. Cotter pin	14. Nut
3. Cam	9. Nut	15. Lockwasher
4. Spring	10. Lockwasher	16. Washer
5. Brake shoes	11. Washer	17. Lever
6. Bolt	12. Bolt	18. Bolt
7. Brake rod	13. Cotter pin	19. Wear indicator

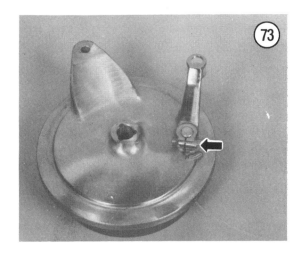

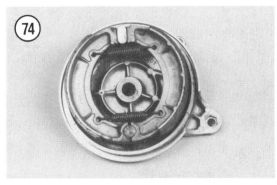

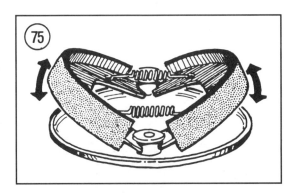

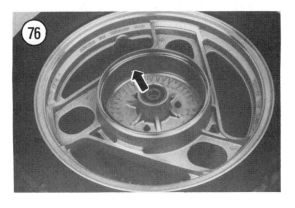

by operating the lever or pedal several times.

15. Test ride the bike slowly at first to make sure that the brakes are operating properly.

REAR DRUM BRAKE

Pushing down on the brake foot pedal pulls the rod which in turn rotates the camshaft. This forces the brake shoes out into contact with the brake drum.

Pedal free play must be maintained to minimize brake drag and premature brake wear and maximize braking effectiveness. Refer to Chapter Three for complete adjustment procedure.

Disassembly

Refer to **Figure 72** for this procedure.

1. Remove the rear wheel as described in Chapter Ten.

2. Pull the brake assembly straight up and out of the brake drum.

3. Remove the bolt (**Figure 73**) securing the brake arm and remove the brake arm and wear indicator from the camshaft.

NOTE
Mark the shoes in relation to the backing plate prior to removing them. If the shoes are to be reused, they must be reinstalled in the same location.

4. Pull the brake shoes (**Figure 74**) and springs up and off the pivot pin and camshaft as shown in **Figure 75**.

5. Withdraw the camshaft from the brake plate.

6. Use needlenose pliers and remove the return springs from the brake linings.

Inspection

1. Thoroughly clean and dry all parts except the brake linings.

2. Check the contact surface of the drum (**Figure 76**) for scoring. If there are grooves deep enough to snag your fingernail, the drum should be reground.

3. Measure the inside diameter of the brake drum with a vernier caliper. If the measurement is greater than the service limit listed in **Table 2** the rear wheel

11

must be replaced (the brake drum is an integral part
of the wheel).

4. If the drum can be turned and still stay within the
maximum service limit diameter, the linings will
have to be replaced and the new ones arced to
conform to the new drum contour.

5. Measure the brake linings with a vernier caliper
(**Figure 77**). They should be replaced if the lining
portion is worn to the service limit dimension or less.
Refer to specifications listed in **Table 2**.

6. Inspect the linings for imbedded foreign material.
Dirt can be removed with a stiff wire brush. Check
for any traces of oil or grease; if they are contaminated they must be replaced.

7. Inspect the cam lobe and pivot pin area of the
backing plate for wear or corrosion. Minor roughness can be removed with fine emery cloth.

8. Inspect the brake shoe return springs for wear. If
they are stretched, they will not fully retract the
brake shoes. Replace as necessary.

9. Inspect the oil seal in the camshaft receptacle in
the backside of the brake plate. Replace if necessary.

Assembly

1. Grease the camshaft with a light coat of lithium
based soap grease. Install the camshaft into the brake
plate from the backside.

2. From the outside of the brake plate, align the wear
indicator to the camshaft and push it down all the
way to the brake plate.

3. When installing the brake arm onto the camshaft,
be sure to align the dimples on the two parts. Tighten
the bolt securely.

4. Grease the camshaft and pivot post with a light
coat of lithium based soap grease; avoid getting any
grease on the brake plate where the brake linings
may come in contact with it.

> *NOTE*
> *If new linings are being installed, file off
> the leading edge of each shoe a little
> (**Figure 78**) so that the brake will not
> grab when applied.*

5. Hold the brake shoes in a "V" formation with the
return springs attached and snap them into place on
the brake plate. Make sure they are firmly seated on
it.

6. Install the brake panel assembly into the brake
drum.

7. Install the rear wheel as described in Chapter Ten.

8. Adjust the rear brake as described in Chapter
Three.

REAR BRAKE PEDAL

Removal/Installation
(Radian Models)

Refer to **Figure 79** for this procedure.

1. Place the bike on the centerstand to support the
bike securely with the rear wheel off the ground.

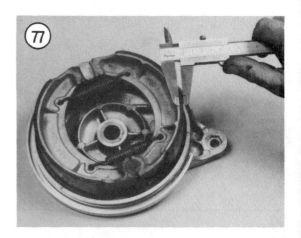

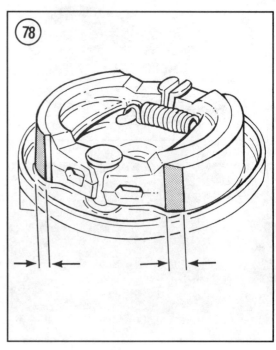

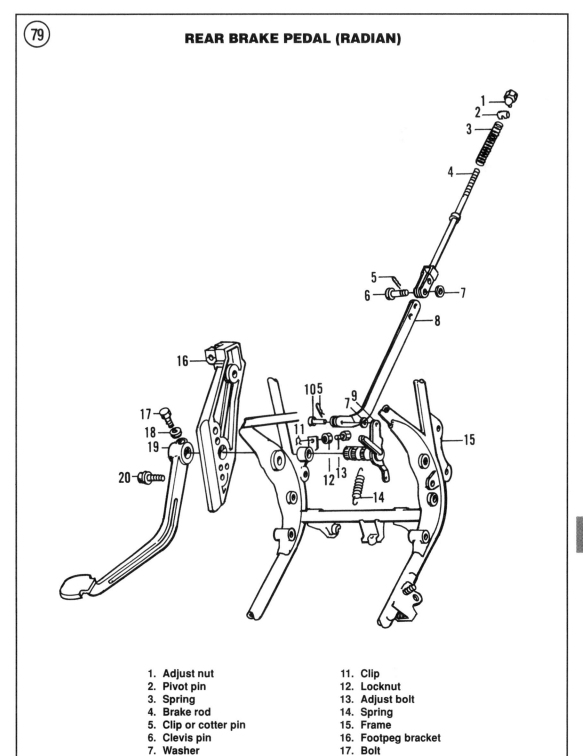

(79)

REAR BRAKE PEDAL (RADIAN)

1. Adjust nut
2. Pivot pin
3. Spring
4. Brake rod
5. Clip or cotter pin
6. Clevis pin
7. Washer
8. Joint rod
9. Pivot shaft
10. Pivot pin
11. Clip
12. Locknut
13. Adjust bolt
14. Spring
15. Frame
16. Footpeg bracket
17. Bolt
18. Washer
19. Brake pedal
20. Bolt

11

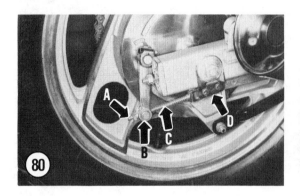

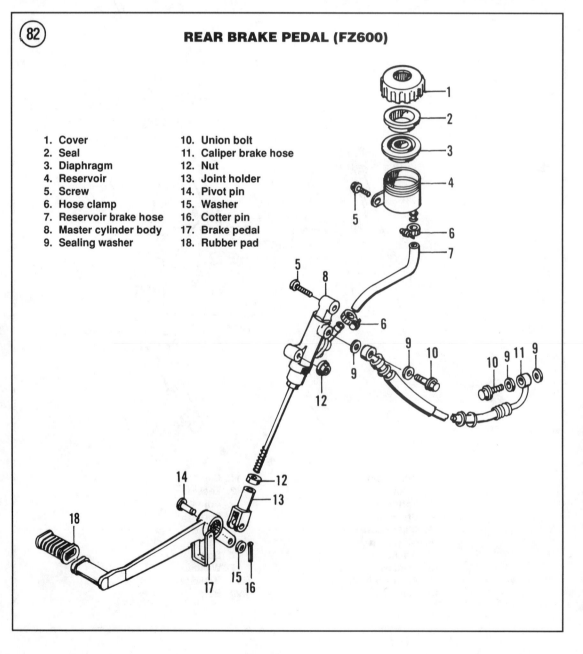

REAR BRAKE PEDAL (FZ600)

1. Cover
2. Seal
3. Diaphragm
4. Reservoir
5. Screw
6. Hose clamp
7. Reservoir brake hose
8. Master cylinder body
9. Sealing washer
10. Union bolt
11. Caliper brake hose
12. Nut
13. Joint holder
14. Pivot pin
15. Washer
16. Cotter pin
17. Brake pedal
18. Rubber pad

2. Completely unscrew the rear brake adjust nut (A, **Figure 80**). Depress the brake pedal and remove the brake rod from the brake lever on the brake plate.

3. Remove the pivot pin (B, **Figure 80**) from the brake lever, install it on the brake rod (C, **Figure 80**) and reinstall the adjust nut to avoid misplacing these small parts.

4. Remove the bolt and lockwasher (A, **Figure 81**) clamping the brake pedal to the pivot shaft.

5. Slide off the brake pedal (B, **Figure 81**). Reinstall the bolt and lockwasher on the brake pedal to avoid misplacing them.

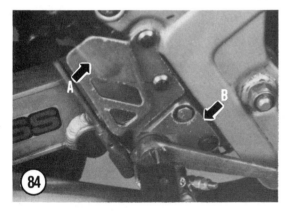

6. Remove the cotter pin, washer and pivot pin securing the joint rod to the pivot shaft and disconnect the two parts.

7. Use Vise-grip pliers and remove the return spring from the pivot shaft.

8. Remove the pivot shaft from the frame.

9. Remove the cotter pins, washers and pivot pins securing the joint rod (D, **Figure 80**) to the brake rod (C, **Figure 80**) and disconnect the two parts.

10. Remove the joint rod and the brake rod from the frame.

11. Install by reversing these removal steps.

**Removal/Installation
(FZ600 Models)**

Refer to **Figure 82** for this procedure.

1. Remove the cotter pin and washer, then withdraw the pivot pin (**Figure 83**) from the master cylinder rod joint holder. Discard the cotter pin.

2. Disconnect the joint holder from the brake pedal arm.

3. Remove the bolts securing the trim plate (A, **Figure 84**) and remove the trim plate.

4. Remove the bolts securing the brake lever and front footpeg assembly mounting plate (B, **Figure 84**) to the frame and remove the assembly.

5. To separate the brake pedal from the footpeg assembly, perform the following:

    a. Remove the bolt from the backside of the footpeg mounting plate.

    b. Remove the footpeg, brake pedal and wave washer from the mounting plate.

6. Install by reversing these removal steps.

7. Apply a multipurpose grease to all pivot surfaces prior to reassembly.

11

Table 1 BRAKE TIGHTENING TORQUES

Item	N·m	ft.-lb.
Brake hose union bolts	25	18
Front master cylinder		
Cover screws	1-2	0.7-0.9
Bracket bolts	8	5.8
Caliper mounting bolt	35	25
Caliper bleed valve	6	4.3
Brake disc mounting bolts	20	14

Table 2 BRAKE SPECIFICATIONS

Item	Specifications	Wear limit
Brake disc		
Thickness	–	4.0 mm (0.16 in.)
Runout	–	0.15 mm (0.006 in.)
Rear drum brake		
Drum I.D.	180 mm (7.08 in.)	181 mm (7.12 in.)
Lining thickness	4 mm (0.16 in.)	2 mm (0.08 in.)

CHAPTER TWELVE

FRAME AND BODY

This chapter includes procedures for the replacement of components attached to the frame that are not covered in the rest of the book. Also included are the body panels for the FZ600 models.

This chapter also describes procedures for completely stripping and repainting the frame.

Torque specifications are listed in **Table 1** at the end of this chapter.

SEAT

Removal/Installation (Radian Models)

Refer to **Figure 1** for this procedure.

1. Insert the ignition key into the seat lock (**Figure 2**) on the left-hand side of the seat.
2. Turn the ignition key *clockwise* until the seat lock is released.
3. Pull up on the rear of the seat and move the seat toward the rear.
4. Remove the seat assembly.
5. Install by reversing these removal steps while noting the following:
   a. Make sure the locating tab on the front of the seat is correctly hooked onto the metal seat bracket on the frame.

WARNING
After the seat is installed, pull up on it firmly to make sure it is securely locked in place. If the seat is not correctly locked in place, it may slide to one side or the other when riding the bike. This could lead to the loss of control and a possible accident.

   b. Push the seat down firmly until the seat latch "snaps" into the locked position.

Removal/Installation (FZ600 Models)

Refer to **Figure 3** for this procedure.

1. Insert the ignition key into the seat lock (**Figure 4**) on the back of the passenger seat.
2. Turn the ignition key *clockwise* until the seat lock is released.
3. Pull up on the rear of the passenger seat and move the seat toward the rear and remove the passenger seat assembly.
4. Remove the bolts (**Figure 5**) securing the rear of the rider's seat to the frame mounting tabs.
5. Pull up on the rear of the rider's seat and move seat toward the rear.
6. Remove the rider's seat assembly.

12

7. Install by reversing these removal steps while noting the following:

   a. Make sure the locating tab on the front of the rider's seat is correctly hooked onto the metal seat bracket on the frame.

   b. Securely tighten the bolts securing the rider's seat.

   c. Make sure the locating tabs on the front of the passenger seat are correctly hooked onto the metal cross bar on the frame.

   d. Push the passenger seat down firmly until the seat latch "snaps" into the locked position.

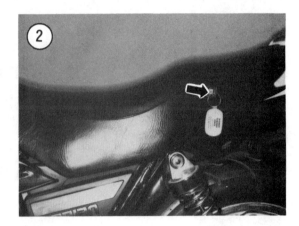

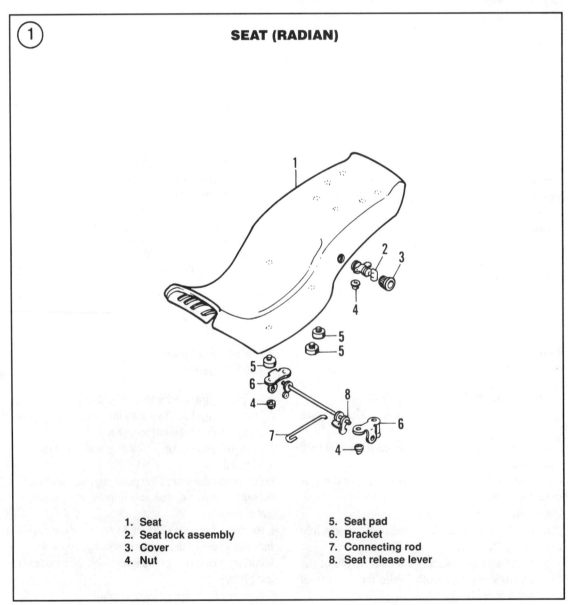

SEAT (RADIAN)

1. Seat
2. Seat lock assembly
3. Cover
4. Nut
5. Seat pad
6. Bracket
7. Connecting rod
8. Seat release lever

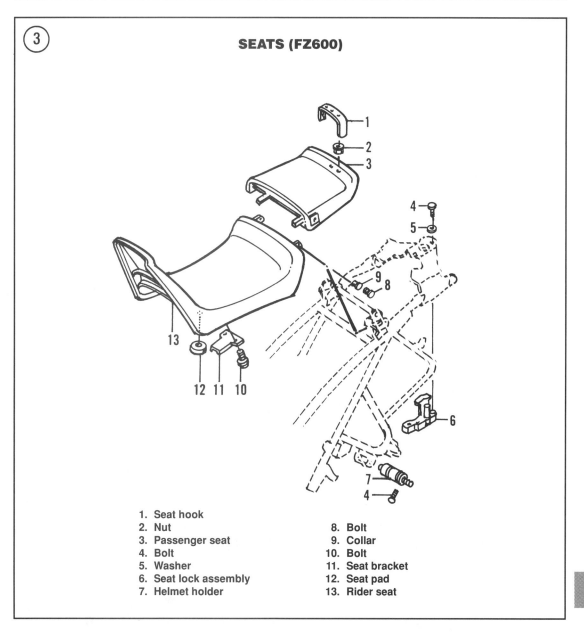

③ **SEATS (FZ600)**

1. Seat hook
2. Nut
3. Passenger seat
4. Bolt
5. Washer
6. Seat lock assembly
7. Helmet holder
8. Bolt
9. Collar
10. Bolt
11. Seat bracket
12. Seat pad
13. Rider seat

12

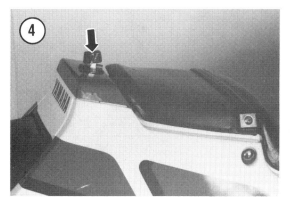

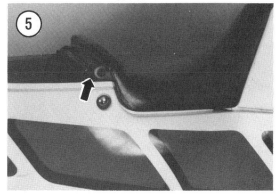

WARNING
After both seats are installed, pull up on each of them firmly to make sure they are securely locked in place. If the seats are not correctly locked in place, they may slide to one side or the other when riding the bike. This could lead to the loss of control and a possible accident.

FRONT FENDER

Removal/Installation
(All Models)

Refer to **Figure 6** for this procedure.
1. Place the bike on the sidestand.
2. Carefully pull the speedometer cable retainer (**Figure 7**) from the fender.
3. Remove the bolts securing the fork brace (A, **Figure 8**) and remove the fork brace.
4. Move the front fender (B, **Figure 8**) forward through the fork legs being careful not to scratch the rear portion of fender during removal. Remove the front fender.
5. Install by reversing these removal steps while noting the following:
   a. Tighten the fork brace bolts to the torque specification listed in **Table 1**.
   b. Attach the speedometer cable retainer onto the fender.

REAR FENDER

Removal/Installation
(Radian Models)

Refer to **Figure 9** for this procedure.
1. Place the bike on the centerstand to support the bike securely with the rear wheel off the ground.
2. Disconnect the battery negative cable.
3. Remove the seat as described in this chapter.
4. Disconnect the electrical connectors going to the taillight/brakelight assembly and to the rear turn signals.
5. Remove the tool kit. Remove the screws securing the tool tray (A, **Figure 10**) and remove the tray.
6. Remove both shock absorbers (A, **Figure 11**) as described under *Shock Absorber Removal/Installation* in Chapter Ten.

7. If necessary, remove the nut on each side securing the side covers (B, **Figure 11**) and remove the side covers.
8. Remove the bolts securing the rear assist bar (A, **Figure 12**) and remove the assist bar.
9. Remove the screws, collars and lockwashers securing the cowl (B, **Figure 12**) to the frame and remove the cowl.

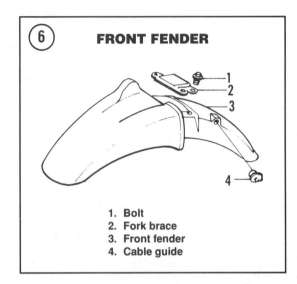

⑥ FRONT FENDER

1. Bolt
2. Fork brace
3. Front fender
4. Cable guide

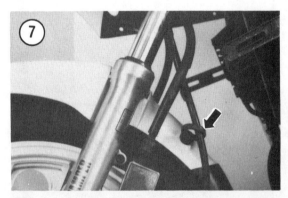

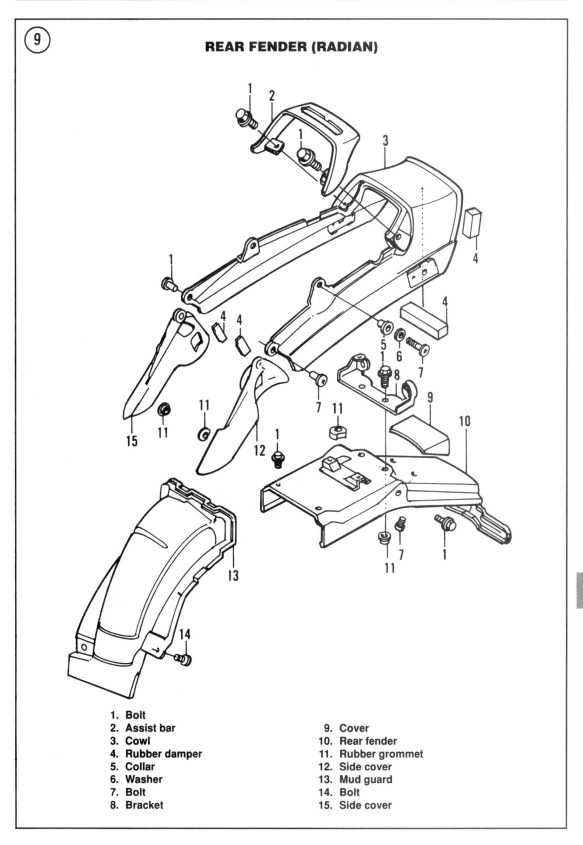

REAR FENDER (RADIAN)

1. Bolt
2. Assist bar
3. Cowl
4. Rubber damper
5. Collar
6. Washer
7. Bolt
8. Bracket
9. Cover
10. Rear fender
11. Rubber grommet
12. Side cover
13. Mud guard
14. Bolt
15. Side cover

10. Remove the bolts and nuts securing the rear fender and bracket (C, **Figure 12**) to the frame. Remove the rear fender and bracket.

11. To remove the mud guard, perform the following:

    a. Remove the screws securing the fuse box (B, **Figure 10**) and move the fuse box out of the way.

    b. Disconnect any electrical cable tie-downs that are attached to the mud guard.

    c. Remove the screws securing the mud guard (C, **Figure 10**) to the frame and slide the mudguard back and over the rear wheel.

12. Install by reversing these removal steps while noting the following:

    a. Make sure the rubber grommets and collars are in place in the mounting holes where applicable. These grommets help prevent the plastic from fracturing at the attachment points.

    b. Tighten all screws securely. Do not over-tighten as the plastic parts may fracture.

Removal/Installation
(FZ600 Models)

Refer to **Figure 13** for this procedure.

1A. Place a suitable size aftermarket swing arm stand under the rear swing arm and support the bike with the rear wheel off the ground.

1B. If a swing arm stand is unavailable, perform the following:

    a. Remove both lower fairings as described in this chapter. Remove the mounting brackets.

    b. Remove the exhaust system as described under *Exhaust System Removal/Installation (FZ600 Models)* in Chapter Seven.

    c. Place wood block(s) under the engine to support the bike securely with the rear wheel off the ground.

2. Remove the side cover on each side as described in this chapter.

3. Remove the seat as described in this chapter.

4. Disconnect the battery negative cable. Refer to Chapter Three.

5. Disconnect the electrical connectors (**Figure 14**) going to the taillight/brakelight assembly and to the rear turn signals.

6. Remove the tool kit.

7. Remove the screws and washers (**Figure 15**) securing the rear fender cover to the frame and remove the rear fender cover (A, **Figure 16**).

8. Remove the screws, collars and lockwashers securing the rear fender and tool box assembly (B, **Figure 16**) to the frame and remove the fender assembly.

9. To remove the mud guard, perform the following:

    a. Remove the screws securing the fuse box (A, **Figure 17**) and move the fuse box out of the way.

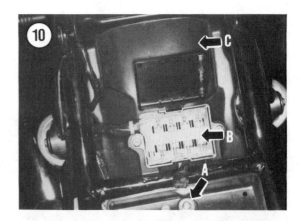

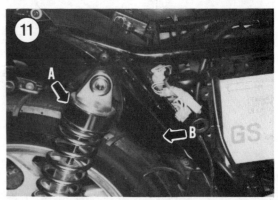

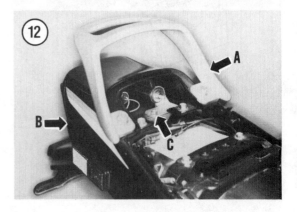

b. Disconnect any electrical cable tie-downs that are attached to the mud guard.

c. Remove the screws securing the mud guard (B, **Figure 17**) to the frame and slide the mud guard back and over the rear wheel.

10. Install by reversing these removal steps while noting the following:

a. Make sure the rubber grommets and collars are in place in the mounting holes where applicable. These grommets help prevent the plastic from fracturing at the attachment points.

b. Tighten all screws securely. Do not over-tighten as the plastic parts may fracture.

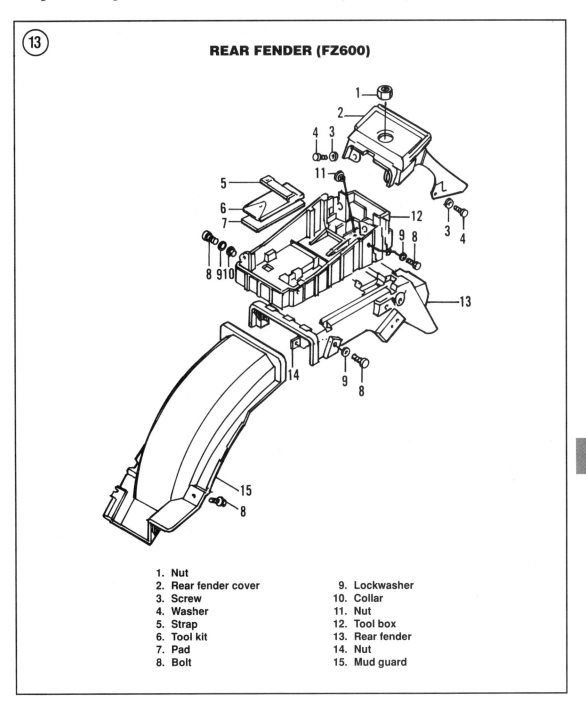

REAR FENDER (FZ600)

1. Nut
2. Rear fender cover
3. Screw
4. Washer
5. Strap
6. Tool kit
7. Pad
8. Bolt
9. Lockwasher
10. Collar
11. Nut
12. Tool box
13. Rear fender
14. Nut
15. Mud guard

12

LOWER FAIRING
(FZ600 MODELS)

Removal/Installation

Refer to **Figure 18** for this procedure.

NOTE
The screw, washer and nut indicated in
A, Figure 19 *are not shown. They are*
recessed in behind the fairing and are
not visible.

1. Remove the screw, washer and nut securing the front upper portion of the lower fairing to the frame mounting bracket (A, **Figure 19**). Don't lose the collar located in the rubber grommet in the fairing mounting hole.

2. Remove the bolt, nut, washer and grommet securing both lower fairing assemblies together at the lower rear.

3. Remove the front lower special screw and washer (B, **Figure 19**) securing the sides of the lower fairing assembly to the frame. Don't lose the collar located in the rubber grommet in the fairing mounting hole.

4. Remove the front lower nut, collar and washer securing the lower portion of the lower fairing assembly to the frame bracket. Don't lose the collar located in the rubber grommet in the fairing mounting hole.

5. Remove the rear upper special screw and washer (C, **Figure 19**) securing the sides of the lower fairing assembly to the frame mounting bracket. Don't lose the collar located in the rubber grommet in the faring mounting hole.

NOTE
Have an assistant hold onto the lower
fairing assembly prior to removing the
upper screws. The fairing is not heavy
but is bulky and may fall from the bike
and get scratched.

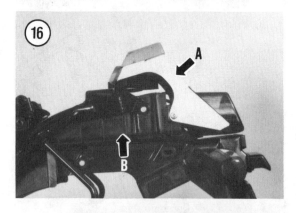

6. Remove the 2 upper special screws and washers (D, **Figure 19**) securing the sides of the lower fairing assembly to the front fairing. Don't lose the collar located in the rubber grommet in the fairing mounting hole.

7. If necessary to separate the upper and lower portions, remove the 3 screws, lockwashers, washers and nuts securing the upper portion to the lower portion of the lower fairing assembly. Separate the 2 parts.

LOWER FAIRING (FZ600)

1. Screw
2. Washer
3. Mounting bracket
4. Upper portion
5. Rubber grommet
6. Collar
7. Bolt
8. Nut
9. Rubber grommet
10. Collar
11. Mounting bracket
12. Mounting bracket
13. Washer
14. Bolt
15. Lower portion
16. Collar
17. Nut
18. Collar

8. If necessary, remove the fairing mounting brackets as follows:

a. Remove the bolt and lockwasher securing the rear upper mounting bracket (**Figure 20**) and remove the bracket.

b. Remove the bolts and lockwashers securing the front upper mounting bracket (**Figure 21**) and remove the bracket.

c. Remove the bolt and lockwasher securing the lower mounting brackets (**Figure 22**) and remove the brackets.

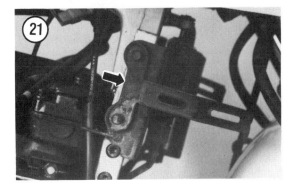

12

9. Install by reversing these removal steps while noting the following:

    a. Make sure the rubber grommets and collars are in place in the mounting holes where applicable. These grommets help prevent the plastic from fracturing at the attachment points.

    b. Tighten all screws securely. Do not overtighten as the plastic parts may fracture.

FRONT FAIRING
(FZ600 MODELS)

Removal/Installation

Refer to **Figure 23** for this procedure.

1. Remove the lower fairing from both sides as described in this chapter.

2. Remove the nuts, lockwashers and washers securing the rear view mirror to the front fairing. Remove both mirrors (A, **Figure 24**).

3. Within the front fairing, remove both headlight covers.

> *NOTE*
> *Do not disconnect the electrical connectors going to the headlights. The headlight assembly is attached to the front fairing mounting bracket and will stay in place when the front fairing is removed.*

4. Disconnect the electrical connector containing 2 wires going to each turn signal assembly. Repeat for the other turn signal.

5. Remove the nut securing the front turn signal assembly to the mounting bracket. Remove the turn signal assembly from the fairing. Repeat for the other turn signal.

> *NOTE*
> *Have an assistant hold onto the front fairing assembly prior to removing the mounting nuts. The fairing is not heavy but is bulky and may fall from the bike and get scratched.*

6. Remove the 2 nuts (**Figure 25**) on each side securing the front fairing to the mounting bracket. Don't lose the collar located in the rubber grommet in the fairing mounting holes.

7. Pull the front fairing (B, **Figure 24**) forward and off of the headlight assembly.

8. Install by reversing these removal steps while noting the following:

    a. Make sure the rubber grommets and collars are in place in the mounting holes where applicable. These grommets help prevent the plastic from fracturing at the attachment points.

    b. Tighten all screws securely. Do not overtighten as the plastic parts may fracture.

SIDE COVERS
(FZ600 MODELS)

Removal/Installation

Refer to **Figure 26** for this procedure.

1. Remove the seats as described in this chapter.

2. Remove the special screws (A, **Figure 27**) securing the side cover to the frame. Don't lose the collar located in the rubber grommet in the side cover mounting holes.

3. Carefully pull out on the upper front (B, **Figure 27**) to disengage the cover's front tab from the rubber locating cushion on the side of the fuel tank.

4. Pull the rear of the side cover down to disengage the locating tab from the rear fender cover (C, **Figure 27**) and remove it from the frame.

5. Repeat for the other side.

6. Install by reversing these removal steps while noting the following:

    a. Make sure the rubber grommets and collars are in place in the mounting holes. These grommets help prevent the plastic from fracturing at the attachment points.

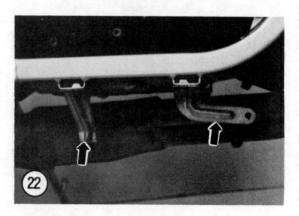

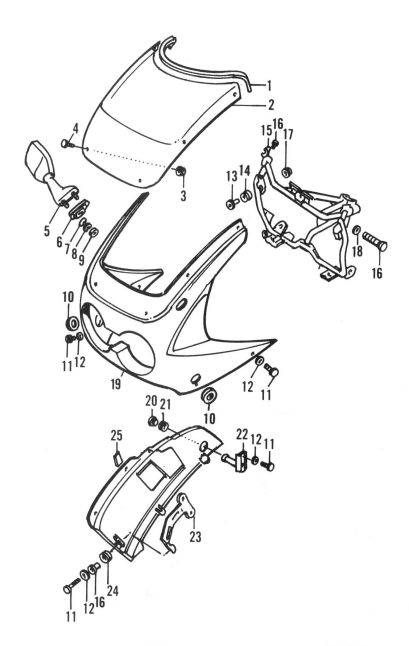

FRONT FAIRING (FZ600)

1. Trim strip	9. Nut	17. Nut
2. Windscreen	10. Rubber grommet	18. Lockwasher
3. Nut	11. Screw	19. Front fairing
4. Screw	12. Washer	20. Collar
5. Rear view mirror	13. Collar	21. Rubber grommet
6. Rubber pad	14. Rubber grommet	22. Mounting bracket
7. Washer	15. Mounting bracket	23. Mounting bracket
8. Lockwasher	16. Collar	24. Rubber grommet

b. Tighten all screws securely. Do not over-tighten as the plastic parts may fracture.

SIDE STAND
(ALL MODELS)

Refer to **Figure 28** for this procedure.

1. Move the side stand to the raised position.

2A. On Radian models, perform the following:

   a. Use Vise-grip pliers and disconnect the return springs (A, **Figure 29**) from the pin on the side stand.

   b. If necessary, remove the springs from the link plate (B, **Figure 29**) and frame.

   c. Remove the bolt (C, **Figure 29**) and nut securing the side stand to the frame mounting bracket.

   d. Remove the side stand (D, **Figure 29**) from the frame.

2B. On FZ600 models, perform the following:

   a. Use Vise-grip pliers and disconnect the return spring (A, **Figure 30**) from the pin on the side stand.

b. If necessary, remove the spring from the frame.

   c. Remove the bolt (B, **Figure 30**) and nut securing the side stand to the frame mounting bracket.

   d. Remove the side stand (C, **Figure 30**) from the frame.

3. Install by reversing these removal steps while noting the following:

   a. Apply a light coat of multipurpose grease to the pivot points on the frame mounting area and the side stand prior to installation.

   b. Tighten the bolt and nut securely.

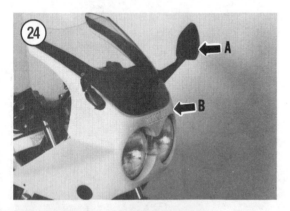

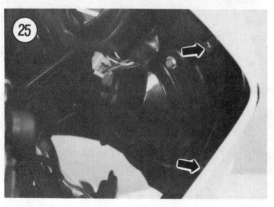

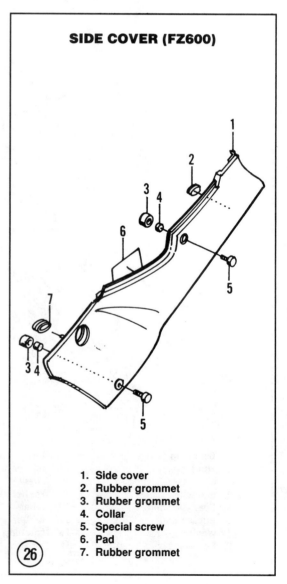

SIDE COVER (FZ600)

1. Side cover
2. Rubber grommet
3. Rubber grommet
4. Collar
5. Special screw
6. Pad
7. Rubber grommet

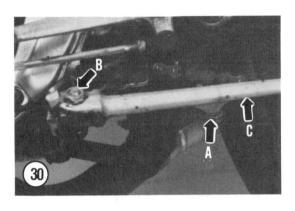

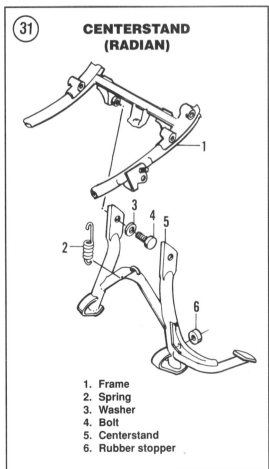

CENTERSTAND
(RADIAN MODELS)

Refer to **Figure 31** for this procedure.

NOTE
The FZ600 models are not equipped with a centerstand.

SIDE STAND

1. Frame
2. Linkplate (Radian only)
3. Pivot bolt
4. Spring (2 on Radian, 1 on FZ600)
5. Self-locking nut
6. Side stand

CENTERSTAND (RADIAN)

1. Frame
2. Spring
3. Washer
4. Bolt
5. Centerstand
6. Rubber stopper

12

NOTE
This procedure is shown with the rear wheel removed for clarity. Do not remove the rear wheel for this procedure.

1. Place wood block(s) under the crankcase to support the bike securely with the rear wheel off the ground.

2. Place the centerstand in the raised position.

3. Use Vise-grip pliers and disconnect the return spring (A, **Figure 32**) from the hook on the centerstand or frame.

4. Remove the bolt and washer (B, **Figure 32**) securing the centerstand to the frame on each side.

5. Remove the centerstand from the frame.

6. Install by reversing these removal steps while noting the following:

    a. Apply a light coat of multipurpose grease to the pivot points on the frame mounting area and the centerstand prior to installation.

    b. Tighten the bolts securely.

FOOTPEGS

Front Footpeg Removal/Installation (Radian Models)

1. To remove the rubber pad only, remove the nut securing the rubber pad to the footpeg bracket assembly and remove the pad.

2. To remove the entire assembly, remove the shoulder bolt (A, **Figure 33**) securing the footpeg and bracket assembly to the frame.

3. Remove the footpeg bracket assembly (B, **Figure 33**) from the frame.

4. Install by reversing these removal steps while noting the following.

    a. Be sure to index the locating pin on the bracket assembly into the locating hole in the frame.

    b. Tighten the bolt to the torque specification listed in **Table 1**.

Front Footpeg Removal/Installation (FZ600 Models)

1. To remove the rubber pad only, remove the top screw and end bolt securing the rubber pad to the footpeg bracket assembly and remove the pad.

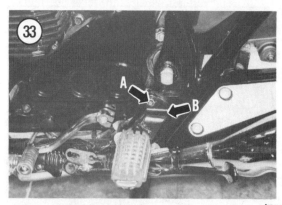

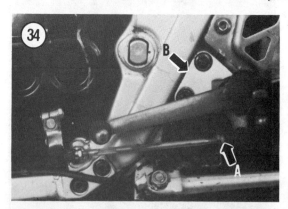

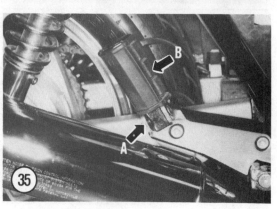

2. To remove the entire right-hand assembly, refer to *Rear Brake Pedal Removal/Installation (FZ600 Models)* in Chapter Eleven. The footpeg is part of the rear brake pedal assembly.

3. To remove the entire left-hand assembly, perform the following:

    a. Loosen the locknut (A, **Figure 34**) on the shift linkage and disconnect the linkage from the shift lever.

    b. Remove the bolts securing the footpeg and bracket assembly (B, **Figure 34**) to the frame.

    c. Remove the footpeg, shift lever and bracket assembly from the frame.

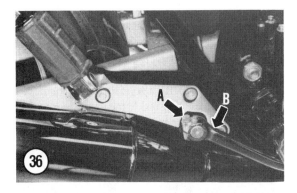

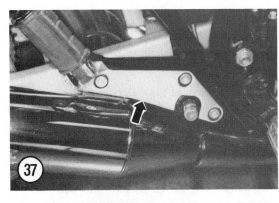

4. Install by reversing these removal steps while noting the following.

    a. Be sure to index the locating pin on the bracket assembly into the locating hole in the frame.

    b. Tighten the bolt to the torque specification listed in **Table 1**.

    c. On left-hand side, adjust the shift linkage as described in Chapter Three.

Rear Footpeg Removal/Installation (Radian Models)

1. Remove the cotter pin from the pivot pin and remove the pivot pin (A, **Figure 35**).

2. Remove the footpeg from the mounting bracket and remove the spring washer.

3. Slide the rubber pad (B, **Figure 35**) off of the footpeg armature.

4. To remove the footpeg bracket, perform the following:

    a. On the right-hand side, remove the bolt and lockwasher (A, **Figure 36**) securing the brake pedal to the pivot shaft. Remove the brake pedal (B, **Figure 36**).

    b. Remove the Allen bolts securing the bracket (**Figure 37**) to the frame and remove the bracket.

5. Install by reversing these removal steps while noting the following:

    a. Tighten the bolt(s) securely.

    b. Install a new cotter pin and bend the ends over completely.

Rear Footpeg Removal/Installation (FZ600 Models)

1. To remove the rubber pad only, remove the top screw securing the rubber pad to the footpeg bracket assembly and remove the pad.

2. To remove the footpeg assembly, remove the bolt, (**Figure 38**) nut and washer securing the footpeg to the frame mounting tabs.

3. Remove the footpeg assembly. Don't lose the collar, spring and ball.

4. Install by reversing these removal steps while noting the following:

    a. Tighten the bolt(s) securely.

12

b. Install a new cotter pin and bend the ends over completely.

FRAME

The frame does not require routine maintenance. However, it should be inspected immediately after any accident or spill.

Component Removal/Installation

1. Remove both side covers and the seat as described in this chapter.
2. Remove all body components as described in this chapter.
3. Remove the fuel tank as described in Chapter Seven.
4. Remove the battery as described in Chapter Three.
5. Remove the instrument cluster as described in Chapter Eight.
6. Remove the hydraulic brake system flexible hoses as described in Chapter Eleven.
7. Remove the wiring harness from the frame.
8. Remove the front wheel, handlebar, steering head and front forks as described in Chapter Nine.
9. Remove the rear wheel, shock absorbers and swing arm as described in Chapter Ten.
10. Remove the engine as described in Chapter Four.
11. Remove the steering head races from the steering head tube as described in Chapter Nine.
12. Inspect the frame for bends, cracks or other damage, especially around welded joints and areas that are rusted.
13. Assemble by reversing these removal steps.

Stripping and Painting

Remove all components from the frame. Thoroughly strip off all old paint. The best way is to have it sandblasted down to bare metal. If this is not possible, you can use a liquid paint remover and steel wool and a fine, hard wire brush.

> *CAUTION*
> *Some of the fenders, side covers, frame covers and air box are molded plastic. If you wish to change the color of these parts, consult an automotive paint supplier for the proper procedure. Do not use any liquid paint remover on these components as it will damage the surface. The color is an integral part of*

some of these components and cannot be removed.

When the frame is down to bare metal, have it inspected for hairline and internal cracks. Magnaflux is the most common and complete process.

Make sure that the primer is compatible with the type of paint you are going to use for the finish color. Spray on one or two coats of primer as smoothly as possible. Let it dry thoroughly and use a fine grade of wet sandpaper (400-600 grit) to remove any flaws. Carefully wipe the surface clean and then spray a couple of coats of the final color. Use either lacquer or enamel base paint and follow the manufacturer's instructions.

A shop specializing in painting will probably do the best job. However, you can do a surprisingly good job with a good grade of spray paint. Spend a few extra dollars and get a good grade of paint as it will make a difference in how well it looks and how long it will stand up. It's a good idea to shake the can and make sure the ball inside the can is loose when you purchase the can of paint. Prior to applying the paint, shake the can as long as is stated on the can. Then immerse the can *upright* in a pot or bucket of *warm* water(not hot—not over 120° F).

> *WARNING*
> *Higher temperatures could cause the can to burst. **Do** not place the can in direct contact with any flame or heat source.*

Leave the can in the water for several minutes. When thoroughly warmed, shake the can again and spray the frame. Be sure to get into all the crevices where there may be rust problems. Several light mist coats are better than one heavy coat. Spray painting is best done in temperatures of 70-80° F (21-26° C); any temperature above or below this will give you problems.

After the final coat has dried completely, at least 48 hours, any overspray or orange peel may be removed with a *light* application of Dupont rubbing compound (red color) and finished with Dupont polishing compound (white color). Be careful not to rub too hard or you will go through the finish. Finish off with a couple coats of good wax prior to reassembling all the components.

It's a good idea to keep the frame touched up with fresh paint if any minor rust spots, chips or scratches appear.

Table 1 CHASSIS TIGHTENING TORQUES

Item	N.m	ft.-lb.
Front fender brace bolts	8	5.8
Foot peg bolts	70	50

INDEX

13

RADIAN 1986-87 U.S.

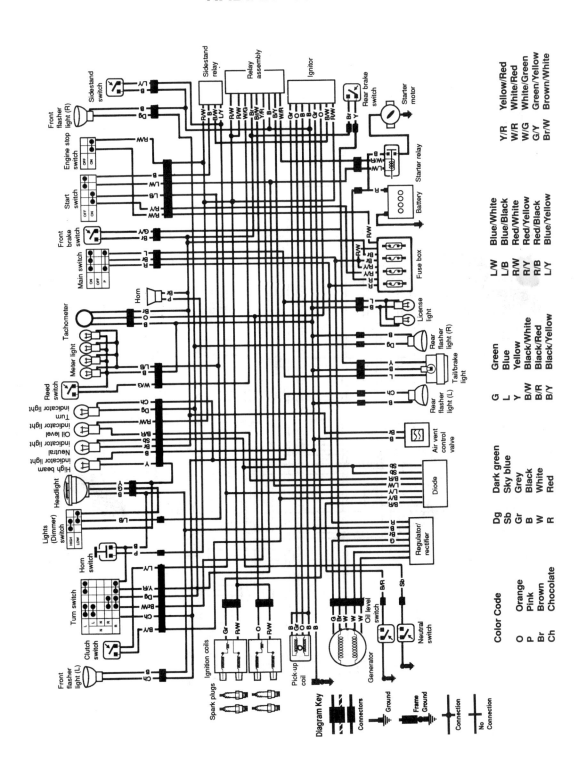

RADIAN 1988-90 (U.S.)

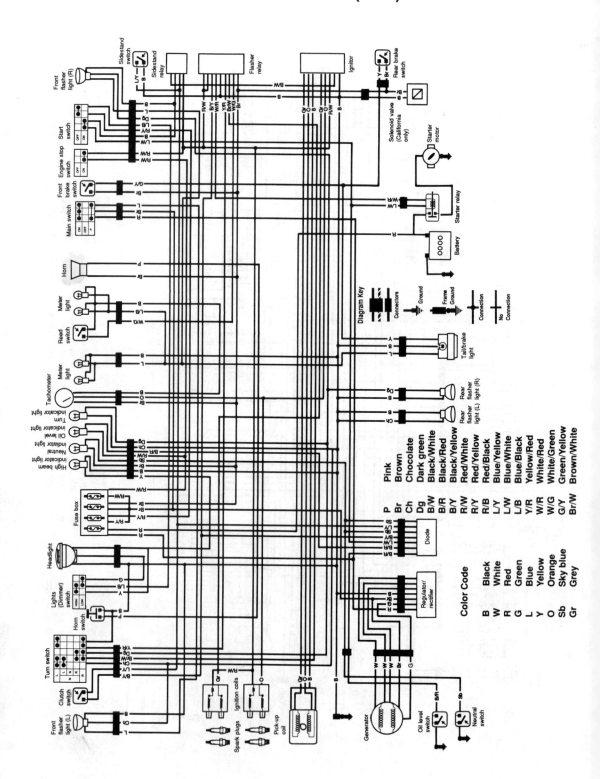

FZ600 1986-88 (U.S.)

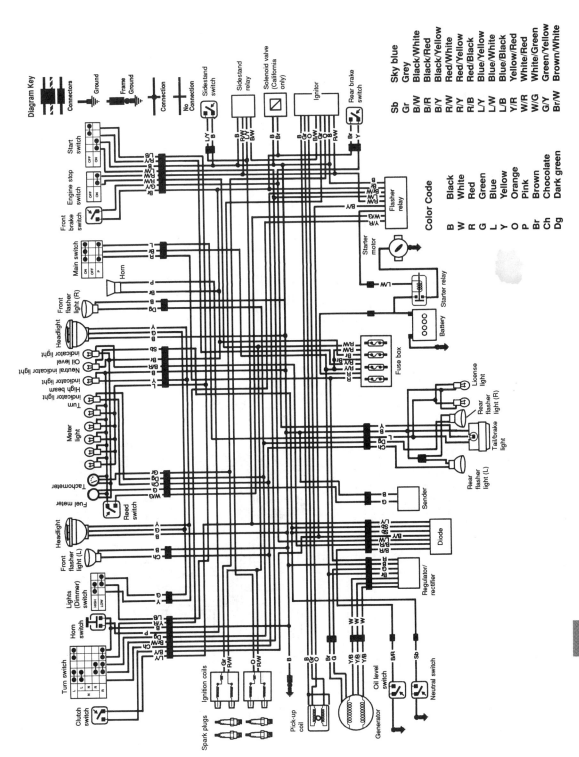

FZ600 1986 (UK)

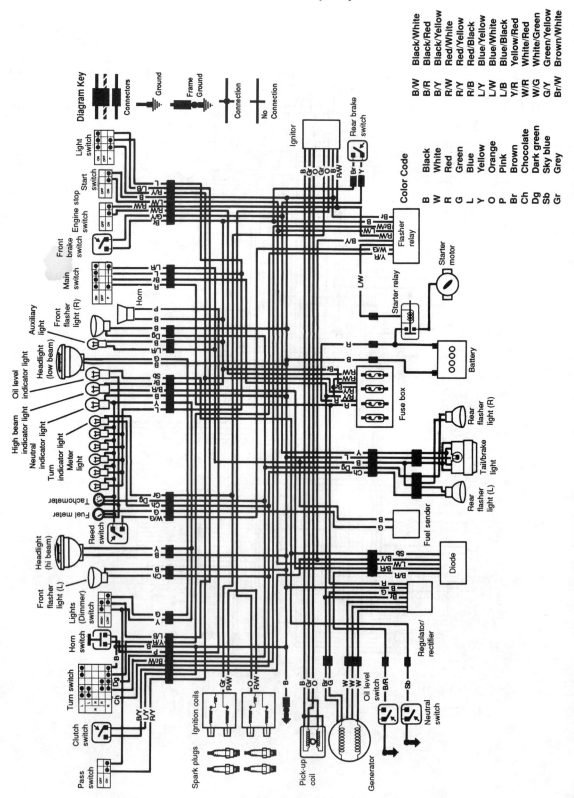

B/W	Black/White
B/R	Black/Red
B/Y	Black/Yellow
R/W	Red/White
R/Y	Red/Yellow
R/B	Red/Black
L/Y	Blue/Yellow
L/W	Blue/White
L/B	Blue/Black
Y/R	Yellow/Red
W/R	White/Red
W/G	White/Green
G/Y	Green/Yellow
Br/W	Brown/White

Color Code

B	Black
W	White
R	Red
G	Green
L	Blue
Y	Yellow
O	Orange
P	Pink
Br	Brown
Ch	Chocolate
Dg	Dark green
Sb	Sky blue
Gr	Grey

FZ600 1987 (UK)

Code	Color		Code	Color
B/W	Black/White			
B/R	Black/Red			
B/Y	Black/Yellow			
R/W	Red/White			
R/Y	Red/Yellow			
R/B	Red/Black			
L/Y	Blue/Yellow			
L/W	Blue/White			
L/B	Blue/Black			
Y/R	Yellow/Red			
W/R	White/Red			
W/G	White/Green			
G/Y	Green/Yellow			
Br/W	Brown/White			

Color Code

B	Black		Br	Brown
W	White		Ch	Chocolate
R	Red		Dg	Dark green
G	Green		Sb	Sky blue
L	Blue		Gr	Grey
Y	Yellow			
O	Orange			
P	Pink			

Start switch, Light switch, Engine stop switch, Front brake switch, Main switch, Horn, Front flasher light (R), Auxiliary light, Oil level indicator light, Headlight (low beam), Neutral indicator light, High beam indicator light, Turn indicator light, Meter light, Tachometer, Fuel meter, Reed switch, Headlight (hi beam), Front flasher light (L), Lights (Dimmer) switch, Horn switch, Turn switch, Clutch switch, Pass switch

Sidestand switch, Sidestand relay, Ignitor, Rear brake switch, Flasher relay, Starter relay, Starter motor, Battery, Fuse box, Rear flasher light (R), Tail/brake light, Rear flasher light (L), Sender, Diode, Regulator/rectifier, Ignition coils, Spark plugs, Pick-up coil, Generator, Oil level switch, Neutral switch

Diagram Key — Connectors, Ground, Frame Ground, Connection, No Connection

14

NOTES

NOTES

NOTES

NOTES

NOTES

MAINTENANCE LOG

Date	Miles	Type of Service

Check out *clymer.com* for our full line of powersport repair manuals.

BMW
M308	500 & 600 CC twins, 55-69
M502	BMW R-Series, 70-94
M500	BMW K-Series, 85-95
M503	R-850 & R-1100, 93-98

HARLEY-DAVIDSON
M419	Sportsters, 59-85
M428	Sportster Evolution, 86-90
M429-3	Sportster Evolution, 91-02
M418	Panheads, 48-65
M420	Shovelheads,66-84
M421	FX/FL Softail Big-Twin Evolution,84-94
M422	FLT/FXR Big-Twin Evolution, 84-94
M424	Dyna Glide, 91-95
M425	Dyna Glide Twin Cam, 99-01
M430	FLH/FLT 1999-2002

HONDA
ATVs
M316	Odyssey FL250, 77-84
M311	ATC, TRX & Fourtrax 70-125, 70-87
M433	Fourtrax 90 ATV, 93-00
M326	ATC185 & 200, 80-86
M347	ATC200X & Fourtrax 200SX, 86-88
M455	ATC250 & Fourtrax 200/ 250, 84-87
M342	ATC250R, 81-84
M348	TRX250R/Fourtrax 250R & ATC250R, 85-89
M456	TRX250X 1987-1988, 91-92; TRX300EX 93-96
M446	TRX250 Recon 1997-02
M346-3	TRX300/Fourtrax 300 & TRX300FW/Fourtrax 4x4, 88-00
M459	Fourtrax Foreman 95-98
M454	TRX400EX 1999-02

Singles
M310-13	50-110cc OHC Singles, 65-99
M315	100-350cc OHC, 69-82
M317	Elsinore, 125-250cc, 73-80
M442	CR60-125R Pro-Link, 81-88
M431-2	CR80R, 89-95, CR125R, 89-91
M435	CR80, 96-02
M457-2	CR125R & CR250R, 92-97
M443	CR250R-500R Pro-Link, 81-87
M432	CR250R & CR500R, 88-96
M437	CR250R, 97-01
M312-12	XL/XR75-100, 75-02
M318	XL/XR/TLR 125-200, 79-87
M328-2	XL/XR250, 78-00; XL/XR350R 83-85; XR200R, 84-85; XR250L, 91-96
M320	XR400R, 96-00
M339-6	XL/XR 500-650, 79-02

Twins
M321	125-200cc, 64-77
M322	250-350cc, 64-74
M323	250-360cc Twins, 74-77
M324-4	Rebel 250 & Twinstar, 78-87; Nighthawk 250, 91-97; Rebel 250, 96-97
M334	400-450cc, 78-87
M333	450 & 500cc, 65-76
M335	CX & GL500/650 Twins, 78-83
M344	VT500, 83-88
M313	VT700 & 750, 83-87
M460	VT1100C2 A.C.E. Shadow, 95-97
M440	Shadow 1100cc V-Twin, 85-96

Fours
M332	350-550cc 71-78
M345	CB550 & 650, 83-85
M336	CB650,79-82
M341	CB750 SOHC, 69-78
M337	CB750 DOHC, 79-82
M436	CB750 Nighthawk, 91-93 & 95-99
M325	CB900, 1000 & 1100, 80-83
M439	Hurricane 600, 87-90
M441-2	CBR600, 91-98
M434	CBR900RR Fireblade, 93-98
M329	500cc V-Fours, 84-86
M438	Honda VFR800, 98-00
M349	700-1000 Interceptor, 83-85
M458-2	VFR700F-750F, 86-97
M327	700-1100cc V-Fours, 82-88
M340	GL1000 & 1100, 75-83
M504	GL1200, 84-87

Sixes
M505	GL1500 Gold Wing, 88-92
M506	GL1500 Gold Wing, 93-95
M462	GL1500C Valkyrie, 97-00

KAWASAKI
ATVs
M465	KLF220 Bayou, 88-95
M466-2	KLF300 Bayou, 86-98
M467	KLF400 Bayou, 93-99
M470	KEF300 Lakota, 95-99
M385	KSF250 Mojave, 87-00

Singles
M350-9	Rotary Valve 80-350cc, 66-01
M444	KX60-80, 83-90
M351	KDX200, 83-88
M447	KX125 & KX250, 82-91 KX500, 83-93
M472	KX125, 92-98
M473	KX250, 92-98

Twins
M355	KZ400, KZ/Z440, EN450 & EN500, 74-95
M360	EX500/GPZ500S, 87-93
M356-2	700-750 Vulcan, 85-01
M354	VN800 Vulcan 95-98
M357	VN1500 Vulcan 87-98
M471	VN1500 Vulcan Classic, 96-98

Fours
M449	KZ500/550 & ZX550, 79-85
M450	KZ, Z & ZX750, 80-85
M358	KZ650, 77-83
M359	900-1000cc Fours, 73-80
M451	1000 &1100cc Fours, 81-85
M452-3	ZX500 & 600 Ninja, 85-97
M453-3	Ninja ZX900-1100 84-01
M468	ZX6 Ninja, 90-97
M469	ZX7 Ninja, 91-98
M453	900-1100 Ninja, 84-93

POLARIS
ATVs
M496	Polaris ATV, 85-95
M362	Polaris Magnum ATV, 96-98
M363	Scrambler 500, 4X4 97-00
M365	Sportsman/Xplorer, 96-00

SUZUKI
ATVs
M381	ALT/LT 125 & 185, 83-87
M475	LT230 & LT250, 85-90
M380	LT250R Quad Racer, 85-88
M343	LTF500F Quadrunner, 98-00
M483	Suzuki King Quad/ Quad Runner 250, 87-95

Singles
M371	RM50-400 Twin Shock, 75-81
M369	125-400cc 64-81
M379	RM125-500 Single Shock, 81-88
M476	DR250-350, 90-94
M384	LS650 Savage Single, 86-88
M386	RM80-250, 89-95

Twins
M372	GS400-450 Twins, 77-87
M481-3	VS700-800 Intruder, 85-02
M482	VS1400 Intruder, 87-98
M484-2	GS500E Twins, 89-00

Triple
M368	380-750cc, 72-77

Fours
M373	GS550, 77-86
M364	GS650, 81-83
M370	GS750 Fours, 77-82
M376	GS850-1100 Shaft Drive, 79-84
M378	GS1100 Chain Drive, 80-81
M383-3	Katana 600, 88-96 GSX-R750-1100, 86-87
M331	GSX-R600, 97-00
M478-2	GSX-R750, 88-92 GSX750F Katana, 89-96
M485	GSX-R750, 96-99
M338	GSF600 Bandit, 95-00

YAMAHA
ATVs
M394	YTM/YFM200 & 225, 83-86
M487-3	YFM350 Warrior, 87-02
M486-3	YFZ350 Banshee, 87-02
M488-3	Blaster ATV, 88-01
M489-2	Timberwolf ATV,89-00
M490-2	YFM350 Moto-4 & Big Bear, 87-98
M493	YFM400FW Kodiak, 93-98

Singles
M492-2	PW50 & PW80, BW80 Big Wheel 80, 81-02
M410	80-175 Piston Port, 68-76
M415	250-400cc Piston Port, 68-76
M412	DT & MX 100-400, 77-83
M414	IT125-490, 76-86
M393	YZ50-80 Monoshock, 78-90
M413	YZ100-490 Monoshock, 76-84
M390	YZ125-250, 85-87 YZ490, 85-90
M391	YZ125-250, 88-93 WR250Z, 91-93
M497	YZ125, 94-99
M498	YZ250, 94-98 and WR250Z, 94-97
M491	YZ400F, YZ426F & WR400F, 98-00
M417	XT125-250, 80-84
M480-2	XT/TT 350, 85-96
M405	XT500 & TT500, 76-81
M416	XT/TT 600, 83-89

Twins
M403	650cc, 70-82
M395-9	XV535-1100 Virago, 81-99
M495	XVS650 V-Star, 98-00

Triple
M404	XS750 & 850, 77-81

Fours
M387	XJ550, XJ600 & FJ600, 81-92
M494	XJ600 Seca II, 92-98
M388	YX600 Radian & FZ600, 86-90
M396	FZR600, 89-93
M392	FZ700-750 & Fazer, 85-87
M411	XS1100 Fours, 78-81
M397	FJ1100 & 1200, 84-93

VINTAGE MOTORCYCLES
Clymer® Collection Series
M330	Vintage British Street Bikes, BSA, 500 & 650cc Unit Twins; Norton, 750 & 850cc Commandos; Triumph, 500-750cc Twins
M300	Vintage Dirt Bikes, V. 1 Bultaco, 125-370cc Singles; Montesa, 123-360cc Singles; Ossa, 125-250cc Singles
M301	Vintage Dirt Bikes, V. 2 CZ, 125-400cc Singles; Husqvarna, 125-450cc Singles; Maico, 250-501cc Singles; Hodaka, 90-125cc Singles
M305	Vintage Japanese Street Bikes Honda, 250 & 305cc Twins; Kawasaki, 250-750cc Triples; Kawasaki, 900 & 1000cc Fours